EDUCATION ON THE WILD SIDE

Oklahoma Project for
Discourse and Theory

EDUCATION ON THE WILD SIDE

Learning for the

Twenty-first Century

by Michael L. Johnson

University of Oklahoma Press
Norman and London

Other books by Michael L. Johnson

The New Journalism: The Underground Press, the Artists of Nonfiction, and Changes in the Established Media (Lawrence, Kansas, 1972)
Prometheus Reborn: Countertechnology, Holistic Education, and the Ecology-Energy Crisis (Roslyn Heights, N.Y., 1977)
(co-editor, with G. Douglas Atkins) *Writing and Reading Differently: Deconstruction and the Teaching of Composition and Literature* (Lawrence, Kansas, 1985)
Mind, Language, Machine: Artificial Intelligence in the Poststructuralist Age (New York, 1988)

Library of Congress Cataloging-in-Publication Data

Johnson, Michael L.
    Education on the wild side : learning for the twenty-first century
/ by Michael L. Johnson.
        p.   cm.—(Oklahoma project for discourse and theory)
    Includes bibliographical references (p. 317) and index.
    ISBN: 0-8061-2546-2 (alk. paper)
        1. Education—United States—Philosophy. 2. Education, Higher—
United States—Philosophy. 3. Education—Social aspects—United
States. 4. Education, Higher—Social aspects—United States.
5. Learning. 6. Teaching. 7. Critical pedagogy—United States.
8. Education—United States—Curricula. 9. Education, Higher—
United States—Curricula. I. Title. II. Series.
LA209.2.J64   1993   93-12365
                                                                CIP

Education on the Wild Side: Learning for the Twenty-first Century is Volume 12 of the Oklahoma Project for Discourse and Theory.

The paper in this book meets the guidelines for permanence and durability of the Committee on Production Guidelines for Book Longevity of the Council on Library Resources, Inc. ∞

To
Jarrett Lawrence Johnson
and
Lauren Elizabeth Johnson

Whoever is a teacher through and through takes all things seriously only in relation to his students—even himself.

Friedrich Wilhelm Nietzsche,
Beyond Good and Evil: Prelude to a Philosophy of the Future,
trans. Walter Kaufmann

In any act of thinking, the mind must reach across this space between known and unknown, linking one to the other but also keeping visible their difference. It is an erotic space. To reach across it is tricky; a kind of stereoscopy seems to be required.

Anne Carson, Eros the Bittersweet: An Essay

*How is it I find you in difference, see you there
In a moving contour, a change not quite completed?*

Wallace Stevens, "Notes toward a Supreme Fiction"

Contents

Series Editors' Foreword

The Oklahoma Project for Discourse & Theory is a series of interdisciplinary texts whose purpose is to explore the cultural institutions that constitute the human sciences, to see them in relation to one another, and, perhaps above all, to see them as products of particular discursive practices. To this end, we hope that the Oklahoma Project will promote dialogue within and across traditional disciplines—psychology, philology, linguistics, history, art history, aesthetics, logic, political economy, religion, philosophy, anthropology, communications, and the like—in texts that theoretically are located across disciplines. In recent years, in a host of new and traditional areas, there has been great interest in such discursive and theoretical frameworks. Yet we conceive of the Oklahoma Project as going beyond local inquiries, providing a larger forum for interdiscursive theoretical discussions and dialogue.

Our agenda in previous books and certainly in this one has been to present through the University of Oklahoma Press a series of critical volumes that set up a theoretical encounter among disciplines, an interchange not limited to literature but covering virtually the whole range of the human sciences. It is a critical series with an important reference in literary studies—thus mirroring the modern development of discourse theory—but including all approaches, other than quantitative studies, open to semiotic and post-semiotic analysis and to the wider concerns of cultural studies. Regardless of its particular domain, each book in the series will investigate characteristically post-Freudian, post-Saussurean, and post-Marxist questions about culture and the discourses that constitute different cultural phenomena. The Oklahoma Project is a sustained dialogue intended to make a significant contribution to the contemporary understanding of the human sciences in the contexts of cultural theory and cultural studies.

Series Editors' Foreword

The title of the series reflects, of course, its home base, the University of Oklahoma. But it also signals in a significant way the particularity of the *local* functions within historical and conceptual frameworks for understanding culture. *Oklahoma* is a haunting place-name in American culture. A Choctaw phrase meaning "red people," it goes back to the Treaty of Dancing Rabbit Creek in Mississippi in 1830. For Franz Kafka, it conjured up the idea of America itself, both the indigenous Indian peoples of North America and the vertiginous space of the vast plains. It is also the place-name, the "American" starting point, with which Wallace Stevens begins his *Collected Poems*. Historically, too, it is a place in which American territorial and political expansion was reenacted in a single day in a retracing called the Oklahoma land run. Geographically, it is the heartland of the continent.

As such—in the interdisciplinary Oklahoma Project for Discourse & Theory—we are hoping to describe, above all, multi-faceted *interests* within and across various studies of discourse and culture. Such interests are akin to what Kierkegaard calls the "in-between" aspect of experience, the "inter esse," and, perhaps more pertinently, what Nietzsche describes as the always *political* functioning of concepts, art works, and language—the functioning of power as well as knowledge in discourse and theory. Such politics, occasioning dialogue and bringing together powerfully struggling and often unarticulated positions, disciplines, and assumptions, is always local, always particular. In some ways, such interests function in broad feminist critiques of language, theory, and culture as well as microphilosophical and microhistorical critiques of the definitions of truth and art existing within ideologies of "disinterested" meaning. They function in the interested examination of particular disciplines and general disciplinary histories. They function (to allude to two of our early titles) in the very interests of theory and the particularity of the postmodern age in which many of us find ourselves. In such interested particulars, we believe, the human sciences are articulated. We hope that the books of the Oklahoma Project will provide sites of such interest and that in them, individually and collectively, the monologues of traditional scholarly discourse will become heteroglosses, just as such place-names as *Oklahoma* and such commonplace words and concepts as *discourse* and *theory* can become sites for the dialogue and play of culture.

ROBERT CON DAVIS
RONALD SCHLEIFER

Norman, Oklahoma

Preface
A Progressive Knotting Into

Let me preface this Preface by quoting from Gayatri Chakravorty Spivak's preface to Jacques Derrida's *Of Grammatology*:

> In an essay on the "Preface" to Hegel's *Phenomenology of the Mind,* Jean Hyppolite writes:
>> When Hegel had finished the *Phenomenology* . . . he reflected retrospectively on his philosophic enterprise and wrote the "Preface." . . . It is a strange demonstration, for he says above all, "Don't take me seriously in a preface. The real philosophical work is what I have just written, the *Phenomenology of the Mind.* And if I speak to you outside of what I have written, these marginal comments cannot have the value of the work itself. . . . Don't take a preface seriously. The preface announces a project and a project is nothing until it is realized."
> It is clear that, as it is commonly understood, the preface harbors a lie. [1]

Other loops and complications can be discovered in this game of prefacing, of course—for example, Spivak's preface precedes and thus prefaces Derrida's own preface to *Of Grammatology*—but let just these Chinese boxes suffice to suggest an unease about prefaces (particularly this one), the textual "phenomenology" of our postmodern world, and the kind of seriousness with which I hope my text on education in that world (if not its preface) will be taken.

This book deals with a multifaceted change in contemporary education, one now under way that promises, if appropriately tended, to make education an enterprise much different from what it has been so far. What follows has developed, sometimes in revisionary or even ironic ways, over twenty years, during which time

Preface

I have published a number of books and articles concerned, wholly or in part, with education. In many respects my work here has evolved most directly out of my book *Mind, Language, Machine: Artificial Intelligence in the Poststructuralist Age* (London: Macmillan; New York: St. Martin's Press, 1988), in which I explored learning as a problem for the interdisciplinary attention of what has come to be called cognitive science. What follows has a more social-constructionist emphasis than the earlier book; but that should not be taken as any simple and immediate supplantation, for I see cognitive science and social constructionism not to be at odds, as a widely held but provincial view has it, but to be dealing with different aspects or moments of the same project: the elaboration of a deeper understanding of the processes, "internal" and "external," involved in learning. [2] Also, though much of what follows mirrors a special interest in American higher education, that interest engages issues global in scale and pertinent to all levels, particularly the "level" of lifelong education. And while much of what I have to say pertains—or may seem to pertain—most directly to what are conventionally called the humanities, which include many of the most pedagogically (and politically) self-conscious fields, its application beyond them (to the social and natural sciences, the arts, even the professions and "vocational" areas) usually can be readily argued; in many cases I do. Otherwise, my exploration ranges widely, freely crossing conventional disciplinary boundaries, all of which are increasingly overlapped and blurred.

Who is my reader? Probably a professional educator, though I would be delighted if he or she were not; for education should be everyone's concern, and I would like to share my exploration with anyone who would like to investigate the "wild side" of education, the deeper problems, stranger complexities, and more extravagant possibilities of education scarcely sounded by popular media. And "wild" should not be taken to imply a lack of rigor, for "education on the wild side" demands more rigor (and more radical and productive creativity) of educators and students than its traditional counterpart, so much so that the reader, especially if a professional educator, may feel challenged too much. But that reader should bear with me: what is difficult is not always impossible, and the stakes are high. If the reader is made uncomfortable, professionally or otherwise, that may be a sign of the need for a refreshment of vision.

Preface

If I am accused of somehow "going too far" in pushing for a better conversation about the theory and practice of learning, then so be it (in certain ways education itself always needs to do so); but the reader should remember my purpose: to survey a restructuring of education already well along and to suggest how it may be continued and expanded. In trying to accomplish that purpose, I must work against the grain; violate the hypnosis of assumptions, conventions, fashions, and ideologies that inhibit the opening and empowerment of the educational enterprise; follow exorbitant trajectories; push the textual toward the metatextual; and at times, to maintain the pressure of key theses in my winding argument, repeat myself. Such a project involves, among other things, what Stefano Agosti finds in Derrida's *Spurs: Nietzsche's Styles:* "*coups de style* (stylistic blows of effects),"[3] rhetorical movements that "spur" the reader (and the writer) onward to grapple with further problems, polemics, and possibilities.

The reader should not expect me to take a simple, consistent position. Such positions are never stable anyway and wind up being clumsy, futile dances choreographed to avoid contradictions. Since the latter are far more interesting, revealing, and, finally, useful, I would rather embrace them, as cannily as necessary, from the start. Education is not a simple matter; far too many people prone to announce the obvious with an air of discovery treat it as if it were. It is precisely the obvious that I want to obvert in order to test its delusions with perspectives and constructions that are perhaps more tentative and difficult but, for all that, also more valuable. If what I thereby discover and advocate does not (yet) seem sufficient, then I would sigh with Roland Barthes, in a "position" thus somewhat similar to mine, "So things are very complicated, but that's the way it is."[4] I would argue in any case that a complex sense of a complicated situation is more productive—and less stressful—than a simple one.

Michael L. Johnson

Lawrence, Kansas

xiii

Acknowledgments

The people who have contributed to the experiences and ideas that shape this book are too numerous to mention, and many of them are cited in it; but I do want to extend special thanks to the University of Kansas for a sabbatical leave that allowed me to complete the first draft, to Becky Eason for research assistance with flair, and to Pam LeRow for word-processing the rat's nest of my typescript into handsome final form.

EDUCATION ON
THE WILD SIDE

PART I

Propaedeutic

Against the background of the familiar, we recognize with astonishment a new pattern.

Barry Lopez, *"The Passing Wisdom of Birds"*

Consider a scene in Steven Spielberg's 1982 movie *E.T.: The Extra-Terrestrial*. After having become acquainted with their celestial friend, whom they have kept hidden from their mother, Eliot and his older brother Michael are alone on the driveway, leaving for school. Concerned that E.T. does not understand why they will be gone for the day, Michael asks Eliot if he explained school to him. Eliot responds with a question of his own: "How do you explain school to higher intelligence?"

The question, rhetorical, eliciting knowing laughter from the audience, obviously presumes a sadly negative and brief answer: "You can't." But suppose, by a less obvious reading, that the question is not just "rhetorical" and seeks a different response. In that case one might have a great deal to say, particularly about why the former reading is the more obvious and what that laughter means.

3

CHAPTER I

Obverting the Ob(li)vious

First, a question from Hunter Thompson, who has made a profession out of grappling with the weird world in which we live: "What do you say . . . about a generation that has been taught that *rain is poison* and *sex is death*?" I say this: a generation that already has been "taught" the multitude of terrible lessons implied by Thompson's synecdoche needs education quite different from that of any previous generation. If the present generation and its progeny are to survive and experience more than "TV and relentless masturbation,"[1] then education in the future must involve not just a preservation of the past but a rereading of it, not just comfortable acquaintance with the known but radical engagement with the unknown. Anyone who doesn't sense the moment of that imperative has somehow managed to ignore the effects and implications of acid rain, AIDS, even TV. The human universe (known or unknown) is different from what it was (once upon a time). It always will be.

Next, an exemplary story from the bad-news side of contemporary American education. It concerns problems that many people regard as "obvious" and certainly deplorable. In "A Little Night Teaching" J. Mitchell Morse, a professor of English, tells of his experiences as a teacher of graduate-level, off-campus evening classes, in which most of his students were themselves teachers of English, at the high school level. He discovers that those teacher-students are appallingly inarticulate, unable to deal with even the basic mechanics of written English. Their spelling is, to use the formulaic epithet, atrocious. They, like "most of our public school teachers and administrators" and "most professors of education," subscribe to—and take as a "working credo"—what he calls "the warm-glow theory of education: the theory that 'the affective domain' is all-important and 'the cognitive domain' all-unimportant, so that emphasis on 'mere cognition' is undesirable." They are profoundly lacking in professional self-awareness and doubtless in their own teaching are busy "numbing the minds of the next generation." Such discoveries lead him to meditate on some of the general cultural-political messes that are interimplicated with the mess of education. And at the end he comes to a telling lament: "Until quite recently I was always ready with ideas for large-scale reform. I agreed with 'the many intelegent sciencetist who are straining their voco chords to encrease our knolege' (*sic, sic, sic*); but now I am beginning to sympathize with a minor character of Maupassant's, who started to write an essay on education but gave it up because he couldn't think of anything to say."[2] Now, what is wrong with the picture this story paints? And—an even more problematic matter—where do I begin in responding to that question?

Well, anywhere, for the moment. With an aspect of context, say. The piece appears under the heading of "Education" in a 1986 issue of *The American Scholar*, a quarterly "Published for General Circulation by PHI BETA KAPPA," according to its masthead. In that journal, whose "general" circulation is open to question for various reasons, pieces concerned one way or another with education are mostly of two kinds, sometimes intermixed: those, usually biographical and under the alternate heading of "Teaching," that celebrate its past and those that bemoan its present and future. Morse's typifies the latter kind fairly paradigmatically and carries earmarks familiar, generically if not specifically, to any regular reader of the journal: a curmudgeonly mood, a Miss Fiddich fussiness about what such people are still prone to think of as "the King's English,"[3] an eagerness to expose and ridicule students' "cognitive" ignorance, smug and unspoken assumptions about how much nicer the situation ought to be and surely was once upon a time, an elitist hauteur typical of people who believe in the gentrification of the intellect, a presumptuousness about literacy, a sense of pedagogical patience at the end of its tether, and a final plague-on-all-their-houses note. Quite apart from characteristics editorially sought and cultivated, there are others, related to those above or recast from them, that trouble even more: the more or less explicit contentions that gaps in learning should have been "fixed" *by someone else long before now,* that the people who should be doing the fixing are themselves badly in need of being fixed, and that there is really no hope for fixing any of that sick, sick, sick mess; a throwing up of hands about "continuing education"; limited, traditional concepts of the teacher's role and the student's; a ready inability to imagine how far-reaching, seemingly intractable, and immediately crucial are all the educational problems that loom on a global scale, beyond the relative comforts, in spite of so much burnout, of the American system of formal education.

I could easily go on teasing out the overtones and undertones of Morse's piece. If I did, I would find—as I already have, really— that I am not completely out of sympathy with the attitude he displays. Doubtless he and I have been somewhat similarly nurtured culturally and professionally. But that attitude, immemorial in its essentials, however it may appear to thrive on the carbohydrates of arrogance and dissatisfaction, will always end up malnourished, uncreatively dis-eased, cynical. Insofar as I am aware of harboring it, I suspect it strongly. Even given its narrowness and oversimplifications, it is not entirely "wrong" and is laudable in its insistence on standards, but it is deplorable particularly in the cloistered, oblivious negativity that prevents a larger vision of the educational enterprise, of how obvious problems might be obverted and reseen as surprising opportunities (so that what is *ob viam,* "in the way," becomes a door or, at least, a window), of how, to borrow from Mina Shaughnessy, "errors" might be refigured as "expectations."[4] That enterprise is at once more complex and more hopeful than Morse would have us believe, but imaginative divergence is required to understand such complexity and hope.

History can be read and reread in a myriad different ways to discover how we have come to "another crest of criticism" of public education, one, complete with abiding cynicism about change (a consistent Gallup-poll message), anticipated by Neil Postman over a decade ago, when bland "back-to-basics" polemics were the hottest thing going.[5] Blame for the state of education in the United States could be laid at the feet of benighted or exploitative interpreters of John Dewey (who is not always wise or easily readable), blame for it in the Third World at the feet of those too quick to export culturally inappropriate (to say the least) models of Western education, and so on—issues of a kind that I engage later and for the further exploration of which my citations and Bibliographic Essay furnish ample resources. But for the moment I want to stress what is at stake in my attempt to help us—especially those of us, whether educators by profession or not, who are on the verge of giving up, one way or another, on the whole business—see education in a different way.

A few suggestive "snapshots," if you will. Anyone who has carefully observed the development of a preschool child, a process puzzled perhaps most comprehensively (and, in the wake of studies revising Jean Piaget's pioneering work, controversially) by Jerome Kagan,[6] knows that the human being is an animal with a tremendously strong predisposition to learn (not only the familiar but, by analytic-imaginative engagement, the unfamiliar, or the familiar, to borrow Viktor Shklovsky's term, "defamiliarized"—think of the gusto with which children played with Transformer toys some years ago) but also that that predisposition must be assisted intersubjectively before its potential, understood differently in different contexts, can be explored and enacted. (That is, there is no getting away from the need for education, a need whose significance and immediacy are vividly inscribed etymologically: the Latin ēdūcere—whose derived and less specialized form ēducare typically gets invoked to argue that to educate means something like "to lead out" or "to draw out" [a child's abilities, say], which is a good enough argument as far as it goes—means "to assist at the birth of a child" and then, by extension, "to rear a child" [to assist at the birth of a person?] and so on.) In classical Greece, according to Werner Jaeger, education, in which "stability is not a sure symptom of health" (pace Morse), "embodied the purpose of all human effort";[7] it does in the postmodern world as well—though with a much less stable and more diverse teleology. Writing specifically of public education in the United States, Postman appraises it as "probably the most important contribution we have so far made to world civilization"; furthermore, extrapolating from Lawrence Cremin's observation that "whenever we need a revolution, we get a new curriculum," he argues that "our public schools lie at the center of our own civilization."[8] More vatically, H. G. Wells pronounces—well over a half century ago—that "human history becomes more and more a race between education and catastrophe."[9] That race, more accelerated, now proceeds, to compound Wells's apocalyptic mood, through a global crisis in education that, according to Philip H. Coombs, has been "intensified by growing maladjustments between education systems and the rapidly changing world all around them" and has recently "acquired new dimensions," of which "the most significant is that *there is now a crisis of confidence in education itself.*"[10] Finally, Gene Lyons, after a devastating exposé of American teacher education, simply declares, "I am sure of one thing. We have to do *something.*"[11]

Indeed, Lyons's declaration roughly summarizes my motive for writing this book, a motive informed, in my more traditional moments, by sympathy with his desire to restore "the dignity of what is, after all, one of the most decent of professions"[12] and, in my more direly postmodern moments, by Coombs's reassurance that "nothing is beyond redemption before educational systems are overwhelmed with ruin. The evidence does not support any such cataclysmic forecast."[13] We have to do something because if a teacher, as Henry Adams avers, "affects eternity" and thus "can never tell where his influence stops,"[14] then we should be fiercely interested in how millions of teachers in our helter-skelter world are affecting eternity, in how their pervasive and enduring influence is formed, informed, enacted, controlled. I *am* fiercely interested, and what I want to do is share a different way of "reading" contemporary education, a way that will help us translate its problems into opportunities, exploit (etymologically, "explicate," "unfold") the possibilities hidden in its frustrations, or—at the very least—understand more comprehensively, patiently, and affirmatively its historical situation. I would even like to argue that the notion that education has failed is a mistaken one—for many reasons, but preeminently because, for most of humankind, education as I conceive it has never really been tried.

I have both planned and avoided the writing of this book for a long time. The planning has had to do with my sense that there is much new and worthwhile to say about education, a topic that usually excites most people about as much as advice on dental hygiene. The avoiding has had to do with my lack, until now, of a way to say it, though I too in more hopeless moments have felt the deeper blankness of "the Maupassant syndrome." That is, I have

9

alternated between two extreme beliefs: that I have far too much to say and that I have far too little. I now believe that I have both just enough to say and a strategy for dramatizing its importance. Let me return to obverting the ob(li)vious.

Though educators are often respected and revered and sometimes even nationally honored, they are more generally regarded, especially in the United States, negatively: as stern and authoritarian (the schoolmarm), as comically irrelevant (the absentminded professor), and so on—the whole inventory of types embraced by anti-intellectualism and resentment toward academics. Their profession is ridiculed (those who can't do, teach), as is, sometimes justifiably, the training for it (those who can't teach, teach teachers). The education they endeavor to provide, whatever its present limits, tends to be taken for granted—and this in spite of all the costs involved—or, when it is a convenient political football, intermittently judged by an anxious public to be somehow not quite what is wanted. And educators as a whole are, of course, appallingly underpaid in comparison to members of other professions.

What is usually forgotten in such recitations, even by educators themselves, is that education is *the* most important profession. People may occasionally need physicians to treat the disturbances that flesh is heir to, lawyers to do the requisite lawyerly things, accountants to count money however the government wants it counted in a given year; but educators, however much their influence is diluted by others, determine much of a person's whole way of life. Everyone has educators of some kind—parents, friends, TV "heroes," whomever—but the best professional educators are continually aware of this responsibility and take it very seriously, knowing that their project is not only "general education" but also the habilitation of all the professions, theirs as well. Indeed, as this book's epigraph from Nietzsche suggests, that seriousness, which should not be confused with sternness or Victorian "earnestness," is what distinguishes the great educator.[15]

I am arguing that education is a profession very much underestimated and misunderstood, too frequently even by its practitioners, who typically see—or let themselves see—little of its importance, complexity, and untried possibilities. Most teachers, no matter how hard they may work, most of the time run on automatic pilot, with little sense of real commitment, and most everybody else in an increasingly automatic world pays scant intelligent attention to that situation. Yet now, as never before, education is crucially important: it is not just a necessity for survival but, through recent tendencies in its evolution, a force for transformation. But that evolution is not automatic (indeed, it entails the "deautomatization" of teaching), and we must "assist at its birth" and nurture it with radical understanding of its potential. In order to do that we must overturn conventional assumptions, ideas, and expectations about education. We might start by noticing how they are already being overturned or even, in poststructuralist phrasing, have "always already" been overturned, their wild side revealed.

The kind of overturn and attendant implications of which we should be aware may be suggested by a passage from Jérôme Carcopino's *Daily Life in Ancient Rome,* which should suggest also that the possibility of overturn is not new. During a discussion of the role of the *paedagogus,* "a slave who served as tutor, guardian, and servant of the child put in his care" (one must remember that education, for the ancient Romans, was more a matter of prestige than of utilitarianism), Carcopino notes the following:

> The spoiled son of a wealthy family had a splendid time putting his so-called "master" in his place, the place suited to a servant, whether he called himself a tutor or not. Already in the *Bacchides* Plautus portrays a precocious adolescent called Pistoclerus who, in order to drag his tutor Lydus with him to his light of love, needs only to remind him sharply of his servile state: "Look here," he says, "am I your slave or are you mine?"[16]

Pistoclerus's question about the relation of pupil to tutor or student to teacher doubtless has been answered in either of the two obvious ways on an untold number of occasions in different cultures and times—but surely never without some of the ambiguity about master-slave relationships, the sense of ironic inversion, that Hegel and others have analyzed.[17] That is, any teacher who answers that question one way or the other must have some awareness of the possibility for the answer being otherwise, for the hierarchy being inverted (and inverted again ad infinitum), and so might in some cases even come to consider that the overturning of such a hierarchy could lead to a further overturning of the institution of hierarchy itself and thus to a relationship involving "heterarchical" elements. Such consideration might well lead to a questioning of the whole notion of "mastery" in the politics, certainly in the epistemology, of learning. (And, of course, the empire that sanctioned the sharpness of Pistoclerus's reminder was overturned.) Any "Nietzschean" educator should be critically and creatively conscious of the possibility of overturn, not just toward the achievement of a different hierarchy, which can be only temporarily advantageous, but toward the achievement of a different balance of contending emphases, one more productive for both the student (who must always become more self-educating) and the educator (who must always be a student). And increasingly we realize, if the term is not problematized out of usefulness, that the role of the educator as "master" is to serve to enable the student to become "master"—that is, by an overturn to turn over a role.

Indeed, that conundrum suggests the principal educational overturn now in process. It may seem slow at times, but it is happening, and has been for quite a while—swiftly enough at times to appall some people. It has many facets and implicates many other patterns of overturn, but for now it can be characterized in broad terms. It involves the overturn of *teaching* in the conventional sense (as it is, unfortunately, predominantly practiced) in favor of *instructing,* in a somewhat unconventional sense of that old-fashioned word. The difference between the two can be illustrated etymologically: the word *teaching* derives from the Old English *tǣcan,* "to show" or "to demonstrate," while *instructing* derives from the Latin *instruere,* "to prepare" or "to equip" (or, by the first step of morphological resolution, "to in-build"). Teaching, then, is showing, demonstrating, proving, imparting "facts" without letting them generate questions, preaching "truth," telling "how it is," "professing," lecturing, giving the answers. Instructing is preparing, equipping, building in. More specifically, in the sense I want to stress, teaching involves presenting information to the student without sufficiently inviting analysis or synthesis: data, dates, facts, rules, whatever. In a word, *tokens* (from the Old English *tācen,* "symbol" or "sign," which is closely related to *tǣcan*): signs (signifiers identified naïvely and, as Stanley Fish would say, antirhetorically with what they are supposed to represent), symbols of authority, souvenirs, substitutes, and (by way of an implicit critique of behaviorist learning theory) "rewards" for certain kinds of conduct. Instructing, more specifically and in the sense I want to stress, involves enabling the student rhetorically *to deal with* information: to discuss, question, interrupt, problematize, negotiate, reinterpret, theorize, analogize it—to relate it as richly as possible to what he or she already knows. Instructing helps the student learn how to turn over the token and see what motivates it, what constitutes its meaning, what range of signifieds (suppressed or foregrounded or outdated, themselves signifiers) is implied by the signifier, what complexities are entangled in representation; it helps the student build the capacity to understand how authority operates, how vital knowledge is not a matter of souvenirs but of revisionary activity, how "reality" is constructed by substitutions, how "rewards" are rationalized. In computerese, teaching is like storing information in memory while instructing is like changing (by rewriting the "*instruction* set" for) the processor of information—to the extent, finally, of giving it the ability to change itself. That difference may be made almost palpable by attentively comparing the nominal stasis of the word *teaching* (a gerund accepted as a noun) with the verbal movement of *instructing* (a gerund more consciously formed from a verb).

This overturn should not be taken to mean a wholesale overthrow—and certainly not any absolute demonization—of teaching by instructing (nor should those terms be equated in any simple way with what are called in the post-Deweyan tradition "content" teaching and "skills" teaching, respectively). Lectures, I would note, function at their best not just to transmit information but to set the stage for students' negotiation of its meaning; they certainly function that way for Derrida, for example, who—oddly enough, given his reputation, for some, as an iconoclast—uses them primarily in the classroom. Indeed, in many instances (though not all), I hope that *overturn,* as I use the word, carries some of the mood of its rough French equivalent, *renversement,* as used by some Marxists, and thereby implies "turning upside down," "upsetting," "inversion," "reversal," "turning inside out" as "a corrective redistribution of emphasis in dialectic."[18] That is, teaching and instructing always require and involve each other, thesis and antithesis each haunted by the other, but there is now a strong shift of emphasis toward instructing that mandates a new and more complicated (balance in their) interrelationship, one that—if I may somewhat facilely play through this Hegelianism—holds the promise of a synthesis in the form of an educational practice quite different from what is now customary.[19]

The purpose of such practice or, more accurately, *praxis* (self-consciously theorized practice), as I envision it, would be what I call *apeironic learning:* a process whereby one learns what is "known" (in a given culture) but then questions it, subjects it to the pressure of alternate interpretive perspectives, theorizes and re-theorizes it as radically as possible, self-consciously revises it (think, perhaps, of Oscar Wilde's inversion of commonplaces into startling aperçus), so that the limited, local, and familiar is forced to reveal its problematic unlimitedness (even, however motivated, its arbitrariness), its global implications, its strangeness. By that process—very much a "practical" one—the known is continually stretched in its horizon, opened, and freshened by incorporating and being transformed into the unknown, teaching and instructing, each enriched by the other. (The *apeiron,* ἄπειρον, turns up frequently in pre-Socratic philosophy, most notably in the writings of Anaximander, where it is the primal indeterminate matter from which all things come; but the word's semantic field includes many other meanings as well: "the endless," "the indeterminate" [generally], "the indefinite," as well as "the untried," "the untested," "the unaccustomed," even "the different"—all of which, at one time or another, with various shadings, singly or in combinations, my use of *apeironic* brings into play.)[20]

Such praxis—already under way, in spite of a sense of "not-yetness," as I will show—is thus both traditional (in that traditional knowledge, even when traditionally "taught," is certainly part of its province) and quite nontraditional (in that what it enables the learner to *do* with or to any knowledge is not traditional, is even antitraditional). This antinomy necessarily involves complex tensions and delicate balances, with teaching and instructing, mild side and wild side (Apollonian and Dionysian, if you will), interdependent and interimplicated, both supplementing and tending to supplant each other. Teaching, too frequently textbook-driven, offers the student what is (putatively) settled; instructing helps the student unsettle it. Teaching reinforces un(self-)conscious myths; instructing (self-)consciously demythologizes or re-mythologizes. (Or, to borrow from Robert Scholes, teaching inculcates "orthodoxy"; instructing, like "joking and wit," encourages the student "to challenge orthodoxy, to trouble the [interpretive] codes, to force the orthodox out of their codified grooves of thought.")[21] Teaching is concerned, in the terminology of cognitive science, with definite or well-scripted situations (those whose sequence of events is typical), instructing with indefinite or ill-scripted situations and with the student devising metascripts in order to understand and participate in the process of (re-)scripting. Teaching tells the student "facts"; instructing enables the student to expose their conventions, to see how they are constituted as situated and motivated fictions. Teaching helps the student adapt old knowledge (or, to turn again to cognitive science, schemata or frames) to new circumstances; instructing helps the student create new knowledge (or schemata or frames) for new circumstances. Teaching instills the dominant ideology; instructing opens the student to counterdominant possibilities (counterstatements, countertechnologies, countercultures). Teaching builds a structure for the student; instructing enables the student, by what René Thom might call a cognitive "catastrophe," to rebuild or build beyond it.

From another point of view, teaching is concerned with what the psychologist Gregory Bateson calls "Learning I" or "protolearning," the kind of learning involved in finding "the simple solution to a problem," whereas instructing is concerned with what he calls "Learning II" or "deutero-learning," the kind of learning (how to learn) involved in becoming "more skilled in solving problems in general" or "figuring out what the context itself is—learning the rules of the game." Instructing is concerned also with what he calls "Learning III," the kind of learning (how to learn how to learn?) involved in understanding both how any problem and its context are defined by a paradigm and how such a paradigm is formed—a breakthrough level, however paradoxical, at which the student "gets a perspective on his or her own character and world view."[22] With instructing, the student grows as both a self-teacher with wide interests and a self-instructor with evolving, deepening abilities—because instructing develops strategies for engaging, caring about, being alert to the unpredictability and surprises (without which powerful learning cannot occur) of what is taught, for *having interest* in it.

While enabling Bateson's Learning II certainly involves the cultivation of more complex intelligence than that associated with Learning I, instructing works always to trigger and augment Learning III. Learning II, as Floyd Merrell observes, "appropriately exists at a metalevel with respect to learning I" and thereby makes possible "transfer of learning," but Learning III entails an apeironic conversion into a "metaperspectival framework," "a radical reorganization of what a human being previously learned." Learning II is the level at which alternatives are engaged, but Learning III is the level "from which the alternatives are *generated*" (my emphasis). It is concerned, in his construal, with "a broader system," and it functions "to cultivate a capacity for deviating from normal thought channels" and "the ability to bring about . . . transformations at increasingly more complex metalevels," to "combine and recombine sets and classes of schemata and relations," to create "new superordinate rules" for the game of knowledge.[23]

But, as Merrell further observes, instructing for such learning too frequently encounters a ubiquitous hindrance:

> Learning I, II, and III do not correspond directly to levels of "intelligence," at least insofar as it is "measured" in our society. An ape can learn to do menial operations more effectively than a child. A computer can be programmed to play a better game of chess than most adult human beings. If "intelligence" is determined by the amount of new information that can be assimilated and the number of problems that can be solved by use of an invariant set of rules within a closed system, then humans have little to no advantage over the higher animals and machines. The vexing syndrome we confront is that success in our modern society is most rapidly achieved by following fixed procedures; we learn that it is wise not to look beyond the barriers of our closed systems lest we and our "superiors" become aware of our "ignorance." That is, use of learning III, which entails creativity in general, is discouraged, if not repressed.

Merrell relates this discouragement or repression, as prevalent in education as anywhere else, to human beings' tendency "toward dogmatism and totalitarian minds. This is understandably the pathway of least resistance, where all is crystal clear, and where there are no unresolved problems. It is also indicative of a need all human beings have for regularity." Doubtless a deluded security and comfort may be found in unproblematic regularity but, just as doubtless, he observes, paraphrasing Ludwig Wittgenstein, "prolonged loss of problems would over the long haul spell death to all creative human efforts." Thus, Merrell concludes, "Tension, problems, uncertainty, vagueness, ambiguity, contradiction, and paradox are ultimately necessary, for without them ever-increasing metalevels of thought and language would be severely limited."[24] This conclusion might be called the Wittgensteinian imperative.

How does one enact this imperative and thus avoid the mentality that opposes it? Merrell's recommendation, indebted to Karl R. Popper, is very much for apeironic learning, which proceeds, in his words, "by the active and conscious search for problem situations that place acquired hypotheses in jeopardy, by criticism of the errors in those hypotheses, by maintenance of an open attitude of criticism such that all hypotheses and expectations are constantly improved and perpetually new problem situations are always met with new alternatives." Such learning exemplifies the creativity involved in "all human learning," which, according to Popper, "consists of 'the modification (possibly the rejection) of some form of knowledge' possessed previously," and it "entails *changes in modes of thinking and subsequently in modes of action.*"[25] And such learning requires instructing that carefully— always carefully—offers problems as a challenge.

Thus instructing fosters creativity. Whatever the controversies concerning what constitutes creativity (and there are many, especially among educationists and psychometricians), however it is discussed (in terms of Arthur Koestler's "bisociative thought," J. P. Guilford's "divergent production," Ernest G. Schachtel's "allocentric perception," Albert Rothenberg's "janusian [or homospatial] thinking," Silvano Arieti's "tertiary process" that blends "primary" [irrational] and "secondary" [rational] processes of thought, Kenneth Burke's "perspective by incongruity," or some other nomenclature, such as Edward DeBono's popular notion of "lateral thinking"), and whether or not it can be "explained" (a misconceived issue for the most part),[26] creativity is the paramount concern of instructing. Whatever disagreements about how to encourage creativity may flourish, instructing strives, one way or another, to do so. Conventional education, "teaching," does not. Merrell has addressed some of the reasons for that situation, but it requires further discussion—this time by a consideration of the work of Roger Schank, an artificial-intelligence theorist and researcher who offers his own version of those reasons as well as practical advice for fostering creativity.

Schank, like Merrell, regards the issues of creativity as essentially those of intelligence. He characterizes "the creative attitude" as, "among other things, the desire to go against the mainstream," a desire opposed "nearly everywhere." That attitude "entails posing one's own questions, not answering the questions of others," and it makes up new rules for the thinking game.

Though typically believed to be an attribute only of the gifted, it can be developed to an indefinite extent, he rightly argues, by virtually anyone; but "the problem is that a great deal of effort, usually quite unintentionally, goes into stopping people from being creative." That effort—and, I would add, one must not be deceived about the extent to which it is guided by intention—originates in cultural institutions that "thrive on rules and on ready answers" and that "abhor wave makers." Schools are greatly to blame, for they do not help students toward "knowing how to teach yourself" (pretty much Schank's definition of *creativity*): "Instead of encouraging children to formulate their own knowledge, we teach by handing down knowledge that is seemingly cast in stone." Such teaching relies on the passive acceptance of formulas. Schank stresses that there is nothing wrong with formulas as such: they can play a "creativity-enhancing" role if we learn them "so that we can adapt them later, move them around like pieces in a game." What *is* wrong is that schools generally ignore this purpose and expect students to acquire formulas "because that is what they are tested on and measured by" most readily, the skills involved in that larger purpose being ones that "cannot in principle be examined by standardized tests, at least not until artificial intelligence has really arrived"[27]—a problem to which I will return later.

Schank's recommendations for countering this situation do not address the politics of testing and measuring, but they do otherwise make useful advice for both students and educators. To promote the creative attitude, he suggests, one must "consider the differences" of new experiences rather than reduce them to versions of familiar experiences; "actively look for anomalies in the world," experiences that do not fit one's present model; think about one's own thinking; "learn to play with the rules as well as follow them"; "tweak" (modify) old knowledge (explanations, proverbs, whatever) so that it comes "into relevance or applicability"; practice "the process of constructing explanations" (hypothesizing); find out "what the questions are, *not* what the answers are"; and dialogically explore what is not understood. Turning more directly and summarily to educators, Schank recommends that the process of education, if it is to nurture creativity, must be

1. An active process, not a passive one
2. Student initiated, not teacher initiated

3. Interactive with an environment
4. Free of the fear of failure[28]

He advocates, in other words, a stronger emphasis on instructing. Contemporary educationists are fond of the notion that teachers teach not the *subject* but the *student*. However sensibly holistic in intent, that notion has had a severely qualified enactment. That is so for many reasons, to some of which Morse alludes, but surely in large part because that notion, as typically invoked, fails to distinguish carefully between teaching and instructing. The first involves making a subject available; the second involves developing the means to *study* it. (How many educators know that that word derives from the Latin *studēre,* "to be eager," "to be enthusiastic," "to be serious" about something, "to strive after" or "to be busy with" it? In our pedagogical doldrums we need to remember the image of the student, the "studier," implicit here and enhance instructing so as to vivify and multiply it. We need to remember also that this image is pretty much that of the child before he or she becomes, as Buckminster Fuller used to say, "de-geniused" by cultural institutions, including, to a scandalous extent, as Schank argues above, those of education—pedagogues as "ped-arrests," M'Choakumchilds, etiolated avatars of the Marquis de Sade's executioner-educators.) One cannot *educate* the whole student or "teach" the student his or her self (that is, help the student explore—and continue to explore—that self) without instructing, and educationists tend to conceive of instructing as, at best, a watered-down, most likely denatured or neutered, version of instructing as I am considering it. Let me stress this point: one may teach *a* subject (in the sense of "object," "topic," whatever), but one must instruct *the* subject (in the sense of "person" as "mind," "sensorium," whatever)—a distinction that, however it might be questioned philosophically, is pedagogically quite fruitful at all levels.[29]

Indeed, that distinction is crucial to the education that we have never really tried. Though there are promising indications that we are beginning to understand the significance and usefulness of that distinction—for instance, in Paulo Freire's theory and practice of education as the cultivation of *conscientização,* critical consciousness of contradictions that liberates the student into informed political action—there is also abundant evidence that we have been slow to do so. The revolution in elementary- and secondary-level mathematical pedagogy heralded by the so-called new math three decades ago did not occur, I would argue, not because the subject (set theory) was too complex for the students but largely because most teachers *taught it* instead of *instructing the students;* thus was lost an opportunity to initiate a generalized and burgeoning "literacy" in the conceptual language of mathematics—at exactly the time when the more recent "computer revolution" was embryonic. And now, unfortunately, computer "literacy," an idealization that has degenerated through years of confused educational intentions to mean little more than what used to be called "secretarial skills," involves a mission very much more of teaching than of instructing, with the result that the vast majority of people who use computers of various kinds have virtually no comprehension of how they work, let alone of how to use them more innovatively or even, perhaps, more appropriately.[30] They "learn" computers in much the same way they do mathematics—or writing, history, physics, and so on—by rote, unimaginatively, with no sense of underlying conceptuality and no apeironic capacity for interpretive revision or appetite for theoretical elaboration.[31] They learn generally through (self-)teaching and not (self-)instructing; and that is a shame, because they were born self-instructors as well as self-teachers—as a child's acquisition of language vividly shows.

In an age when the AIDS virus appears to be almost as busy changing its molecular labels as the Germans were resetting their Enigma coding machines during World War II, when nuclear arsenals and the world economy are intertangled with and even "controlled" by computer networks that operate largely without enlightened human intervention, and when our planet's ecology is being ruined acceleratively, education has to become different from what it has been, not only in kind but also in scale. And that change will not be initiated or carried through—not yet, anyway— "at home," because that is where most people in the world spend their lives more or less illiterate (in one sense or another), believing whatever the pope or an electronic evangelist or their government wants them to believe, relentlessly driven to consume whatever they have been conditioned to consume, unwilling or unable to think about their lives or imagine them other than they are, ignorantly unconcerned with or even opposed to the transformative possibilities of education (in the United States parental indifference or uninvolvement is a major problem, especially at the elementary and middle levels). That change, still inchoate, will have to be effected, first at least, by professional educators (even those who train people "on the job"), who must continually re-educate themselves about those possibilities and be ever willing to inform, seek support from, and see their efforts extended and amplified through the increasingly interconnected and mutually problematic publics of the world. Given the worldwide "failure" of education, educators now must design and begin to implement a pedagogy for the twenty-first century, one appropriate to the growing magnitude and complexity of the human experiment.

Since that experiment is more and more apeironic in its own way, education also must be so, especially if "continuing education" (continual "re-in-building" to learn more and learn differently) is to become the lifelong process it should be. Only continuing and global apeironic self-education, however given momentum and sustained, can empower people to live with engaged understanding of the increasingly multicultural, interdisciplinary, equivocal, paralogical universe now being discovered and invented. Without it, that experiment will involve, indefinitely, only a very limited measure, collectively and individually, of the well-being and deep life that still elude most of humankind. As much as I admire and agree with John Holt's criticisms of conventional lockstep schooling and his advocacy of self-directed learning through "home schooling," an alternative he eloquently rationalizes and thoroughly documents as successful on a small scale in his 1982 book *Teach Your Own: A Hopeful Path for Education* and elsewhere, I think that it is simply not feasible for the vast majority of people in the United States or, for that matter, the world; therefore I believe that the role of professional educators in the human experiment will end no sooner than when the role of the police does—though those roles should not be (and certainly have been!) confused with one another (along with the misprision of confusing school and prison). And the effectiveness of that role depends on its changing, mostly by the self-critical and creative furtherance of a broad shift of emphasis already occurring.

In the chapters ahead I consider many specific aspects and versions of this *renversement* in terms of their histories, difficulties, and possibilities, always, I hope, in the spirit of obverting the ob(li)vious. Rather than outlining those chapters, a tediously bookish procedure, I refer the reader to the Appendix, a chart that suggests the range of my concerns and that the reader is invited to peruse in preparation for the investigation that follows and thereafter to use, like my Bibliographic Essay, as a reference. The chart is not intended to be exhaustive (though it may appear to pretend to be, I could easily make additions—and the reader, who doubtless will quibble with some entries, is invited to do so), but it does generously abstract this chapter and those ahead (including notes), whose sequence of development it mirrors. Some of the chart's terminology already has been introduced more or less explicitly; the rest—much of it, I think, accessible by analogy—will come into play later and thus become more comprehensible and, in most cases, be attributed more formally. For the sake of economy, I leave it to the reader to discern the sense, parallel in predication for each pairing (an item of which may, for good reason, recur in some form in one or the other of the columns), of how teaching or instructing "involves" given items in the columns under the main headings. The citations for most of the pairings indicate direct quotations, though some indicate indirect or implicit connections or may be associated with only one of the items in a pairing; a slashed citation indicates the respective attributions of items in a pairing or of a slashed item, and a parenthesized citation acknowledges further derivation of one or both of the items in a pairing. Pairings without citations are so either because their allusiveness seems too general for specific documentation or because they are of my own making. Finally, let me reiterate, here by quoting from Karlis Racevskis's discussion of Michel Foucault's technique "of tactical reversals," how most of the pairings that exemplify the shift should be interpreted: "As with all metonymical relationships, . . . this process of substitution does not work to eliminate the first term of the enumerated pairings: it keeps it in mind while producing a new conceptualization made possible by the second term"[32]—an activity much akin to Rothenberg's janusian or homospatial thinking.

Let me caution the reader against concluding that this shift entails little more than warmed-over progressive education. Though it does entail some of John Dewey's emphases (many of which have been badly translated through several generations of apostles), as I read them, it ranges far beyond them as well, both in overall pattern and in particular aspects. The pedagogy of it is more self-conscious than that of his progressivism, less scientistic, more sophisticated theoretically; the curricular implications are more complex; and so on. The token has been turned over before, but now the scale is larger; the stakes have grown with the postmodern drive to question the given and quest for the new; the kinetics of the torque bringing the turn, like the taste of what is being invented and discovered, is different. The shift has the feeling more of a mutation in human culture, in how humankind makes sense of the universe, than of a reform movement.

The last distinction is crucial. There have been many educational reform movements in many different cultures during the last century or so. Indeed, in the United States they have occurred, with attendant versions of liberal-conservative conflicts, since the beginning of nationhood. Few have had wide or lasting impact; nearly all were wrongheaded in one way or another. The most recent one that can be seen with enough historical perspective to be assessed—and whose effects have provided occasion for ill-researched nostalgias and misplaced accusations from the likes of Allan Bloom and William J. Bennett—occurred during the late 1960s and early 1970s. Most prominent in the United States, though certainly evident elsewhere, it began, as Postman describes it, with "a firm hold on the facts" but ended in "ridiculous flights of fantasy." The question of why that movement—of which Postman's own book *Teaching as a Subversive Activity,* written with Charles Weingartner and first published in 1969, remains an important document—went awry makes for interesting speculation. Postman offers some cogent "guesses about what happened" that, if correct, may provide "a lesson or two to be learned—for next time around." First, the movement was closely linked to opposition to the Vietnam War and lost momentum when American troops were withdrawn from that conflict. Second, "there was an insufficient understanding of the complexity of the school as a social institution." Third, some of the key personalities in the movement, such as Ivan Illich, who wanted to abolish all schools, were captivated by utopian visions of "total change" that could never have been implemented; their disappointments led to social indifference and more private forms of guruism. Fourth, many reform-minded critics "had a well-developed contempt for teachers and administrators, the very people who would have to carry through

the proposed reforms," and they viewed "the student population
. . . as through a Rousseauian glass, unrealistically." Fifth, the
movement had only a tenuous connection with schools of education and governmental educational agencies, so that "the official
routes of influence remained relatively untouched by new ideas."
Sixth, along with the movement arose "what may be charitably
described as the Age of Self-Improvement"—still with us, albeit
in more conservative habit and on the wane—that encouraged young
people to withdraw "in large numbers from the social arena to
tend the windmills [now more the stock portfolios and fitness
programs] of their own minds" and forget the whole business of
educational reform. Finally, there was an economic decline that
"led to education cutbacks and frozen staffs" and that otherwise
dampened the zeal and hope for change.[33]

By and large, Postman's guesses seem accurate, and as I will
try to show, the problems and limitations they implicate do not
figure significantly in—or are being effectively avoided or overcome by—the *renversement* with which I am concerned. This "next
time around" promises, so far, to be different. There are persuasive reasons to believe that the shift now in the offing will have
a wider and more lasting impact than any past reform movement
and that that shift already is proceeding with the "sustained and
rigorous criticism, accompanied by the invention of multiple alternatives of a practical nature," that Postman argues is required
"to change what . . . students and teachers do to each other, or
how and where they do it."[34] That multiphasic shift promises, if
carried through, to do more than *re*form education: it promises to
*trans*form it.

CHAPTER 2

Homo Deludens: The Trivial Pursuit of Paideia

Why, in this context, *Homo deludens*? Because "mostpeople," to use e. e. cummings's telling fusion, continue to delude themselves about education. This "bad game," to follow the etymology of *delude,* involves many kinds of (self-)deceptive beliefs. Among them are these: that education, all lip service aside, is or ought to be a relatively simple (and unicultural) matter that largely takes care of itself; that what it inculcates (values, meanings, attitudes, skills) is or ought to be somehow universal and timeless; that it is or ought to be, after all, essentially preparation to join the work force; and that its problems require or ought to require only modest, straightforward, commonsensical, readily technicalized solutions. Such beliefs invariably implicate, subtly or otherwise, a forgetting or failing to understand that education is *the* enterprise on which the survival and enrichment of the whole diverse human experiment depend—so extensively, intimately, and complexly that, indeed, it virtually *is* that experiment. Enacting beliefs such as those above, virtually all cultures, sooner or later, have embraced reductive versions of that equation—a perseverance now not only deluded but increasingly disastrous.

The classical Greek notion of paideia, though culturally specific in many ways (the classical Roman notion, for instance, bears less relation to public life), capsules the general equation of education with the human experiment and suggests its significance—and what is at risk in forgetting it—as Werner Jaeger explains:

As man becomes increasingly aware of his own powers, he strives by learning more of the two worlds, the world without him and the world within, to

25

create for himself the best kind of life. His peculiar nature, a combination of body and mind, creates special conditions governing the maintenance and transmission of his type, and imposes on him a special set of formative processes, physical and mental, which we denote as a whole by the name of education. Education, as practiced by man, is inspired by the same creative and directive vital force which impels every natural species to maintain and preserve its own type; but it is raised to a far higher power by the deliberate effort of human knowledge and will to attain a known end.

Though parts of this statement might well be questioned (the easy distinctions between the worlds without and within and between body and mind, for instance), it provides a cogent emphasis, one that entails certain corollaries: that education (even in today's more utilitarian versions) concerns not just "the individual alone" but "is essentially a function of the community," that "The formative influence of the community on its members is most constantly active in its deliberate endeavor to educate each new generation of individuals so as to make them in its own image," and that, "therefore, education in any human community (be it a family, a social class, a profession, or some wider complex such as a race or a state) is the direct expression of its active awareness of a *standard.*" Thus education as paideia—to which word Jaeger frequently but not unproblematically, as he admits, apposes "culture" and similar synonyms—tends strongly to idealize and thereby ideologize human development, the molding of character. (And thus from his own idealized Hellenic perspective, "what we call culture to-day is an etiolate thing, the final metamorphosis of the original Greek ideal. In Greek terms, it is not so much paideia, as a vast disorganized external apparatus for living, κατασκευὴ τοῦ βίου"—a clumsy and uninternalized artifice.) Finally, "the decisive factor in all paideia is active energy";[1] enabled by such energy, paideia is man's "only real possession," without which he is a creature of " 'unculture,' . . . apaideusia."[2]

More contemporarily and cynically—though quite accurately—the function of education as paideia (*not* as custodial service) "in most societies, especially at the primary and secondary levels, is the conservative one of inculcating in children the ideology of the established social order," according to Donald Lazere. In the United States, for instance, where attendance at those levels, as in many societies, is compulsory, "that order is overwhelmingly biased in support of American ethnocentrism; a capitalist economy; organized religion; and a white, male, middle- to upper-class view of the world."³ According to Jules Henry's even more severe view, the function of education is one of "drilling children in cultural orientations" and of thereby invading and "binding the intellect" with "cultural obsessions" so that *Homo sapiens* gets "from his children acquiescence, not originality"—with the consequence that, for instance, "Learning social studies is, to no small extent, whether in elementary school or the university, learning to be stupid" rather than learning "to play among new social systems, values, and relationships"; that is, learning in terms of this function is "learning to be *absurd.*"⁴ In a more sophisticated and seemingly detached fashion, this function may be defined as the installation of a modeling system—however stratified and providing for the interaction of the individual and the culture—that causes "reality" to be interpreted or constructed and, because of the evolutionary "exaptation" of that system, shared communicatively in terms of its constraints.⁵ However defined, the function of education as paideia for the most part remains dominantly what it has been: preservative, culturally specific, and conservative.

But that situation is beginning to change—radically, globally, and rapidly enough to cause the mossbacked to dig in their heels, at one extreme, and to propel the incautiously innovative into dithering experimentation, at the other. In the chapters ahead I deal with both of these extremes, as well as with the important possibilities in between, but for now I want to focus attention on the conservative reaction to this changing situation, especially in the United States, where the attendant climate of controversy is manifoldly relevant to the rest of the world. That reaction has manifested itself in a plethora of commissions, remonstrations, proposals, turf wars, confusions, and—foremost, as I will show—delusions. In all the shouting there are also useful arguments, balancing vectors that must be included in the play of forces if change is to be both productive and corrective. Mostly, however, particularly in the public realm within the last decade, there are reports. Though many of them concern higher education, they all bristle with implications for all levels. And mostly, whoever their official signatories may be, they have been issued by—or have "come out" from—compilers who are beigely multiple, impersonal, always already dispersed and only obliquely responsible.

The watershed event in the building of this protracted "crest of criticism," to use Neil Postman's phrase again, was the 1983 publication by the Government Printing Office of *A Nation at Risk: The Imperative for Educational Reform,* a report to the secretary of education by the Commission on Excellence in Education. Its thesis: American students are being poorly educated in virtually all areas, so much so that "the established social order," to use Lazere's phrase again, is under threat of dissolution; the American way of life, the nation itself, is "at risk." Late in 1984 the National Institute of Education released *Involvement in Learning: Realizing the Potential of American Higher Education,* a report of the Study Group on the Conditions of Excellence in American Higher Education. Much more directly concerned with education beyond high school than its predecessor and less hysterically conceived, it engaged, fairly trenchantly but sometimes in question-begging fashion, a number of worthwhile issues—faculty morale and collegiality, standards and objectives, curricular coherence, enrollment trends—with a laudable special focus on the need to enhance the "involvement in learning" of an increasingly diverse national student body. And it offered a vertiginously idealistic list of recommendations—most, however difficult or impossible to implement, quite defensible—concerning student retention, student responsibilities and attitudes, contact between students and faculty, support services, defining institutional goals, liberal-education requirements, assessment of students' proficiencies, remediation, faculty scholarship, evaluation of academic programs, professional awareness of the history of higher education and of pedagogical principles, roles for external agencies, and related matters. On the whole, the report was a useful document for stimulating informed discussion of genuine problems and some measure of hope for grappling creatively with them, though the staggering fiscal implications of some recommendations (the conversion of part-time positions to full-time ones, for instance) were not addressed.

Involvement in Learning was quickly followed, however, by a report with a different tone—accusatory, acid, relentlessly conservative. Publication in 1984 of *To Reclaim a Legacy,* a report from the National Endowment for the Humanities written by William J. Bennett, who was then chairman of NEH, marked the end of nice-guy reports and began an era of nervous combativeness about educational issues that still continues. Whatever constructive debate Bennett's text—and his subsequent publicized complaints and anathemas while he was secretary of education and afterward—may have occasioned, surely in large part indirectly and even inadvertently, that text was a minor monument of invective, animus, and patent ideological bias that charged educators and administrators at all levels with pedagogical irresponsibility, cultural negligence, and moral bankruptcy. Although the report stressed the importance of "teaching," it did so with a rancorous eye on faculty research and in terms of a parochial, nostalgic notion of paideia: the traditional "humanistic" values and skills of Ronald Reagan's fantasy of an America that never quite existed. And it berated American education not only for not inculcating those values and skills in students but for not exemplifying them, for forgetting them in its preoccupation with curricula that Bennett viewed as faddish, budgetarily convenient, and irrelevantly or perversely abstruse.

To Reclaim a Legacy was followed in 1985 by a report from the Association of American Colleges entitled *Integrity in the College Curriculum: A Report to the Academic Community,* which was followed by another report and another and another—until by now even the most electronically oriented Marxist must be considering investing in the ecologically brutal capitalism of the paper industry. Whatever useful professional self-consciousness this ongoing blizzard of largely redundant criticisms and recommendations may promote, their idealizations show little grasp of the daily work of educators and administrators, of problems of morale and money, of the need not for a paideia that simply recovers an imaginary past but for one that complexly encounters an unimaginable future. Not only do such reports tend to "gloss over . . . fundamental problems": in their attempts at comprehensiveness, "they turn out sometimes diffuse, with serious disconnections between their stated problems and proposed solutions," and "their cures for some well-known problems range from the ephemeral to the facile."[6] Each successive report, questionable as a plan for action and already being forgotten, makes yet another chapter in a book of delusions.

This storm of conservative criticism has included not only reports from commissions and study groups but also a number of individual voices, many more informed and articulate—and less shrill—than that once emanating from Bennett's bully pulpit. Anyone who cared to pay attention would have heard them in the 1970s, growing in number toward the end of that decade, unconsciously prophesying the reports to come, and then to some extent resonating with them. Let me single out two that are representative, particularly in being initially persuasive (or seductive) but then betraying the telltale signs of *Homo deludens*.

Temperamentally conservative, about as articulately so as one could wish, Gene Lyons in 1976 published an essay entitled "The Higher Illiteracy: On the Prejudice against Teaching College Students to Write." It concerns "the coming plague of semiliteracy." American college students, he argues, "are not learning to write because nobody bothers to teach them how." Nobody bothers because universities have become self-contained, self-justifying bureaucracies in which departments of English are preoccupied with "the worship of literature" and "protecting the holy texts." The faculty members in such departments are careerists who are "rewarded less for what they *do* as teachers than for *who they are*" and who have no interest in teaching students how to write because they are engaged continually "in hobbyhorse 'research' of a kind that used to be done primarily by potty Church of England vicars when it was too rainy for croquet." There is thus an unfortunate gap between "pedantry" and "illiteracy," which situation harbors the irony that *both* contribute "to the declining prestige of imaginative literature." To correct this situation Lyons proposes a number of essentially legislative measures, the net effect of which would be to stop what he regards as "useless and superfluous 'scholarly' publishing ventures" and to require "that senior faculty teach a certain number of basic courses in all disciplines . . . and be evaluated primarily as *teachers*."[7] Insofar as this line of criticism applies—and to some extent it certainly still does—it offers a pointed reminder about some of the (lesser) foibles of academia; though the proposed measures for correcting them could be oppressive, counterproductive, even politically dangerous.

Much as I may sympathize with Lyons's critique, I am troubled by its rancorous tone, its uninformed overgeneralizations, its artless invocation of top-down and typically ineffective legislative solutions. Its odd fury about English departments spills in non sequitur fashion onto other disciplines, and the powerful and sometimes subtle importance of research to fresh and innovative (self-) instructing is never given due consideration. But what most troubles me is an assumption that runs through much conservative criticism of education: that somehow "everyone" knows what needs to be taught and how. In other words, educators ought to cease noodling around with issues of paideia and pedagogy and just get on with what they are paid (inadequately) to do—in "basic courses." The complexity of those issues is swept aside; the significance of much research for dealing with them is misunderstood or ignored.

Lyons's 1979 essay "Why Teachers Can't Teach," from which I quoted earlier, takes to task schools of education, primarily those in Texas but also, by his frequent extension, virtually all of them in the United States. Here Lyons has done his homework better, and his impressive gift for phrasing serves his purpose well. He is less tangled by question-begging ill will, and, though exceptions and qualifications can usually be adduced, the arguments for his case are persuasive: teacher colleges "turn out hordes of certified ignoramuses whose incompetence in turn becomes evidence that the colleges and the educators need yet more money and more power" (though I know of many such institutions that are miserably underfunded and of educators who enjoy no excess of "power"); "teacher education in Texas—as everywhere else in America—is a shame, a mammoth and very expensive swindle of the public interest, a hoax, and an intellectual disgrace"; that situation finds its historical roots in the beginning of this century, when " 'progressive' educators anxious to reform the authoritarian rote and memorization practices of the time" began the misrepresentation and misapplication of John Dewey's theories about student-centered learning and a stress on "method over subject matter" that now has led "the Educationists to create a tax supported empire of cant"; the non-nominal functions of that empire are "to grow, to protect the profession from competition, and to ward off outside scrutiny"; educators are too much occupied with "secondary" matters such as driver training, drug counseling, and family socialization; the method-oriented "puffed-wheat curriculum" of schools of education is such that "gifted students are forced to choose between certifying to teach and getting a decent education"; and so on. This system "for insuring mediocrity" can be pruned and changed, Lyons proposes, only by opening it to competition, "other paths to certification."[8] That proposal involves high stakes, of course, but Lyons, in his frustration, is not sanguine about its enactment—appropriately enough on the whole, since the same proposal comes forward again, through much the same biting arguments, in Lynne V. Cheney's 1990 NEH publication *Tyrannical Machines: A Report on Educational Practices Gone Wrong and Our Best Hopes for Setting Them Right.*

Eight years later, however, as if in response to Lyons's cry in the wilderness, Texas legislators apparently were not so timid—at least not after being pressured by H. Ross Perot and others—and passed legislation that virtually eliminated the traditional undergraduate degree in education all across the state, an action that put the writing on the wall nationally for schools of education, many of which have problems of accreditation, and thereby triggered a good deal of program revision and curricular housecleaning. Such legislation, in Texas and elsewhere, or widespread talk of it had the generally salutary effect of encouraging more interest in graduate-level programs in education and in undergraduate subject-area preparation for them. But, like Lyons's muckraking, it really does not address the complex issues, underlying those concerning certification, of what and how teachers should teach, provided they *can.* Critics like Lyons, legislators, and many "Educationists" are prone to take paideia for granted, to be unreflective about pedagogy, and to be unaware of the manifold and frequently quite subtle interrelationships through which they govern each other. Conservative prescriptiveness about such issues certainly is fraught with dangers, and so is the conservative assumption that everyone more or less knows what ought to be taught and how.

Many of Lyons's concerns and much of his mood may be found in the writings of Richard Mitchell, who began publishing his journal *The Underground Grammarian* in 1976. Incorporating and expanding upon several years of periodical criticism of abusers of "the Mother Tongue" and the "clear thought [that] is the most important benefit of education," he published in 1981 *The Graves of Academe,* a book flavored throughout by an almost frontiersman intellectual traditionalism not easily labeled by the term *conservative* as it applies to Bennett and his ilk. Mitchell takes pride in the description of *The Underground Grammarian* as "a journal of radical, academic terrorism" that pursues in language use "the thoughtlessness that more and more seems to characterize our culture," finding "the most egregious examples of mindless and mendacious babble neither in the corporation nor in the Congress but in the schools." There "educationistic humanism" (which attempts to free students from the "cruel" rigors of traditional "knowledge, scholarship, and logic") contends with "the iron law of behavior modification" (whose charm for educationists Mitchell traces to the psychological experiments of Wilhelm Wundt, who taught and conducted research at the University of Leipzig from the 1870s until his death in 1920 and who is far more to blame for our woes than Horace Mann or John Dewey); that irreconcilable contention is "at the heart of our educational disorders." So educationists are both soft on intellect and guided by stimulus-response notions of learning. "Thus it is," as Mitchell puts it, "that educationistic thought and language have a disconcerting hermaphroditic quality, for the educationist is committed on the one hand to the proposition that human qualities are quantifiable and predictable (through the work of the intellect, presumably, for how else can we quantify and predict?), and on the other hand to the proposition that the practice of the intellect is of less significance and 'value' than the possession of certain human qualities."[9] Needless to say, this situation engenders much gathering of quantitative data whose theorizations are codified in a jargon so at war with itself that it obscures not only technical issues but "humanistic" ones as well.

That is to say, I sympathize to some extent with Mitchell's argument—up to this point. The next step entails an enlargement of his denunciation of Wundt and his tradition of educational psychology, for that tradition has led the Lyons-like "empire of the teacher-training establishment" into a lucrative "preoccupation with pathology," learning disabilities of various kinds. Mitchell's impatience with this development, as he elaborates it, exposes both his conservatism and his (willful?) naïveté. The delusion implicated by them is figured in a rawly mechanical analogy that counters both the Wundtian tradition and that of "educationistic humanism":

There would be little hope of such things in a simpler calling like plumbing. Plumbers install plumbing, and, when something goes wrong with the plumbing, they fix it. They don't care how the pipes feel about it. Teaching reading and arithmetic is much more like plumbing than you probably think. If you know how to read and cipher, you can, if you want to, teach those skills to

Propaedeutic

almost any child in America. . . . if the teaching of children were handled that way, . . . then a vast and comfortable empire would fall.[10]

Apparently the "human qualities" mentioned earlier should be of no importance whatsoever to the teacher, whose job is to get on with fixing students' mental plumbing so that they can "read" the way Americans are supposed to and "cipher" (surely the near-archaism tells its own tale) well enough to keep the books in the family store. Here in a few ignorant moments Mitchell nostalgically restores the classroom of Thomas Gradgrind, the fact-and-calculation authoritarian in Dickens's *Hard Times,* sweeping away 150 years of tremendous and complex changes in the human experiment—certainly in our understanding of "reading" and "ciphering"—as well as elementary humaneness (a golden-rule notion that comes as close to a moral universal as one can get).

Attracted to H. L. Mencken's suggestion that the way to improve American education is to "hang all the professors and burn down the schools," Mitchell, in a less mechanistic mood, argues that the problems now plaguing education were occasioned by a national shift in attitude early in this century. He measures the torque of that shift, as have others for their own purposes, by contrasting two texts: the *Report of the Committee of Ten on Secondary School Studies* (Washington, D.C.: Government Printing Office, 1893) and the *Cardinal Principles of Secondary Education: A Report of the Commission on the Reorganization of Secondary Education, Appointed by the National Education Association* (Washington, D.C.: Department of the Interior, Bureau of Education, Government Printing Office, 1918). The first report, from a group established in 1892 and chaired by Charles W. Eliot, then president of Harvard University, proposed that public schools should dedicate themselves to cultivating students' intellectual powers of observation, reasoning, and judgment; to encouraging their acquisition of traditional humanistic knowledge and scientific habits of mind; and so on. The second report, edited by C. D. Kingsley and from a much larger and more heterogeneous group of educationists established in 1913, "found that proposal an elitist's dream" and proposed that the public schools should concern themselves with the more democratic goal of educating "most schoolchildren"—that is, those who "are *not* capable of such things and should stick to homemaking and the manual arts."[11] The biting of that apple of

34

anti-intellectualism, according to Mitchell, signaled the beginning of the present woes of American education. In sympathy with that argument, I would add that the size and makeup of the commission, along with the chain of information about the publication of its report, direly foreshadows the educationist bureaucracy that would proliferate to implement its counterproposal.

But however persuasive Mitchell's case as to how that shift promoted the institutionalization of courses in home economics, civics, and physical education and of questionable notions of so-called minimal competency, his reaction to it leads him, in spite of passing emphasis on an exploratory independence of mind, to stressing the importance of students' learning "facts." If the *Cardinal Principles* set the stage for public education to turn too much away from the cognitive-intellectual and toward the affective-vocational domain, Mitchell would set the stage for something equally questionable: the teaching of the "facts" and "skills" that constitute his unexamined notion of the intellect. I agree that American schools have become too much "an instrument for socialization" rather than "an incentive to thoughtfulness,"[12] but I disagree with Mitchell's argument that they cannot be both; for if "thoughtfulness" were a larger and more radical activity than he suggests, then it would be itself "an instrument" of a "socialization" far more self-aware and creative than either he or most of the educationists he despises can imagine. Mitchell's conservatism motivates him to criticize poignantly an educational system in need of change, but it also causes him to analyze its problems in terms of simple dichotomies and to look to an idealized past (that fortress of simple dichotomies) for the alternative.

If conservative critics like Mitchell and the "ordinary citizen" whom he both berates and would persuade could break the delusion maintained by their nostalgic assumptions about the "traditional" paideia and overcome their knee-jerk despair about the "progressive" one, then they might begin to envision the possibilities of the apeironic paideia now tentatively developing, partly in response to the problems with which they are preoccupied. Were that to happen, "all questions of education and schooling" would not be "hideously boring"; public educators could no longer be, as Mitchell labels the commission members, "Sunday-school supervisors *manqués*"; "the anti-intellectual dogmatism that characterizes our schools today" would wonderfully attenuate; "the professors of everything else" besides education would have a more committed interest in it; the "guardians of education and monitors of texts and techniques," whom a not-so-conservative Mitchell sees as being as "thoughtless and self-serving" as educationists, would fade into irrelevance like dunce caps and paddles; and "a way of the mind, the *individual* mind," one far less restricted than that encompassed by his anachronistic notion of "literacy," would open.[13]

The conservative delusion has nourished criticism of American education not only from the outside, as it were, but from the inside as well. Primary and secondary education have long included a significant proportion of conservative temperaments in their ranks, where one easily can find agreement with the arguments of Bennett, Allan Bloom, and E. D. Hirsch, Jr. Recently, however, the voices of conservative post-secondary educators, usually a reticent minority, have become more strident and more choral, as evidenced by, among other things, the pronouncements and activities of the presumptuously named National Association of Scholars (NAS), a growing, dominantly white-male organization formed in the mid-1980s and dedicated to the reactionary propositions that higher education in America has become too radically egalitarian, too "tainted by political ideology," too feminized, too culturally diversified in its core curriculum (thus too concerned with, to invoke the fashionable term of conservative opprobrium for progressive orthodoxy, one already embroiled in ironies beyond the point of self-parody, "political correctness") and that something must be done to "reclaim the academy"[14]—presumably mostly for self-important and self-serving white males who want to inculcate a traditional and "unpolitical" white-male paideia.

Even as enlightened a spokesperson for education as the late A. Bartlett Giamatti, former president of Yale University, once sang a variation of this song. In his book *A Free and Ordered Space: The Real World of the University,* he explores the character of the university and its relationships to other institutions, drawing upon several decades of academic and administrative experience. Much of what he offers in the way of arguments, ideas, and advice is pluralistically tempered, imaginative, useful, even wise. He has a keen aversion to the "Apocalyptic or Coercive Style" of "the Simplifiers" (not a bad synonym for *Homo deludens*), but he argues—quite accurately, as far as he goes—that the more or less conservative criticism of American higher education is a symptom of a general waning of "the American people's faith in the institutions of education." That waning has been caused, at least in part, by a "smugness that believes the institution's value is so self-evident that it no longer needs explication, its mission so manifest that it no longer requires definition and articulation." The consequence of such an attitude during the tremendous changes of the last half of this century is that universities have tended to "stiffen up and lose their evolving complementarity to other American institutions." In doing so, they have failed to reexamine themselves and, concomitantly, "failed to reeducate the public," on which they greatly depend, as to the value of their activities. This "vacuum of definition," lacking resistance to attack, thus invites criticism: "The critiques, rarely encountering an institutionally generated countervailing point of view, colonize the vacuum created and maintained by higher education about itself."[15] And, of course, those critiques, however colored politically, are, by the logic of this whole situation, necessarily uninformed to one extent or another. According to Giamatti, American higher education itself has contributed unwittingly to the nurturance of *Homo deludens*.

Except for offering some qualifications (among which, were I to pursue them, would be observations, I believe in the spirit of articulating a "countervailing point of view," concerning the public's reciprocal unwillingness to be re-educated), I cannot refute that conclusion; indeed, it surely applies, mutatis mutandis, to lower-level education as well, though not as strongly. But associated with that conclusion are some assumptions and opinions that must be examined. While they hardly expose Giamatti as a full-blown example of rightist *Homo deludens,* they do indicate a conservative bias that blinds him somewhat to the exigencies and opportunities of an unconventional paideia.

For Giamatti, universities are "profoundly conservative institutions, meant to transmit the past, built to remember (despite a tendency within themselves to amnesia)," and the subtitle of his book betrays his hard-nosed positivism about "the real world of [in, around, in relation to] the university," which ignores the subtlety of the cultural forces constituting that world and the possibility of its being productively constituted otherwise. Certainly one function of the university is "to transmit the past," but it has others as well, including the anamnestic one of *rereading* "the past" (reading against the grain or between the lines of its discourses [sets of interrelated texts], raveling them or, to use another double-edged word, one more closely related to *reading, riddling* them) and exploring alternatives to the "real world" accepted as its (textual) legacy. In any case, such assumptions about the conservative nature of the university and its world entail corollary opinions about the disruptiveness of those who dissent from traditionalism and about the kind of consensus that somehow must be achieved. Giamatti comes down hard on the dissenters:

> For these people, all traditional institutions are sexist plots or capitalist instruments designed to deny Rights and Freedoms. Such people are found (among other places) in the student bodies and faculties of many colleges and universities. While their essentially redistributionist and leveling impulses, vaguely compounded of New Left, Old Left, and narcissistic postures, hardly represent more than a fraction of any campus, hardly more than a special flavor to various Special Interests, they do—paradoxically—impede the process of institutional redefinition by baying so stridently for radical change that they spark counterreformations that invariably go back to the recoverable past for their counterproposals.[16]

Problems abound in this characterization. First of all, "these people" are frequently much more ideologically complex than Giamatti portrays them as being; their attitudes and concerns range far beyond those of the few who might be considered paranoid feminists and Marxists. Surely they should be vigilant about "Rights and Freedoms" in an increasingly reactionary, conscienceless, and morally unimaginative society. Their "impulses," which generally could be more tolerantly portrayed as egalitarian and democratic, are leftist in many respects—but what else would one expect from conscionable, intelligent, and feeling people in a diverse and intricately changeful society many of whose leaders, plenty of whom are given to "narcissistic postures," are hell-bent on continually (re)establishing a masculine uniculture dictated by a feverish, near-hallucinatory nostalgia? Furthermore, those impulses "flavor" the world of the university (in the several senses of that phrase) a great deal more than Giamatti recognizes or grants. And while some nontraditionalists may be "baying so stridently" for extreme change that their efforts counterproductively provoke "counterreformations" of the kind spearheaded by Bennett, Bloom, Hirsch, and the NAS, it is more accurate and hopeful to see their efforts—once the range, magnitude, and purpose of them is more generously understood—as indeed articulating a "countervailing point of view." Not the one Giamatti might wish, of course, and one still inchoate in many ways, sometimes shrill in distinguishing itself from a powerful and enveloping cultural environment, but one whose articulators are—"paradoxically" in an opposite respect—not impeding but *enabling* the most "radical," far-reaching, and important "process of institutional redefinition" ever undertaken in American higher education.

Giamatti advocates a point of view traditional enough to seem not "countervailing" at all. Wisely stressing a lesser role for fashionable "management strategies" in guiding the academic mission, he urges "debate on each campus, led by its leaders, as to what the purposes and goals of each campus are." He sketches the possibility of such debate as "the open arrival at some shared consensus of what the contour, the shape, the tendency, of the campus or of higher education will be." Though his language is muddy (how could a "consensus" not be "shared," and what is the difference between a "contour" and a "shape"?), he presses for such consensus: only through it "can the drift of American higher education be halted; can the further internal fragmentation of campuses be forestalled; can the rush to special interest be reversed; can the public's faith that these places know what they are about, know why they exist and where they are going, be restored." Or, as he puts it later and perhaps better in the same essay, which was delivered, in an earlier version, to the 1987 meeting of the Association of School Administrators, "The deepest need is for the permanent parts of the place—the members of the faculty and the administration—to reforge common aims, to establish again a common set of goals and values, to lay aside the mistrust that corrodes the capacity to educate the young and to discover and share new knowledge, and to speak to the public of the nature and purpose of an education." The nostalgic wishfulness of this mandate, its lack of careful specificity, its axiological vagueness, and its setting of the stage for like statements, in the following paragraph, concerning the need "freely to pursue the truth" (one can feel the uppercase, univocal intent of that last word) and "the goal of our common and universal impulse"[17]—all strongly suggest the operation of a now-familiar delusion.

Institutional debate, as Gerald Graff and many others have argued, is of paramount importance; indeed, the call for it is being
seriously answered. Such debate will continue and, given the increasingly polemical atmosphere about educational issues, doubtless will broaden, become more complex and politicized, entail
higher stakes—though I hope not to the point of shifting from
enlivening exchange to the destructive "battle" etymologically
inscribed in the word. But the call for a consensus somehow
grounded in the "common and universal" is now being and more
and more will continue to be questioned and opposed; it will not
be answered as Giamatti would have liked. Such a consensus is no
longer possible, if it ever really was. It *may* be possible, from time
to time, to achieve a "metaconsensus"—that is, some agreement
on the rhetorical stylizations, the mechanisms, the protocols of
disagreement—but that agreement will be always provisional,
itself a springboard for further debate. Debate, to invoke Graff
again, is now what higher education is about; what, I would argue, *all* education should be about; what, on its constrained wild
side, it has been about all along. Increasingly, "to speak to the
public of the nature and purpose of an education" will be to communicate to it—as much as possible, I hope—an ongoing debate.

And "the drift" that Giamatti wants checked is increasingly one
empowered by debate. Really, the whole of human history has
always been some such empowered drift. People who wear the
blinders of a static, unicultural paideia or whose fearful lives are
defined by Jaeger's "vast disorganized external apparatus for living" have always clamored for a consensual destination; others,
who exercise the wider vision of a dynamic, multicultural paideia
or whose lives are characterized by a complexly organized and
very much internalized "apparatus" (which Richard Lanham
would call *sprezzatura*), have always made a creative quest of the
voyage itself. An ever-changing balance of the two temperaments—
indeed, their continual debate—is required for the survival and
enrichment of the human experiment; that is precisely why a swing
in favor of the latter is now, through education, occurring. The
obverse of what Giamatti presents as a ubiquitous problem is a
pervasive opportunity.

But that opportunity does not come without difficulties, a principal one of which is the continuing accusation, directed in various versions at higher education, of a *trahison des clercs,* of the

faculty's betrayal of what should be its values and purposes. That accusation frequently targets, in shotgun fashion, the same "these people" who worried Giamatti, and it tends to have a strong rightist flavor, something one finds, to an extent, in Lyons's protestations against academic ivory-towerism. That accusation has been made in reports of the kind I discussed earlier. Parrotings of it turn up in the popular media, and hysterically hyperbolic, meanspirited, misinformed variations are available in recent books that, like Charles J. Sykes's *ProfScam: Professors and the Demise of Higher Education* and *The Hollow Men: Politics and Corruption in Higher Education,* ride the wave of journalistic noise about educational apocalypse. (The quality of recent reporting on educational issues suggests that schools of journalism also need some program revision and curricular housecleaning.) That same accusation figures significantly in Dinesh D'Souza's *Illiberal Education: The Politics of Race and Sex on Campus,* an ill-researched and sanctimonious book that sets out to develop a balanced view of the large issues underlying debates about curricular choices and political correctness but winds up facilely demonizing leftists as the enemies of academic freedom, reciting routinized plaints about scholarly careerism and parochialism, and playing to predictable anxieties about multicultural "revolution" on campus— besides sometimes simply, as a journalist would say, "getting the facts wrong." And as we will see, the left too sings its variations, though with a less deluded sense of target and intent—and with less notice from the public. But the *Meistersinger* of that accusation, an honor gauged by any of the usual seismographs of general public disturbance, is the late Allan Bloom, whose 1987 book *The Closing of the American Mind* long haunted best-seller lists and still continues to be read by nostalgic alarmists curious about, as the subtitle goes, *How Higher Education Has Failed Democracy and Impoverished the Souls of Today's Students.*

Bloom's book has been embraced as a godsend, a much-needed jeremiad on American education that offers a clear-headed and novel traditional or classical paideia in place of a curricular hodgepodge based on, as Bloom sees it, teen culture, Germanic nihilism, warmed-over Vietnam-era politics, and other fashions he disdains. It has also been criticized as naïve, smug, insensitively elitist, blatantly WASPish, question begging, facile, confused, preposterous, pseudophilosophical, unself-consciously self-parodical, and itself hodgepodgelike—among other epithets. Certainly his book is polemical, productively so in some respects, particularly in that its monumental exemplification of how the inflexible, unself-critical, and nostalgic idealizations spun by at least one subspecies of *Homo deludens* has encouraged the fuller development of a "countervailing point of view."

What is Bloom's accusation, exactly? How does he go about formulating and presenting it? If the faculty of American higher education has gotten the paideia wrong, how, according to Bloom, has that happened? What are the implications of the alternative he proposes? Let me conduct a sort of Cook's tour of *The Closing of the American Mind,* offering an occasional gloss or query and ignoring Bloom's more fatuous explorations (of popular music, for instance, which he discusses mostly with an alienated ignorance, or of racial politics, which he analyzes with appalling intolerance and ideological numbness), and then consider some cogent reactions to the book, all of which grapple with the issues of paideia involved.

Bloom's text begins, after a somewhat incautiously eulogistic foreword by Saul Bellow, a fellow professor at the University of Chicago, the seedbed of Great Books thinking, with the announcement that "this essay—a meditation on the state of our souls, particularly those of the young, and their education—is written from the perspective of a teacher." Such a project is wholly appropriate, for "the teacher, particularly the teacher dedicated to liberal education, must constantly try to look forward to the goal of human completeness and back at the natures of his students here and now, ever seeking to understand the former and to assess the capacities of the latter to approach it." That "attention to the young . . . is the essence of the craft," and the teacher's task, a matter more of "midwifery" than of "socialization," is to assist in the "fulfillment" of "human nature" in the young. It follows, by a suspicious telescoping of logic, that "there is no real teacher who in practice does not believe in the existence of the soul." Furthermore, liberal education, which entails preeminently the teacher's midwifing of human nature through the soul, exists "especially" for "a small number" of students who "will spend their lives in an effort to be autonomous"; presumably, their elite autonomy will be "against the grain of . . . our times" but not against Bloom's way of thinking for them.[18]

Bloom asks that his book "be taken as a report from the front," though he seems to know little of that area as most educators know it—a conclusion evidenced by, among other things, his insistence that most freshmen hold to some version of the belief "that truth is relative." (I have met plenty who at least *think* they don't: a testimony to the remnant effectiveness of teaching, as opposed to instructing, in the public schools.) He attributes that debatable situation to the "education of openness," which disperses and disorients learning to the point that "men [always *men,* for him] are not permitted to seek for the natural human good," a summum bonum to which Bloom knows the way. Thus "relativism," in his naïve and smugly nonspecific sense, "has extinguished the real motive of education, the search for a good life."[19] In other words, according to Bloom, the "relativistic" paideia promulgated by teachers, particularly those in higher education, has distracted students (hence, most Americans?) from the quest, through Reason, for Virtue. (Most such terms in his book have an uppercase aura, whether or not he capitalizes them.)

Having named his bugaboo, a vaguely characterized relativism, Bloom finds its avatars malignantly tentacled through modern Western culture and contemporary education. One of those avatars is "historicism (the view that all thought is essentially related to and cannot transcend its own time)," whose "truth," he argues, "a proper historical attitude would lead one to doubt . . . and treat as a peculiarity of contemporary history." (For "proper" read "Bloomian," the epithet of an "attitude" blind to how this proposition undermines and refutes itself; that is, since any "contemporary history" has various kinds of "peculiarity"—including, of course, "thought" that idiosyncratically privileges as "proper" [from the Latin *proprius,* meaning "one's own" or "peculiar," the opposite of *transcendent* or *universal*] an attitude that doubts the truth of historicism—the historicist attitude is the only *im*proper recourse. Surely some thought, especially if mathematical, does "transcend its own time"—all human minds are instantiated in roughly similar brains—but Bloom's snotty dismissal hardly advances our dealing with the issue.) Another avatar is "dogmatic skepticism," which has supplanted "nature herself" with "a gray network of critical concepts, which were invented to interpret nature's phenomena but which strangled them and therewith destroyed their own *raison d'être.*" It follows from this romanticism

43

that "our first task," "our educational challenge," is "to resuscitate those phenomena so that we may again have a world to which we can put our questions and be able to philosophize." In other words, we must strip the world of an interpretive apparatus gone haywire in aporia so that we can know things "again" *as they really are*—that is, as Bloom's own interpretive apparatus, his presumably less critical questioning and philosophizing, knows them. His simplism here troubles, of course, but not nearly so much as its associated pedagogy: he has tried "to teach my students prejudices, since nowadays . . . they had learned to doubt beliefs even before they believed in anything"[20]—a paradox that itself might be doubted, I would add, but only if one believed something else to be the case, since doubt thus paradoxically involves belief.

Bloom worries especially about "*value* relativism," his discussion of which leads him, by a predictable twist, into anxious explorations of nihilism. What he calls the "new language" of that relativism is "preventing us from talking with any conviction about good and evil anymore." (Apparently "we," by which he means Americans, used to do so—and in Bloomian terms.) Consequently we are continually engaged in axiological shuffling, floating, water treading. We have gotten "beyond good and evil" as Bloom's American absolutism understands them, a condition for which he strongly blames Nietzsche, who "told modern man that he was free-falling in the abyss of nihilism," and his German progeny. That construal impels Bloom into a frenzy of epigrammatic indictments of such figures as Freud, Weber, Heidegger, Marcuse (for instance, "Herbert Marcuse's accent has been turned into a Middle Western twang; the *echt Deutsch* label has been replaced by a *Made in America* label; and the new American life-style has become a Disneyland version of the Weimar Republic for the whole family"), most of which suggest that America cannot really understand such "German things" and so has ingested them in bad faith: "American nihilism is a mood, a mood of moodiness, a vague disquiet. It is nihilism without the abyss." It is only a self-centered "pose," he concludes on behalf of all Americans, but "the language derived from nihilism has become a part of their educations and insinuated itself into their daily lives."[21]

The cumulative effect of these avatars of "relativism" on higher education is, according to Bloom, that it "now offers no distinctive visage to the young person," who finds, during the postsecondary years that "are civilization's only chance to get him," merely an "anarchy" of disciplines. The purpose of the university, "to impose a point of view on the student," fails to be carried out. The "unwillingness" of higher education "to think positively about the contents of a liberal education" has its consequences: "on the one hand, to ensure that all the vulgarities of the world outside the university will flourish within it, and, on the other, to impose a much harsher and more illiberal necessity on the student—the one given by the imperial and imperious demands of the specialized disciplines unfiltered by unifying thought." While Bloom seems momentarily wistful about the absence even of "a set of competing visions"—and thereby faintly echoes Giamatti or Graff—he is essentially uneasy with what he calls "the diversity of perversity" and "the diversity of specialization" and longs for "a unified use of the university's resources."[22]

Thus, in Bloom's view, the disciplines in the university "do not address one another." Each is a "sideshow" incapable of contributing to a "general education" whose courses should make students aware of "the permanent questions." His "only serious solution" to this problem is one biased strongly toward teaching and away from instructing: "the good old Great Books approach, in which a liberal education means reading certain generally recognized classic texts, just reading them, letting them dictate what the questions are and the method of approaching them—not forcing them into categories we make up, not treating them as historical products, but trying to read them as their authors wished them to be read." This solution, with its notion of the reader as a nonpositional tabula rasa, is astonishingly naïve. And it tangles Bloom into one of his many thoughtless contradictions: he condemns "composite courses" (with titles such as "War and Creativity") that now figure in many general-education curricula for having "nothing to do with any program of further study" at the same time that he praises the "special experience" of the Great Books for leading "nowhere beyond itself"—though he does urge that the latter offers students "a new alternative and a respect for study itself." However much trouble one may have in accepting a "good old . . . approach" as a "new alternative" or "just reading" as anything like real "study," Bloom apparently believes that "the tepid reaction of humanists to Great Books education" involves, at least in part, their "defending recent scholarly interpretation of the classics rather than a vital, authentic understanding"[23]—as if all understanding, including his, were not a matter of interpretation, of something always more than "just reading."

Incoherent and incompatible as his arguments are, Bloom nonetheless marshals them in support of his repeated claim that "the crisis of liberal education is a reflection of a crisis at the peaks of learning, an incoherence and incompatibility among the first principles with which we interpret the world, an intellectual crisis of the greatest magnitude, which constitutes the crisis of our civilization." In other words, a crisis of paideia, one caused by lack of the sort of synoptic cultural and educational unification that Bloom longs for, hawks as obvious, but articulates as more a frustrated confusion than a creative synthesis eclectic and flexible enough to powerfully transform living and learning not only in "our civilization" but in "the world." And he finds evidence for this crisis everywhere: in the mutual alienations of the humanities, social sciences, and natural sciences; in the traditionlessness of the humanities; in history reduced to disparate historicisms; in science at odds with philosophy; and especially in "deconstructionism," a "fad" that "will pass, as it has already in Paris," which "is the last, predictable, stage in the suppression of reason and the denial of the possibility of truth in the name of philosophy," for it involves "a cheapened interpretation of Nietzsche" that reduces all text and all reality merely to matters of interpretation, dissolving tradition and leaving only "fancy German talk [that] fascinates us and takes the place of the really serious things."[24] Bloom's peremptory condemnation of deconstruction is ironic, for if he were to investigate its development thoroughly (which I would urge its enthusiasts as well to do), he would discover that Jacques Derrida, its putative father, is hardly an enemy of tradition, which he insists one must know in order to understand deconstruction, and that its ancestors stretch back much further than Nietzsche, indeed to the "serious" philosophical works of Heraclitus and Boethius, even Plato, among others, works that Bloom surely would include in the Great Books.

Pessimism, ignorance, and misconception abound in the foregoing catalog and invite counterargument. Interdisciplinary education is expanding in many institutions, in part because of historicisms that have created a fresh, multiperspectival interest in history and tradition. Scientific and philosophical projects tend increasingly to dovetail in their theoretical preoccupations. Deconstruction, which Bloom direly misconstrues, is not so much passing—a nonevent its critics relentlessly p. oclaim—as becoming a broadened and generalized enterprise, an increasingly, albeit problematically, assimilated strategy of analysis, one that does not so much reduce text and reality to interpretation (though, in a way, it does that) as refigure (somewhat as Althusserians do Marx's oeuvre) reality and interpretation (in any discipline) as textuality. And so on.

But even if one grants Bloom his idiosyncratic crisis of paideia, what does he propose as remedy? At times he appears to suggest an almost apeironic paideia, as when he declares that "true liberal education requires that the student's whole life be radically changed by it" and that it "puts everything at risk and requires students who are able to risk everything." Always, however, his anxieties about relativism and historicism intrude, and he returns to his inability to see how they are stimulating exactly the sense of risk, the impulse to inquiry, the creativity that he believes higher education, especially in the humanities, now lacks. As he begins the conclusion of his book, he briefly does another such oscillation, first arguing, with twisted grammar, that "liberal learning . . . does not consist so much in answers as in the permanent dialogue" and then proposing that "men" who read the Great Books "are participating in essential being," that those "books in their objective beauty are still there," and that "we must help protect and cultivate the delicate tendrils reaching out toward them through the unfriendly soil of students' souls." What he proposes by such precious assertions is a protective paideia, one that seems much more concerned with peculiarly Bloomian "answers" than with "permanent dialogue." Such an assessment is justified further by the dreamily idealistic emphases that sprinkle the final paragraphs of Bloom's conclusion. His paideia involves "that magic Athenian atmosphere reproduced, in which friendly men, educated, lively, on a footing of equality, civilized but natural, came together and told wonderful stories about the meaning of their longing." Bloom's ideal students are *already* "educated," male (though he does not consciously address the issue of whether or not to "reproduce" the homosexuality typical of his Athenian models), and—as his further qualification goes—somehow not so "dependent on his-

47

tory and culture" as most students are today. In principle this paideia may engage many, "the community of those who seek the truth," but in practice it is for "only a few," whose disagreements unite them in a "common concern for the good" and make them "absolutely one soul." This paideia is Bloom's version of that outlined for the philosopher-kings in Plato's *Republic,* a paideia, by a convenient but nebulous logic, somehow wholly appropriate for the present "American moment in world history, the one for which we shall forever be judged."[25]

Thus Bloom's peroration. The relevance of this exclusionary, invaginated Bloomocratic paideia—with all its unexamined assumptions, paranoid pseudoanalyses, and naïve anachronisms—to the daunting project of global higher education is a problem left to the reader. That reader, one must remember (lest Bloom seem only my straw man), has too frequently been so persuaded by the simplistic sophistry of Bloom's Athenian retreat as either to forget that problem or to believe that he has offered the solution to it—just as he has offered the remedy for his crisis of paideia promoted by insufficiently Athenian faculty members.

But other readers, however much they may grant the value of Bloom's book for spotlighting certain issues about the faculty's role in shaping the postsecondary paideia, are not so persuaded. Robert Scholes finds Bloom's discussion of what "teachers have failed to teach" to be, among other things, partly an indulgence "in parlor psychologizing of a truly lamentable sort," especially in its treatment of student attitudes, and partly "well worth reading" but to offer "no conception of the alternative" to cultural relativism "and how this persuasion might actually function either in education or in society at large"[26]—no absolutist paideia, in other words. Martin Gardner finds Bloom's moralizing vague and question begging, his excoriation of the Nietzschean tradition "Teutonic baloney," his tracing of American philosophical history woefully wrongheaded in its emphases and out of date—with no worthwhile paideia on the horizon.[27] Kenneth Alan Hovey notes that, among his other faults (such as basing his "generalizations about the characters of European countries . . . largely on anecdote and unsupported assertion"), Bloom "creates the illusion" that the authors of the Great Books are all sufficiently in agreement for him to derive from them "a single set of transcendent principles by which he condemns American higher education"[28]—a suspiciously unified reading of so much diversity. William K. Buckley, while admitting that he "can say yes" to a number of Bloom's criticisms, judges them as frequently too easy, obvious, or unspecific, the book "more howl than argument," at times "the leisured and cranky lament, characteristic of the small-town editorial page," its popularity due to its attack on nineteenth-century science; and he sees Bloom himself as a self-deluded Don Quixote whose unrealism leads him to plan "to encase the imagination within prescribed consensus and to secure the university against change."[29] Helene Moglen critiques the book, largely from a feminist perspective, as a confusion of "autobiography" and "educational and intellectual history" in which "Bloom's strategy is to essentialize the traditional values and practices he approves" and to deplore "as 'unnatural'" any that subvert the "old hierarchical orders," with the result that he displays "all the anxious misogyny of the late Victorian patriarch," wishing to affirm the "machismo" that he sees expressed and justified by "the Western tradition," rejecting difference (in paideia as in culture, without realizing that he thereby indicts his own philosophy of education), and defining "learning as an unreflective accommodation to professorial and social authority."[30]

And even Sidney Hook, certainly a more conservative and sympathetic reader of Bloom than the company above, readily detects that he "confuses subjectivism with moral relativity" and "seems not to have heard of the notion of objective relativism," which confusion and ignorance account in large measure for his holding the "demonstrably false" position that, to borrow Hook's crisp summary, "good is good and right is right—and that's the end of it." Hook is appalled at Bloom's distortions of history, "the glaring gaps in his argument," his indifference to the complexities of the tensions and conflicts that characterize American culture, his failure to define key terms in his implausible contentions, and so on. His reply to Bloom's vague and chaotically conceived curriculum is one of his own making. Unrevolutionary though it may be, it at least stresses that education should help students "become intelligently aware of . . . the alternatives of development still open to us" and "be informed . . . of the conflict of values and ideals in our time"[31]—imperatives of exactly the kind endorsed and enacted by many of the educators whom Bloom attacks in his mania for the simplicity of a pre-Nietzschean past.

Well, I could go on with such citations, but what of the accusation of a *trahison des clercs* from the left (the word itself suggesting the "sinister," the opposite of "right," the wild side itself)? It may be discovered in various versions but perhaps most typically in two books: Paul A. Bové's *Intellectuals in Power: A Genealogy of Critical Humanism* and Russell Jacoby's *The Last Intellectuals: American Culture in the Age of Academe.*

Bové's book began with his desire "to write a history of the institution of academic literary criticism," but it expanded, by an inexorable Marxist logic, into an attempt to treat its subject "as situated within an entire range of discourses and institutions whose own metier is power and interest." Far from the long-surpassed workers-of-the-world stuff that some neoconservatives still gird their loins against, his exploration exposes and grapples with the political resistance (or indifference) and self-blindness that characterize the critical practices of the traditional humanism that he sees as still—but precariously—dominant in "advanced literary education and criticism." According to Bové, those practices are so resistant to admitting their involvement with specific structures of power and interest that "critical humanism can no longer function legitimately as the toolbox of oppositional intellectual practice." Consequently, he is attracted by figures such as Michel Foucault and Edward W. Said, "who embody both the strengths of a politically progressive critical humanism and the most concerted and rigorous effort to think against it." The "antihumanist" Foucault is important "precisely because he concerns himself with the materiality of humanistic practice" that traditional humanists avoid by subordinating politics to reason or by taking refuge in the argument that "things are more complex" than Bové's accusation admits (surely in many ways they are, I would venture, risking exactly the sort of irony Bové relishes analyzing). Said is important because he "has produced the most powerful model of oppositional critical practice within the American literary academy." Both figures provide strategies for examining "the darker side" of institutionalized humanism: how it creates and maintains its heroes, how it "makes a self-understanding of the profession materially difficult to achieve," how "it supports the worst elements of an imperialistic and repressive society while justifying itself under the sign of 'liberal humanism,'" and so on. The betrayal on which Bové focuses is, however, slippery with ironies, for "traditional and oppositional intellectuals alike" are generations of his "humanistic genealogy."[32]

Institutionalized humanism, without sufficient oppositional practice, thus tends to exhaust itself in nonhumanism, according to Bové, because it fails to struggle against—indeed, it works for—hegemonic power structures. Its practitioners, whom Bové terms "mendacious innocents," hardly serve "political struggles for self-determination." This situation is pandemic in academe, for "even the most revisionist, adversarial, and oppositional humanistic intellectuals—no matter what their avowed ideologies— operate within a network of discourses, institutions, and desires that . . . always reproduce themselves in essentially antidemocratic forms and practices."[33] Even oppositional practice repeats what it would deconstruct.

What recourse does Bové propose? His skeptical critique, which ingeniously points out the paradoxical political self-entrapments of critical humanism, really envisions none, though he, like Bloom, offers unelaborated hints: "critics should try to move away from the oppositional humanistic tradition"; their "new burden is to struggle for openness"; Said's insistence "on the political necessity of critical consciousness as the ground for justice in the world" and Foucault's hope "to challenge the very priority of the subject," whose activity is blunted by the "doubling back" of inscribed humanistic tradition, emphasize positions that "require not only that we see practice and theory as specific and situated—discursively and culturally—but also that we find precise and definite ways to evaluate the relative political efficacy of various forms of opposition as these exist in humanism and as they either signal the need to escape it or try, as in Foucault's case, to destroy and go beyond it"; "some effort must be made to make more precise judgments . . . , judgments that will permit us, as we must, to acknowledge and support those forms of skeptical, oppositional humanism directed toward political self-determination"; and "the crisis in education" must be addressed as involving a "dehistoricization," the result "of the founding and persistence, especially in the United States, of an institution more interested in reproducing itself and gaining its own rewards than in preserving the skills, values, and knowledge of historical research"[34]—a notion that (with a difference, to be sure) echoes Lyons, Bloom, and others of more rightist bent. I sympathize with Bové's critique of academic betrayal a great deal more than I do with Bloom's—the former pursues its issues with considerably more informed intelligence and self-awareness—but both fail to investigate sufficiently strategies for undoing it and developing an alternative. Both are truncated at a certain point, one by aporia and the other by dogma.

Jacoby's book, published about the same time as Bloom's, in many ways sings a leftist counterpoint to it. More journalistic than Bové, Jacoby lacks his rigor, repeats himself maddeningly at times, and invites all manner of quibbling (for instance, he offers only casual definitions of "intellectuals" as "those who cherish thinking and ideas" and "public intellectuals" as "those who contribute to open discussions"). But Jacoby does offer a generally well-documented, historically oriented discussion of the too-insular absorption of the intelligentsia into academe, of the delusions of much (mostly rightist) criticism of higher education, and of the need for the kind of public education (in the broadest sense) afforded by vernacular intellectual discourse—all with cautious qualifications, commendable self-awareness, appropriate appeal to a general audience, and no Bloomian jeremiad or nostalgia. His thesis is simple enough: a whole generation of urban-bred, public-minded intellectuals (including such people as Lewis Mumford, Edmund Wilson, Jane Jacobs, Lionel Trilling, Paul Goodman, and John Kenneth Galbraith) who wrote for the general educated reader has been on the wane for some time and now has "been supplanted by high-tech intellectuals, consultants and professors—anonymous souls, who may be competent, and more than competent, but who do not enrich public life." In amplifying that thesis he readily admits that his "critique of the missing intellectuals is also a self-critique" (he has been something of a floater among academic institutions) and that his ambiguous title may be read as harboring the prophecy (about which he is pessimistic, though I am not) of a *next* generation of intellectuals. That is to say, among other things, he hopes that what he perceives as the boredom and demoralization haunting the faculties of American universities might undergo a sea change, that their "subterranean discontent might surface, reconnecting with public life," and become exactly the kind of catalyst for cultural self-awareness that conservatives "suspect and fear" and "continuously rail against."[35]

"The restructuring of cities, the passing of bohemia, the expansion of the university" over several decades are not the only processes implicated in the demise of public intellectualism, but they are the foci of Jacoby's attention. And in all of them he discovers, for the most part, triumphs of conservatism and forces promoting the privatization of intellect. The consequence? "Younger intellectuals . . . are almost exclusively professors" who inhabit essentially conservative institutions and communicate largely only with themselves and in an idiom opaque to the public. Jacoby grants that the American audience for intellectual discourse has been shrinking for some time—perhaps for more than a century—but he is adamant that it "has not evaporated" and puts his emphasis "less on the eclipse of a public than on the eclipse of public intellectuals." Since this "eclipse," which threatens to break the transmission of America's "larger culture,"[36] suggests more something that has happened to contemporary intellectuals than something they have brought about, what is their betrayal?

Jacoby avoids oversimplifying the issue. He both forgives and blames: "Younger intellectuals have responded to their times, as they must; they have also surrendered to them, as they need not." However much their situation may be an understandable development of historical forces, he still holds them responsible for bad choices. Academic intellectuals generally opt for professional conformity rather than the independence of spirit that Jacoby argues, without undue lionizing, characterized their free-lancing public-intellectual precursors (and he is careful to note that this tendency is not new but is certainly worse, at least quantitatively, now than it was in Lewis Mumford's heyday). He particularly derides leftists for quiescently buying into university power structures, for producing scholarship of little value (or in the case of Fredric Jameson and his proselytes, scholarship that is fatuous, morally and otherwise), for failing to create an intellectually oppositional momentum that could influence their colleagues and students (not to mention the public). The polemical iconoclasm of the old intellectual left has been succeeded, in other words, by the timid (and, with another twist, "politically correct"?) careerism of the new—a result perfectly congruent not just with such changes as the media dominance of television over print but with the gentrification of the inner city (the end of bohemia), the suburbanization of the outer city, the corporatization of academe, and the academization of intellect. As Jacoby puts it, more apothegmatically, "If the western frontier closed in the 1890s, the cultural frontier closed in the 1950s"[37]—and seemingly transpersonal history alone is not to blame.

Reviewing the conservative critique of academic intellectualism—the kind to be found in, for example, somewhat dated works like Robert Nisbet's 1971 book *The Degradation of Academic Dogma* or in journals like *The New Criterion, Commentary,* and *The American Scholar*—Jacoby sympathizes with its condemnation of careerism (self-promoting "sophistry," grant grubbing, and so on), and he appreciates conservative critics' adoption of "a public idiom," a "lucid prose" that makes them widely read (and, I would add, doubtless serves, more problematically than they know, their penchant for oversimplification). But while applauding conservatives for sniffing out corruptions real or imagined, he also judges them counterproductive, self-defeating, unself-aware. They betray a tendency "toward anti-intellectualism." Their critique "turns into its opposite, a defense of special interests and fields," and "they do not allow that an independent intellectual can also be a critic of society." For conservatives "politics can only mean left-wing politics. Their own politics is not politics." Blind to the implications of their own ideological hegemony, they constantly nourish "the fiction that the universities have been politicized by some left scholars." "For conservatives"—Bloom readily comes to mind here—"a critical vision is itself evidence of personal failings or foreign ideas." Perhaps most telling of all, their "critique of big universities and big bucks is also more than a bit compromised by their embrace of big universities and big bucks." Thus conservatives dominantly control the institutions they accuse the left of taking over. They call the tune and are irritated when the left won't dance to it or plays another tune and thrives at all by doing so. More committed to economic determinism than the Marxists they condemn for "the subordination of mind to matter," conservatives are appalled by the "intolerable contradiction" of people living off the society they denounce.[38]

Like Bové, Jacoby offers a subtler—and a more balanced—analysis of the *trahison des clercs* in American higher education than does Bloom, but none of them proposes a well-considered, practical, affirmative alternative. Though Jacoby apparently would advocate that leftist academic intellectuals stand up to, in Mencken's phrase, the "rich ignoranti" who control higher education and thereby become a public force for oppositional ideas, he finally sees them as trapped in their institutions as Bové's "mendacious innocents" or Bloom's "relativists." And none of the three critics treats any of the recent positive and hopeful changes, however much still inchoate, in higher education toward a more self-conscious professionalism, less insular specialization and more open and creative interdisciplinarity, a more multicultural (and courageous) social conscience, and indeed a more engaged relationship with the public (including K-12 schools, legislatures, students' parents, even the business sector). Jacoby imposes too tight a definition on his search for important young public intellectuals and so overlooks many individual voices (what of figures like Carl Sagan and Henry Louis Gates, Jr., who are also academics?) as well as voices, most notably those of feminism, whose powerful effects cannot be accounted for by his model "of single voice and general public."[39] Thus he—like Bennett, Lyons, Giamatti, Sykes, and others, in their own ways—misses crucial issues or just-emerging possibilities of paideia that have much to do with the coming generation of public intellectuals. Like most leftist critiques of American higher education, Jacoby's is more cogent than comparable rightist works, but both sides are subject to delusions that limit the balance, perceptiveness, and comprehensiveness of their analyses and hamper innovative and hopeful vision. Nor is the perspective of those institutionally either inside or outside privileged in this regard; as we have seen, there is, to quote perhaps hazardously from Jonathan Swift, "a strong delusion always operating from *without* as vigorously as from *within*."[40]

PART 2

Curriculosclerosis and Related Problems

The canonical or "Great Books" curriculum finally sought to present the humanities curriculum as a stable, finished work of art. The curriculum I have tried briefly to sketch can be thought of as a work of art too, but a work of postmodern art, unstable, unfinished, interactive, not a certified canon of revealed cultural truth but a participatory drama in which the student must take part, a drama which is set on a stage but not set in concrete, with dialogue which is there to revise and a plot which licenses us to collaborate with chance— all these together aiming to teach not only knowledge but the way knowledge is held. And this, of course, is how Whitehead defines wisdom.

Richard Lanham, "The Rhetorical Paideia:
The Curriculum as a Work of Art"

Given the delusions at play in critiques of contemporary American education, higher or otherwise, it is important in countering those delusions and in more productively understanding and, in some cases, changing the situations that trigger such critiques to address specific issues, to question them, to explore something of the complexity and extent of their contexts—and then respond to them as informedly and creatively as possible. Virtually any educational issue can be construed as one of paideia, of "cultural literacy" in some sense (not just E. D. Hirsch's, which pertains largely to unicultural, commonplace knowledge), but here I would like to consider issues particular to each of the broad multidisciplinary areas conventionally denominated as the natural sciences (including mathematics), the social sciences, the humanities, and the arts.

CHAPTER 3

The Natural Sciences

As we have seen, diatribes and jeremiads about the systemic failure of American education are omnipresent. Many of them thrive on percentage-based data, frequently gleaned from surveys of one kind of another, concerning high school dropout rates (especially in the inner city), how many people cannot meet the minimum-literacy standards for postal clerks or assembly-line workers, belief in angels, job dissatisfaction among educators (frequently exposed in some percentage as being ignorant of the subjects they purportedly teach), and so on. Business-world media like the *Wall Street Journal* place major emphasis on the dwindling percentage of people qualified to hold jobs of various kinds, complete with statistics from the Department of Labor that demonstrate how America is "falling behind" Japan or Germany. A balance-of-trade apocalypse may be invoked to stimulate interest in the problem. The "decline" of basic communication skills always makes for a cause célèbre since such skills are the sine qua non of an ever-enlarging white-collar service industry; but the highest stakes in the national economic game invariably are associated with "math and science," that aggregate of industrially (and militarily) useful knowledge of which "they" seem to have increasingly more than "we." And "our" relative loss usually is gauged by the waning, starting in the mid-1960s, of the post-Sputnik frenzy of education in such knowledge through which America hoped to "catch up with" and "surpass" the Russians. But the implications of the matter go well beyond such competitive quantification.

In July 1988 the Public Opinion Laboratory (POL) at Northern Illinois University conducted a widely publicized national telephone survey of just over two thousand adults (people eighteen and older), asking each person seventy-five questions concerned with knowledge conventionally regarded as "scientific." The results of such surveys are always questionable for a number of reasons (not the least of which is the usual margin-of-error voodoo), but still there is cause for appall: less than half the group knew that the orbital period of Earth is a year; nearly a third either believed that the sun orbited Earth or were uncertain as to which one orbited the other; few had any sense of the traditional methods of science or any conceptual grasp of phenomena like the greenhouse effect. Such results corroborate the oft-quoted truism—much lamented by organizations like the National Science Foundation (NSF) and the National Science Teachers Association (NSTA)—that fewer than 10 percent of American high school graduates have sufficient scientific education for postsecondary study in any of the natural sciences. (The similar oft-quoted truism for the former Soviet Union is that there the number is close to 90 percent.) And such results are not unrelated to problems evidenced by standard primary and secondary (and, in some instances, even postsecondary) natural science textbooks: "dumbing down" of concepts, pandering to creationists, all manner of errors, unengaging formats, and a great deal of insipid writing.

A similarly gloomy picture emerges from *The Science Report Card: Elements of Risk and Recovery,* a study undertaken as part of the congressionally mandated National Assessment of Educational Progress (now in force over two decades) and published in 1988 by the Educational Testing Service, which implements the NAEP. Though the ETS is a controversial agency in many respects—rightly so, given recent questions about its standards and procedures—the results of this study, based on tests administered to a sample of some thirteen thousand students (nine-, thirteen-, and seventeen-year olds), are generally congruent with those of the POL survey: most such students have little understanding of the traditional methods and discipline-specific knowledges of the natural sciences. Congruent with my oft-quoted truism, fewer than 10 percent demonstrated any sophistication about those matters. Also, though some minority students, on the average, showed "gains" over earlier comparable test groups, minority students typically performed less well than Caucasians—and women in all ethnic groups less well than men.[1]

Such surveys and studies abound. None is significantly at odds with any other. In spite of their simplisms and ideological baggage (which typically doesn't pretend to be invisible), especially concerning the national work force and foreboding comparisons with other countries, they do indicate and crudely inventory a serious situation. And such instruments document a like situation for mathematics education. A 1989 report from ETS entitled *A World of Differences: An International Assessment of Mathematics and Science,* whose conclusions are based on the testing of approximately twenty-four thousand thirteen-year-olds in the United States, four Canadian provinces, and four other countries (including South Korea), ranks American students comparatively low in mathematical ability.[2] A 1988 NAEP report, *The Mathematics Report Card: Are We Measuring Up?,* argues that about a fourth of American thirteen-year-olds lack elementary computational skills, that only a small proportion of American seventeen-year-olds can solve multistage algebraic and geometric problems, and that most American students learn mathematics in rote fashion and have little conceptual comprehension of principles—and, of course, there are the usual signs of small gains by minority students.[3] And another 1989 report, *Everybody Counts: A Report to the Nation on the Future of Mathematics Education,* produced by a seventy-member panel that included a wide range of educators and researchers and issued by the National Research Council (NRC), a part of the National Academy of Sciences, acknowledges the embarrassment of American mathematics education but also attempts to explain its causes and proposes remedies. The principal causes at all levels are an outmoded curriculum that takes little account of modern (let alone contemporary) mathematical research and an authoritarian lecture-oriented pedagogy that discourages deep engagement by students. The report urges that mathematics educators (especially those in schools of education) reach beyond the curriculum in which they were trained and develop one more currently informed, that curricular decisions be decentralized, that standards of instruction be raised at all levels (especially, I would suggest, at the elementary level), that calculators and computers be integrated into instruction at all levels, that more conceptually involving methods of instruction be tried (especially in introductory-level courses, where the patients are easily etherized), and that colleges and universities should take the lead in building a plan for mathematics education that is national in scope but not top-down in its execution.[4]

Such urgings may or may not come to much, but they are commendable in several respects. They are notably sanguine and generally democratic in spirit. They avoid—indeed, oppose—the muchtouted Japanese model (incarnated in a few hundred American schools as Kumon Mathamatex), one that, however successful in improving public numeracy in Japan, has significant drawbacks: it relies largely on rote techniques of learning, stifles creativity, is rigidly authoritarian, requires a cultural homogeneity hardly characteristic of the culturally hyphenated United States, and promotes the stressful competitiveness that contributes to high truancy rates and vandalism in Japanese primary and secondary schools (not to mention the sociopathy and suicides associated with the exit-entry "examination hell" that decides which students can attend universities or the burnout of students who do).[5] And they encourage curricular enrichment and more productive pedagogy. *Everybody Counts* sees no point in substituting fear for boredom, and it suggests strongly that mathematics education in the United States shift its emphasis from reproduction to invention, from teaching to instructing, from routinized memorization to conceptually engaged learning.[6]

The NRC's report and others, including the NRC's 1991 report *Moving beyond Myths: Revitalizing Undergraduate Mathematics,* have elicited useful response. The National Council of Teachers of Mathematics, as reflected in its 1991 report *Professional Standards for Teaching Mathematics,* has revised its standards for mathematics education and continues to rethink curricular and pedagogical issues toward the end of broader, deeper, and more exciting learning—for both educators and students. In its 1991 report *A Call for Change: Recommendations for the Mathematical Preparation of Teachers of Mathematics,* the Mathematical Association of America encourages mathematics educators themselves to become more active learners. And in yet another 1991 report, *Counting on You: Actions Supporting Mathematics Teaching Standards,* the Mathematical Sciences Education Board offers practical ideas for implementing the kind of changes in mathematics education urged by earlier reports. Whatever the disadvantages of international publicity, the numeracy crisis in America, which now rivals the much-worried literacy crisis for popular attention, has exposed for interrogation several assumptions held long enough to have the feel of "facts": that mathematical ability is far more a matter of nature than of nurture (a privileging, responsible for fomenting anxiety in many a student, that the Japanese system, to its credit, has proven, except for extraordinary instances, largely fallacious), that women and many minorities have little talent for mathematics, that mathematics is inherently boring or alien to most people, that students who use mathematical prostheses like calculators will never learn the operations such gadgets perform for them.

In the wake of such interrogation have come resounding calls for mathematics educators not only to update themselves but to cross specialty lines and cultural boundaries; to help students understand the historical development of mathematics, study collaboratively, and use calculators and computers (through conceptually oriented programs like Mathematica) as learning tools and not just number-crunching slaves; to emphasize mathematical reasoning and conjectural thinking and not memorization and the mechanical derivation of "right answers," particularly in multistage problems; to concentrate on the analytical treatment of problems rather than on front-of-the-room lecturing and template exercises; to help students find authority in the evidence of operations performed rather than in the person at the blackboard; to open up their professional debates and research to students; to combat the notion that mathematics is the province of only a talented elite; to illustrate the variety and fun of mathematics; and, above all, to encourage students to contextualize mathematics in its broadest applications and relevance.

Some of these imperatives may be translated readily into more specific, practical suggestions. The history of mathematics should deal with contributions not only from European but also from Egyptian, Mayan, and other cultures, and it should be studied through its controversies (concerning, for instance, who invented the calculus) and colorful personalities (Pierre de Fermat, for instance, or Srinivasa Ramanujan) as well as its concepts (that, say, of what constitutes a number). Cooperative learning should be encouraged by helping students discover aspects of a problem that may be individually investigated and then collegially discussed (the question of why Fibonacci sequences, easy for even elementary students to grasp, occur so widely in natural structures would serve well). Machine computation should be used by students not just to "solve" problems but to explore them (for instance, by using a calculator to assay Christian Goldbach's conjecture that every even number is the sum of two prime numbers or by writing a simple program to do so). The power—and limitations—of mathematical reasoning and the significance of conjectural thinking should involve studying how mathematical problems have been and can be approached (Eratosthenes' measurement of Earth's circumference provides a classic example for the first, as does the history of grappling with the apparently "solved" four-color problem; a variety of contemporary theories about the shape of the universe offers God's plenty of apeironic speculation for the second). The instructor should be always willing to work analytically with students on a problem to which he or she has no textbook solution (a so-called intrinsically difficult problem, say, or even just a spontaneously generated algebraic equation). The instructor should welcome students' discussion of ongoing controversies in mathematics (concerning, among many other things, issues of computability, the status of Gödel's Theorem, the constructed rather than discovered nature of mathematical phenomena, enduring topological riddles). The instructor should prompt all students to recognize and develop further the mathematical skills and instincts they already, perhaps quite unself-consciously, exploit in their daily lives (when shopping, taking a trip, and so on). The fun of mathematics inheres, for some students, in certain kinds of exercises (building one of Blaise Pascal's arithmetic triangles, for instance, or searching for the rule by which a geometric pattern in Arabic tiling proliferates or a sequence of numbers is generated), but most students should be helped to know it through the virtually endless, hardly trivial or isolated applications of mathematics, especially those that spur critical thinking (the use of statistics in polling, say, or of probability theory in calculating the changes of all manner of events) and analogical elaboration (any geometry as a paradigmatic system of relationality, Klein bottles and Möbius strips as models of paradox generally, catastrophe theory as a tool for describing and better understanding radical changes in many different kinds of systems, the fractal as a ubiquitous characteristic of spatial irregularity, and so on). Higher mathematics may never be comfortable territory for most Americans, but there is increasing hope, as such recommendations are put into effect, that a more numerate culture, American or global, can have a larger appreciation of those seemingly abstruse regions and of the significance—epistemological or cultural, potential or otherwise—of their enterprise.[7]

Indeed, I see no reason why one should not feel hope generally for education in the natural sciences, even in the United States, with its history of wavering and typically unimaginative commitment to such education, of anti-intellectualism, and of alienation between the "hard" sciences and "softer" or more humanistic disciplines. The NSTA is very much concerned to implement curricular changes that will allow primary and secondary students a more protracted and more theoretical involvement with the natural sciences, and it has the financial support of the NSF. The lavishly endowed Howard Hughes Medical Institute is now funding projects for innovative undergraduate education in biology, especially for women and minority students. Among many other, similarly hopeful efforts that could be mentioned is Project 2061, whose futuristic affirmativeness is inscribed in its title's reference to the date when Halley's comet will return to the vicinity of Earth, an event most of the present generation of primary-level students could, in a world of intelligent science, live to witness. Sponsored and directed by the American Association for the Advancement of Science, Project 2061 intends, through well-executed research, well-considered proposals to the educational community, and pilot-site training, radically to redefine and reconstitute the curricula of the sciences, social as well as natural, in such a way as to emphasize conceptualization and theorization and devalue the memorization of vocabulary lists and "facts" and the performing of predictable experiments. The project's attempt, very much in the spirit of Project Kaleidoscope's recent recommendations for postsecondary science education, to turn American educators away from the deluded pedagogy of science as an inert catalog of information to collaborative hands-on (whether "kit-based" or laboratory-based) approaches has been slowed, as one might imagine, by institutionalized habits and disciplinary turf wars, but the momentum of more apeironic pedagogical thinking is growing and may convert even some of the anti-intelligentsia—by appeal to, if nothing else, their nationalistic spirit of competition. It is encouraging that the AAAS's overview report on the project, *Science for All Americans,* was previewed, with a sympathetic reception, at the 1989 national meeting of the Holmes Group, a consortium of ninety-odd research-oriented universities dedicated to improving schools of education and enhancing the status of the profession of education.[8]

In the early 1980s Edward A. Feigenbaum and Pamela McCorduck expressed extreme concern about the state of American education, most notably in regard to "knowledge engineering" and American response to Japan's Fifth Generation Project for computer development. Their concern was multiply motivated. It was certainly occasioned by a climate of anti-intellectualism that they argued, somewhat simplistically, had been bolstered by "a large-scale revulsion against the intellect, especially as it was supposed to be embodied by rationality and formal education," in the 1960s. But a perhaps more troubling cause for alarm was their observation that "American intellectuals" (that is, mostly academic humanists) were willfully ignorant of artificial-intelligence work, saw "the computerization of university campuses . . . as the new barbarism," and lived typically in "a dream world" of snobbery and indifference toward the revolutionary science and technology of the Fifth Generation world. A representative consequence of this alienation: "virtually no professors of English know anything about the discoveries knowledge engineers have made in their efforts to represent ideas in language" (a gap I tried to help close with my book *Mind, Language, Machine*). Intellectuals and knowledge engineers trapped in that latest version of C. P. Snow's two cultures, Feigenbaum and McCorduck announced, had "no common language," an unfortunate situation since "no plausible claim to intellectuality can possibly be made in the near future without an intimate dependence upon this new instrument [the computer]."[9]

However incautious and preposterous that exclusionary hyperbole, a commonplace of what I would call the cybernetic sublime, the scientific-humanistic alienation Feigenbaum and McCorduck observed seems to be increasingly moderating and even changing into (at least) a rapprochement that involves enlarging measures of mutual respect, understanding, and curiosity. Knowledge engineers have come to recognize the daunting complexities of natural language that professors of English have been grappling with, and professors of English have learned to take advantage of the utility and power of computers—not just in word processing but in computer-assisted learning and other applications. But more important, in a broader perspective there recently has come about a remarkable thickening and intensification of the sense of complementarity between the sciences and the humanities, a process that I would argue, against Feigenbaum and McCorduck's reading of the 1960s as a dark age, was promoted—in no simple way, sometimes indirectly, frequently through proliferant (self-)critiques—by the cultural mood of that time and has continued, admittedly by fits and starts, ever since. In 1970 the late Northrop Frye pertinently characterized that complementarity in these terms:

> It does not seem to me that the really important difference between the humanities and the sciences is in the difference in their subject matter. It is rather that science exhibits a method and a mental attitude, most clearly in the physical sciences, of a stabilized subject and an impartial and detached treatment of evidence which is essential to all serious work in all fields. The humanities, on the other hand, express in their containing forms, or myths, the nature of the human involvement with the human world, which is essential to any serious man's attitude to life. As long as man lives in the world, he will need the perspective and attitude of the scientist; but to the extent that he has created the world he lives in, feels responsible for it and has a concern for its destiny, which is also his own destiny, he will need the perspective and attitude of the humanist.

This characterization involves considerable idealization (not to mention naïveté and sexism), but it occurs in the context of—and concludes—a discussion that suggests, already, an ongoing complexifying of the sciences-humanities complementarity: Frye speculates that "science, as a form of knowledge, could even be thought of as a gigantic human narcissism, the reason falling in love with its own reflection in nature," and he remarks that "in history, in philosophy, in criticism, a scientific detachment and a humane engagement are fighting each other like Jacob and his angel."[10] Indeed, over the next two decades Frye's idealized complementarity would mutate into a more interactively tangled relationship, the sciences and the humanities each a limit case of the other and each shot with issues that more traditionally might have been relegated to the other. For instance, the sciences have been compelled to confront, ever more nervously, the implications of the thinking of John Archibald Wheeler and others concerning the ineluctably human and cultural dimensions of scientific observation and theorization (uncertainty and metaphoricality), while the humanities have had to struggle with the implications, crucial for their self-definition, of the rigorously analytical exposures, by Derrida and others, of how profoundly their activities are determined by textual forces (semiotic logics) beyond the ken of traditional humanism.

Evidence of that changing relationship is not difficult to discover. Examples especially pertinent to science education may be found in the writings of Paul Feyerabend and Lewis Thomas, both of whom, in different ways, urge apeironic approaches. In his 1975 book *Against Method: Outline of an Anarchistic Theory of Knowledge,* Feyerabend criticizes conventional science for its pretensions to objectivity, universality, factuality, and methodological purity—pretensions that inevitably involve delusive simplification, inattention to intersubjectivity, interpretive authoritarianism, repression both epistemological and political. Concomitantly, "scientific education . . . simplifies 'science' by simplifying its participants." Such simplification separates by both disciplinary and historical isolation, institutionalizes certain "facts," works "to inhibit intuitions that might lead to a blurring of boundaries," eschews the unscientific (religion, humor, and so on), and restrains imagination. Such education promotes an explainable mystification about the difficulty of science: "A subject such as medicine, or physics, or biology appears difficult only because it is taught badly, because the standard instructions are full of redundant material, and because they start too late in life." He exhorts us to "free society from the strangling hold of an ideologically petrified science just as our ancestors freed *us* from the strangling hold of the One True Religion." He proposes that "a mature citizen . . . will study science as a historical phenomenon and not as the one and only sensible way of approaching a problem." Science educators should acknowledge, in spite of the artful hegemony of conventional science (think, I would suggest, of the entrenchment of big-bang cosmological theory), that "the world we want to explore is a largely unknown entity" and that "we must, therefore, keep our options open and . . . not restrict ourselves in advance." Along with this acknowledgment Feyerabend stresses the need for science education to be reconciled with "a humanitarian attitude," sympathizes with John Stuart Mill's desire for it to cease deleterious conflict with the cultivation of individuality, and calls for skepticism about "the ideals of rationality that happen to be fashionable in science." Toward those ends he outlines a "methodology" (or antimethodology?) of science—and, mostly implicitly, of science education—that is "anarchistic" or, as he qualifies that epithet in a note, dadaistic.[11] His detailed outline of that wild-side methodology, tasting distinctly "humanistic" as well as "scientific," comprises most of his book and so is too extensive to be fairly capsuled here, but I will later touch on its countercurricular purport.

In his essay "Humanities and Science," in his 1983 book *Late Night Thoughts on Listening to Mahler's Ninth Symphony,* Thomas offers a discussion less revolutionary in tone than Feyerabend's but not necessarily in its implications, a discussion that suggests some incorporation of Feyerabend's seemingly jarring perspective into a less-radical reflection on science and its pedagogy. Thomas begins with two dicta from the influential physicist Lord Kelvin (William Thomson) in the late nineteenth century: that "no observation of nature was worth paying attention to unless it could be stated in precisely quantitative terms" and that physics "was an almost completed science." As Thomas argues well, both have proven subsequently to be problematic, to say the least; but their delusional force has remained in effect in the public mind and in science education, and scientists have done too little to dispel it, to break its spell. In consequence there are unnecessary misunderstandings between the sciences and the humanities "as to the place and importance of science in a liberal-arts education, and the role of science in twentieth-century culture," that have contributed to a saliently Gradgrindian pedagogy:

> Over the past half century, we have been teaching the sciences as though they were the same academic collection of cut-and-dried subjects as always, and—here is what has really gone wrong—as though they would always be the same. The teaching of today's biology, for example, is pretty much the same kind of exercise as the teaching of Latin was when I was in high school long ago. First of all, the fundamentals, the underlying laws, the essential grammar, and then the reading of texts. Once mastered, that is that: Latin is Latin and forever after will be Latin. And biology is precisely biology, a vast array of hard facts to be learned as fundamentals, followed by a reading of the texts.
>
> Moreover, we have been teaching science as though its facts were somehow superior to the facts in all other scholarly disciplines, more fundamental, more solid, less subject to subjectivism, immutable. English literature is not just one way of thinking, it is all sorts of ways. Poetry is a moving target. The

facts that underlie art, architecture, and music are not really hard facts, and you can change them any way you like by arguing about them, but science is treated as an altogether different kind of learning: an unambiguous, unalterable, and endlessly useful display of data needing only to be packaged and installed somewhere in one's temporal lobe in order to achieve a full understanding of the natural world.[12]

What emerges here is a characterization of science that is false—science, as Thomas is quick to point out, is "not like this at all"—and one of science education that reveals it as its own caricature of mechanical and philosophically naïve "teaching."

Thomas argues cogently as to how science is otherwise than portrayed above and as to how, concomitantly, education in it ought to be so. Lord Kelvin was mistaken a century ago and still is: "every field of science . . . is incomplete." Certainly in the life sciences, Thomas's own area of specialization, knowledge is not set and static; indeed, "it is required that the most expert and sophisticated minds be capable of changing those minds, often with a great lurch, every few years." In the sciences generally, "hard facts tend to soften overnight," so that "the conclusions reached in science are always, when looked at closely, far more provisional and tentative than are most of the assumptions arrived at by our colleagues in the humanities." Given that, Thomas stresses the importance of a Graffian attitude toward strongly polarized scientific controversies: "The essential lesson to be learned has nothing to do with the relative validity of the facts underlying the argument, it is the argument itself that is the education: we do not yet know enough to settle such questions." Elaborating this deconstructive strategy, he contends that "it is the very strangeness of nature that makes science engrossing. That ought to be at the center of science teaching." Having suggested that the peripheral become the central, he inverts the usual hierarchical relation of precise sciences and imprecise humanities: "There are more than seven-times-seven types of ambiguity [an allusion to William Empson's pioneering New Critical work *Seven Types of Ambiguity*] in science, awaiting analysis. The poetry of Wallace Stevens is crystal-clear alongside the genetic code." And he undermines scientific arrogance by another inversion: "Science, especially twentieth-century science, has provided us with a glimpse of something we never really knew before, the revelation of human ignorance." Lord Kelvin's emphasis on the mathematicization of knowledge is surely relevant to this situation, but so is another quite different emphasis: "For getting a full grasp, for perceiving real significance when significance is at hand, we shall need minds at work from all sorts of brains outside the fields of science, most of all the brains of poets, of course, but also those of artists, musicians, philosophers, historians, writers in general."[13]

That necessity (for a heterosis of disciplines) prompts Thomas to "press for changes in the way science is taught" to both those who "will be doing the science themselves" and "pretty nearly everyone else," the people who must think about the enterprise of the first group. Those changes should involve, among other things, the development of "a new group of professional thinkers . . . who can create a discipline of scientific criticism"—a suggestion that speaks to some of Jacoby's concerns. Thomas's pedagogy following from his characterization of science, he proposes that "introductory courses in science, at all levels from grade school through college, be radically revised. Leave the fundamentals, the so-called basics, aside for a while, and concentrate the attention of all students on the things that are *not* known." In other words, motivate first the interestedness of an apeironic appetite—for, say, what remains unknown about gravity—informing introductory students that the details, the mathematics and whatnot, can serve its tropisms later, to whatever appropriate extent. Instruct students in how to discover problems—in different physical conceptions of time, for instance—and wonder about them. In doing so, Thomas stresses, the instructor should help students question "the promises sometimes freely offered by science" and the notion that science, in its task of gradual comprehension, is "a search for mastery over nature." He fervently advocates a deeper education in the sciences for humanists and, in a nostalgic mood, a recovery by science education of "the great fun [that] has gone out of it," the sense of "the high adventure" of science as "the shrewdest maneuver for discovering how the world works" (a sense, I would add, that public television, through numerous series, has tried assiduously to inspire in its viewers). Students should learn that their "bafflement" about science is not "simply the result of not having learned all the facts," that "everyone else—from the professor in his endowed chair down to the platoons of postdoctoral students in the laboratory all night—is baffled as well," that "every important scientific advance that has come in looking like an answer has turned, sooner or later—usually sooner—into a question." Thus Thomas urges that education in the sciences should be an apeironic enterprise profoundly mindful of the human(istic), one that can enable "an educated person" to have "a feel for the queernesses of nature, the inexplicable things."[14]

Thomas's thrust contrasts somewhat with that of more conventional thinking about so-called scientific literacy, widely taken to mean something like the ability to understand science as a presence in one's daily life. Literacy in that sense is fine as far as it goes, particularly if it involves the grasp and application of principles and not just a passive store of unquestioned background material that, perhaps all too briefly, allows some feeling of acquaintance with scientific enterprise. Robert M. Hazen and James Trefil should be credited for emphasizing such principles in their 1991 book *Science Matters: Achieving Scientific Literacy,* but they, like many advocates of scientific and other literacies, conceive such literacy too much as a relation to the known and too little as a relation to the unknown. Even principles change or become qualified, and science is not so much a body of knowledge, of principles—though it necessarily is that—as it is an *attitude* toward what baffles or eludes explanation. Thus general science education should help students not only "achieve" a certain useful knowledge but also develop a growing apeironic ability to, among other things, engage wonderingly Thomas's "queernesses of nature."

What, in the practical terms of the classroom and laboratory, does that involve? It ought to involve, as in mathematics education, instructors sharing their own research and disciplinary controversies with students, inviting ideas from them, doing research with them; likewise, authority should derive not from the instructor but from the evidence of discovery. The computer, already a redoubtable influence in updating the natural science curriculum, should be used to implement a pedagogy of experimentation and discovery sensitive to individual learning styles (the kind of pedagogy enabled by, for example, the CUPLE [Comprehensive Unified Physics Learning Environment] system). The dialogical/dialectical character of science should be stressed, its activity as a conversation between the student/scientist and the realm of inquiry (a notion vividly illustrated by the uncertainty principle, Niels Bohr's insight that physics concerns not so much what nature is as what kinds of statements can be made about it, and the anthropic principle, for instance) and among students and scientists as an interpretive community (dramatic examples of which may be found in the development of atomic fission, the mapping of DNA, or the recent polemics concerning the verification of cold-fusion experiments). Scientific "laws," such as those of electromagnetism and thermodynamics, should be investigated in terms of their biographical-historical and continuing evolution and never treated as givens brought down from a mountain. Dullness should be avoided at all costs and can be partly by helping students see and do science as an activity of imagination as well as of iterative technique, of startling insights into phenomena that violate, at least initially and sometimes revolutionarily, conventional desiderata of regularity, predictability, or quantifiability (classic examples being Bohr's breakthrough remodeling of the electronic structure of the atom in quantum-mechanical terms, Paracelsus's revisions of sixteenth-century medicine, and Johannes Kepler's reconception of planetary motion that made Copernicus's system mathematically precise). The fallibility, limits, and changefulness of science as inquiry and institution should be highlighted (qualities well exemplified in successive revisions of Dimitry Mendeleyev's periodic table or the history of medical diagnosis), the impact of its mistakes (in weather or earthquake prediction, say), as well as of its remarkable ingenuities, on day-to-day life. But above all, the pedagogy of general science, as of science generally, should concern itself with the apeironic leap from the known to the unknown, with helping students discern the kinds of interconnections that make it possible (that enabled Galileo to induce the planets' orbits from those of the Jovian moons, celestial physics from terrestrial, or Gregor Mendel to elaborate simple binariness into genetic logic) and then encouraging them to create their own.

The proposals of Feyerabend and Thomas in the decades following the 1960s address issues in the natural sciences that have continued to enlarge in scope and complexity, with the result that such proposals are increasingly persuasive—avatars of them are certainly evident in the recommendations of *Everybody Counts* and the plans for Project 2061. That situation burgeons with controversies, many of them arrayed by the traditionalist-postmodernist axis; a similar situation, the array of whose controversies frequently may be more tellingly discerned in terms of the parallel

rightist-leftist or revanchist-revisionist axes, may be found in social science education. There, too, more and more educators are
discovering that, as James Boyd White's counsel has it, "when
. . . we have in this world no earth or rock to stand or walk upon
but only shifting sea and sky and wind, the mature response is not
to lament the loss of fixity but to learn to sail."[15]

CHAPTER 4

The Social Sciences

In American education the social studies curriculum, especially at the elementary level, has long catalyzed debates, most of them dreary, localized, lacking in ideological self-awareness, and concerned predominantly with "content." Issues of content typically involve conflicting notions of usefulness (immediate relevance) and substantiveness (enduring historicalness). Such conflict almost invariably polemicizes the role in the curriculum of "history," a discipline constituted uneasily, sometimes with the feel of an intellectual free-fire zone, at the interface of the humanities and social sciences—though that polemicization usually (and naïvely) has more to do with *whether* it is learned than with *how* it is learned.

Diane Ravitch, a well-known conservative critic of American education, formerly an adjunct professor of history and education at Columbia University Teachers College and assistant secretary for the Office for Educational Research and Improvement, provides an entrance into this arena. In her experience the social studies curriculum in the early grades (K–3) "is virtually content-free," though also, seemingly paradoxically, "overwhelmingly sociological and economic." But the paradox is explicable: the curriculum is "content-free" because it concerns "the child's own world" and nothing beyond it. Presumably the child already knows this world and therefore learns little by studying it (probably a safe presumption, since the student is typically taught it as a given and not encouraged to explore and question its constitution), though that child may gain some self-esteem by having its importance institutionally recognized. Unsurprisingly, Ravitch discovers "a welter of dubious assumptions" behind such a "curriculum of 'me, my family, my school, my community.' " Introduced in the 1930s with the blessing of the American Historical Association and still officially supported in principle by the National Council on Social Studies (though opposed by the newly formed National Council for History Education), this curriculum is, according to Ravitch, largely a product of "the 'social reconstructionist' wing of progressive education" that wanted public education following the Great Depression to become more realistic and practical, especially for " 'nonacademic' students." As devised by Paul Hanna, generally regarded as its originator, and as implemented early on and ambitiously in Virginia, the curriculum was part of an effort "to replace traditional subject matter with real-life problem solving." Known later as the curriculum of "expanding environments" (or some similar nomenclature), it initially entailed a quasi-Piagetian pedagogy of "building from the known to the unknown," that "unknown" finally to include "the world"—that is, history. Thus this formalization of a not-entirely-novel approach involved a gradual pedagogical movement from the expository description of increasingly less local places to the narration of increasingly less immediate times, from (to borrow from Ravitch) "tot sociology" to (what it seems appropriate to call) "tot history." The sociological part of this moving curriculum soon became more emphasized, however, with a consequent truncation of "the historical part." All this has come about, according to Ravitch, because of an approach that "was established not as a result of the findings of cognitive or developmental psychology, but as a result of specific social and political values."[1] Well, whatever one may infer about her attitude toward those values, that does appear to be the case.

I agree with Ravitch that what has come about—insofar as it has come about without a thoughtful, well-researched pedagogical rationale and to the extent that she argues (generally cogently) that it has—is unfortunate and needs to be changed. But her proposal for a remedy betrays and is motivated partly by a typical conservative nostalgia about the good old days of history education—which, in the manner of Bloom, she documents as much by wistfulness as by (seemingly idealized) particulars—and it also lacks a sufficient rationale, as well as ideological self-consciousness, methodological specificity and imagination, and an informed sense of recent issues redefining both history as a discipline and the social sciences at large. While it may be true that, before the expanding-environments curriculum became dominant, "children in the early grades in most public schools learned about primitive peoples, heroes, myths, biographies, poems, national holidays, fairy tales, and legends," Ravitch offers no evidence that such learning "about" productively engaged those children; indeed, she says little about how it proceeded, how it prepared them "for the study of history and literature in the later grades" (which grades many of them never reached). It would be difficult to disagree effectively with her contention that the present social studies curriculum is not underwritten by any well-conceived learning theory (Piagetian or otherwise) and that it bores educators and students alike: "Imagine the plight of the typical first grader: She has seen television programs about space flight, wars, terrorism, foreign countries, and national elections, but her social studies textbook is about neighborhood helpers and family roles." Small wonder that increasingly less time and energy are given to implementing such a curriculum. But one must remember that "history" itself, as "learned about" in public schools (and surely in the private ones that Ravitch touts as offering a better curriculum in history), was a potent classroom anesthetic for most students (at all levels) long before the expanding-environments curriculum was installed. It still is, and will remain so if not transformed by a more reflective pedagogy than she suggests by speaking of students who need "a far more interesting immersion in history" in order to be more thoroughly imbued with (in her direct appeal to the notion of cultural literacy as popularized by Hirsch) "the background knowledge that a literate person has available to him as he goes through daily life." If history is "a good story," why aren't students enthralled by it? If it is "an opportunity to exercise the imagination and live in another era," why don't more students embrace that opportunity? Why doesn't it help a child in a public school develop "a broader knowledge of other cultures as well as his own"? Very likely, I would argue, because most of the educators whom Ravitch criticizes—and to whom she offers nothing essentially different in this respect—suffer from an imprisonment, into which they induct their students, that is tellingly characterized by the language of their and her pedagogy (such as it is): history as "historical and cultural content"[2] (rather than as, say, narrative cultural formations), as "background knowledge" (rather than as assumptions to be brought to the foreground for discussion), as "a good story" (rather than as many stories or versions of a story, some conflicting, some not so "good"), and so on. Names, dates, places, events—all idealized, to be "learned about" rather than apeironically explored, memorized rather than critically questioned.

The principal limitation of this conception of history and its pedagogy is adumbrated in colloquial fashion by Ben Sippy, the narrator of Larry McMurtry's novel *Anything for Billy*, in a passage where he is puzzling about the many different versions of the story of Billy the Kid: "Even the simplest events grow mossy with the passage of years. If the students accepted the simple view of events in past times, how would their stiff brains ever get any exercise?"[3] The principal limitation of Ravitch's conception, so like that of the public-education system that has displaced history from its curriculum, is that it instantiates and promotes "the simple [and largely Euro-American] view." How can the "stiff brains" of students, K–3 or otherwise, "ever get any exercise" if they aren't encouraged to discover the problems of history (of historicizing) and challenged to explore them? Certainly students should learn the "data" of history—but in the context of an instructing that habilitates them to puzzle what is given, outline its tensions and contradictions, ask what has been left out (since history is always synecdochic and thus excludes) and what motivates the teller of the tale, look for hidden assumptions, and likewise investigate and theorize other versions and their interrelations. Such instructing, informed by intelligent learning theory and research and sensitively enacted, is hardly beyond the mission of educating grade school children, who are far more driven by curiosity than by hunger for the cold pasta of "facts" dished up by educators who, even if they want only to propagandize the "official" view of history, cannot thereby do it effectively.

Indeed, why not instruct those children, who are aware of how events may be variously "told" (by sincere, if frustrated, efforts at truthfulness or by exaggeration, coloring, and other kinds of "lying"), in how to *read* the biographical "history" of a legendary figure like Billy the Kid (or George Washington, Sitting Bull, Martin Luther King)? If some have difficulty with that idea, the instructor might offer them the analogue of a map: however projected, it always distorts the territory it represents (and throughout history plenty of maps have been made intentionally to distort their territory). McMurtry's book is perhaps a little out of range (its colloquialness belies its narrative sophistication—though that deceptiveness is the point here for anyone capable of subtly studying it), but it suggests engaging issues whose implications quickly spread. What causes events to "grow mossy with the passage of years"? Isn't all history mossy? Are there different kinds of "mossiness"? Why? Who accepts "the simple view"? Why? And why are there so many versions of the history of Billy the Kid? Is McMurtry's novel a version? How is a history like or unlike a novel? How can Ben Sippy be a character in the story he is telling? Isn't a historian always somehow *in* the story he or she is telling?

Such an expanding pattern of interrogation and theorization, however adapted to grade level, could lead students to consider, among other things, how they themselves figure in the varying and conflicting histories of Billy the Kid (which ones appeal to them, which don't and why) and how those histories are part of their own present culture, of themselves (in terms of differing romanticizations of the gunslinger, beliefs about individual freedom, aspects of the frontier mentality in a world that even in Billy the Kid's time was becoming a "global village," and so on). They might then come to realize in a moment of surprise how profoundly (the study of) history *informs* them (makes them [see themselves as] the historical persons their own lives write them as being). It is the sort of moment that occurs, to follow Guy Davenport's interpretation, in Edward Gibbon's *History of the Decline and Fall of the Roman Empire* "when, late in the work, he himself [Gibbon] realizes that he is one of the barbarians he is talking about in the mists of Britannia, remote from the Italian sun."[4] And it is the sort of moment—when students discover that Americans, like the Maori, like people anywhere at any time, to a great extent create history to fit the needs of their culture; that they themselves both historicize and are historic(ized)—from which the transformatively apeironic learning of "history" can really begin.

What I am suggesting is that the social studies curriculum in public schools, from the "tot" level on up (including, mutatis mutandis, postsecondary institutions as well—and, for that matter, private institutions at all levels), should strive for a more radical and creative integration of sociology and history than Ravitch or most of the educators she criticizes have foreseen. Such a curriculum would involve a pedagogical strategy of oscillation: combining synchronic and diachronic studies, it would help students learn their own place and time through the perspectives afforded by other places and times, and vice versa. (Such a curriculum necessarily would address the glaring inadequacy, at all educational levels, of the study of the interrelationships between the history of the United States, usually presented as a sort of Ptolemaic diorama, and the parallel and antecedent histories of other nations and cultures—Latin American and Native American, for instance.) Differentially comparative, it thus would be alternately both an expanding-environments and a *contracting-environments* curriculum. Students would not merely assimilate some univocal textbook description or history of their own or another culture; rather, they would read such a version in order to search out its implications about the interplay of cultural values and attitudes, translating the "content" of the text into an exploratory *dis*content about what it omits, avoids, suppresses, hides, twists.[5] Learning the dialogue of etic (observational) and emic (participational) perspectives, students would learn what it means to historicize and sociologize (archaeologize and anthropologize), what is at stake in doing so, and they would not be just learning "about" something but building a strategy of learning that reflects the strategy of instructing and that they can continue to use for the discovery and critique of cultural issues, for the invention of defamiliarizing interpretations of them, perhaps for the revision of the strategy itself.

By the traditional metaphor of education as nourishment, this approach might seem to Ravitch and others to be one that would encourage students to play with their food instead of eating it. That metaphor is open to question in any case; but if I had to respond in terms of it, I would say that this approach could encourage students to study their food (playfully) in order to make eating it a richer experience. If students are bored with social studies, that is because they are being taught settled answers (by equally bored teachers) rather than being instructed in how to deal with unsettled questions (such as, to suggest really vital and interesting possibilities, given Operation Desert Storm and its disastrous aftermath, the perennially troubled interrelations of Middle

Eastern cultures, about which the world generally understands very little, or, given recent events in the former Soviet Union and eastern Europe, the nature of communist regimes and of the nation-state itself).

And those made uneasy by what they see as the political implications of this approach—with its shift from History to historicism(s) (something whose subatomic analogue no longer makes physicists in their dealings with multiple, simultaneous quantum "histories" queasy), its interrogation of the historicizing subject, its treatment of history as a problem, its thrust from the assumed known to the troubling unknown—should not be too quick to identify it as necessarily leftist or Marxist. Though many historians or social scientists who are also educators may define themselves as such, this approach, however much like what they use, makes *any* simple political positioning, "correct" or otherwise, quite provisional and unstable. Indeed, this approach derives from and further promotes the recent general polemicization of social-scientific theory and practice, a polemicization very much aware of its attendant educational issues that is proving, gradually, productive more of continuing, open explorations than of dug-in, closed advocacies. Invidious contestation has hardly all changed to fruitful debate, but some useful pedagogical insights, interdisciplinary in character, are emerging from the fray.

Brook Thomas, for instance, argues with patent polemical intent that "one of the most exciting developments in the study of literature has been the rise of new historical analysis." For New Historicism, which he defines succinctly as "the renewed interest in the historical analysis of literature in the wake of the poststructuralist attack on traditional historical criticism," the time has come. And that needed radical analysis—much indebted to Foucault, prone to read history as complexly as the literature it contextualizes, and practiced perhaps most notably by Stephen J. Greenblatt—ought to figure more, Thomas contends, in the American classroom. Why? He responds: "Because our cultural amnesia has left us with no perspective on the present, thus making it more difficult than ever to shape the direction of the future. Alienated from history, our students are confined to a series of fragmented, directionless presents." If that is the case, then, he asks, "How does one teach historically in an ahistorical culture?" Certainly "the most obvious solution—add a little history to our instruction of literary texts—is itself a symptom of our problem. Students will read literature historically only when they are historically aware. To think of history as some *thing* that we can add to literary texts is the very opposite of historical awareness." Thomas proposes that "the only way out of this dilemma is to confront it historically"—that is, to start with the situation of students in "a culture that suppresses their contact with history" and causes it "to be considered something that we add to the study of literature," and then use that situation pedagogically "to move towards a more genuine historical awareness." Such a strategy would counterbalance the still-dominant New Critical tendency to teach literary works as if they were aesthetic objects isolable from history. It also would encourage us "to think of a historically-based study of literature as a discipline that can relate separate realms of knowledge," perhaps through "a literature-across-the-curriculum program." By analyzing specific works, Shakspeare's Sonnet 87 and Keats's "Ode on a Grecian Urn," Thomas demonstrates convincingly how a close reading of a text involves also a close reading of history and how students with a refined historical awareness can be helped "both to reconstruct the author's intention . . . and to read against the grain of his intention." (Such an approach, I would add, functions wonderfully well with Shakespeare's history plays, which are rich in problematic historical self-reflection, and may be applied, of course, not just to "literature" but to a diary, journal, public document, and so on.) And Thomas emphasizes the importance, for educators who would use this pedagogical strategy, of cultivating a "sense of social context" and the historical self-awareness to take advantage of the remarkable opportunity the New Historicism has made possible, "a perspective from which we can judge the very conditions of our judgments."[6]

Approaches such as Thomas's are not without their critics, of course, but some of those critics are motivated not by conventional (conscious or unconscious) political advocacy but by the belief that the scholarly and pedagogical enterprise of the New Historicists proceeds in a fashion only superficially interdisciplinary—that is, that the disciplines involved lack sufficient mutually informing interaction.[7] Probably more dialogue among them gradually will weaken the warrants for that kind of criticism, which does not detract from the promise of that enterprise nor from the significance of what has given rise to it, what Philippe Sollers calls "a new consciousness capable of scrutinizing the texts of official history and discovering what they exclude, what they censor, what their gestures serve to exorcise."[8] This "new consciousness," overcoming Thomas's "cultural amnesia," engages the past not as a repository of timeless (and, in the West, mostly Eurocentric) truths and values but as a text already revised that must be reinvented (again and again) for the future. Such a shift of interpretive emphasis, which has been under way in American education since the 1960s, which reached an ethnohistorical watershed with the Columbus Quincentenary, and which can trace its ancestral line at least as far back as Nietzsche, implies—even mandates—tremendous changes in the history curriculum and its pedagogy, indeed in the whole (always already historicized) paideia, the culture's evolving self-consciousness.

To the extent that those changes are in process—they certainly are in postsecondary education in the United States (and elsewhere), and primary and secondary educators are beginning to feel their influence, to sense their possibilities—they constitute a first-magnitude cause célèbre. Much is at stake, for such changes involve the questioning of texts that represent and endorse established systems of dominance. As Sollers's characterization of the "new consciousness" suggests, many historians are rereading "the texts of official history" to explore their gaps and rewriting them in terms of elided subjects and their buried or repressed stories— the experiences of women, marginalized ethnic groups, "ordinary" people (rather than the usual "big players"—think how students might rewrite the "official history" of events in Beijing in June 1989, indeed rewrite the popular image of facile heroism, from the perspective of that lone, unarmed protestor who halted a column of tanks near Tiananmen Square, an act immortalized, however anonymously, in a well-known press photograph). Their activities (for instance, the numerous recent revisions, against the traditional conception of Frederick Jackson Turner, of the history of the American West—most notably Patricia Nelson Limerick's 1987 book *The Legacy of Conquest: The Unbroken Past of the American West*) provoke charges from other historians, typically more conservative, that they are neglecting broad trends, becoming estranged from the public, fragmenting the profession into minor specialties, or making coherent and univocal historical accounts (desired for whatever reason) impossible. Such polarization reflects a power struggle within the profession between, as Joan W. Scott sums it up, "conservatives, those for whom history is an orthodoxy, true and immutable," a position exemplified by the Victorian historian Gertrude Himmelfarb, among others, and "democrats, who argue that history, as well as historical practice and knowledge, is heterogeneous, and constantly changing," a position recently endorsed officially by the Organization of American Historians. The former exemplify a guardian mentality, the latter an insistence that "history consists of many irreconcilable stories." But Scott stresses that the "democrats" have transcended "a simple pluralism in which every man, or woman, is his, or her, own historian" in order "to analyze the ways differences among groups are constructed in history."[9]

Certainly this enlarging of the historical arena has been occasioned mostly by response to crucial moral issues, however much it may be fueled by opportunistic political correctness or scholarly careerism, but it must be seen also as part of a general complexifying of knowledge in the twentieth century—a point stressed by Lawrence W. Levine, who, after invoking the work of Einstein as a precursive example, defends his nontraditional colleagues by arguing that "the complexity of our writing is not the complexity of specialized and esoteric languages, but the complexity of peoples in the past, and the cultures they created."[10]

Well, the debate goes on, but those sympathetic to the conservative point of view need to recognize that the divergence from orthodoxy is not a matter of intellectual or political perversity, just as Scott's "democrats" need to recognize that orthodoxy itself is not only a matter of willful ignorance. As I said, much is at stake: the meaning of the past, at the very least. Whether conservatives like it or not, "history" is now shot through with knotty issues of diversity; there is no going back, and it is surely a delusion to believe that students, at whatever level and in all their increasingly intermingled cultural diversity, can—or ought to—be excluded, by a "protective" curriculum and pedagogy, from experiencing the complexity of which Levine speaks. They need to know what's up. Borrowing from Graff, who advocates the same for students in English courses, I would say it is high time for children to start listening to their parents' quarrels—and even join in.[11] If allowed and helped to do so, they will become a new kind of public, one no longer "ahistorical" and alienated from what were once seemingly specialist issues.

And I would broaden this line of argument to encompass social studies generally; for synchronic research on cultures is, for quite similar reasons, just as charged with complexity and multiplicity as the diachronic, and, to complicate the situation further, the two more and more intertangle their perspectives. Sociology, anthropology, political science, psychology, and other disciplines, hybrid disciplines, and subdisciplines more or less gathered under the umbrella of the social sciences have, like history, undergone a far-reaching loss of innocence and simplicity during the last few decades, however much some would deny it. The characteristics of that loss, which demonstrate how much has been gained by it, recall analogous and related characteristics of the loss/gain in the natural sciences discussed by Feyerabend and Thomas: a skepticism about the objectivity and universality of social-scientific knowledge; an ideological sensitivity to the position, orientation, and interests, unconscious or not, of the observing/theorizing/writing subject (and thus to all issues of interpretive perspective); a severely questioning attitude toward traditional methods of investigation and reportage, along with an increasing interest in theories of chaos and self-organizing open systems to model and explain nonlinear and seemingly disordered patterns of behavior; an uneasy awareness of the provisionality of knowledge, its problematic textualization, and its probabilistic limitedness; and an interdisciplinary openness, especially, most recently, toward the humanities.

Though these characteristics are typical of all the social sciences (old hat to some practitioners), contemporary ethnography manifests them perhaps most acutely. That subdiscipline of anthropology bristles with polemics concerning subjectivity and partisanship in the study of cultures, "the kinds of 'hidden agenda' that both researchers and informants bring to anthropological field work" (patterns of informational suppression, evasion, silence, and so on), the problematics of so-called participant-observation, the extent to which ethnographic writing—and, increasingly, film and videotape—is "as much invention as transparent representation" (literature, say, rather than science), and the relentless ironies inhabiting the notion of scientific neutrality.[12] For Gordon Hewes, most of whose fieldwork has been archaeological, this situation, particularly in regard to issues about the truth status of ethnographic texts, has reached a point of unacceptability. He chafes at the way Clifford Geertz reads the ethnographic texts of anthropologists such as Claude Lévi-Strauss and Ruth Benedict from what Hewes construes as "a subjective idealist position that the world's ethnographic literature is just that: literature." By such practice, Hewes hyperbolizes, "Brobdingnag is just as real as the pueblo of Zuni." Thus " 'experimental' interpretations" like Geertz's inspire in younger anthropologists a rejection of "all claims to objectivity, or even the legitimacy of investigating other cultures" (an enterprise rife with somewhat Gödelian snarls in any case), and "it is not unusual to find anthropology students these days who regard all the ethnographic documentation that has been accumulated in the West as part of the apparatus used to control, exploit, and oppress Third World peoples, and to doom them to a kind of cultural genocide." Doubtless such students also hyperbolize in their own ways, though evidence to document the political use of ethnography—and not just "in the West"—abounds. But however hyperbolic (and even partisan) they may be, they are at least responding seriously to issues of interpretive equivocality opened up by this "Rashōmon Problem"[13] (named after the film by Akira Kurosawa in which an event is reported by four different and mutually contradictory witnesses) that Hewes seems intent on dismissing into absurdity or irrelevance by holding to a naïve notion of objectivity and a deluded belief that social-scientific texts (mis)read as "literature" are thereby open to any arbitrary interpretation.

Hewes's conservativism in reacting to what looms for him as a possibility for professional anarchy blinds him to the important opportunities for fresh, revealing, and insightfully evidenced (re)interpretations of both ethnographic texts and the texts of the cultures they interpret (never, needless to say, as a matter of "transparent representation") that are exposed by this *renversement* of the taken-for-granted. And he misjudges Geertz, who (to give him the last word here) is not spinning experimental hermeneutics out of subjective idealism but responding to, participating in, contributing to what he calls, in the subtitle to one of his best-known essays, "The Refiguration of Social Thought." In that essay Geertz observes that "something is happening to the way we think about the way we think." Among other things, "the casting of social theory in terms more familiar to gamesters [and not just traditional game theorists] and aestheticians than to plumbers and engineers is clearly well under way," with "society less and less represented as an elaborate machine or a quasi-organism and more as a serious game, a sidewalk drama, or a behavioral text"; through the work of Irving Goffman and others, social life is coming increasingly to be theorized not as any kind of conventionally formal system but as "just a bowl of strategies" textualized or text-analogized to the extent that "we live immersed in meta-commentary"; and "it is not [pace Hewes] that we no longer have conventions of interpretation; we have more than ever, built—often enough jerry-built—to accommodate a situation at once fluid, plural, uncentered, and ineradicably untidy."[14] The science of that situation, like the "science of texts" as Robert de Beaugrande and Wolfgang Dressler characterize it, requires conventions concerned more with "realistic modelling of the diverse but systematic strategies people actually apply when using texts in everyday life" and less with dogmatic philosophizing and psychologizing. In that enterprise

probabilistic models are more adequate and realistic than *deterministic* ones. Dynamic accounts of *structure-building operations* will be more productive than static descriptions of the structures themselves. We should work to discover *regularities, strategies, motivations, preferences,* and *defaults* rather than *rules* and *laws. Dominances* can offer more realistic classifications than can *strict categories*. . . . It is the task of science to systematize the *fuzziness* of its objects of inquiry, not to ignore it or argue it away.[15]

Like social thought generally—even "dismal" economics, which is beginning to supplement neoclassical theory, now inadequately descriptive of global behaviors, with less positivist, more textualist approaches, especially in the classroom—ethnography is turning apeironic. Perhaps its students would be less apt to opt for easy or obvious partisanship if those who educate them helped them, all along, to engage that situation fearlessly and intelligently. I would not wish anything less for all students at all levels, for they are all students of culture.

CHAPTER 5

The Humanities

Recent controversies concerning American social science education overlap, especially in the area of "history," with those concerning humanities education. Indeed, that overlap—involving not only history but many other disciplines and, increasingly, professions as well, insofar as they participate in the interdisciplinarity of what has come to be called cultural studies—has a good deal to do with those latter controversies, which concern preeminently issues about the nature, province, and role of the humanities in the whole process of education. Such issues are complex, but because their implications spread on a large sociocultural scale and are, frequently in simplified or distorted form, generally comprehensible, they have been widely publicized and worried. Hence I need to treat them more extensively than those in natural and social sciences education.

In 1970 Frye could define the humanities, with some confidence, by distinguishing them from the sciences: exemplified by history and philosophy, they "are almost purely verbal, non-experimental, and non-predictive," though they nonetheless require, like the sciences, "accuracy of statement, objectivity of description and dispassionate weighing of evidence, including the accepting of negative evidence"; they differ from the sciences, "increasingly a communal and corporate activity," in being "more individualized"; and so on.[1] No one informed of developments since then can offer such a confident definition, though it remains useful in some particulars. In his 1988 book *Education's Great Amnesia,* Robert E. Proctor laments that "no one today knows what the humanities are. . . . The phrase 'the humanities' warms almost everyone's heart. But why can't we define them? Because the original humanities are dead, and we have found nothing to replace them." Frye's negative definition has become general but bereft of any addendum—or, more nostalgically, foundation—of seemingly positive attributes, so that the popular notion of the humanities is powerfully haunted, to the point of conceptual dominance, by the opposite that enables the definition. Thus, according to Proctor, "when you mention the humanities today, it is not the Greeks and Romans that come to mind, but, ironically, science and technology: most people are able to think about the humanities only in terms of their opposites, the sciences."[2]

Though one may readily argue that this definitional problem (very much one of language or, in Derridean terms, *écriture*) does not uniquely typify the humanities, Proctor finds it most severe in them. And his diagnosis is quite specific. First of all, what we have lost in the death of the "original humanities" is "not just a nonscientific or even a 'prescientific' way of looking at man; they had a precise content: the *studia humanitatis* [the term from Cicero's *Pro Archia*], as they were originally called, began in fifteenth-century Italy as a cultural revolution calling for the imitation of classical, as opposed to medieval, Latin, and for the study of Roman, and to a lesser extent Greek, literature, history, and moral philosophy as guides to individual and collective behavior." Proctor unintentionally problematizes the matter of originality here and ascribes a questionable univocality to the classical canon, but he knows peremptorily the cost of losing that "precise content": a "void created at the very center of our curriculum" that he identifies with "our current 'crisis of the humanities.'" Furthermore, "we have simply found no unifying focus to replace the one they provided," so that, "if you try to discuss the humanities today, chances are you won't talk about specific books and authors at all, but will spend your time debating questions of methodology." He compares this obsession with methodology, as he construes it (as if "talk about specific books and authors" were not always already methodized, albeit usually unwittingly), to the "fervid interest in the *techniques* of research" that obsessed universities in the late medieval period, "the period in which the humanities emerged," to such an extent that "the ability to 'play' with Aristotelian syllogisms inevitably became an end in itself."

This comparison enables him, with a short step, to make the de rigueur conservative sneer at those who invent "new techniques of analysis and research" like "postdeconstructionism" and to bemoan "the vogue for 'quantitative reasoning' in the social sciences." From there he generalizes: since "all the disciplines of modern universities" do not address the issue of "substantive *content*," we are in danger of creating a situation, for which some argue, in which "the essence of education [in the humanities and otherwise] is exposure to different methodologies and disciplinary perspectives."[3] Though such a possibility hardly seems dire, Proctor abhors it and, completing his comparison, takes it as a sign that the times are ripe for the reemergence of the "original humanities."

In (re)turning to the humanists, for him both "early" and "original," to find "an answer to this dilemma," Proctor foregrounds many of what Kenneth Burke would call the "terms for order" of recent humanities education controversies. And while what he proposes is not as deluded (nor as arrogant) as what Bloom proposes, it nonetheless tends to be nostalgic and naïve, at times appallingly so. Bothered by what some regard as the "healthy pluralism" of the current postsecondary humanities curriculum, Proctor studies the Renaissance humanities "to discover why the early humanists were able to create a coherent curriculum, while we are not." That study does not lead, as does Bloom's quite different one, to a simple corroboration of bias: "one of the unexpected results of my research has been to force me to change my understanding of the original humanities. The humanities, I have come to see, grew out of a particular and historically unique perception of human existence which we no longer share today. And this discovery leads me to conclude that we cannot revitalize the humanities today simply by trying to reinstitutionalize earlier humanistic educational ideals." How then to revitalize them? We must start, he argues, by recognizing a crucial philosophical disjunction between the work of Cicero and that of Proctor's Renaissance exemplar, Petrarch: one discovers in the former "a sense [readily detected in Dante as well] that the 'center,' the goal or final resting place, of a human being lies *outside* of himself"; one discovers in the latter a frustrated but dedicated attempt "to find a center and a resting place *within* himself." Thus, according to Proctor, "the humanities emerge, in part, out of Petrarch's attempt to do what Cicero and Dante would have never conceived of doing: triumph over contingency ('chance,' 'Fortune') by distancing himself from it in his inner life. " By this logic Petrarch's own (re)turning to the past, like that of his fourteenth- and fifteenth-century followers Coluccio Salutati and Leonardo Bruni, was motivated by an interest in "emulating what he believed was the *inner* strength of his ancient heroes." Untroubled by the wobble of this distinction between inner and outer "centers," admitting that Petrarch's project "was more of a hope . . . than a reality" and that he "lived in constant fear and anxiety," Proctor nonetheless asserts that through this project the early humanists discovered in their multiply unstable world "a refuge, of sorts, in the new 'humanities.' "4

Petrarch's saliently literary *studia humanitatis,* as Proctor construes them for his purposes, thus "contain this ideal of forming, shaping, molding one's inner self through the study of other human lives, especially the ancient Romans," along with "a conception of an autonomous 'personal self,' which was a Renaissance creation." That ideal determines the "goal of education as the shaping of character"—a less specific and less cynical version of Lazere's characterization of the function of contemporary education as paideia, also one that tempts Proctor to quote Leonardo Bruni and Lionel Trilling on lives and selves "as works of art" that can be consciously "perfected, and completed." That ideal and the educational practice enabled by its curriculum and pedagogy have, for him, virtually disappeared, an event he relates "in part, at least, to a changing experience of the 'self.' "5

What to do? Since, as Proctor open-mindedly notes, "there is no biologically predetermined experience of what it means to be 'human,' " and " 'humanity' is a cultural and historical experience," his response takes the form of a challenge "to rethink and define what we mean by the word 'human,' a task which demands, I believe, questioning the usefulness of the concept of an exclusively personal, inward-turning 'self.' " Unlike Bloom, he takes that challenge "as an opportunity for us to appropriate the past in new ways." And he realizes that such an opportunity suggests education not to recover forgotten Truth but "to investigate the Renaissance's problematic relationship to classical antiquity and our own increasingly problematic relationship to the Renaissance," especially in terms of the modern adaptation of its concept of the self.[6] So far, so good. Scarcely conservative, his thinking here manifests a somewhat apeironic flavor. But what curriculum and pedagogy does he propose?

Now the issues get stickier. For Proctor the humanistic tradition insists that "the primary purpose of education is moral"; it follows "that the most important instruction we can give our students is that which will help them seek wisdom and virtue." Though he never adequately defines those regularly paired notions for classical, Renaissance, or modern—let alone American or global—culture, he nonetheless organizes his postsecondary curriculum to accentuate the "moral philosophy" instantiated in his version of the history of humanism. The result is a mixed bag, fraught with both commendable emphases and deluded idealizations. For instance, surely "we still need a dialogue with the Greeks and Romans," but I doubt the usefulness of the idea that Petrarch's response to the fragmentation of the "ancient unity" of the curriculum in his day "must be ours, at least until we can find a new unity of all the areas of learning." Surely the "activity of trying to understand, revise, and reappropriate" the humanistic tradition is worthwhile, but I doubt that that activity "could, in itself, give continuity and coherence to the liberal arts curriculum, and moral consciousness to our students"—unless such terms were construed in a far different way than Proctor apparently intends. And surely that activity can help students achieve some measure of historical consciousness, "understand and evaluate the moral and intellectual life of the present," and "find other ways of experiencing our humanity," but I doubt that such projects can proceed productively if guided by Proctor's peremptory and filiopietistic maxim that "it is impossible to be modern and moral." Furthermore, in elaborating his four-year curriculum, he appears to vacillate about the pedagogical role of Petrarch's perspective, first advocating that it "must be ours" and then advocating that it must be avoided in order not to "miss the new perspectives" that come, paradoxically, from "the ancient ideal of the unity of the individual with something greater than himself."[7]

When Proctor occasionally breaks out of his Petrarchan tangles, some of his proposals appear quite useful. He proposes, for instance, that the secondary and postsecondary history of science be radically revised within a humanistic counterperspective that exposes the fallibilities and limitations of a kind of knowledge regarded by most students as quasi-magical and absolute (Thomas would heartily approve) and that the humanities and social sciences "begin a fruitful dialogue." But he founders, as do many of his conservative peers, whenever he invokes—repetitively—any version of the naïve and problematic equation of the old and the moral. How are students "to put aside modern categories of thought" as if they were as removable as clothing? How are they to interpret without profound misgivings the variegated texts of classical societies that, whatever else they did, kept slaves, degraded women, fought terrible wars in the name anthropomorphic deities, and so on? Proctor may call for a dialogue of present and past, but either he has already decided which side will win or he really wants only a monologue. In either case he espouses the Bloomian belief that the present relevance of his humanistic tradition "concerns issues which transcend gender and race"—even though that tradition, variously far more at odds with itself than he discerns, was begun and has been promulgated relentlessly, except for recent signs of abatement, by Caucasian males, mostly of privileged classes. As if this drawback to Proctor's "reappropriation" of the humanities were not enough, consider the purblind absurdity of his proposal for high school students to learn Greek and Latin as "the first step" toward "the kind of serious instruction in moral philosophy which the humanities can provide" and which, he triumphantly assures us, "can be used to address the problem of drugs in our schools" and perhaps even decrease the "number of teenage suicides."[8] I would be the last person to argue that high school students should not be encouraged—though hardly expected—to learn Greek and Latin, but it is sad indeed to encounter an educator entertaining such a provincial and bluntly insensitive application of "the humanities."

Thus Proctor, like many conservatives, winds up arguing for a teaching-as-preaching approach to moral education through the humanities, a model that a respectable (and little-heeded) volume of research on moral development, if nothing else, has demonstrated to be far less effective than an approach that helps students engage moral issues more apeironically so that they may discover humane decisional principles for themselves and refine them as they grow in experience.[9] But, of course, this latter approach involves imputing to the self and cultivating exactly the autonomy that he abhors. For him the tropism of the modern autonomous self is almost always away from "wisdom and virtue" and toward "drugs," "teenage suicides," and universal MTVland.

Though Proctor assays Bennett's proposals for humanities education, first set out in *To Reclaim a Legacy,* as too broad, amorphous, and historically undefined and the Great Books approach he embraces as unaware of the profound discontinuities in the humanistic tradition (problems similar to those he finds in *Integrity in the College Curriculum,* problems of "amnesia," diversity, too much choice and fragmentation),[10] he is very much aligned with Bennett in his simplistic emphasis on content (what is read) rather than method (how it is read) and on the humanities as a means for moral recovery. And the two share various vague nostalgias about unity, harmony, wholeness, and so on, as well as an anachronistic sense of the complex forces and knowledges that shape contemporary culture. On the other hand, Proctor lacks Bennett's militant stridency. But whatever their differences, Proctor, like many other critics of humanities education with conservative agendas for reform, is riding the wake stirred by Bennett in the 1980s during his tenure as chairman of the National Endowment for the Humanities and then as secretary of education.

Perhaps the most salutary result of those years of fear and loathing, during which Bennett alienated so many educators (from his own staff members to the president of Stanford University),[11] was the gradual emergence of the humanities from educational marginalization—though surely not in the way he wished. By the late 1980s the powerful voices in the arena of debate about humanities issues seemed to be more those of leftist "theorists" (who always sounded more "ideological") than those of rightist traditionalists. In other words, in spite of the efforts of people like Proctor and Bloom (with whom Bennett, after leaving the Department of Education in 1988, established, through grants from conservative foundations, the still-disarrayed Madison Center for Educational Affairs, which is devoted to the study of public policy and the Great Books), another sort of marginalization, internal to the humanities, was occurring. Many postsecondary students disillusioned after the lemminglike rush for market-fashionable degrees like the MBA had turned to humanities courses for deeper learning experiences (a trend that still continues). But in the brief heyday of campus "marathon readings" they were far more likely to share James Joyce's *Finnegans Wake* or Thomas Pynchon's *Gravity's Rainbow,* quintessentially modern and postmodern works, than any of the Great Books. Many students of the humanities, like many of their professors, hungered for texts and strategies of reading that reflected, engaged, and enriched patterns of consciousness unknown to or not explored by the authors of the Great Books or those who taught them as containers out of which one could pluck "wisdom and virtue." Such ancient Mediterranean notions, translated and displaced through a hundred generations, did not lack interest or merit, but they could hardly be incontestably apt or sufficient in an age poised for nuclear holocaust (a situation, like the present mortally conflicted mess of the Middle East, historically linked to Roman militarism) and fearful that the cost of sexual pleasure (something the Periclean Greeks took for granted) might be certain, agonized death.

Contrary to Bennett's belief that the humanities are in danger of becoming recondite and irrelevant to public life, their diversifying, complexifying, and contemporizing have contributed to making them more publicly visible and connected. And demarginalization implicates other processes as well, processes that respond to Susan Sage Heinzelman's imperatives for the profession of the humanities as they move beyond a place analogous to that of "the silenced woman": "to restructure the relationship between the dispossessed humanities and the income-generating scientific, legal, and business communities"; "reimagine its own discipline so that it demystifies those interpretive strategies that have both manufactured and disguised its narrative of marginalization"; and "insist on the value of exactly that which feminism asserts: a discourse that speaks of both public and private, of both objective and subjective, of both masculine and feminine, of both what the poet-lawyer Wallace Stevens terms 'labials [and] gutturals.'" Other "restrictive oppositions" dear to the hearts of conservatives— canonical and noncanonical, Western and non-Western, and so on—are being dismantled as boundaries blur and dissolve in the formation of this new "professional narrative."[12] What Bennett and others see as a problem of fragmented diversification and alienation from the public, Heinzelman and others see as an opportunity for the humanities to become a more comprehensive, more tolerant, more balanced, and more influential intellectual enterprise, academically and otherwise. To borrow from and paraphrase Robert Graves, where he finds "clear images" of chaos, she finds "broken images" of a new order.

Variations of that difference have figured in many controversies involving those who hold to some version of Proctor's "original humanities" (Great Books, the standard canon, and so on) and those who indeed strive for something "to replace them"—or, more typically, to supplement (without trying wholly to supplant) them. Such controversies have blossomed nowhere more noticeably than they have around issues concerned, directly or indirectly, with the humanities canon (a word, by now deeply ironized, that we inherit, through early Christians bent on selecting and listing orthodox texts and, then, arguably inappropriate eighteenth-century usage, from the Alexandrians, who used it to refer to *their* Great Books—mostly as grammatical models—which, at that time, twenty-three hundred years ago, were more "modern" than "classical"), especially that part of it conventionally regarded as "literary." Gerald Graff's 1987 book *Professing Literature: An Institutional History* makes a useful starting place for considering what is at stake at this site of curricular and pedagogical struggle—and for countering some conservative nostalgias.

Graff's admirable account of the evolution of literary studies in the United States repeatedly triggers a sense of déjà vu and subvocalization of *plus ça change . . .* as he retrieves past versions of present controversies. He strives for balance in his presentation of the recurring conflicts of traditionalists and innovators, but clearly he intends to offer a lesson both to traditionalist critics like Bloom and to academics stuck in the tar pit of institutionalized complacency. Thus, he admonishes, "whatever the sins of recent theory [which he conceives, by a useful enough definition here—though not in the sciences, where a more formal and positivistic definition still, albeit less and less strongly, dominates—as self-conscious discourse concerning the multiple forces that organize and legitimate texts], those who blame the problems of the humanities on them—and on other post-1960 developments—only illustrate their own pet maxim that those who forget the past are condemned to repeat it." And he hopes that his resurrection of earlier critics who complained of research displacing teaching or bureaucracy ousting community or method taking primacy over literature "can at least cure us of the delusion that academic literary studies at some point underwent a falling-away from genuine Arnoldian humanism." That delusion persists troublesomely, partly because of "the habit of thinking of institutions as if they were unmediated projections of the values, methods, and ideologies of major individuals and movements." This seemingly commonsensical habit entails, according to Graff, a blindness to changes in how those projections are constituted, so that what goes into them in the way of "isms" winds up little resembling what comes out, "often to the point of subverting their original purpose, or so deflecting them that they become unrecognizable to outsiders."[13] The internal self-evidence of the institution thereby contributes significantly to its appearing externally like a black box housing perverse curricular and pedagogical mechanisms—a portrayal that recalls Giamatti's critique of the university's unself-awareness and insularity.

The egregious consequence of this situation is not that conflicts have been muffled, hidden, or "gone unresolved—unresolved conflict being just the sort of thing a democratic educational system should thrive on—but how little of the potential educational value of such conflicts the professional system has been able to turn into part of what it studies and teaches, instead of a source of paralysis." Such is not always the case, as Graff readily admits, mentioning "the current cold war between theorists and humanists" as an example of a somewhat "esoteric" conflict that has gained a good deal of public attention—and I would argue, perhaps more sanguinely than he, that it is less and less the case (much to his credit)—but still most of the "educational-cultural battles" take place in professional journals and conferences rather than in classrooms or public arenas. This backgrounding, by a "pretense," informing both administration and curriculum, "that humanism and the cultural tradition preside over the various dispersed activities of literary studies," has prevented many students and professors alike, as well as the public, from engaging crucial issues in the humanities in more than token fashion.[14]

Also indicted here is the "field-coverage model of departmental organization." Instituted widely in the late nineteenth century in an attempt to modernize and professionalize education, it effected, whatever its seeming conveniences, a rigid disciplinary balkanization whose problematic artificialities still plague literary studies and the humanities generally—indeed, mutatis mutandis, much of the whole machinery of formal learning. Its principle, until recently almost invisible, "created a system in which the job of instruction could proceed as if on automatic pilot, without the need for instructors to debate aims and methods." Application of the principle "made the modern educational machine friction free, for by making individuals functionally independent in the carrying out of their tasks it prevented conflicts from erupting which would otherwise have had to be confronted, debated, and worked through." And such disjointed compartmentalization or modularity of the curriculum—into periods, nationalities, themes, genres, critical approaches—gave rise to complacency: "It was as if categories existed in order to make it unnecessary to think about them and to recognize that they were the product of theoretical choices." Through this largely unconscious suppression of inter-connection, of openly positional conversation among diverse courses and disciplines, "the illusion could be kept up that nobody had a theory"—but at the considerable cost of depriving students and faculty "of a means of situating themselves in relation to the cultural issues of their time."[15]

Coupled with the ideology of "the humanist myth," the field-coverage principle perpetuates the notion that literature is "self-interpreting," hence *"teaches itself."* Bloom patently embraces this notion; so does Proctor, finally, though he pays much lip service to the idea of contextualizing literature through historical dialogue. Graff aptly points to the persuasive counterexample of Robert Scholes, who argues "that to teach the literary text one must teach the 'cultural text' as well." (Thus, for example, the instructor should help students relate Shakespeare's *Tempest,* a play profoundly concerned with imperialism, to the "cultural text" of the New World colonialism of the time or relate Salman Rushdie's *Satanic Verses* to that of contemporary Islamic belief.) And Graff seems surprised that traditionalists have not been more concerned about the extent to which the field-coverage principle "tends to efface the larger cultural conversation to which works of literature refer" and thus been more sympathetic to arguments like Scholes's. But surely the reason is that, by putting students in what they regard as " 'direct' contact with texts themselves," tra-ditionalists can control the way the conversation goes, "with a minimum of contextualizing interference" by other, less cooper-ative, more questioning voices. In any case, without the "better contextualizing" that Graff advocates, a more capacious apeironic mediation, "the student's 'direct' experience of literature itself tends to result either in uncertainty or facile acquiescence in an interpretive routine."[16]

Graff's analysis, informed by his somewhat deconstructionist concern "with the way idealizations such as 'humanism' have functioned rhetorically to mask the conflicts that constituted them," his sense of the lack of a "metalanguage" for interrelating proliferant disciplinary dialects, and his skepticism that coherence in the humanities can "be grounded on some restored consensus"[17] (conservative or otherwise), is corroborated by Karen Lawrence's diagnosis that the undergraduate core curriculum in English suffers from "curriculosclerosis." She defines this "hardening of the categories" as an "apparent condition" which "suggests that the vitality of much recent research within and across disciplines has not infused the English major." Though she discerns signs of the disease abating—as faculty in many institutions "seem to be seeking a more complex and powerful historical analysis . . . that questions the ideology behind acts of interpretation and treats 'periods' as constructs rather than givens"—she feels the threat of "forces outside the discipline of English that affect the humanities greatly." Two of special concern, which she finds combined in Bennett's philosophy (or whatever it is), are "a pressure on the humanities to prove its [sic] relevance and practicality" (for example, in helping students get jobs) and an insistence that by reading "the classics" in an unmediated fashion anyone can somehow absorb (and learn to make practical use of) their eternal verities. The first derives from the continuing—though perhaps slowly vanishing—American "romance" with practicality. The second, involving a "view of the classics acquired by osmosis," may have stronger bearing on curricular and pedagogical (and finally cultural) issues, for that view "distorts history (as if Plato were ever easy to interpret) and reduces all that is complex and potentially subversive in the 'tradition' itself to accessible, even self-evident truths." Considered together, they shape a reaction from Lawrence that addresses the perception by some, like Proctor, that the humanities, if not dead, are in danger of dying for one reason or another: "What is most unfortunate about the neoconservative response to the declining prestige of the humanities is that it encourages an unthinking consolidation of tradition at a time when crucial developments in literary theory and criticism could bring about a different kind of 'relevance': a relevance that derives from the revisioning of disciplinary boundaries, and discussion of the relation between power and knowledge that is a major part of the intellectual climate today."[18] Graff's call for debate still may be eliciting more sequestered stichomythia than productive public interaction, but Lawrence's proposal for the new "relevance" of the humanities demonstrates that his call—and others more or less resonant with it—is being heeded.

Though they may well understand and fear its implications in some respects, conservative critics of recent innovation in humanities education have been too quick to misconceive issues concerning the literary canon, worrying that its expansion entails dilution, its drive for present relevance a neglect of the past. They thus forget a feature fundamental to the logic of virtually all projects in the humanities: what Martin Mueller terms the "moment of return." He elaborates:

> This moment of return marks a major difference from science, where discoveries are typically absorbed into a cumulative, expanding, and progressive body of knowledge, although the author's writings are discarded or forgotten. Newton on gravity is not a text a scientist needs to read, but one returns again and again to Thucydides, Machiavelli, or Hobbes on power. This inescapable moment of return creates for scholars in the humanities dilemmas of repetition that do not exist in the sciences or many of the social sciences.

Still "inescapable," this moment nonetheless has changed. The notion of remembrance as repetition involves a different sense of relevance than obtained in the past: "In the earlier stages of Western society, the literal memory of the text was hard to achieve and worthy of recognition. The mere reproduction of the text is not sufficient in the modern world: the scholar's task is to repeat it in a manner appropriate to the times."[19] That task, involving a balanced tension of progressive-scientific and retrospective-humanistic imperatives, is, I would emphasize, the educator's as well.

How does one enact this interpretive repetition? By recognizing, first of all, that it "is caught between the Scylla of routinization and the Charybdis of faddish innovation," extremes that Mueller exemplifies analogically by, on the one hand, the performance of a Beethoven symphony that sounds like all the other performances of it (because of too conservative a desire to *preserve*) and, on the

other, the performance of a Shakespeare play that bears little resemblance to any other performance of it (because of too extravagant a desire to *transform*). Given these pitfalls, Mueller stresses
the need for balanced enactment. Orchestras should not, like their
analogues among traditional humanists, strive simply for "original performances" (an effort he regards as "dubious") but should
attempt performances that "sound refreshingly and illuminat-
ingly different from the ways in which we are used to hearing the
work." And this preserving repetition *with a difference* may be
enacted also—again with the humanities analogy in play—through
disciplinary or interdisciplinary conflicts of interpretation. Mueller
suggests the latter possibility, particularly, by his observation that
"clashes between the ethos of musical and theatrical interpretation have become the norm," a situation illustrated by how "some
of the Ring cycles at Bayreuth, by embodying such clashes of
interpretive practices in an extreme form, may serve as unwitting
paradigms of the dilemmas of repetition that confront cultural
memory in our time."[20]

Mueller's argument concerning the humanities' continually
nuanced repetition compulsion, which could be evidenced easily
and extensively, counters strongly the conservative claim that the
traditional canon, "literary" or otherwise, is being neglected or
jettisoned. But what about the expansion of the canon? In that
process too he sees not loss but gain:

> Expansion of the canon provides one form of escape from repetition. Work
> on the current margins of the canon—whether it is new works or older works
> marginalized by previous generations of scholars—is an extremely important
> part of our activities. By the nature of the activity, much of it may appear to be
> a "waste," but whatever the value of an individual contribution, the collective
> work on the margins of the canon performs the essential function of drawing
> and redrawing the boundaries of the canon and of submitting its internal
> differentiation and hierarchy to a continuing critique.

No knee-jerk leftist, Mueller believes such a critique should deal
with the whole spectrum of canonical interestedness, from that of
"a singularly meanspirited and strident complacency" (at times
characteristic of adherents to the now-traditional New Criticism)
to that of "current movements for a narrowly sectarian concept of
the cultural sociopolitical dimension they want to restore to literary scholarship" (which movements tend to operate by, in a phrase

echoing Paul Ricoeur's judgment of Freud, "a hermeneutics of suspicion and contempt"). Acknowledging his indebtedness to Graff, whose analysis of the profession of literary studies he describes as "a study in the pathology of tolerance," Mueller condemns present "climates of corrosive suspicion, inquisitorial arrogance, dogmatic certainty, and strident complacency" and points to the need for "more mutual engagement across the wide range of political thought that is embodied in the canon."[21] If Mueller's labeling of those climates seems exaggerated, that is because the climates themselves are exaggerated—an indication of what is at stake in canonical issues (for they involve, in Peter Carafiol's words, "critical 'tastes' . . . enmeshed with so many of our other beliefs, attitudes, and intuitions" as to be, "as Stanley Fish has said, . . . what we see with")[22] and of the need for less shallow dialogue.

Efforts to enlarge the literary canon are hardly new, as Graff's history abundantly demonstrates; and though such efforts inevitably have resulted in changes of curricular emphasis, they seldom have entailed the wholesale deletion of works. To the contrary, expansion, as the word suggests, functions by an inclusionary impulse. Responding to charges by Bennett, Jonathan Yardley, Stephen Balch, and others that many contemporary literary humanists are debasing or gutting the curriculum, eminent spokespersons for those humanists have countered to that effect. Cary Nelson, editor of *Theory in the Classroom,* a book that has manifoldly enriched thinking about literary pedagogy, finds "very little evidence of people arguing that the classic texts should be eliminated." And Gary Waller, coauthor, with Kathleen McCormick and Linda Flower, of *Reading Texts: Reading, Responding, Writing,* a book concerned with strategies for reading texts in terms of their overdeterminations—the "reading" of reading—whose influence on innovative pedagogy has been even greater than that of Nelson's, argues, with countless others, "that teaching new works, as well as teaching old works in new ways, encourages students to think critically about contemporary society." Speaking specifically of his own theory-oriented English department at Carnegie Mellon University, whose poststructuralist curricular reorganization, especially at the undergraduate level, has served as a model for other departments, Waller re-presents the issue as one, implicated in any notion of canonicity, not simply of

what texts are read (and what they mean) but of *how* they are read
(how their meaning is assigned): "We're educating to make students aware they have choices—that they're agents in an increasingly complex and deterministic society. . . . We don't want students to just passively receive the wisdom of the ages."[23] And
therein lie both the real rub for neoconservative traditionalists
and the real mission for canonical revisionists: a canon expanded
and diversified (to include more works by women, African Americans, Native Americans, Latin Americans, non-Westerners, white
males marginalized for any number of reasons) *and* an activist,
counterdominant way of reading it.

Graff too has readily identified and analyzed the doubleness of
this situation. He relates it to a now-familiar problem invariably
generated when "educational fundamentalism," especially the
Great Books brand, proposes some "unifying principle": that
principle "always ends up being defined either too narrowly to
secure agreement or too broadly to be meaningful." And the delusional dynamic of the principle fosters a wearisome historically
recurrent cycle:

> Fundamentalist unification projects don't simply fail, however. They even-
> tually provoke a reaction that ushers in an even more extreme state of frag-
> mentation than the one they set out to cure. Furthermore, the broken con-
> tinuity resulting from alternating rebellion and backlash erases the memory
> of previous failures—which helps explain why the educators who defend the
> values of the past never seem to learn anything from the past.
> The fundamentalists are right in identifying the curricular problem as
> incoherence. Their mistake is to think that the only way to counteract incoher-
> ence is to legislate a common content. Educational fundamentalism, in other
> words, needlessly confuses content with agreement about content, coherence
> with consensus. Since no such consensus is available (probably not even
> among fundamentalists), the fundamentalists' ideal curriculum could be
> institutionalized only by forcing it down everybody's throat.

In order to escape from this cycle and thereby avoid its Bennett-
like final solution, Graff proposes that we "recognize that ideological conflicts" about the curriculum "are probably here to stay"
and that we "begin asking how such conflicts might be made educationally productive." Such a project, already well under way in
many institutions, necessarily involves dealing with canonical
questions, but it hardly neglects the Great Books; indeed, for
Graff, "the question of what it means to read or teach the great

books (as well as what it means to call a book 'great') is precisely what the current conflict in the humanities is all about." Such questions are not just a matter for specialty theorizing: they have everything to do with building a useful and stimulating context in which students can (learn to) read all manner of books, Great or otherwise. The point is to help students "get a sense of what is at issue in the cultural controversies they have a stake in." They can do that only if "the principle of difference," which Graff sees as a more powerful principle of university organization than any pretending to be unifying, is not suppressed but dramatized—in curriculum, pedagogy, departmental structure—for "difference can't be understood by students unless it is experienced as difference." He even suggests, as a mechanism "to increase the internal responsiveness of the curriculum," the development of a special capstone course, of "what could be called a 'metacourse,' whose aim would be not so much to expound a particular subject as to correlate issues raised in other courses."[24]

But the troubling implications of the educational-fundamentalist imperative extend well beyond the university-level course in "literature," with its increasingly diverse student population, to intersect larger cultural, social, and economic issues that cry out for Graff's differential curriculum, an open literary canon, humanities education (including, crucially, "foreign"-language instructing, especially, now, in Arabic, Russian, and Chinese)—and finally a whole paideia, at all educational levels and not just in the United States—that embraces and thrives on diversity. Criticizing what he calls "the canonical orientation," Mike Rose eloquently discusses that intersection, along the way suggesting that the criteria for building canons, however much matters of authority, derive from other imperatives as well:

> There is a strong impulse in American education—curious in a country with such an ornery streak of antitraditionalism—to define achievement and excellence in terms of the acquisition of a historically validated body of knowledge, an authoritative list of books and allusions, a canon. We seek a certification of our national intelligence, indeed, our national virtue, in how diligently our children can display this central corpus of information. This need for certification tends to emerge most dramatically in our educational policy debates during times of real or imagined threat: economic hard times, political crises, sudden increases in immigration. Now is such a time, and it is reflected in a number of influential books and commission reports.

After briefly citing as examples the arguments and calls for action of Hirsch, Ravitch, Bloom, Mortimer Adler and the Paideia Group, and others, Rose observes that, historically, heightened concern about the maintenance of the canon "was explicitly elitist, driven by a fear that the education of the select was being compromised." Though this traditional elect/preterite dichotomy could readily be, as Derrida would say, "desedimented" from the texts (particularly Bloom's) cited above (a possibility Rose certainly senses, as we will see, but does not actualize in specific terms), Rose argues that now "the majority of the calls are provocatively framed in the language of democracy." Thus such calls declare that the traditional canon can save "disadvantaged youngsters" from the restrictions of a pedestrian curriculum and, by their exposure to works "central to the discourse of power," help them overcome their cultural "disenfranchisement." Such calls, forgetting the multiplicity of the students' own traditions, are "forceful," promising a common heritage, "a still center in a turning world."[25]

But Rose disputes this facile application of a traditionally elitist canon still shaped, however much its hierarchy has been loosened, by a potent rationale of marginalization and haunted by the violence of its past excludings. Himself once labeled and treated as a "disadvantaged" student (because of a clerical mix-up), he also knows that to "redress past wrongs" requires more than expansion: "the very reasons for linguistic and cultural exclusion would have to become a focus of study in order to make the canon act as a democratizing force." But he discerns a deeper problem: the inherent tendency of the canonical orientation to prompt "a narrowing of focus from learning to that which must be learned." And that valorization manifolds in effects, for it ignores or represses the student's own specific life, "simplifies the dynamic tension between student and text," "reduces the psychological and social dimensions of instruction," and frequently makes education a matter of mere "transmission" of already completed Truth from text to student—with the result that "learning is stripped of confusion and discord" and of "strong human connection."[26] Such "transmission" (in the sense of "teaching" as "handing down" or "bequeathing" through a text) is one definition of the Latin *trāditio;* another is "betrayal."

Opposed to the notion that the disadvantaged student can be educated in the humanities merely by transmissive exposure to the canon, Rose proposes a divergent approach, a more transactional one that mutually projects text into context, context into text. Since the canonical orientation—with its implicit "model of learning" that "seems, at times, more religious than cognitive or social"—proves alienating for such students, he points out the need for "an orientation to instruction that provides guidance on how to determine and honor the beliefs and stories, enthusiasms, and apprehensions that students reveal" and on "how to build on them" and make productive discussion of their conflicts with the curriculum. This pedagogical sensitivity to—indeed, Shelleyan moral imagination concerning—the "discordance between the message and the audience" in turn requires a more socially contextualized understanding of literacy and its development. With that, humanities educators who fear cultural balkanization can stop preaching a faith in an impossible "cultural unanimity" (by which they nonetheless measure their students' learning) and instead extend "an invitation for people truly to engage each other at the point where cultures and classes intersect"—a canonical coherence based not on authoritarian (Mosaic) consensus but on democratic (mosaic) interconnectedness. Something of a Freirean and a Graffian, Rose thus envisions education as vitally a matter of "cultural dialogue and transaction" that the canonical orientation, with its tropes of exclusion, suppresses, along with its tendency to "squelch new thinking, diffuse the generative tension between the old and the new." Judging the authority of that orientation to derive from "a misreading of American cultural history" and to depend on "a mythologizing act" of invoking phantasms of past cultural stabilities and uniformities, he calls, finally, for apeironic learning:

> Democratic culture is, by definition, vibrant and dynamic, discomforting and unpredictable. . . . A truly democratic vision of knowledge and social structure would honor this complexity. The vision might not be soothing, but it would provide guidance as to how to live and teach in a country made up of many cultural traditions.
>
> We are in the middle of an extraordinary social experiment: the attempt to provide education for all members of a vast pluralistic democracy.[27]

And, I hasten to add, just as Rose's experiences in his hometown, Los Angeles (where public school students speak eighty-odd languages), help him understand the imperatives for education nationally, so does the American multiethnic experiment, for all its faults still the most successful in the world, help us understand those of its burgeoning global counterpart—even the unusual homogeneities of race and class that have made possible Japan's educational system are beginning to leak.[28]

Surely Rose would agree with Myra Jehlen that the reformation of the literary canon must not proceed by a play of differences that only "distinguish but do not relate—since they are not seen as emerging from relations." To avoid an expansion that creates an inclusive, pluralistically representative curriculum and yet one that is static, she advises that revisionary reforms should "embody relations, dramatize interactions, define and describe interdependently." Indeed, as she convincingly suggests, literature itself comes into being through such processes of relation: literary creation occurs at the dialectical interface of differences, and it instantiates their dynamics. The reading of literature, at another time and place, involves still more encounters with difference. Given this manifold, it must be treated as "a calculus" rather than as "a multiplication," so that students do not "come to believe themselves universal beings" through a facile inclusiveness. Thus "the first issue" is not curricular content but "the way any subject defines itself in relation to others, identifying itself at its limits, where challenges to its identity can lead to rethinking." Echoing Graff's concern with how students experience difference, she reminds us apothegmatically that "reading new things is not the same as arriving at new readings: the curricular model we need will embody and teach that distinction *first*."[29]

Though the broad disciplinary area of literary studies continues to be the most salient battleground of humanities education polemics—and educators in that area perhaps the most publicly engaged in those polemics—the whole conflict, well exemplified in disagreements between canonical traditionalists and revisionists, continues to unfold on a larger scale. Considerable momentum, more exacerbating than productive (and productive mostly by indirection), was added to that conflict by Lynne V. Cheney, Bennett's successor at the National Endowment for the Humanities, in the late 1980s. In February 1988 she convened an NEH-sponsored panel of assorted "experts" to diagnose what she regarded as the ailments of the humanities in America. Though no unanimity resulted, apparently she gleaned from—or imposed upon—the proceedings a vague diagnosis confirming her suspicion that too many humanists, pretty much the same people Roger Kimball would later nastily assail as opposed to humanism in his *Tenured Radicals: How Politics Has Corrupted Our Higher Education,* were entangled in recondite (equal leftist, theoretical, innovative) pursuits and so not properly serving the real (equal neoconservative, practical, traditional) needs of the American community. As remedy for this irresponsibly unbalanced academic/public antinomy she suggested that perhaps the NEH should work to promote projects that would address those neglected needs.[30]

The meeting elicited an astute response from Barbara Herrnstein Smith, then president of the Modern Language Association, who found in its deliberations an indication of "the ambivalent and to some extent self-contradictory perspective—condescending conservatism crossed with querulous populism—from which the current examinations of the health of the humanities are being conducted and recommendations for its cure generated." Herrnstein Smith defended the humanities professoriat against Cheney's charges of ivory-towerism, pointing out that, even if the scholarship of humanists seems "obscure to nonacademics or nonspecialists," they are "nevertheless responsive, in their *teaching and other professional activities,* to the situations and perspectives of women, blacks, children of immigrants, and other minority or non-elite social groups and, furthermore, that a larger number of professors than in previous years are themselves members of such groups—as are, of course, increasingly, our students." She reminded "public officials" that the humanities, particularly literary studies, involve much more than just "reading great books and affirming their greatness" and that the NEH was established to encourage exactly the kind of important scholarship (with, I would add, its possibly far-reaching implications for humanities education) not "mediated and managed by commercial sponsors" long interested in the general readership. Herrnstein Smith's counterclaim was not that the humanities in America "are without problems" but that, as they grapple with the immense cultural changes of the late twentieth century, their problems cannot be "cured" by government regulation of humanists "seen as enemies of the people."[31]

Whatever attention she may have paid to such dissenting voices, Cheney had a navigational lock on her mission. In her report issued in September 1988, *Humanities in America,* she almost "talks their talk" at times, but her pretense of comprehensiveness only lightly veils dismissive gestures. Her simple message, in the imperialist, interdictory mood of the time just before Bennett was crowned "drug czar" of all the Americas (largely in response to a national preoccupation with, in the media phrase, "drugs in the schools"), threads like a leitmotif through the whole text: just say no to theory (or other categorical bogeymen subsumed under that term: esoteric specialism, political activism, skepticism, and so on) and yes to her brand of public-minded humanities education (a coherent traditional curriculum, predictable Shakespeare productions, politically beige chautauquas, and so on—what I am tempted to term "humaninanities" education).

Let me be more specific. In her report Cheney offers convincing numerical evidence that the humanities are healthy and thriving in the public sector: millions of people each year participate in state-sponsored humanities programs; in 1986 Americans apparently spent more money on "cultural events" than on "sports events"; art museums are attracting record numbers of visitors. The culture of the few is becoming more and more available to the many; still, of course, much remains to be done. (Compare many European countries' expenditures on the arts, I would add.) But then the smile turns to a frown: "It is not possible to make such a positive assessment when one looks at our colleges and universities." There the number of bachelor's degrees in humanities disciplines has declined over the last twenty years or so (actually a reversal began in the mid-1980s, which she admits—but with no sense of how dramatic it has been); most students, increasingly favoring business as a major (in fact a trend on the wane), graduate without knowing "how the ideas and ideals of our civilization have evolved" and without "studying a foreign language" and so lack (now the mild blandishments for those not yet on board) "a basis for understanding other cultures" and "a framework for lifelong learning about ourselves and the world in which we live."[32] A moderate argument so far, not all wrongheaded and, taken in a generous spirit, irrefutable in some particulars.

But who is to blame? The professoriat, of course. According to Cheney, the humanities in the academy have become too esoteric an enterprise, too specialized, too willing to practice activist politics rather than revere beauty, to expose "timeless matters" as "transitory notions" instrumental in cultural hegemony. The neglect of "broad learning" she attributes largely to the humanities' adoption from the sciences of an emphasis on "narrowly focused research" underwritten by an incestuous system of peer review that discourages "generalized, synthetic" work. (I would agree with this last point and acknowledge the need for change, though I find quite problematic any suggestion here that the sciences are inherently narrow and the humanities inherently broad. Cheney appears to have little awareness of the fruitful cross-pollination between deeply detailed research, on the one hand, and generalized thinking, on the other—or of its necessity in any process of learning that is more than disjunctive memorization or unreflective idealization, a necessity clearly acknowledged by the Carnegie Foundation for the Advancement of Teaching in its 1990 report *Scholarship Reconsidered: Priorities of the Professoriate,* which urges the integration of *teaching into research,* with the latter expansively conceived.) She endorses the argument that "new theoretical approaches have further isolated scholars, making it difficult even for colleagues in the same discipline to understand one another," and contributed to the mutual alienation of "the academy and society."[33] Apparently uninformed of the extent to which these approaches have not only intellectually galvanized research *and* instructing in individual humanities disciplines but also opened a whole new interdisciplinary agenda that continues to enrich relations both among humanities disciplines and between the humanities and other professional and public enterprises, Cheney goes on to excoriate the professoriat, as she stereotypes it, for rewarding research over teaching, for overemphasizing publication, and so on—notes she later sounds again in *Tyrannical Machines.* The analysis runs shallow—and aground at times—but it does bring into view imbalances, even hypocrisies, that the academy needs to address.

One might have more sympathy with Cheney's criticism of the tendency to read "humanities texts as though they were primarily political documents" if she would not peddle eternal verities so hard. In my experience most humanities educators do not dismiss "questions of intellectual and aesthetic quality," and even those strongly theoretical in orientation may show signs of ennui at the thought of guiding their students through yet another reading of a text as a product of gender, race, or class. But there is a general desire to help students situate texts and engage intellectual, aesthetic, political, and moral questions they raise that cannot (and, I would argue, *should* not) be seen as disconnected—once we have, as we now do, the shared theoretical apparatus (including a vocabulary that some find esoteric) to see otherwise. If there is bias toward political interpretation, it is in response to an overdose of Cheney's "truths that pass beyond time and circumstance" with suspicious smoothness. Indeed, that corrective, part of a larger investigation of variegated "truths" (political or otherwise) enabled by "new theoretical approaches," is beginning to provide for students precisely what she laments the academy losing (if it ever had it): an "overarching view of how the separate courses they have taken relate to one another."[34] Graffian curricular and pedagogical experiments, among many others undertaken with theoretical self-consciousness, have helped in that regard, though the debates that energize such projects are not the vanilla ones she condescendingly advocates as the path to immortal and illocal truths. There may, in some sense, *be* such truths in the humanities—Cheney never says what they are—but contemporary humankind will have to deal with them in all their slippery complexity and not merely rely on interested versions of supposedly universal axioms from an ever-differing past.

After excoriating the professoriat, Cheney turns to a more public but certainly related issue: the fate of reading. Like Neil Postman, she is concerned "that reading might become an endangered activity"—not because of censorship and book banning (though repressive factions have done both aplenty) but because of so few people wanting to read. "What is the fate of modes of thought that reading encourages: complex, probing, reflective ways of thinking that have long been identified with the humanities?" she asks, apparently oblivious to how the educators she criticizes are working to encourage and enrich those modes. The bugaboo is predictable: television, which has become "our national obsession" to the extent that "our common culture seems increasingly a product of what we watch rather than what we read." And "we" (most people) watch (or read in another sense) mostly "dismal" stuff—endless soap operas, sitcoms, exercise shows, electronic evangelists, news shows dominated by reportage of personal and grander disasters, and so on ad nauseam. As she rightly notes, this stuff is packaged so that "it allows little time for the mind to double back on itself and question" and thus is passively received;

but she fails to acknowledge that many educators in the humanities, especially those criticized for their concern with popular culture, are working to help their students discover or invent practices of critique that enable them to read any text, in whatever medium, more actively and creatively. She also recognizes the "positive aspects to television," applauds them, and stresses (since television "is not going to go away") that "the object . . . is to keep in mind its potential"[35]—but without ever addressing the issue, crucial to the humanities theorists she pillories, of *how* to experience more actively programming of whatever quality.

Cheney's encompassing emphasis is on how the humanities, as she amorphously idealizes them, should figure in American public life. She conceives their public activities as constituting "a kind of parallel school, one that has grown up outside established institutions of education." Since such activities are so diverse, however, that school "cannot provide the coherent plan of study, the overarching vision of connectedness, that our schools and colleges can." In her view they often fail to enact that complementary role, largely because they promote and reward specialist research and do not value work in the "public humanities" that for her "has evolved into an intellectually rigorous pursuit." She concedes that "there will probably always be in our colleges and universities some sense of estrangement from society, a sense that flows from a critical attitude toward human affairs which is crucial to preserve," but she also suggests that "the extreme alienation of some faculty members may well be tempered by closer involvement with our culture."[36] That seemingly sweet reasonableness immediately precedes her vision, near the end of the report (just before she distills specific recommendations from what has gone before), of an America where public teaching proceeds in many unassuming fora—in New Jersey, Arkansas, Montana—and the whole nation glows from its permeation by Arnoldian energies.

What has been the response to Cheney's report? Some weeks after it was released, David Laurence, then director of the Association of Departments of English, published a rejoinder expressing qualified sympathy for Cheney's concerns but also taking her to task for misrepresenting specialization as the "main culprit" in getting the academic humanities "in an abnormal condition." Laurence very much doubts that the condition is abnormal and notes, with amusing documentation, that, regarding the attribution of culpability, "every generation has said the same of its scholars." He defends specialization for its grappling with the difficult and telling details that Cheney sees as obstructions to the quest to "confirm a particular set of known general truths." That grappling may lead to some such truths, but it leads also to an encounter with the apeironic, as Laurence explains:

> Insofar as *Humanities in America* suggests that study in the humanities always leads to the same abiding insights or answers, . . . the pamphlet leaves a way open for claims that it endorses active discouragement of scholarship that does not presuppose or reproduce those insights. Yet, empirically speaking, reading has always produced what it seems fair to describe not only as abiding insights but also as glorious, if on occasion annoying, swarms of partial, mutually incompatible answers whose antinomies we sometimes may not know how to resolve.

He is appropriately anxious about the suppression of specialization because of discomfort with the "social, intellectual, even emotional conflicts" to which it gives rise, for that "can only have a chilling effect on inquiry in general" and discourage, in particular, one of the purposes of scholarship as inquiry: "to examine commonplaces as well as to transmit them, to question orthodoxies rather than to promulgate them, to challenge our own intellectual and especially our emotional loyalties more than to defend them." As a humanist intent on that purpose, he examines Cheney's commonplace that the results of specialized research are supposed to be assimilated into an "architectonic whole." He finds it wanting and wonders "whether specialization, with all its problems, may nonetheless have been pointing to an awareness that knowledge never can be other than fragmented and to the intellectual and moral task of learning to embrace the fragmentariness without melancholy, nostalgia, or rage." Thus, he concludes, specialization, whatever its failures, leads to what "may even deserve to be called success, when it directs us to an awareness that may be arguably better for us than the mirage of a totality."[37]

Responding to the report about the same time but less philosophically, Phyllis Franklin, then executive director of the MLA, faulted Cheney's numerical data for their historical insufficiency, questioning the assumptions by which they were interpreted and trying generally to articulate the complex issues (which Cheney much oversimplifies) entailed in diagnosing the health of the academic humanities on the basis of data about course enrollments and bachelor's degrees conferred. She also took Cheney to task for not defining what she means by *specialization* and for obscuring "the central role specialized research plays in ensuring the vitality of the humanities."[38]

And many others, in various media and fora, reacted to Cheney's report, typically from fairly polarized positions. But surely the most eloquent and balanced statement of, to use Giamatti's phrase, the "countervailing point of view" was the early-1989 report from the American Council of Learned Societies (ACLS) entitled *Speaking for the Humanities,* a document that addresses not only Cheney's attack but also the similar ones mounted by Bennett and Bloom. Though all its authors are professors in the sprawling bailiwick of literary studies (predominantly English), they strive assiduously to represent academic humanists in all the humanities disciplines. Expressing concern that differing humanists have not responded adequately to such attacks, the report attempts to do so. It deals at length with the contrasts between those who deludedly believe that the activities of humanists should be somehow traditional—simple, clear, universal—and those engaged in such activities, from the most rigorous projects of poststructuralist theory to the most ad hoc gestures of classroom practice, who experience them as increasingly (and appropriately) complex, entangled with equivocalities, culturally self-conscious. The authors are deeply aware of those contrasts (whose analogues may be found abundantly not only, as we have seen, in the natural and social sciences but also in the professions and certainly in the arts) as indications of a powerful positive change in education, one much more complicated, necessary, and fruitful than Cheney imagines.

Interested both "in confronting negative criticism directly" and "in revising the popular understanding of the humanities," the authors very much disagree with Cheney's "story of the abandonment of the humanities by undergraduates." Their story concerns "a revival of the humanities" that is attracting students away from the mammonish pursuit of degrees in business and high-technology fields. They argue that attacks such as Cheney's, "which would be comic in their incongruity if they were not taken so seriously by so many people, . . . actually obfuscate the ways in which the humanities can be and are socially and intellectually important." Thus dangerous irony inheres in the humanities being attacked, incongruously, "at a moment when for many of us their significance and strength have never been greater." Gaining perspective by this incongruity, the authors obvert the ob(li)vious and argue that "precisely those things now identified as failings in the humanities actually indicate enlivening transformations." On the other side of the token: a pervasive wild-side activity of interrogation that, while "inevitably uncomfortable" (so it was "at Socrates' feet"), involves a discomfort that "teachers of the humanities tend to encourage," finding in it "a source of creativity"; a self-consciousness (and self-criticism) that is not a symptom of the humanities' ailments but "one of the signs of their health"; "problems . . . almost always more complicated than the popular interpretation allows"; and "difficulties stigmatized in recent indictments [that] are the consequence of the virtues of the system" (so that, for example, the much-assailed practice of assigning a large proportion of humanities courses to part-time faculty members, however lamentable, "is not a consequence of bad faith, or professional self-interest, as is often charged, but of the sheer size and cost of the enterprise of higher education in America," an enterprise dedicated to "the attempt to create a genuinely democratic system of higher education").[39]

More specific counterarguments expose shortcomings and flaws in Cheney's criticisms and illustrate those "enlivening transformations." The work of "general significance" for which she calls "only develops from specialized and particularized research." Humanities educators specialize and professionalize because "they take their subject seriously" and want to avoid being belletristic amateurs "who unself-consciously sustain traditional hierarchies, traditional social and cultural exclusions, assuming that their audience is both universal and homogeneous." The humanities check narrow specialization by their tendency to interdisciplinarity, a tendency that should be encouraged as their thought "tests limits," enriches through debate, and achieves "the most advanced, most self-reflective, most rigorous, most subtle work possible." For such achievement they "are better conceived as fields of exploration and critique rather than materials for transmission." If the future promoted by that wild-side view is "divided and contentious," it is still surely more "engaging and productive" than whatever Cheney foresees.[40]

The authors sensitively treat the problem for many, both inside and outside the academy, of the challenge posed by contemporary humanism "to the positivist ideal of objectivity and disinterest." Critiques of that ideal, with their imperative to theorize the positionality and conditionality of thought, threaten conventional notions of moral order and trigger fear of its subversion. Once such theorization begins to proliferate, however, there seems little possibility of ignoring its power as a learning strategy, of regaining some premodern innocence. But, the authors assert, only undemocratic authority bent on suppressing choice need feel alarm at this situation, for "a system of thought that is alert to the way interests generate thought and ideological assumptions govern the most self-evident truth has a better chance to understand and analyze arguments effectively than a system that does not question assumptions." And they are quick to add, for anyone on the lookout for a single-minded political agenda, that "to locate ideology is not necessarily to condemn," that the best scholarship and instructing try to clarify their own "ideological blindspots," and that, "at its best, contemporary humanistic thinking does not peddle ideology, but rather attempts to sensitize us to the presence of ideology in our work, and to its capacity to delude us into promoting as universal values that in fact belong to one nation, one social class, one sect." Thus the authors hardly oppose students' reading Great Books—quite the contrary—but such reading should be done "while simultaneously pursuing an inquiry into how we understand what we read," so that, for example, *The Merchant of Venice* should be read in relation to the social circumstances of European Jews in Shakespeare's time and *Paradise Lost* in the context of seventeenth-century Christian beliefs, always with a readiness for "renewed debates on value."[41]

This latter effort involves also the articulation of new contexts for reading that account for historical change and cultural and linguistic diversity and "allow the best contemporary thinking, including theory, to be reinvested in the teaching of classic texts in the most productive way." As the authors explain, the analytical counterforce of that thinking, particularly as represented by theory, has arisen not in order to undo shared curricular and cultural values but in order to respond creatively to their already having been unsettled and found wanting by the historical work of modern thought. To participate in that response is "to live with uncertainty"—in the apeironic contingencies of "new reflection on our condition." The commitment to do so suggests something quite the opposite of what neoconservatives construe as "moral cowardice." Indeed, from this point of view, "it is precisely the unwillingness to live with uncertainty, the desperate need to return to old verities that seems the real failure of nerve."[42] Moral courage inheres in not saying no to theory, in not avoiding the difficulties it enables one to see (the word derives from the Greek θεορία, "a [mental] viewing") more complexly and understandingly, and in helping students do the same. It inheres, I would argue, in working for the possibility of a generalized consciousness so self-aware that the distinction between a "theorist" and a "non-theorist" would have little meaning—a metanoia from which there would be no regression.

By a similar logic of inversion, the authors argue that curricular disagreement in the humanities should not be "taken as evidence of incoherence and self-doubt" but should be recognized as a continuation of the debates that characterize the most vigorous periods in the history of the humanities. The argument echoes some of Cheney's lip service concerning that recognition, but with the crucial difference that it recommends, "not retreats to traditions which in their own time were inadequate, but rethinking." Such rethinking valorizes "instruction in otherness: vivid, compelling evidence of differences in cultures, mores, assumptions, values." It poses fundamental questions about the forces that constitute any canon, about how much and what kind of cultural and ethnic diversity it can encompass, about whether there now can or should be such a thing as a canon. Such rethinking, radiant with profound implications, requires careful debate. It takes time, sometimes seeming glacially slow. And the institutional changes it suggests are, as Giamatti well knew, "very difficult to effect." The authors, keeping a careful balance, caution that, as this rethinking proceeds, easy assumptions about what is "innovative" or "conservative" should be eschewed. But like most of their sympathetic colleagues, they have no wish that all of this end in aporia and inaction. Rethinking should lead to decisions, but "they should not be made self-delusively, self-righteously, without recognition of the nature of the contemporary epistemological and ideological debate."[43]

Like Franklin, the authors of *Speaking for the Humanities* discover problems with the conclusions drawn from enrollment statistics in both *To Reclaim a Legacy* and *Humanities in America.* They intelligently reinterpret the national decline—not without exceptions—of enrollments in humanities courses and of the number of humanities degrees conferred during the 1970s as having occurred not because of any disenchantment with the humanities (or, for that matter, with the social sciences, whose enrollments show a similar pattern) but because of an interest in business-related courses and degrees in "a period of declining economic expectations throughout the country, when middle class America began to reimagine the possibility of hard times." They argue persuasively that humanities majors are "intrinsically attractive" (though their usefulness in the business world, I would add, may be argued just as persuasively), especially "when the economic pressure is lighter." While the authors admit that recent and continuing positive trends have not been documented adequately, they present enough evidence of their strength and breadth to justify the conclusions that "the humanities are anything but moribund and marginal" and that "the statistical argument for 'decline' is demonstrably spurious."[44] Beyond doubt, the authors aver, the present attractiveness and importance of the humanities for undergraduates (and graduate students) may be attributed in large part to the kind and quality of education that academic humanists practice.

The authors concede that the educational mission of the humanities has been compromised in some respects—by the tendency of the academic marketplace to overvalue scholarship, for example. But they also observe that the humanities professoriat is invariably more involved in undergraduate education than its counterpart in the sciences. And they stress that the problems occasioning compromises, many having to do with the democratic scale of that mission, should not be piously oversimplified. Moreover, they adduce considerable evidence as to the quality of humanities faculties not only in research universities but also, partly because of market forces, in postsecondary institutions generally—faculties very much engaged with curricular and pedagogical issues and ideas.[45]

Thus, for the authors of the ACLS report, the academic humanities continue to thrive, but their activities in doing so increasingly entail apeironic turns that trouble the conservative temperament.

They take seriously their responsibilities for discovering and keeping safe the treasures of the past, but they also "continue to expand our sense of the past and to include those who have hitherto remained on the margins of history: the powerless, the illiterate, the dispossessed." They are very much concerned with human values but as matters for "free discussion" and not for passive reception, and they work "to expose and analyze those values that lie hidden beneath the surfaces of language and art." They "protect and [pace those who think beauty is no longer appreciated] celebrate languages—verbal or visual, in poems or paintings, novels or films, but also in nonfictional writing or in artifacts"—and not with an "inflexible affirmation of past structures" but with "a rigorous self-consciousness about the structure and operations of languages as they transform through history." They don't merely instill meaning: they "investigate the way meaning is created, how we determine what is true or false, how we interpret and define 'reality,'" concomitantly exploring "the uses of the imagination in its creation of alternative worlds through language and the arts." Such activities are carried out not just in discipline-oriented undergraduate and graduate programs but also in nearly three hundred interdisciplinary humanities centers, hardly havens of narrow specialization, that have proliferated nationally. And those activities, organized to help "create the freeing conditions of democracy," should be understood not as manifestations of some political agenda gratuitously or perversely opposed to traditional ideas and values but as part of a larger, momentous shift in human consciousness: "Much of what most matters in modern thought challenges claims to universality and subverts traditional assumptions of authority; and those challenges—from science (relativity and quantum theory, for example), from psychoanalysis, from philosophy, from cultural anthropology, from critical theory—cannot be ignored by way of a simple return to tradition, for they significantly alter the way we can conceptualize 'tradition.'"[46] Participation in that shift involves, to borrow Thomas Pynchon's kinesthetic phrasing, "not a disentanglement from, but a progressive *knotting into*"[47] the great general issues that Cheney accuses academic humanists of avoiding. No retreat in the least, it requires a courage that William Carlos Williams, an exemplary modernist, knew well:

Curriculosclerosis and Related Problems

How easy to slip
into the old mode, how hard to
cling firmly to the advance.[48]

With that sort of awareness, the authors of *Speaking for the Humanities* offer their recommendations. Acknowledging that their variegated profession, like higher education in general, "is obviously far from perfect," they offer them (some superficially similar to those offered by conservative critics but, finally, in most cases, radically different in degree and direction) with a firm "rejection of the notion that the way forward is the way back" and a hopeful affirmation of "the determination to risk the difficulties that follow from profound questioning." At least two of those recommendations have a Graffian flavor: that continuing discussion and debate of humanities curricula be a high faculty priority and that humanities departments focus on how their disciplines have been "constituted and authorized." Others call for small course sections, intensive attention to student work (particularly writing), more faculty positions to increase the proportion of courses taught by full-time staff, more involvement by distinguished faculty in undergraduate education. Since "the most fruitful lines of thinking often traverse previous boundaries," one calls for more opportunities for interdisciplinary instructing and research. Surely the most controversial recommendation and the most important is that "humanities programs continue to teach the great works of the traditional canon in relation to historical scholarship and critical theory" but with the provisions that

> experiments with the canon should be the norm, not the exception, and texts representing traditionally marginal voices or other national contexts should always be taught, and for these reasons: first, because our students are not themselves drawn from a single homogeneous culture; second, because the nation is increasingly involved in cultural and business exchanges with other nations; third, because one of the humanities' most fundamental responsibilities is to expose and question the aesthetic, moral, cultural, and epistemological assumptions which govern our behavior and our society.[49]

The rationale underwriting this recommendation, as well as the others, is informed not just by theoretical sophistication and professional self-awareness but also by a global cultural conscience, a practical sense of the world's transactions, and a positive belief in the future.

The debate that escalated in 1988 continued through 1989, much as it continues now. Cheney's public responses to the ACLS report show little sympathy for its arguments: a little give-and-take on peripheral issues, counterclaims about enrollment figures, and so on—but mostly drumbeating for the usual vague transcendent values and truths she accuses the academic humanities of neglecting in their ideological pursuits.[50] The *New York Times,* the *Wall Street Journal,* and other large-circulation newspapers, already involved in 1988, joined the fray in earnest in early 1989, featuring op-ed pieces and letters by Bloom and others that battled back and forth on issues of canon and curriculum. Many focused on curricular changes at Stanford University, Duke University, the University of Pennsylvania, and other high-visibility institutions. Insofar as the popularized version of the debate can be seen as politically polarized, the left has attended and responded to the right more informedly and intelligently than the right to the left. That generalization holds as well for the more recent squabbles, notably between the NEH and the MLA, over the scholarly credentials of nominees to the National Council on the Humanities, the conservative-packed advisory board for the NEH. And it holds for the further intensification of the debate in 1991 when a number of distinguished educators (again, mostly in literary studies— Wayne Booth, Stanley Fish, Gerald Graff, Henry Louis Gates, Jr., and others) formed an organization called Teachers for a Democratic Culture in order to counter excesses on both sides of the debate (name-calling and the like, especially accusations about political correctness from the covertly politicized NAS), better apprise the public of the issues involved, and promote a balance between tradition and innovation in humanities education. And that generalization, I daresay, still holds.

But however that may be, the dramatizing of the left-right polarization in the public media, which are dominated easily by figures like Cheney with ready access to them, still has created problems of its own. The issues have become oversimplified or misrepresented, so that, for instance, mulish rightists seem to spend all their time promulgating the Great Books to the masses while trendy leftists seem to spend theirs deconstructing minority soap operas or rehashing the niceties of political correctness (should women ever wear pink?) for the entertainment of a cloistered elite. Many important developments have been neglected—for instance, new programs and courses in which students study canonical and noncanonical works comparatively, reading them against each other and thus allowing the familiar and unfamiliar mutually to foreground different or similar cultural assumptions and aesthetic values, or changes in the style of inquiry, scholarly production, and pedagogy in the humanities occasioned by the rapid proliferation of computer technology.[51] (In regard to the former, consider how some students are learning "to produce the canonical and the noncanonical in relation one to the other and to ask questions about their mutual [intertextual] definition, one as a function of the other," perhaps in terms of what Ross Chambers calls a "palimpsestic pedagogy" that invites them to deal with the ironies of canonicity—for instance, that "one cannot strive to change the canon without simultaneously supporting the system of canonicity"—and involves, finally, "teaching that appropriates the system of education in such a way that students learn in turn to appropriate the system for their own purposes."[52] In regard to the latter, consider literary critics' engagement with Hans-Walter Gabler's recent computer-compiled synoptic edition of Joyce's *Ulysses,* a project that, as John M. Slatin argues, raises all manner of questions, easily made pertinent to the classroom, concerning "the fixity of the printed text" and of its correlate "object in mental space." Or consider the widening use in humanities courses of hypertext, which textual form "exists only in the online environment" and prompts reading "as a discontinuous or non-linear process which, like thinking, is associative in nature, as opposed to the sequential process envisioned by conventional text"[53]—a process that redefines the reader, as well as the writer, in some ways but also surely one that finds quick accommodation by students, who live in a video-oriented, shopping-mall world.) And, a problem that in many ways occasions and feeds the two aforementioned, the conservative pole tends (sometimes quite disingenuously) to define the terms of and thus control debate, with the result that many members of the humanities professoriat have no voice and are ignored, disproportionate attention is given to literary studies, and salient contexts besides the overtly political seldom come effectively into play.[54]

Nonetheless, the scale of the debate does provide a large forum for helping the public learn about the academic humanities, and humanistic scholars less and less fear popularization of their concerns as an anathema and are joining in, inviting their public school colleagues also to do so. Their purposes in responding to this opportunity may well be at variance with what Cheney would wish, for they are increasingly intent on not compromising the range and difficulties of the issues involved. They sense the dangers of both formless pluralism and unreflective traditionalism. Recognizing the stakes, they are seeking the balance points of a new dance—so that, for instance, a text be not dissolved in context but opened to engage the student and thus the distinctiveness, the value, even the beauty, of it be not sacrificed but highlighted by interpretation, critique, and theorization.[55] Like Cheney, they know that the absence of what Mark Van Doren calls "intellectual design" is the great bane of education, but they know—at least the most intellectually and morally alert of them know—also that the conservative vision of that design lacks and indeed works to suppress the complexity, variety, and dynamism of the still inchoate paideia they are striving to invent.

CHAPTER 6

The Arts

Controversies about American arts education inevitably overlap with those about humanities education. The two areas manifoldly share aesthetic, moral, political, and cultural concerns—as well as, to some extent, patterns of polarization regarding issues of beauty, truth, value, taste, and so on. But while students of the humanities may study the arts for one reason or another, students of the arts themselves are interested preeminently in artistic creation and performance. So one may speak of arts education as involving both learning somehow *of* them (how to experience them) and learning somehow *in* them (how to practice one or more of them). Anyone who can deeply appreciate and volubly discuss an étude by Chopin but cannot play it or cannot compose a piece for piano certainly knows the difference here, though some people can do all these things; and students at all levels should be encouraged, as appropriate, to appreciate, perform, and create.

In regard to the arts as a matter of artistic production—perhaps the most conventional way of conceiving them—rather than of appreciation or performance, Frye again offers some useful distinctions:

> The role of art . . . is primarily to express the complex of human existence, humanity's awareness of being itself rather than its perception of what is not itself and is outside it. . . . It does not quantify existence like science: it qualifies it: it tries to express not what is there but what is here, what is involved in consciousness and being themselves. . . . The stabilized subject of science is usually identified with the reason; the unstabilized subject [of art] is normally called the imagination. . . . So while science deals with the consolidating of what is there, the arts deal with the expanding of what is

here; the circumference of science is the universe, the circumference of the arts is human culture. . . .
   Science is increasingly a communal and corporate activity. The humanities are more individualized, and the arts are intensely so.[1]

However debatable such distinctions might be, one probably would have little trouble finding general agreement on them or, for the most part, on the conventional categories of the artistic—though one might well find considerable dissent as to whether or not a particular painting, say, is or is not "art," and the issue of the difference between art and craft might arise, as might that concerning what makes an art "fine" (as opposed to popular, middle-brow, whatever) or that concerning whether or not or how to include the "verbal arts," such as drama, poetry, or fiction. One could multiply and problematize such distinctions indefinitely, but still one cannot quite say, paraphrasing Proctor's lamentation about the humanities, that no one today knows what the arts are. Rather, the problem here is, according to the 1988 report on arts education of the National Endowment for the Arts, that "the arts are in triple jeopardy: they are not viewed as serious; knowledge [in this context, either of or in the arts, I presume] itself is not viewed as a prime educational objective; and those who determine school curricula do not agree on what arts education is."[2]

   That report, mandated by Congress in 1985, undertaken by the NEA with the help of the National Council on the Arts, and somewhat preciously entitled *Toward Civilization,* litanizes the causes of that triple jeopardy and recommends measures to counter them. Issued without an author's name that might lend it polemical conservative cachet, it nonetheless makes prefatory bows to *A Nation at Risk* and the works of Bloom and Hirsch. Still, though simplistic or wrongheaded in some respects and prone to promote even more suffocating bureaucratization of public education, many of its recommendations, if taken in an apeironic mood, persuade. Likewise its brisk condensation of the triple-jeopardy problem: "basic arts education"—as an enterprise that "aims to provide *all* students, not only the gifted and talented, with knowledge of, and skills in, the arts," that includes all the interdisciplinary arts, and that is pedagogically well rationalized, supported by sufficient resources, and effectively evaluated—"does not exist in the United States today."[3]

How so? Generally, in that public education fails to fulfill the four purposes, according to the report, of arts education: (1) "to give our young people a sense of civilization" (that is, of the cultures that have contributed to American civilization—whose art, the report admits, affectedly acknowledging a role for interpretation, "needs to be 'unwrapped' "), (2) "to foster creativity" (for creating "a personal vision," for developing "reasoning and problem-solving skills essential to a productive work force and to the learning of other subjects," and for engaging "actively in the process of worldmaking," the alterity of poets, whom, the report observes, paraphrasing Jerome Bruner, "tyrants hate and fear" more than they do scientists), (3) "to teach effective communication" (verbal and otherwise, especially in "television's vocabularies"), and (4) "to provide tools for critical assessment of what one reads, sees and hears" (so that one may make "better choices" or "reasoned choices" among consumer products and ideas, perhaps "even influence the marketplace of both"—but surely not, the report's silence on the possibility suggests, to the point of criticizing and advocating an alternative to "marketplace" as a deeply problematic cultural metaphor and reality).⁴

The report attributes failure in fulfilling those purposes to several "impediments": Americans' tendency (documented by a 1986 Gallup poll) to devalue knowledge not related to "job skills" and thus to neglect "education in what those skills are to be used for," their tendency to "confuse the arts with entertainment which can be enjoyed without understanding," a tendency by some "to think of the arts as potentially threatening or even blasphemous" (surely an ironic judgment, given the NEA's—and the NEH's—official approval of 1989 legislation, in the aftermath of the failed Helms Amendment, forbidding federal funding, through grants or subgrants, of artistic projects deemed obscene by yet another self-righteous commission, a responsibility subsequently relegated, by 1990 legislation, to the courts), and, of course, disagreement, even among those committed to it, "on what arts education should be."⁵ The report argues variously that overcoming the last impediment is the key to overcoming the rest. Thus much of it concerns taking inventory of specific problems that contribute to that impediment and recommending solutions to them.

What are the problems? High school graduation requirements in the arts (established in only a fourth of the states) are generally vague and evadable, and colleges and universities frequently do not accept them for credit. Elementary-level teachers have little training in the arts, and they lack adequate instructional materials. In high school, especially, attention focuses mostly on talented students. Certain of the arts, such as dance, are virtually ignored at all levels. NAEP data from the 1970s indicate declines, perhaps continuing, in student knowledge of the visual arts and music that the report implicitly attributes to "confusion about learning goals," a situation that it correlates with the fact that "nowhere in the country is there any systematic, comprehensive, and formal assessment of student achievement in the arts." State certification programs ignore some of the arts and are spotty in their concern about others. And so on—the whole inventory capped, I would say, by one item: "a severe lack of research about how young people learn about the arts and what they can be expected to learn at what ages."[6]

The recommended "solutions"? Predictably, many of them are referred for action to state and school district bureaucracies and to schools of education, apparently with scant interest in the financial costs implied. Predicated on the aforementioned purposes of arts education and addressing directly, if idealistically, the above problems, they are numerous but may be synopsized as follows: design and implement policies on a sequential arts curriculum for all K-12 students; agree on specific arts knowledge and skills minima to be learned; make requirements substantial and inescapable; hire experts to develop and evaluate the curriculum and to engage the help of artists and institutions beyond the school; provide budgets for appropriate instructional materials; test students to measure learning outcomes against objectives; enhance the NAEP so that it can assess nationally all the principal arts; establish more rigorous certification requirements for all arts teachers; recruit such teachers (including minorities) more vigorously and provide them with opportunities for professional development, adequate salaries, facilities and materials, and administrative support; enlarge and improve research on all aspects of arts education, encourage long-term studies of arts learning, and make findings generously available to teachers; and have the NEA facilitate the implementation of its recommendations in a variety of ways (by helping redesign the NAEP, providing some funding for state-level assessment and for translating research findings into classroom practice, conducting further studies of its own, serving as an exemplar of the collaborative effort it advocates, and so on).[7]

For many reasons I applaud the NEA report. It discusses with general accuracy public attitudes toward the arts and how they contribute to the neglect of arts education. Its spirit and intent are largely democratic. It emphasizes the interdisciplinarity of much artistic enterprise and encourages, to some extent, multiculturalism in arts education. It is concerned that Americans not lose a sense of the enduringly beautiful in the contemporary welter of tawdriness and that profoundly "media-ized" students not be media illiterate. It reminds us of the seriousness of the arts and calls for a tremendous commitment to the future of arts education.

And yet delusions abound in the report, and it ignores, side-steps, or appears unaware of some crucial issues. First of all, its dominant advocacy, in spite of its touting "creativity," is of the preservative function of arts education; it avoids dealing with the implications of the powerfully de-automatizing, apeironic, transformative dynamic of the arts—probably not surprising in a document engendered under the aegis of conservatism. Also, it tends to conceive of the arts more as closed, static knowledges to be acquired than as open(ing) experiences to be pursued changefully. (Thus one imagines the authors of the report made quite uneasy by the controversial 1991 exhibition "The West as America" mounted by the Smithsonian Institution at its National Museum of American Art, an exhibition that radically questioned traditional, heroically idealized interpretations of westward expansion in the nineteenth and early twentieth centuries and encouraged reconception of the standard ideologically constructed images of Western "development.") It fails to articulate a role for in-the-field educators themselves as researchers, apparently in the conventional and wholly questionable belief that educational research ought to be conducted by somebody else. Nor does it deal with the well-recognized need for such research and the practice it would urge to be guided not by long-useless (or worse) behaviorist theories of learning, which concern mostly the repetitive and nervous-making business of performance, but by those informed by the theoretical insights of, among other productive fields of inquiry, cognitive psychology, general cognitive science, semiotics, and—especially in this case— all manner of interdisciplinary studies of the processes of creativity. Heedless of the fiscal implications of its recommendations, the report, in its press for an official curricular consensus and uniformity, standardized evaluation, and (inevitably) bureaucratic quantification, runs counter to the complexly interiorized, qualifying, imaginative, and individualized spirit of artistic enterprise. Certainly it does not engage the problems attendant upon the diffuse curriculosclerosis in arts education (in music at the postsecondary level, for instance) promoted by the hypertrophy of a preservative mentality that cleaves to Mozart but sneers at zydeco or monumentalizes Michelangelo but disdains R. C. Gorman. And it never even touches on the continuing controversy as to whether or not (or to what extent) formal education at any level, however rationalized, actually can help develop artists.

Probably in large part the polemics about arts education lack the breadth and stridency of those about humanities (or natural or even social sciences) education because the arts, as *Toward Civilization* argues, "are not viewed as serious." That situation can and should be changed. Certainly the arts curriculum and its pedagogy have long suffered neglect, much more than those in the other areas with which I have been concerned. That situation too can and should be changed. In both cases *Toward Civilization*, through responses (though far from dramatic or much publicized) to its recommendations, may prove useful. But in some ways, as I have tried to show, it will not. What is needed now is not so much a new arts curriculum as, prior to and then evolutionarily along with that (doubtless in a form the report only accidentally adumbrates), a new way of thinking about the arts (or any other) curriculum. Not so much the pretense of a monological consensus on the curriculum as an authentic engagement in debate about it. Not so much a preservative movement "toward civilization" (of the past) as a transformative movement toward an apeironic paideia (of the future).

PART 3

From Cultural (Il)literacy to Re(-)mediation

*The difference between one and more than one is all the difference in the world.
Indeed, that difference is the world.*

Ursula K. Le Guin, *"The New Atlantis"*

Concerned about the level of adult illiteracy in the United States, a real estate developer named John Corcoran goes public for the Associated Press in mid-1988, confessing that (by strategies no less agonizing than oddly brilliant) he graduated from high school and college, taught in a public school system, and became wealthy—without ever learning how to read. Following the release of *Toward Civilization,* the report's most portentous data and conclusions are published in newspapers and broadcast nationally with an air of pique, shame, and despair about the state of cultural literacy in America. A Gallup poll taken on Columbus Day in 1989 indicates, among other such findings, that one-fourth of college seniors in the United States do not know when Columbus "sailed the ocean blue," that 42 percent cannot place the Civil War in the second half of the nineteenth century, that 55 percent cannot identify the Magna Carta. Immediately in the wake of that poll, Cheney's *50 Hours: A Core Curriculum for College Students* is released, and in bookstores appears, just in time for the holiday market, Hirsch's *A First Dictionary of Cultural Literacy: What Our Children Need to Know*—to be followed, in the next few years, by (note the pronoun change) *What Your 1st Grader Needs to Know,* then *What Your 2nd Grader Needs to Know,* and so on.

Of the kinds of "stories" above, surely those like the first, of such a fundamental inability going unnoticed and unaddressed, should be the most alarming, and yet the kinds represented by the rest, not unrelated to the first, have been more important to the American public in recent years. Americans are obsessed with what they "know"—or don't "know"—in common, especially about their "heritage." Hardly new, certainly expectable, and having counterparts in other cultures, that obsession recently has been intensified and shaped for the popular mind more by E. D. Hirsch, Jr., than by any other person (including multitudinous clones with or without his blessing), largely because he has codified and particularized its object, "cultural literacy," simplistically and in a finite and (that solidest of American attributes) practical inventory. But that obsession, especially as nurtured by Hirsch and company, raises questions far more profound, complex, and far-reaching than any of the answers supplied by a seemingly forthright rationale for cultural literacy and the lists of what one needs to "know" in order to be a culturally literate American. What beyond or besides the items on some standardized list should an American know? Standardized by whom? Why? *Know* in what sense? What are the implications of such an obsessive list for an educational system and a society becoming willy-nilly more multicultural? Wouldn't its institutionalization guarantee a quick-fix curriculum? (Remember that the word means "race course" as well as just "course" in Latin.) Wouldn't its pedagogy be based predictably on rote memorization and testing by the list? To what extent would teaching or socialization involve nothing more than, to borrow (while hearkening to the darker overtones of) Walter Lippmann's phrase for a key requirement of democracy, the "manufacture of consent"? To what extent would the possibilities of global acculturation be sacrificed to the projects of nationalistic propaganda?

Such questions readily entail others with broader and deeper implications. To what extent in an increasingly diverse world can anybody—American or whatever—know the same things (in the same way?) as anybody else? To what extent do we really *need* to? Given the vastness of information more or less available from which one might select to construct knowledge (or make knowledge claims) and an astounding ability to generate more, shouldn't common—and increasingly richer—strategies for dealing with (critiquing, supplementing, transforming, applying, synthesizing, and so on) particular knowledges be given a much higher priority in education? That is, shouldn't education involve pre-eminently the elaboration (both vertically and horizontally, as it were) of metaknowledges? If one still may speak of it, won't wisdom increasingly inhere in, to borrow from Gilbert Ryle, not just any particular knowing (declaratively) *about* but also—and more importantly—a general, flexible, and expansive knowing (procedurally) *how?*

The point of such questions is not simply to express antipathy toward an obsession (in which I doubtless unwittingly share more than I would wish) and its prominent exploiter but to suggest its limitations and delusions, especially as exploited by Hirsch. His project is not wholly wrong, and he has helped foreground key issues about cultural literacy and stimulate much useful debate about them; but he also has encouraged reductive curricular thinking, flash-card pedagogy, and a self-righteous obliviousness about many of the profound and difficult problems of multicultural education—so much so that the cultural literacy he proposes must be construed, by yet another inversion, as a far more problematic kind of cultural *il*literacy than the kind he combats. This last argument requires development, first by a closer look at his *Cultural Literacy: What Every American Needs to Know* in terms of the concerns that motivated it, then by a survey of its reception by educators, and then by a consideration of alternatives to his project. That line of development will occasion discussions in subsequent chapters of controversies about evaluation, assessment, accountability, and remediation, leading to some thoughts on alternative curricula and pedagogies.

CHAPTER 7

Cultural (Il)literacy

Though one could go back further, my Hirschian history and *Rezeptionsgeschichte* begins in 1983. In that year Hirsch published two widely read essays that adumbrated embryonically the shape of things to come, "Cultural Literacy" and "Reading, Writing, and Cultural Literacy." Since they say much the same thing, let me treat the latter, shorter one first, by my own lights, and then turn to a consideration of John Warnock's 1985 treatment of the former.

Hirsch opens "Reading, Writing, and Cultural Literacy" by arguing that the assumption that reading and writing are skills that "can be applied to *any* content" has created a situation in which "our [pedagogical] theorists pay little attention to *particular* contents in the classroom"—with the result that "we have necessarily fallen short also in imparting the formal skills of reading and writing." Then, before going further, he sings a sort of palinode to ease the reader familiar with his earlier work: he has changed his mind about the thrust of his 1977 book *The Philosophy of Composition,* where his "emphasis was strongly on the teaching of skills in writing—and, by extension, in reading"—and on the need for research in composition "into the most efficient ways of teaching its various subskills." Why the (cognitive-to-cultural) change? Because, to make his brief account briefer, his own subsequent research, which began with the assumption "that reading and writing are transferable skills" and sought "to base the stylistic evaluation of writing on its actual reader effects," contradicted that assumption by finding "that it was not possible to separate reading skills from the particular cultural information our readers happened to possess." Thus he now sees the error of his formalist ways and, all too clearly, of the formalist pedagogy that, however attractive for its seeming political neutrality, has long promoted the teaching of "forms and principles" with the mistaken hope that "the contents will take care of themselves."[1] Then what does he propose? Taking charge of "the contents"—as if their separability from skills, forms, and principles, which he himself has problematized, were a suspended (however perennially and naïvely recurrent) issue.

Drawing on the reading research of Richard C. Anderson and others, Hirsch contends that what has come to be called the current-traditional linguistically or rhetorically oriented teaching of writing, with its (from his point of view) neglect of vocabulary, is "inherently incomplete." Assuming that there is "knowledge about the world contained in knowledge of words" and that such knowledge is "an essential aspect" of "underlying cultural information," he argues that "we cannot do a good job of teaching reading and writing if we neglect, by concentrating on technique, the *particular* cultural vocabularies we want to teach." Assuming further that "we" agree with his notion of particularity, he asks, "Is there a central canon of cultural information that is analogous to the central canon of literature?" Indeed there is, he supposes, and he terms "its possession 'cultural literacy.' " Furthermore— and not surprisingly—without it "you cannot have linguistic literacy." And "we" cannot afford to be "vague" about this shared knowledge, so must "take explicit, political account of the concept of cultural literacy and make it an explicit goal of our teaching. This is a politically difficult move, of course—dangerous because it smacks of a ministry of culture." Indeed! It smacks of cultural democratization as an imposition of *our* culture, however much always dispersed, disputatious, and decentered, on *them*. Nonetheless, he calls on the MLA and all manner of other agencies to join him in his politically "dangerous" project of fighting an illiteracy that involves a "deficiency," by his medical metaphor, not just of skills but of information as well. Moreover, he argues, enlarging his arena, that, since "our strictly functional and aesthetic conception of literature is hardly more than a century old and can easily be swept aside in favor of a more serviceable concept bound up with general culture," teachers of literature should join with teachers of writing not only in the mutual teaching of literature and composition but in the mutual exemplification of cultural literacy.[2]

In his study of "Cultural Literacy" (a study that takes account of other Hirschian documents that precede *Cultural Literacy,* including personal communication), Warnock expresses concern about the implications of that essay, especially since by 1985 Hirsch, with support from NEH and Exxon and encouragement from numerous quarters, was well along in building a list to concretize what he thought Americans should know in order to be culturally literate. Apparently despairing of the possibility that such a list might be compiled by professional consensus, he was doing it more or less on his own, at the same time developing some sort of correspondent cultural-literacy test. The thrust of the project, like that of the essay itself, Warnock implies, seemed guided more by a political attitude than by carefully articulated theory and thoroughgoing research. However much he was waffling, in any forum, on the politics of cultural-literacy education, Hirsch fervently advocated national control of such education. And his hell-bent momentum, as Warnock observes, entailed a significant silence beyond such easily discerned problems, since his project already seemed insufficiently sensitive to "the representation of people and groups not hegemonic in education today" or unaware of "the difference between hegemony and cultural validity."[3]

For Warnock, as for me, that silence has to do with pedagogy, though it is finally a matter of paideia in the broadest sense. He sympathizes with Hirsch's concern about the traditionlessness occasioned, in part at least, by a habit of living only "in our new improved, modern world of today," but he discerns a troubling absence of specificity in Hirsch's proposal as to how cultural literacy is to be taught—that is, how it is to be learned. Though Hirsch's notions of "extensive" and "intensive" learning seem conventional or "traditional" enough, Warnock is "not sure what kind of pedagogical scene is imagined here," largely because "Hirsch is all but silent on a crucial point: the nature of the learner and the relation of the learner to the thing learned." For Warnock the key question concerns how students are to be motivated to learn (beyond, say, by fear of a cultural-literacy test that many teachers doubtless would allow bluntly to determine their pedagogy). He highlights the insufficiency of Hirsch's Horatian simplism in regard to the question—that teachers somehow should make such learning fun—by contrasting it to C. A. Bowers's extended exploration of the learner-learned relation in his 1974 book *Cultural Literacy for Freedom: An Existential Perspective on Teaching, Curriculum and School Policy.* Warnock argues that, while "Hirsch replaces one formalism with another," Bowers in that work grappled with a problem that "was not educational formalism and the need for a canon so much as it was the mismatch between the cultural assumptions fostered in the school and the culture the student would actually encounter, added to the lack of support in education for both students and teachers in their existential encounter with learning." The focal terms of Bowers's work— "words like *active, actual, critical, dialectical, rhetorical, writerly*"—suggest strongly to Warnock what Hirsch (still, I would say) has left out of his scheme: an account of "the relation between knower and known . . . in which the self is at risk—in relation to itself, in relation to others, and in relation to the Other." [4]

Warnock advises that "educators for literacy" accept Hirsch's critique of educational formalism and, perhaps partly because he is a professor of law and therefore aware of the value of consensual criteria, sees no reason "to reject out of hand" a cultural-literacy list recommended by a respected national group of such educators. [5] But, as a professor of English as well, he immediately singles out one of Bowers's words in order more specifically to thematize his concern about Hirsch's silence. His springboard is a passage from Roland Barthes's *S/Z* that contrasts "the writerly" (*le scriptible*) and "the readerly" (*le lisible*):

> Why is the writerly our value? Because the goal of literary work (of literature as work) is to make the reader no longer a consumer, but a producer of the text. Our literature is characterized by the pitiless divorce which the literary institution maintains between the producer of the text and its user, between its owner and its customer, between its author and its reader. This reader is thereby plunged into a kind of idleness—he is intransitive; he is, in short, *serious:* instead of functioning himself, instead of gaining access to the magic of the signifier, to the pleasure of writing, he is left with no more than the poor freedom either to accept or reject the text: reading is nothing more than a *referendum.* Opposite the writerly text, then, is its countervalue, its negative, reactive value: what can be read, but not written: the *readerly.* [6]

Apparently uneasy about the possibility that Hirsch's silence implicitly recommends (or surely does not discourage) a readerly rather than a writerly (read, in my terms, teacherly rather than "instructorly") approach to cultural-literacy education, Warnock adduces findings from the research of James Britton and his colleagues in support of his argument that "unless we incorporate the writerly into our conception of our destination in education for literacy, we will fail to reach our destination even in the way that destination is imagined by Hirsch." Such research indicates that an actively engaged, writerly relationship between the learner and the learned is far more productive than a passive, readerly one of the kind that Warnock sees in the 1960s (a time that Hirsch, like Bloom, judges educationally pernicious) as having been exposed in a general reaction against the Nietzschean *ressentiment* engendered by the long dominance of inactive, alienated learning. "If *ressentiment* is the symptom" against which the 1960s, an age that for Hirsch anomalously neglected the extensive (can we call it the readerly?) curriculum (in favor of the more intensive or writerly?), reacted, then, Warnock asks, "what is the disease?" Admitting that the question "cannot be quickly or easily answered," he nonetheless responds askance by troping Hirsch's own medical metaphor, with a vengeance: "Let's just say here that the disease is obviously not just Hirschean cultural illiteracy. And let us recognize that certain kinds of efforts to address the symptom of cultural illiteracy—cultural imperialism, for example—might well eliminate the symptoms, for a while, anyway, as they exacerbate the disease."[7]

Such issues are shot through with "politics." Hirsch may have cunningly abjured any politicization of the classroom, and Warnock may reject the idea that writerly learning "is directly tied to action in the world"; but one cannot escape the fact that education, as a profession and a practice, is political. In the case of a national cultural literacy, crucial questions inevitably arise: "What is the nation we are talking about here? Whose is it? For whom is it?" Warnock warns educators not only to avoid cultural formalism but also to suspect any proposition to the effect "that writerly relations are for some and not for others," to follow Jerome Bruner's advice to "act as if children can learn anything" (provided that "we don't assume that the child begins where we do"), and to be ever mindful that educational institutions and their affiliated organizations "have a notorious tendency to be self-reproducing, at the expense of everything but themselves." And he couples such warnings to sobering reflections:

If developing writerly relations with what is being learned turns out to be subversive of cultural institutions, including institutions of higher learning and the cultural literacy, that is as may be. Perhaps I should fear this eventuality, but I do not, not nearly as much as I fear a world where our institutions are allowed to stand beyond the writerly relation with the people they deal with. Writerly relations are protection against the indoctrination we rightly fear and against the inanity of skills teaching. The price paid is that action must be sanctioned and anything given must be seen as subject to revision.

A canon will not ipso facto prevent writerly relations. Nor will it, ipso facto, promote them. . . . Unless the business of selecting and maintaining the canon is political in the sense that it is from the beginning aimed toward writerly relations in the community it supposedly supports, it will ipso facto militate against writerliness.[8]

Thus, in this last sentence, does Warnock make more explicit and foreboding his unease about Hirsch's silence on a critical pedagogical question. And thus does he make a case for his own version of cultural-literacy education that emphasizes the apeironic, somewhat Freirean wild side of learning.

Though in retrospect Warnock's assurance that we should not "raise false fears" about Hirsch's "recommendations" or about his list becoming the basis of a universally taught "iron-clad curriculum" seems a little too sanguine in view of events since 1985,[9] his warnings and reflections above have proven prophetic in at least two ways. First, Hirsch's project has enlarged, but with a continuing silence on—or apparent indifference to—pedagogy (beyond lambasting, somewhat in Richard Mitchell's spirit, formalism in several avatars—the *Cardinal Principles,* the educational philosophies of Rousseau and Dewey, the romantic version of the 1960s—and vaguely advocating a complementarity of intensive and extensive curricula). Second, many educators (though *far* from all), especially those who try to foster writerly learner-learned relations (or their analogues), have since become concerned not only about how such relations were not defined as a goal at the start of current cultural-literacy efforts prompted in part by Hirschian urgings but also about how they continue to be forgotten, misunderstood, even avoided. *Cultural Literacy,* published in 1987, dramatically evidences the enlargement and ongoing pedagogical and political issues of Hirsch's project; the history of its reception stories the concern of educators who, to say the least, see it "as subject to revision."

Hirsch certainly has agitated a multitude of educators and parents with that best-selling book, which carries the subtitle *What Every American Needs to Know* and contains an appendix, co-compiled with Joseph Kett and James Trefil, entitled "What Literate Americans Know: A Preliminary List." Hirsch makes much of the apologetics concerning "preliminaries," but he seems unaware of how much he contradicts himself about the prescriptiveness of his list. For instance, he argues that his notion of "cultural literacy is represented not by a *prescriptive* list of books but rather by a *descriptive* list of the information actually possessed by literate Americans," but the book's subtitle suggests a drive to arm Americans with what they *have* to know. (Also, he may be somewhat aware of the possible "misuse" of such a list, but he fails to foresee the extent to which the American—nay, human—appetite for ready-made solutions to complex problems might compel its being baldly taught.)[10] That suggestion is writ even larger in Hirsch's establishment, later in 1987, of the Cultural Literacy Foundation, whose function is to design standardized tests, allegedly to be used without regard to any specific pedagogy, of students' knowledge of the kinds of items included on the list (or some evolving version of it), a function that Hirsch then described as "a little simple, a bit anti-intellectual, but in the best pragmatic American tradition."[11] And that suggestion indubitably underwrites the rationale for his 1988 book, coauthored by Kett and Trefil, *The Dictionary of Cultural Literacy,* which offers definitions of list items, and, of course, for his *First Dictionary of Cultural Literacy,* which I mentioned earlier—both of which, as dictionaries of a kind, hardly present themselves as (and are not taken, by many people, as) merely "preliminary" and "descriptive." Small wonder that the cause of this professor of English was championed by Bennett, who was as intent on simplistically controlling education as his yuppie peers were on similarly controlling diets, exercise, lovemaking, the stock market, even outer space. Unsurprisingly, a heavy load of contradictory consequence arises from enacting such a fetish for control. (As the French etymology of the word hints, its most fundamental procedure is the act of checking or testing "against" [*contre-*] a "list" [*rolle*], a primitive and linear cybernetics.)

Now surely, to recall Warnock's more forgiving moments, no one could object, in principle, to Hirsch's desire to guarantee that Americans, especially those belonging to what James Wolcott has termed "the Blank Generation,"[12] share enough knowledge (or is it just "information"?) to read with some level of understanding the sorts of texts that are commonly encountered. But by playing Trivial Pursuit with Hirsch's list in *Cultural Literacy,* one discovers peculiar biases of omission and inclusion. For example, "AIDS" does not appear, while "Graham, Billy" does; "blues, the" does not, while "Fresno, California" does.[13] I could easily go on in this vein. The list is, of course, "a little simple" and, no matter how much revised, would show numerous biases, no matter who compiled it, but such examples are pertinently revelatory. Still, in spite of such disadvantages, Hirsch cites respectable, if somewhat narrowly positivistic, research on reading to rationalize his mandate. Doubtless he should be applauded for drawing attention to the chicken-egg problem involved in students' knowing the "meaning" of the words they read in order to develop the reading "skills" that preoccupied him earlier in his career, though others have done that before, albeit on more modest scales. But his formulation of cultural literacy is naïve, ignorantly conservative, and authoritarian, especially when compared to that of Mike Rose, say, or of Richard Lanham, both of whom engage the topic with more theoretical sophistication, multicultural sensitivity, and—by a long shot—pedagogical awareness.

While Hirsch's agenda has been variously praised, supported, and enacted in the classroom by countless teachers and administrators, mostly at the elementary and middle levels, many others, mostly at the postsecondary level, continue to criticize it, along with his book, for its arrogance, failure to acknowledge diversity, counterproductive oversimplifications, threat to academic freedom, pedagogical naïveté, and so on.[14] But it has met with strong criticism from other levels as well. For instance, in 1987 at the English Coalition Conference, which consisted of representatives from all educational levels and all the major organizations of the English profession, these problems were much discussed. Though some disagree about the exact character of the unanimity of response to them, few dispute its general negativity, which Wayne Booth, in his foreword to the extended report on the conference, emphasizes in recounting the opening session. He relates that "An official of the Department of Education . . . charged us to join in a grand national repudiation of the 'skills movement'" and "either to embrace Hirsch's list of nearly 5,000 'cultural literacy' terms, or to come up with a list of our own." Booth finds the reaction extraordinary:

> I've never seen an audience more effectively united by one hour-long speech. We all knew that whatever else we might want to say to each other, we must repudiate that spokesman's narrow, misinformed, programmatic vision of ourselves, our history, and our charges. To be asked to impart bits of isolated information, to be asked even to think about that kind of goal in isolation from all the difficulties and complexities every teacher faces, simply trivialized the work we all do and love. Whether we were thinking of graduate students or of first graders, whether we had light teaching loads or heavy, whether we taught honors sections or remedial sections, whether our training was in linguistics, language arts, media studies, or critical theory, we knew that the last thing American education needs is one more collection of inert information, a nostrum to be poured raw into minds not actively engaged in reading, thinking, writing, and talking. Not only did we believe that abstracted lists of terms would not motivate our students to become spontaneous learners; we were sure that they would increase the tendency of too many of our schools to kill whatever spontaneity the children bring when they enter school. [15]

Hirsch himself got "a chilly reception" when he spoke at the conference, [16] and the problems of his approach became the conferees' touchstones for formulating statements of principles—"a list of our own," so to speak—quite different from his. Those statements, to which I will return, carefully address such issues as the cultural heterogeneity of American students, their need to experience a variety of "content" (traditional and otherwise), the importance of their developing subtle and powerful strategies for understanding the technologized blizzard of competing messages in which they live. [17]

To give Hirsch his due, one has to admit that *Cultural Literacy,* while advocating his "Ciceronian ideal of universal public discourse" made possible largely by a "consciously conveyed extensive curriculum," does allude to those kinds of issues and even takes account of them—though somewhat vaguely and halfheartedly. "What is required," the text proclaims at one point, "is education for change, not for static job competencies." It urges that "we should resist the extreme views of pragmatists [Deweyans who have turned history into social studies and overstressed the child's self-concept and education as practical socialization] and traditionalists alike." Since, according to Hirsch, "The anti-traditional goals of the progressive movement have turned out to depend on traditional information," there is opened, through that paradoxical result, "the possibility of a compromise—a curriculum that is traditional in content but diverse in its emphases, that is pluralistic in its materials and modes of teaching but nonetheless provides our children with a common core of cultural information." Thus he provides for an "intensive curriculum, . . . equally essential," presumably complementing the extensive one, which "ensures that individual students, teachers, and schools can work intensively with materials that are appropriate for their diverse temperaments and aims." But he does not elaborate on that curriculum and its pedagogy, and he fails to engage deep contradictions in this curricular marriage between wholly traditional "content" and "education for change," between inculcating "a common core of cultural information" and accommodating "diverse . . . aims." Instead, he performs again the swerve rightly so distressing to Warnock: "Schools can find means."[18]

No surprise then, in spite of Hirsch's conciliatory gestures, that *Cultural Literacy* too has had "a chilly reception." And no surprise that one of the earliest professional-journal reviews of it is by Warnock, whose response to its proposals "is like that of the maid to the passionate shepherd." He criticizes Hirsch for not recognizing that the schools' stress on skills and neglect of common content "are better seen as symptoms, not causes," though he acknowledges the imbalance involved, attributing it in part to the desire of school administrators and the public "to dodge" the political controversiality of content issues (and he accuses Hirsch of making "a similar move when he declares that his interest is in 'competence' and not in 'cultural politics' "). He is concerned that Hirsch "does not reveal the criteria" for deciding who would serve as consultants in compiling his list, which Warnock fears "will come to be used as yet another way of blaming the victim," and he repeats his argument that Hirsch has omitted any consideration of the writerly, here codified as "critical and constructive abilities."[19]

Many other reviews and critiques fault Hirsch's book for its default advocacy of cultural-literacy education as, more in my terms, the (perhaps necessary but certainly not sufficient) teaching of tokens rather than instructing that enables writerly strategies of learning. Besides exposing wholesale omissions from the list and pointing out the mechanical simplicity of Hirsch's notion of an information-sharing community (which would be better modeled, by analogy with "Wittgenstein's idea of family resemblances," as a variegated pattern of overlapping sets than as one all-inclusive set) and other problems (like "the degree to which the book supports the ideology of the dominant class"), Robert D. Denham, like Warnock earlier, worries the problem of motivating students to learn (memorize) "bits of information" apart from any engagingly meaningful context. If educators resist the "innocent optimism" of Hirsch's proposals, he argues, that will be because they know that becoming culturally literate is more complex than learning a list and that "the constructivist view of education, as advocated by, say, Bruner, provides a more accurate account of how learning takes place and a more inviting picture of what the classroom can become."[20] Writing "from a Holmes Group perspective," Robert J. Yinger criticizes Hirsch for not emphasizing that "cultural literacy does not constitute cultural competency," which entails "engaging, representing, orchestrating, and acting upon knowledge."[21] Patricia Bizzell astutely observes that "Hirsch's candidate for privileged ideology of literacy is not as context-free as he claims: it is an academic ideology of literacy." More specifically, she argues,

> the academic canon is now performing for Hirsch exactly the same function that Standard English did in *The Philosophy of Composition*: he imagines that it has been granted by history the power to transcend and hence to control local cultural canons. Hirsch detaches the academic canon from its own social origins, which are systematically suppressed—for example, in his forgetting to mention that the turn-of-the-century lists he admires were first promulgated by Harvard, a highly race-, sex-, and class-determined institution.

The most salient consequence of this control ethos, for Bizzell, is that it implies a "prescriptive" pedagogy rather than a "collaborative . . . one that successfully integrates the professor's traditional canonical knowledge and the students' non-canonical resources," a pedagogy that makes education "something done to one person by another" rather than a "truly reciprocal" experience.[22] According to Scholes, in *Cultural Literacy* "culture has been commodified . . . and packaged for handy consumption," a solution that "is both absurd in itself and eerily disconnected from the material Hirsch presents to support it"; that depends, through its notion of schemata, on a confusion of "syntax and semantics" analogous to the one involved in "assuming that we hold in memory individual patterns for all the sentences we encounter in speech and writing, rather than that we hold in mind a grammar of our language"; and that, especially as instantiated in Hirsch's list, "is voodoo education, offering a quick, cheap fix for massive educational problems, while ignoring the intractable realities that underlie those problems."[23] Patrick Scott questions in more detail Hirsch's translations of others' research and notes, among other oddities, his "apparent narrowing of the psycholinguistic concept of the schema, when he identifies it for purposes of curricular discussion with 'cultural information' rather than . . . with 'scripts' or structural/generic expectations." And Scott avers that "for many teachers full literacy is seen as a (primarily psychological) liberation from the shared culture that alone, Hirsch claims, makes reading in his sense possible."[24]

The reception of the book has not been, however, unrelievedly chilly. Scott, for instance, grants that "Hirsch has successfully communicated to a wide public, as an empirical finding, the idea that reading, even for limited practical purposes, requires cultural education," and he is somewhat distressed that the English profession has reacted to Hirsch's book with such strong negativity, finding the response "not only intellectually shortsighted . . . but also politically inept."[25] Certainly there has been a mix of negative reactions, themselves sometimes mixed, about, say, the extent of the cultural chauvinism in Hirsch's notion of linguistic and cultural standardization, but there has been also a general readiness among thoughtful educators to point out the pedagogical problems and implications of the book and its proposal. (Thus, for instance, Donald Lazere, "a leftist . . . more sympathetic to the criticisms of Hirsch by American cultural pluralists," shows himself "also sympathetic to Hirsch's arguments on national language and national culture" but finds him to "err in believing the critical thinking movement at present is opposed to cultural literacy" when, to the contrary, it works toward "incorporating cultural literacy into *critical* literacy.")[26] That readiness evinces itself nowhere more forcefully than in *Profession 88*, the 1988 annual of the MLA, that year focused principally on the topic of cultural literacy.

Of the articles collected in *Profession 88*, that by Jeff Smith is the least negative, indeed the most positive. His attempt to treat

Hirsch and his opponents evenhandedly lends his text a tone of moderate reasonableness, but it also imputes to Hirsch a pedagogical rationale only dubiously implicit in his proposal and gives insufficient credit to or misconstrues the position and practice of anti-Hirschians. Thus Smith asserts unqualifiedly that Hirsch "does subscribe to a progressive political agenda," that all he proposes is that "training students in dominant cultural ideologies" be made "systematic and rational in ways that might ultimately create space for resistance to those ideologies," and that "he wants to conserve information *about* the culture so that people can more adeptly negotiate their way through it, or even past it"—his "ultimately" and "or even past" surely strained (and insincere?) optatives. Smith's problematic portrayal of the opposition can be represented fairly in a passage where he elaborates on one of the "honorable opposed views." Since that elaboration harbors predictable misconceptions about apeironic pedagogy that need addressing, I quote it at length:

> One is that pedagogy ought to foster the construction of a new discourse altogether, an oppositional discourse that is built out of our students' "natural" ways of being and talking and that would give voice to the legitimate but unvoiced demands of the world's oppressed, which many claim includes those students. In other words, it could be argued that the point is not to enter the existing discourse and change it from within but to overpower it from without.
>
> This view makes sense (assuming leftist political goals), but nobody is really trying it, including the anti-Hirschians. It . . . is a revolutionary road that is talked about but not taken. Instead, a third way is implicitly followed: what students come to us with is naively affirmed as if it somehow were a natural and spontaneous expression of their inner selves, or as if the subcultures that evolved those youthful or ethnic ways of being and talking are somehow "authentic" and truly human—unlike the national common culture that Hirsch argues for teaching.

Smith argues that the extreme form of this view "would give us a classroom where the language of the video parlor [our fin-de-siècle opium den] is privileged and the language of the Bible or Shakespeare isn't"—a vision of monstrosity to make even the least Bloomian wince. He admits that "I don't know that anyone currently does take it to that extreme," but he nonetheless finds the logic of his argument binding and warrants its seemingly inevitable consequence by professional experience of a kind: "colleagues of mine are loath to explain in any detail what they actually do in the classroom by way of not validating some artificial cultural style or other."[27]

Quite apart from the question of *why* Smith's colleagues "are loath to explain" how they avoid the Scylla he fears (as well as, I would hope, the Charybdis Hirsch proposes), I would guess that many of them could—though perhaps not to *his* satisfaction—if offered sufficient circumstances to do so. If by "colleagues" he means, as he seems to, those less Hirschian than he, their typical explanation might well begin with a rejection or qualification of the pseudo-Rousseauian attitude he ascribes to them; and it surely would attribute the unrealized extremity that he logically envisions to the extremity of the misconceptions from which it derives. Few of those colleagues would accept their students' "ways of being and talking" as simply "natural" (rather as largely cultural) though many would respect those ways and, as Rose suggests, try to figure them as cognitive styles in a pedagogy, to whatever extent apeironic, that would enable those students in *other* such ways. That respect necessarily would begin with a willingness to learn, in Margaret Mead's term, "prefiguratively" (from the young) or at least with the recognition, as Herrnstein Smith has it, that

> contemporary students . . . are not merely deficient versions of us but quite distinct creatures, who, in fact, know—for better or worse, and not always worse—some amazing things we don't know: in part through their coming of age in a society already decisively shaped by, among other things, civil rights, Vietnam, feminism, the environmental crisis, AIDS, television, and computers; in part through their informal education in demotic—or, as we say, "ethnic" and "street"—cultures quite alien to most of us; and in part also (as we often forget) through their formal education in fields such as biology, anthropology, and history that are themselves quite different from what they were the last time . . . *we* dropped in on them.[28]

Furthermore, few would be naïve enough to believe that "oppositional discourse" can somehow transcend "existing discourse" and "overpower it from without"; many would know, from Derrida or elsewhere, of the problematics of within/without distinctions and the impossibility of a totally exterior discourse. Most would espouse some version of "the social-constructionist position," as understood by Patricia Bizzell, that "we can become at least partially aware of what we have learned, question it, and change it, but . . . it is highly doubtful that we could ever achieve a methodological purchase on what we have learned such that we could study it from a 'distance' or from 'outside.' "[29] In other words, acknowledging that all sorts or reductive extremes are imaginable but not—in this case, as Smith himself admits—realized in practice, they would, quite rightly, deny that they follow his "third way," question his version of the "revolutionary road" their pedagogy may open, and (even the most skeptically apeironic among them) insist on the importance in their enterprise of a far more complex sense of balance than Smith allows them.

The other contributors to *Profession 88* move far beyond Smith's confused apologetics, attacking Hirsch's book persuasively, even fiercely, and suggesting apeironic alternatives to supplement or, mostly, supplant his project. I will consider some of those alternatives shortly; for now, let me sample the critiques.

Paul B. Armstrong argues that "Neither 'culture' nor 'literacy' . . . is as monistic or as codifiable as Hirsch assumes," and he shows how contradictions in Hirsch's book (concerning, for example, the political neutrality of cultural literacy) "expose errors in some of his central assumptions about language" (such as equating "linguistic competence with vocabulary") and thus "undermine his pedagogical proposals."[30] Besides criticizing the "odd, homemade linguistics" that underwrites the book, Andrew Sledd and James Sledd detect numerous misuses of sources and sloppy citations, and they demonstrate persuasively that Hirsch's "reasoning suffers from obvious contradictions and non sequiturs, that he constantly makes rash claims, unsupported assertions, and false promises, and that he conceals his failures in logic by bully-boy rhetoric and genteel sneers." The pedagogy of his proposal is not only flawed but dangerous as well, they contend, because "he offers the ideology of bureaucratized assent, disguised by the denial of ideology. His plan would limit and trivialize the education of the young and the reeducation of some of the middle-aged."[31] William K. Buckley berates the book, along with Bloom's, for its facile "sloganeering."[32] Helene Moglen takes Hirsch to task for supporting the too-prevalent view that "cultural diversity is a social disease for which cultural literacy is the appropriate cure" and for presenting a farcical proposal whose Gradgrindian pedagogical method, such as it is, "eliminates any reflective and interactive process" and whose system, if adopted, "would certainly ensure 'the trivialization of cultural information,' which

Hirsch himself acknowledges as a 'near certainty.' "[33] And James
A. Schultz offers a general critique of the list mentality exemplified by Hirsch, arguing that students should be taught "to reflect
on what they are told and on what they say" and that lists, like
tests, "teach them just the opposite: they teach them to do what
they're told."[34]

Critical responses to Hirsch have continued since the watershed
of *Profession 88,* at times to the extent of protesting too much—
that is, avoiding the problems he has exposed and the issues he has
forced or, more disturbing, swerving from the challenge of proposing cogent alternatives to his project. But many of his opponents have indeed proposed such alternatives, both in broad terms
and in specific, even programmatic, terms; for the most part,
through considerable variety, they accord in stressing (writerly)
instructing over (readerly) teaching and in calling for a more apeironic approach to cultural-literacy education.

Let me turn first to concerns and recommendations of the English Coalition Conference that have special relevance to the
Hirschian challenge. "Active learners, not passive receivers" was
an overarching, recurrent emphasis, according to Booth, who
defuses any accusation of mere warmed-over Deweyism:

> Such language obviously is not brand new in our educational history. But the
> echoes in that language of John Dewey and other "progressive" theorists
> should not lead any reader to see us, as some of our critics have suggested, as
> falling back into the tired formula, "Teach the child, not the subject." To do
> so would be to engage in precisely the kind of polar thinking that has plagued
> too much recent criticism of the schools. We do not choose between "the
> child" and this or that "subject." We choose subjects which, by their nature,
> if taught properly, will lead the child eagerly through increasingly indepen-
> dent steps toward full adult, self-sustained learning.[35]

Furthermore, as Richard Lloyd-Jones and Andrea A. Lunsford
observe, discussion directed by that emphasis worked purpose-
fully beyond negative reactions to Hirsch and other critics in order
to generate "a constructive response" to them, a Graffian one that
proceeded by "a thorough hearing of many conflicting views."
The emergent theme of "Democracy through Language" aptly
rubricates the conferees' efforts to confirm "the importance of
the humanities generally and the specific value of English studies
in the education of citizens who live in a democratic and increas-

ingly complex information society." Participants concluded that
broad literacy could best be achieved in "the interactive classroom" by "encouraging students to articulate their own points of
view, and encouraging them to respect different perspectives."
Such appreciation of diversity should involve, among other things,
helping students understand "how and why different ways of reading can find different meanings in the same text" and "expand the
capacity of students to imagine and value worlds other than their
own." Along with this differential curriculum should go a differential pedagogy that does not leave a blank role for educators (who
by default, as Warnock feared, tend to become "givers of knowledge") but suggests for them the role of interactive enablers who
foster active learning by "sensitive integration of what students
study formally with what they bring to the classroom from outside
it."[36]

Such pedagogy would be a great deal more effectively public
than any envisioned by Hirsch—or Cheney, for that matter. Accounting for student experiences both inside and outside the classroom, it would provide a multicultural "scene of dynamic transactions and interactions." In that scene students would not be
subjected to rote learning but would engage in the regular "practicing" of language in incrementally various modes and in self-
consciously reflecting on the power and limitations of each usage.
Participants conceived of "this second kind of learning as a theoretical activity" and concluded that it should be enacted at every
educational level toward the apeironic goal of enabling students to
"adapt what they know to a variety of situations." Anticipating
the possible reductionisms of prescription, participants offered
no reading lists, recommending rather that "students read widely
in both traditional literature and literature that reflects the diversity of American culture" and that they read in as many genres as
possible. They regarded "the skills/content debate as resting on
an overly simple, and ultimately false, dichotomy" irrelevant to
learning that "inevitably unites skills and content in a dynamic
process of practice and assimilation." Lloyd-Jones and Lunsford
thus construe conference participants as very favorably endorsing
Hazard Adams's anti-Bloomian idea of "knowledge as process,"
an idea that catalyzes learning as questioning and reformulation.[37]

Congruent with this endorsement, the three "strands" of the
conference—elementary, secondary, and college—offered dis-

tinctly un-Hirschian recommendations for promoting active learning. Those of the elementary strand arise from a sensitivity to the difficult emotional and economic backgrounds of many children, to the "mixed blessing" of media influences on them, to the knowledge and sense of peerage they bring to the classroom. Intelligent humility checks any impulse to mandate exactly what children should know when they leave the elementary level in the twenty-first century, but they should leave not only with new knowledge but also "with curiosity, a sense of wonder, and imagination" that will help them "maintain an enthusiasm for learning, both in school and in their homes and communities." (That enthusiasm, I would add, is precisely the *ganas* ["appetite"] for learning that thematizes *Stand and Deliver,* the 1988 film—based, as the saying goes, on a true story, that of Jaime Escalante—about a class of barrio high school students who are helped to learn calculus well enough to pass the Advanced Placement tests in it. That appetite, the motivation that Warnock found wanting in Hirsch's plan early on, is the sine qua non of any such apeironic adventure of breaking out of the given.) The recommendations, moving beyond the usual debates concerning phonics and whole-language learning, urge self-confident abilities and attitudes in the use of language that enable students to "use prior knowledge to comprehend new oral or written texts," to respond to such texts critically and aesthetically, to recognize and respond to manipulative language, to "become language theorists" aware of their own language activities, to appreciate and respect their own languages and cultures and those of others. The strand recommends that students should develop a balanced sense of both "common humanity" and social diversity. It makes a number of particularized suggestions about curriculum, pedagogy, teacher education, administration, assessment, and conditions of the scene of instructing (for encouraging, for example, different "ways to construct reality" and "risk-taking");[38] but it clearly wants educators to explore alternatives (orientations based on problem solving, brainstorming, whatever is locally pertinent) far beyond mere memorization.

The secondary strand also recognizes the importance of taking into account students' diversified cultural backgrounds, observing, for example, that many, increasingly, are non-native speakers, have immigrated from countries ravaged by war, use drugs, and live in poverty. The strand addresses nuts-and-bolts issues of coping with such a student population in a context informed by three key principles:

1. Learning is the process of actively constructing meaning from experiences, including encounters with a broad range of print and nonprint texts (films, videos, TV and radio advertisements, and so on).
2. Others—parents, teachers, and peers—help learners construct meanings by serving as supportive models, providing frames and materials for inquiry, helping create and modify hypotheses, and confirming the worth of the venture.
3. Learners at different ages and stages of development may well learn in different ways.

Opposed to "rote exercises" and the "passive ingestion of 'facts,' " the strand recommends, among other things, that secondary students should learn to "use language effectively to create knowledge, meaning, and community in their lives"; to "reflect on and evaluate their own language use"; and to "recognize and evaluate the ways in which others use language to affect them." The educator's role in such critically and imaginatively active and interactive learning should be that of "a coach" committed to the individualized enabling of students.[39]

The thrusts of the college strand follow consonantly from those of the previous strands. Since postsecondary students "often have dramatically different backgrounds, goals, and work experiences from those of previous college generations"—by virtue of being typically older, more diverse in language and culture, profoundly shaped by the media, and so on—they need an education itself "dramatically different." That education should encourage them to be "active learners" who can "reflect critically on their own learning," have "a high degree of practical and theoretical literacy," and understand how "meaning is negotiated and constructed." They should be engaged with the "*practices*" of language through a curriculum characterized by a canon broadened in terms of race, gender, class, and textual media. Traditional texts should be learned "in relation to theoretical concerns," with entry-level courses stressing "an *active, interactive theory of learning* (rather than a theory of teaching)." Theory-informed educators should enable students "to transfer what they learn." General-education courses in the humanities certainly should deal with specific texts and issues but also "should be organized around problems through which 'knowing about' becomes an occasion to raise questions about 'knowing how' and 'knowing why.' " Students in such courses should learn not merely to revere traditional texts but to "dramatize differences" and "explore cultural diversity" in an interdisciplinary setting. Helping students, especially English majors, become more self-reflective, confident, and creative readers and writers requires a shift in the pedagogical scene that changes "the classroom from a place in which knowledge is disseminated to one in which—as students examine and criticize the production of knowledge—learning occurs and knowledge is created" through a curriculum that is "issue-centered," "learning-centered," "student-centered"[40]—a shift from teaching students to absorb traditional "cultural information" to instructing them to make apeironic cultural *knowledge*.

Several of the contributors to *Profession 88* echo English Coalition emphases. Armstrong argues that "what students need is 'pluralistic literacy'—the ability to deal effectively with cultural differences and to negotiate the competing claims of multiple ways of reading"—to "equip them for the novelty and diversity ahead of them." He too calls for an apeironic shift, one mandated by a more complex theory of the operation of schemata than Hirsch offers: from "memorizing vocabulary" to "learning how to control and generate synthesizing patterns." This shift, in some ways parallel to that in foreign-language education from an emphasis on *langue* (grammar, vocabulary) to an emphasis on *parole* (communicational situations), requires students to confront difference, otherness, since "a language or a mode of understanding can seem 'natural' and self-evident unless it is juxtaposed against an opposing set of terms and conventions, which organizes the world according to different principles that seem equally obvious to its adherents. As Robert Scholes notes, 'the way to see one discourse is to see more than one' "—in whatever sense *discourse* is taken (as text, text-world, culture, knowledge, and so on). By virtue of this shift, a concept of cultural literacy less mechanical than Hirsch's emerges. And such literacy is no less assessable, once its "most important indicators," of which Armstrong defines three, are established: "(1) the ability to construe and create new sentences, (2) the capacity to extend prior knowledge to make sense of something unfamiliar, and (3) the power to translate a different use of language into one's own vocabulary and conventions (and to recognize the limits of translatability)."[41]

Hirsch has paid nonspecific lip service to this "ability to deal with novelty," of course, but he has stopped far short, perhaps warily, of facing its largest implications and proposing how students might achieve it. Armstrong grants him his due, perhaps more generously than I, but stresses the minimalism of what Hirsch proposes: "Altering and extending interpretive categories to adapt to new challenges cannot be accomplished without a large supply of schemata to experiment with, but . . . memorized content is only necessary and not sufficient." Quite apart from the issue of what "content" Hirsch wants students to memorize looms the issue of how students are to become "prepared for the unknown." Elaborating on the second of his indicators above, Armstrong stresses the importance of Peter Elbow's "metaphorical thinking" in that preparation:

> students need to develop an ability to invent new ways of fitting things together by recognizing and even creating new analogies, new patterns of similarity and difference. New combinations cannot be created without old materials, of course—a stock of existing categories to alter and extend. But mastery of content alone will not give students confidence in their capacity to generate good guesses about how best to configure unforeseen situations. An educational program that combines wide reading with interactive experimentation as the teacher and students try out responses to a variety of problems is the best way to develop an ability to discover analogies and to use what one knows to meet unexpected challenges.

The "unknown" here is not traditional unicultural information that the teacher knows and the students do not (yet or ever): it is a space they must investigate together. Whatever "stock of existing categories" they share should comprise not some Hirschian national heritage (or Bloomian universal Truth and so on) to be absorbed for its own sake (or for the sake of those in power) but, more productively, "old materials . . . to alter and extend." Without the power to alter and extend those materials, students cannot learn "how to ask questions about puzzling irregularities," a crucial aspect of Armstrong's third indicator, and, no matter what they share culturally, will not know "what to do when we find an absence of commonality." Thus, for him, "what is *not* shared is

the issue. . . . Negotiating different perspectives when one discovers that common ground is lacking is essential to using language effectively. It is also a requirement for participating in a
democracy."[42] Armstrong's concept of pluralistic literacy appears
to embrace (at least a penultimate version of) Jean-François Lyotard's "ultimate vision of science and knowledge today as," in
Fredric Jameson's phrasing, "a search, not for consensus, but
very precisely for 'instabilities,' as a practice of *paralogism.*"[43]

Sledd and Sledd offer recommendations for cultural-literacy
education similar to Armstrong's, but more strident. Their counterproposal to Hirsch's extensive curriculum is "not to impose,
but to escape the limitations of middle-class, middlebrow Middle
Americans" by having schools "*attack* endemic cross-cultural
illiteracy." That attack would involve, not only for white middle-
class students but for all United States citizens, "constant practice
in the reading of just those texts that are hard to read, and essential
to read, because they do presuppose knowledge and beliefs that
are alien to us." Such reading requires the development of an
apeironic skill because, "unless readers are content to limit their
reading narrowly, it is impossible to predict with any precision
what knowledge the next text they encounter will demand. No
lexicon of pseudodoxia will serve." Only practice in dealing with
instances of textual otherness can prepare one "to spot the causes
of acknowledged puzzlement and to search out ways of solving the
puzzle"—an argument Sledd and Sledd find patently adumbrated
in the work of John Dewey, whom Hirsch "unfairly scorns" in
Cultural Literacy. For them, what most obstructs this kind of
"significant educational reform in the US is the structure of the
very society within which Hirsch would do his bit to imprison
students—the society to whose mind-set he appeals."[44]

For Moglen, alternative cultural-literacy education began with
"two pivotal events" that unfolded during the late 1960s and early
1970s, that time Hirsch and Bloom (not to mention Bennett, the
NAS, and so on) regard as the origin of our present retrograde
curricular evils: "The admission into the university of a heterogeneous, often poorly prepared student population, which necessitated a new emphasis on literacy education, and the demands of
women and minority faculty members for all forms of institutional representation and expression." Moglen explains the impact
of those events:

Cultural (Il)literacy

These faculty members, who had either chosen or been relegated to the ghettos of writing programs and women's and ethnic studies departments, accepted the task of educating students who had been marginalized and disempowered: students who had little sense of social or intellectual entitlement and believed neither in the authority of their own judgments nor in the validity of their experience. The worlds that had been constructed for them by the educational systems by which they had been processed—the "facts" that they had been taught, the canonical traditions that had been introduced to them as theirs, even the language that they had been assumed to speak—had effectively silenced them while encouraging them to develop strategies of alienated survival.

As those strategies evolved, as more students became "self-conscious readers and writers of themselves and their societies," a very much un-Hirschian concept of cultural literacy took hold. Its imperative was not for a convergent, static sharing of unicultural information but for a divergent, dynamic engagement with and creation of multicultural knowledges. It encouraged students to learn "from decentered perspectives"—feminist, Marxist, poststructuralist, deconstructionist—"so that they could see how interpretive, methodological, and rhetorical practices are influenced by the politics of gender, race, nationality, and class." Such strategies empowered them—and, increasingly, continue to empower them—to make visible the invisible cultural forces that multidimensionally shape their lives; to question texts, teachers, cultural practices; and to work interactively, collaboratively, toward the "reconceptualization of hierarchical structures that had previously been perceived as necessarily inflexible and inevitably oppressive." "A significant alternative to the conservative agendas," this kind of cultural literacy appeals to "a remarkable coalition" that Moglen urges to be—and foresees as—"committed to enlightened self-consciousness and radical social change."[45]

As we can see from the above synopses, alternatives to Hirsch's agenda typically stress a liberatory enabling of students through the cultivation of reading (and writing) strategies variously called "strong," oppositional, self-conscious, writerly, and so on—without which Hirschian cultural literacy, as rote acquaintance with unicultural information, amounts to little more than another kind of imprisoning *il*literacy. Like many of those who have proposed such alternatives, I too find my own educational theory and practice increasingly concerned with the larger development and application of such strategies. Thus, while my students' initial reading of a text may well be Hirschian (denotative, receptive, univocal, unaware of "gaps," governed by positive logic, and so on), I try to help them move to a second level of reading "differently" (*autrement*), a rereading (connotative, conflictive, equivocal, critically aware of gaps, governed by either/or logic) that multifariously interrogates the text and allegorizes it (makes it, by etymology, "speak other[wise]"), and then to a third level of fully writerly reading ("stereoscopic," integrative, dialogical, creatively filling gaps, governed by both-and and fuzzy logic) through which they can achieve a double or janusian perspective on the interrelationships of the other two readings. This apeironic approach to cultural literacy, which pushes students "to alter and extend" the known and accepted, to supplement and even supplant it, works especially well with poetry, though it may be used with virtually any text.[46]

Let me offer an example of how this approach works, one from my own classroom practice with, in this case, first-year college students. Many such students are familiar with, perhaps even have studied to some extent, Robert Frost's poem "The Road Not Taken," widely read in the United States for decades, enough so that it has the status of a cultural icon with a taken-for-granted meaning; indeed, Hirsch includes its title in his list of "What Literate Americans Know."[47] Even if the students have not encountered the poem before, they tend to accept it on a first reading, discussion reveals, as a more or less transparent statement of traditional American wisdom about the positive consequences of being (morally) independent of mind, of not traveling with the herd, wisdom apparently synopsized in the oft-quoted last three lines:

> Two roads diverged in a wood, and I—
> I took the one less traveled by,
> And that has made all the difference.

But when the students are urged to read the poem closely, more questioningly—to reread it differently—they begin to notice problems, not only with the poem, as it were, but with their initial reading of it. Not arbitrary perversity but critical attentiveness, prompted by the text, leads them to ask whether the poem, no longer univocal, is more concerned with, as the title has it, "the road not taken" (which "bent in the undergrowth") or with "the other, just as fair," that the speaker did take; how the other road, "the one less traveled by," could have "wanted wear" if "the passing there / Had worn them really about the same"; how the taking of one of two quite similar roads could have "made all the difference"; why the speaker "kept the first for another day!" when he doubted he would return to it; what the speaker means by the "sigh" (of weariness? relief? mourning?) with which, he predicts, he "shall be telling this . . . / Somewhere ages and ages hence"; whether the "difference" at the end of the poem is to be interpreted as a positive or negative value (or neither or both).[48]

Discussion of this second-level reading then gradually opens for the students the possibility of a third-level reading through which they (re)construct the poem as a more integrated pattern of flip-flopping instabilities by which its meanings both complement and supplement/supplant each other. The poem thereby becomes for them both a statement of conventional wisdom (but how much imposed by cultural assumptions?) and a qualification of it, both a solemn romantic "sigh" and a subtly mocking parody of it, both an upbeat exemplum for school children and a riddle (from the Old English *rædels,* a "reading" or "interpretation") perhaps revealing the dark side of Frost that has come to intrigue his critics and biographers. Discussion of this writerly reading, with its engagement in the (writer's and the reader's) detailed production of the poem, easily broadens into other, related issues concerning authorial intention, the positionality of the reader, the complexities of "difference" (and sameness), the ironies of choice, the paradoxes of (American) romantic individualism, text as (a reflection, privileged or not, of) culture and vice versa.

This approach works much the same way with a standard anthology poem such as Keats's "Ode on a Grecian Urn" (by concentrating, again, on the problematic concluding lines), but it can be applied effectively to dramatic and narrative texts (Native American folktales, advertisements, jokes), newscasts, op-ed pieces, legal documents, technical manuals, sports events, what have you. Also, its three-stage progression recurs in similar strategies developed by others. An approximate analogue may be found in one offered by Scholes, who stresses that students must be given not "readings" but "tools for producing their own": "In *reading* we produce *text within text;* in *interpreting* we produce *text upon text;* and in *criticizing* we produce *text against text.*"[49] And Lanham's distinctions among three kinds of "vision" of the text (verbal or otherwise)—looking *through* it (referentially), *at* it (rhetorically), and (oscillatorially, as readily exemplified by the operation of a pun) *through/at* it—suggest a related, parallel progression.[50]

Indeed, Lanham was thinking through the implications and applications of this sort of alternative cultural-literacy pedagogy (of text-as-culture/culture-as-text) before I was—and certainly before the Hirschian Sturm und Drang struck—and he oversaw its integration into the UCLA Writing Programs in the early 1980s. Certain key interdisciplinary insights, partly derived from the rhetoric of Kenneth Burke, principled that thinking and the project into which it was translated, these among them: that by its utopian predisposition "curricular debate never ends"; that "humanism was [and is] a characteristic attitude and endeavor, not a list of canonical texts"; that, in Lanham's dynamic, style-oriented "Post-Darwinian" view of culture and the self (which he opposes to the static, purpose-oriented "Edenic" view—very much that of the typical neoconservative), "social reality . . . possesses no independent ontological security guaranteed by God," so that, "if the social drama stops, reality stops"; that, consequently, we must "construct our social human nature self-consciously, . . . construct our own social reality, construct it as drama, and by playing social roles gradually accrete around ourselves a felt identity, a 'real' self"; and that, though "mankind has invented a culture which aims to control his biogrammar," still "the wild-card impulse continually struggles against this conception of culture as *suppression* and threatens to turn it into *expression* instead," and thus "threatens to take over culture and play it just for fun."[51]

In Lanham's Post-Darwinia, surely now our world far more than the Hirsch-Bloom-Cheney camp can understand or admit, such insights about the fluid, contingent, dramatistic, ludic makeup of culture mandate more educational attention not to so-called content but to "style" and to "the leftover evolutionary baggage, the impulses of game and play from which style emerges." They suggest that mankind is involved in "a crisis of self-consciousness rather than a crisis of ethics." And they indicate the need for a more rhetorical (and, at that, more Gorgian than Platonic) and less philosophical paideia—for humanism especially but also for cultural literacy and, finally, perhaps, all education—a possibility much neglected, since "the thinking about the core [curriculum] has been all 'serious' rather than 'rhetorical' thinking, all *Through* and very little *At.*" Implemented through "a poetic pedagogy," such a paideia, which has been realized at least to some extent at UCLA and variously adapted elsewhere (mostly at the postsecondary level, though one can easily imagine its potential at lower levels), emphasizes not "a naive Arnoldian sublimity" but an intricate dialectic of playfulness and earnestness that Lanham finds prototypically exemplified in the poetry of Geoffrey Chaucer, "the self-conscious, ever-shifting reestablishment of temporary stays against confusion which constitutes the true Chaucerian seriousness, a kind of biogrammar which finally proves so complex that it does not so much take over culture as become isomorphic with it."[52] However playful/serious and complex, Lanham's cultural literacy (though he may not use that later-fashionable term) is very much, to borrow Burke's well-known formulation, "equipment for living"—not in the nostalgic past but in the uncertain future.

More recently, David S. Kaufer, enacting the reading progression I mentioned above, has engaged the Hirschian challenge quite directly in an attempt both to grant the significance of Hirsch's project and "to alter and extend" it. He concedes that, by virtue of its intended explicitness, "Hirsch's answer is already better than any modern alternative," and he believes that critics who dismiss him "will miss the intellectual challenge he is issuing." He admits that Hirsch addresses serious shortcomings in education. He observes that "it is easy to criticize Hirsch, but not to out-implement him." Still, Kaufer successfully attempts the latter in offering "the seeds of a practical alternative to Hirsch's challenge."[53]

That attempt begins with much the same Hirschian silence that troubled Warnock, more specifically that concerning the relation between extensive and intensive curricula. As Kaufer puts it, "Hirsch offers not a whisper of information on how the one curriculum speaks to the other—how fact learning speaks to more reflective learning"—a crucial gap, since "Hirsch's extensive curriculum makes sense only as input to the intensive curriculum and to a theory of mature literacy." Thus Kaufer's task, once he has discovered and critiqued that gap of silence, is creatively to fill it: "to make this link explicit" by means of a theory that "embodies many of Hirsch's ideals for culturally shared knowledge but extends them and significantly alters their focus." The logic of his theoretical strategy involves a complementation that shades into supplementation, even supplantation:

> Sharing, within this alternative, remains a goal: writers surely can't be expected to contribute to a culture that they don't share. But contributing now becomes a parallel aim: writers can't be expected to share a culture to which they can't contribute. Without sharing, as Hirsch notes, we have fragmentation rather than freedom. But unless we hope to contribute to what we share, sharing is an authoritarian exercise rather than a legitimate tool of democracy.
>
> I shall refer to this alternative as the "contributing" theory of cultural literacy in opposition to Hirsch's theory of "sharing." The content focus of a contributing theory is—not the list, reference, or text—but the issue. Literate readers and writers may share a cultural background, but the importance of that sharing is that it provides a vehicle for contributing to common issues. Within a contributing theory, "teaching content" finally means teaching issues. The teaching of issues can, of course, work its way into the teaching of specific texts that themselves try to contribute to these issues.

So, by a turning over of the token, "The [other side of the] common coin of literacy is not cultural facts and associations but . . . cultural conversations," the curriculum of each aspect to "be sequenced according to the criterion of parallel difficulty."[54]

Kaufer's contributing theory conceptually bridges "developing and mature forms of literacy" by his notion of "newness." With predecessors (though he does not trace them) in information theory, Ausubelian learning theory, and elsewhere, that notion makes his theory paradigmatically apeironic. He defines newness "as the mechanism by which 'interesting,' 'not fully expected,' or 'surprising' knowledge is discovered, constructed, and foregrounded against a background of old, given, or received knowledge." It thus connects "two complementary notions" or has two "faces," both highlighted by his theory: "(1) accounting for one's cultural givens and (2) constructing the givens in a way that allows one to go beyond them." But that complementarity, in privileging the second notion, neglected by Hirsch, harbors an inversion: it "inserts newness at the center, where Hirsch has placed shared cultural knowledge," and thereby equips Kaufer's theory, unlike Hirsch's, to be "workable for students"[55]—because it provides for exactly the motivation to learn whose absence in Hirsch's theory troubled Warnock.

That workability resides in the role that Kaufer's contributing theory assigns to "culturally shared knowledge": it is not just information to be absorbed but "a vehicle for exerting personal authority, for allowing a student to talk back to his or her culture by exploring beyond the culture's givens." He argues for the importance of this issue-oriented back talk that says "something new" (a sublimated, intellectualized version, for the instructor, of that insolent discourse the teacher abhors but, by an irony of authoritarianism, inevitably invites) by suggesting how it and related provisions of his theory can help avoid and alleviate, respectively, what Robert Pattison calls the "Shakespeare Paradox" and the "Finn Syndrome." Kaufer characterizes them as "two common educational situations that threaten to stop Hirsch's practical program dead in its tracks" and glosses them as follows:

> The Shakespeare Paradox begins with the observation that shared references that once promoted efficient communication may lose their utility after generations of negligible use. In a society where everyone knows *Julius Caesar,* for example, the passage "There is a tide" communicates without elaboration. But once the play is no longer read, the passage is no longer rehearsed and its capacity to support efficient communication diminishes. The paradox rears its head when we decide nonetheless to revive Shakespeare *in order to* correct these and other communicative inefficiencies. In the name of expedience, we have legitimized a rather inexpedient and roundabout practice.
> The Finn Syndrome reflects Huck Finn's attitude that one shouldn't "take stock in dead people." Hirsch suggests that students will learn any fact they are taught. Pattison, citing the Finn Syndrome as his authority, argues that students are much more selective and learn only what they care to learn. The disposition to learn redounds on the disposition to want to learn. Are students ignorant about World War II because they've never had a unit on it—or, as the Finn Syndrome suggests, because they've never been presented with enough personally involving and meaningful experiences to want to confront their ignorance and seek to reduce it?

A sharing theory of cultural literacy, according to Kaufer, does not account for—nor suggest practice for dealing with—the problems that Pattison's phrases so deftly capsule. Educationally enacted, it tends, largely through its emphasis on the traditional, to instantiate and proliferate the Shakespeare Paradox and, since "it leaves undefined the students' personal stake in the learning process," to perpetuate, perhaps even exacerbate, the Finn Syndrome, which indicates a problem of *ganas.* In contrast, contributing theory, thus enacted, avoids the Shakespeare Paradox by stressing that "students should not be forced to learn an isolated phrase or locution or fact if it remains just that—isolated in time and space"—

and that "shared knowledge is powerful because of what it enables (i.e., exploring what remains unshared)," and it alleviates the Finn Syndrome "by insisting that content should be taught when it can efficiently inform issues that remain present and alive for students."[56] In other words, cultural-literacy education, rather than teaching dead "facts," should make content apeironic by instructing students in how to figure it into engaging issues, however old or subtly "relevant" or both, and thereby contribute new knowledge to the ongoing cultural conversations.

And other differences, crucial and dramatic, distinguish Hirsch's proposal from Kaufer's alternative. Hirsch's pedagogy, such as it is, focuses on the specific cultural information, determined by authority, to be transmitted to the student. Kaufer's focuses on empowering the student to deal with virtually any kind of cultural information in terms of its pertinence to the interactive perspectives that constitute and enlarge compelling issues—a pedagogy of particular texts read in a particular way, in contrast to one of a general textuality. No surprise, then, that for Hirsch the extensive curriculum in many ways should drive the intensive one, whereas for Kaufer the reverse should obtain—that is, first "we try to decide on sources that contribute to the issue, sources that can teach students to read and write for newness," and then "we focus on the background (linguistic, cultural, historical) that we believe students require to make their way intelligently through these and increasingly difficult sources." Kaufer does not delude himself into arguing that his approach is inherently more democratic than Hirsch's; but it seems to me it is apt to be more so in practice, if only because it operates, by design, against starting curricular planning from narrowly predetermined background information. Also, Kaufer, unlike Hirsch, believes that "the practicality of a curriculum is measured by more than the simplicity of its implementation." Though it emphasizes the complex *how* of cultural literacy rather than the simple *what* (and he sees "little gain in trying to argue about curricula from a consensus model"), Kaufer's proposal suggests a curricular possibility that measures well even by rather conventionally practical criteria: "it avows worthy goals, provides a reasonable plan for meeting them, and allows evaluation and revision."[57]

Lest the reader think Kaufer's proposal somehow *merely* theoretical, I should underscore his continual concern with and distinctions about the practical. For instance, he observes that Hirsch "bequeaths us a list (a practicum) in lieu of a sound practical theory" and "overlooks the practices of literacy most prized in a free society," through the exercise of which students develop something most practical, "a vision of themselves as empowered to follow and, eventually, to lead our most important cultural conversations."[58] Those conversations, as instantiated in the Great Books and ubiquitously elsewhere, have always involved, at their best, not sharing information toward beige cultural homogeneity but contributing knowledge toward a fuller common understanding, however tentative and eclectic, of and participation in the significant issues that arise from, make for, and enrich cultural heterogeneity.[59] That heterogeneity is crucial not just to democracy but also—as any "practical-minded" ecologist will argue, analogizing from the cruciality of variety in biological systems— to the survival of any cultural system, local or global.

One way or another all the preceding critiques of and alternatives to Hirsch's project recommend that cultural-literacy education should be sensitive and attentive to the cultural literac*ies* that students bring to school, at whatever level. What students already "know," by whatever means, those literacies that Herrnstein Smith asks educators to respect (that Hirsch at least neglects and Bloom ridicules) should define the immediate context for any alternative and guide its implementation. As Eugene R. Kintgen, Barry M. Kroll, and Mike Rose note, "when the purposes of literacy in the classroom can be related to students' other interests, education is much more successful."[60] Therein resides a principle as fundamental as one can get, and yet educators and others bent on the authoritarian molding of students either are unaware of it or choose, for whatever reason, to ignore it, acknowledging only those interests that suit their purpose (too frequently, impossible, alienated idealizations) and hoping that the rest (students' private experiences—emotional, occupational, and so on) can be forgotten, treated as a tabula rasa, perhaps in time extinguished by desuetude.[61] That principle and its implications figure increasingly in reading theory informed by research in cognitive science. Schank, for instance, observes that "One of the very important tasks of the reading instructor is to assess what a child currently knows so that he can build upon it." He argues that "to teach a detailed part of some piece of world knowledge, it is best to personalize it as much as possible," since "reading and personal experience are strongly intertwined." And he recommends that children be taught to read by "the context method," whereby instructing unfolds "within an overall context that is of interest to the child."[62] Indeed, that principle, hardly restricted to the province of any particular notion of cultural literacy, is a universal of a kind far more powerfully applicable than any offered up by neoconservative humanists. Plato exploits it. Piaget's theories of the child's development, however much recently problematized, depend on and illustrate it. It applies—though with a difference—to a rat working its way through a maze, certainly to a human working through arithmetic to algebra, Newtonian mechanics to relativity, accounting to macroeconomics. It pertains to all learning, everywhere.

The most cogent elaborations of that principle may be found in the theory of education that has evolved from the quasi-Kantian educational psychology of David P. Ausubel, whose efforts to encourage educationists out of the dark ages of the "obsolete epistemologies" of positivist behaviorism, which is concerned with learning as behavioral change, and into a conceptually oriented and constructivist cognitivism concerned with *meaningful* learning (learning as change in what and how experience *means*) are gradually becoming more and more influential. Joseph D. Novak, the most prominent Ausubelian (along with D. Bob Gowin) and a major figure in science education, has spent several decades extending and refining Ausubel's model of learning as a process of conceptual assimilation, elaboration, and differentiation. He sees the generalization of that model into educational practice as the most effective way to break out of the cycle of "innovation after innovation" that has left us with nothing but a situation in which "the basic problems in teaching and learning persist." His view of education accounts for both sides of the token: "Every culture has a framework of concepts and practices. The task of education is to transmit to the children in the culture the concepts and practices they will need as adults. Concepts and practices change over time, however, and so education not only must include careful selection of those that are of most lasting value, but also must assist children in acquiring the capacity to generate and use new ones." And neither activity can proceed without identifying "those elements in the learner's existing knowledge store that are relevant to what we hope to teach, or, in Ausubel's terms, . . . the relevant sub-suming concepts that are available in the learner's cognitive structure." Novak's argument, surely supportive of its analogues in proposed alternatives to Hirsch's project, gains great authority by citing Ausubel's succinct and forceful statement of the principle I have labored: " 'The most important single factor influencing learning is what the learner already knows. Ascertain this, and teach him accordingly.' "[63]

Not only do the aforementioned critiques of and alternatives to Hirsch's project oppose insensitivity and inattention to students' own literacies—part of a general tendency, which Rose eloquently describes, to conceive complex problems reductively in terms of simple solutions—but they also oppose, more or less explicitly, any simple, easy accommodation of new knowledge to students' prior knowledge. Instead, they advocate that students read, write, and think actively, oppositionally, rhetorically; that they grapple collaboratively with difficult issues, decentered views, cultural otherness; that they question, problematize, theorize; that they construct new meanings, knowledges, realities—that, in other words, they learn apeironically. Learning otherwise—say, by memorizing a list and its predictable associations—involves little of engaging importance, little challenge, little intellectual or emotional enlargement, little "newness." It is the kind of minimal learning promoted by textbooks that try to optimize readability, as de Beaugrande and Dressler put it, "simply by striving for the best possible match between text-presented knowledge and prior world knowledge." In information-theoretical terms, such textbooks "possess radically low informativity" and are "devoid of interest"—which "flaw," according to de Beaugrande and Dressler, "pervades much of the reading materials now used in education," including, I would add, those Hirsch is turning out. Interestingly enough, the definition of *readability* "as the expenditure of the least effort," which rationalizes the use of such textbooks, is, as they note, essentially the one endorsed by Hirsch's *Philosophy of Composition* (and, for all his palinodes about that work since its publication in 1977, not repudiated by him). Recognizing that "readers will gladly expend additional effort upon a text if the unexpected occurrences lead to rewarding insights," they offer a less simplistic, more research-informed and instructing-oriented definition of *readability* "as *the appropriate proportion between required effort and resulting insights.*"[64] Those two definitions would serve just as well to characterize a basic difference in how Hirsch and his opponents, respectively, understand "learnability."

Another version of this difference, somewhat quaint and folksy but mostly in the right spirit, may be discovered in Jacques Barzun's *Teacher in America.* "The whole secret of teaching—and it is no secret—consists in splitting the opposition, downing the conservatives by making an alliance with the radicals," he argues a half century ago. Insisting—but without muting their relevance here—that he does not intend these political words "in their workaday sense," he explains that "the conservative part of the pupil's mind is passive, stubborn, mute; but his radical minority, that is, his curiosity and his desire to grow up, may be aroused to action." Thus "the whole aim of good teaching," what I have been calling instructing, "is to turn the young learner, by nature a little copycat, into an independent, self-propelling creature, who cannot merely learn but study—that is, work as his own boss to the limit of his powers. This is to turn pupils into students, and it can be done on any rung of the ladder of learning." Though Barzun admits, of course, that "some facts must be learned 'bare,'" pupils turn into students by learning "principles." The educator's efficacy, I would analogize by adapting the Chinese proverb, inheres in helping students make nets, not in giving them fish, most fish being—for Barzun in 1945 as for anti-Hirschians now—what he calls "hokum" and describes as "the counterfeit of true intellectual currency. It is words without meaning, verbal filler, artificial apples of knowledge." It manifests as "blind hokum, hokum absolute," in pupils' "parroting of opinion." As if foreseeing Hirsch's list and its implications, Barzun inventories hokum at some length:

> All the dull second-rate opinions, all the definitions that don't define, all the moral platitudes that "sound good," all the conventional adjectives ("gentle Shakespeare"), all the pretenses that a teacher makes about the feelings of his students toward him and vice versa, all the intimations that something must be learned because it has somehow got lodged among learnable things (like the Binomial Theorem or the date of the Magna Carta)—all this in all its forms gives off the atmosphere of hokum, which healthy people everywhere find absolutely unbreathable.

Big Daddy, so adept at detecting "mendacity" in Tennessee Williams's *Cat on a Hot Tin Roof,* couldn't do it better! And Barzun, in another prophetically anti-Hirschian moment, conditionally praises Deweyism by declaring that "progressive education in this country, if it has done nothing else, should be forever honored and given thanks for insisting on genuine, hand-to-hand teaching, as against the giving out of predigested hokum," which "older way" he regards as "a hangover from the one-time union of the teaching and the preaching professions."[65]

In the fun of considering possible new additions to Barzun's inventory of hokum, I wonder if—and with what qualifications—the cultural-literacy "crisis" itself should be included. Certainly the argument for doing so has been made, sometimes persuasively. Pattison, for instance, argues that what Hirsch, along with Bloom, has really diagnosed is what he calls "the stupidity crisis," which "meets all the requirements of a genuine American panic" and "has struck a hysterical chord in the population at large," harbingering "the decline and fall of the American way of life." Pattison offers considerable evidence that it is a pseudo-crisis and that "the crisis mongers are wrong in their facts and in their conclusions." Like Rose, he observes that such mongering forgets "what a recent and astounding innovation our system of formal education is," and, even after examining serious problems that plague that system (such as the low salaries typically paid to educators and ludicrously easy certification tests), he defends his position in terms of a widely noted irony that neoconservatives cannot or will not acknowledge:

> So in answer to the question, are Americans stupider now than they were in the golden past, I think the answer is no. In fact, the appearance of stupidity may be fostered by the reality of our success. No one would have noticed the general ignorance of the population if our system hadn't exposed great numbers of the heretofore uneducated to progressively higher stages of schooling, including college classrooms where the very ill-informed students of a suspicious democratic heritage have, over the last forty years, met the very learned professors of a German academic tradition.

And he goes on to show how the crisis mongers, in their proposed solutions to the crisis, have purveyed "ideals for the future" (such as a stereotype of the humanities as "fighting an elitist, rear-guard action in a vulgar culture," a stereotype that—by another irony, I would add—"hastens the disconnection between humanities and everyday life" so troubling to Cheney) as "warped" as their readings of the past.[66] Well, one could object to Pattison's somewhat cavalier characterization of "ignorance" above, but the point is clear enough.

Andrew Sledd makes a similar point—though more shrilly and diffusely—in contending that the "crisis in literacy" (by which he seems to designate, by turns, a crisis both in literacy in the traditional sense and in cultural literacy) doesn't exist or "is a hoax." That is to say, "both the crisis and the means to resolve it have been manufactured in order to serve purposes of which teachers should not be servants"—the purposes of, severally, "forces that foster ignorance and suffering," "national security," "high-tech society," and so on through a thesaurus of epithets sometimes applied with more leftist petulance than accuracy. Sledd reminds us that literacy, in one generation's judgment of the next, "has been declining since it was invented" and that "there will always be a literacy crisis, if for no other reason than because the old never wholly like the young," but in a less I-seen-'em-come-and-I-seen-'em-go mood he also recognizes, with Pattison and others, that during the "reigns of Carter and Reagan" scores on the SAT (Scholastic Aptitude Test) "fell largely because rising numbers were being tested." In any case, he thinks "it is deluded to treat literacy as a panacea" and suspects that "it may be deceptive to discuss it at all, for there is no thing, literacy, only constellations of forms and degrees of literacy, shifting and turning as history rearranges the social formations in which they are embedded." He rightly worries that literacy, as a unicultural practice imposed by the technocratic state, discourages imagination and hardly helps "build stronger minds." Indeed, he sees crisis-management efforts to intensify and universalize education in such fatuous literacy (with its suppression of all language but that "favored by business and the state") as simply furthering "a two-tiered educational system producing at the top a minority of over-paid engineers and managers to design the technology and provide the supervision for a majority of docile data processors and underpaid burger burners at the bottom," both of which "types of lesser hominids are needed to operate the new post-industrial economy being planned for us by our corporate magnates."[67]

Thus, for Sledd, the real crisis is not in literacy but in American "society and government." Counter to the nightmare of educators' more-of-the-same-only-worse continuation, he offers a Marxist-anarchist vision of "a commonwealth of genuine, popular participation" as an inspiration. The realization of such a vision requires not top-down bureaucratic pedagogy and curricula but "a cooperative, dialogic pedagogy that allows students' voices to be heard, not just unending teacher talk," and "curricula not afraid of the forbidden—of the un- or half-told stories of women, minorities, working people, others unlike ourselves; not afraid to name the follies of the learned or the incompetence of the mighty to solve the problems that they cause." Recalling his insistence that educators should abjure the purposes for which the literacy crisis has been "manufactured," his peroration turns on we/they oppositions: "We do need to raise our standards, as they so often suggest, but by using our values, not theirs. Ours should be educational and democratic, not obscurantist and repressive."[68] And so on. However much the petulance—or the hyperbole, even near-paranoia—of his critique may put off some or the utopianism of his alternative seem "impractical," Sledd makes arguments that linger, inviting more consideration and concern; and he proposes a Freirean *renversement* in educational reform very much in keeping with other ideas for more apeironic cultural-literacy education.

Finally, especially in view of Sledd's denunciation of the "obscurantist and repressive" in educational practice, I would like to share a parable, complete with applicable interpretation, concerning the darkest ironies of cultural-literacy education, both as it is being conventionalized by Hirsch and his allies and as it is being redefined by others. The parable and its gloss, along with illustrative narrative, constitute an essay by Richard J. Murphy, Jr., about his experience at the Modern Language Association's Right to Literacy conference, held in September 1988 at Ohio State University. The parable, which opens the essay, is essentially his synopsis of an extraordinary best-seller, and it merits quotation in full:

> At the center of Umberto Eco's novel *The Name of the Rose* stands a library. It is a fortress and a maze. Arranged in fifty-six adjoining rooms on the top floor of a huge tower in a remote Italian monastery, the library houses the greatest collection of books and manuscripts in medieval Christendom. But no one is allowed to enter it except the librarian.
>
> Even the monks who work at the monastery as scribes or illuminators must ask the librarian for permission to consult materials they need, and it is the librarian alone who enters the library to collect or return requested books. There is a catalog of the library's holdings, but only the librarian knows how

to interpret the catalog citations. The books are shelved in rooms that are arranged systematically, but the system is hidden in a code of letters concealed in quotations over the library doors. To make the design even more obscure, the rooms are of different sizes and shapes with different numbers of doors and windows. Some have no identifying quotations. The passageways between some rooms are further confused by walls of mirrors. Every night the library is locked by the librarian to discourage unauthorized entry, and hallucinogenic herbs are set out to disorient and frighten any intruder.

This elaborate puzzle has a very practical purpose: to keep the ideas housed in the library secret. It is a deeply paradoxical purpose. The learned authorities responsible for building and maintaining the library consider books precious. The chief work of the monastery is in fact to copy and illuminate them, on the finest vellum, in the most glorious inks. Painstakingly, generation after generation, the monks keep, care for, and increase the vast store of beautiful books. But at the same time, the monastic authorities consider books dangerous. The ideas expressed in them may be heretical or blasphemous. One book above all others, the book hidden in the room with no doors or windows at the center of the labyrinth, is considered so threatening that if its ideas were to become known, the whole structure of the Catholic world would topple. It is on the attempt to keep this book out of the hands of the uneducated that the series of murders in Eco's story ultimately depends.

Murphy then begins to interpret the parable in terms of its relation to the conference:

A principal theme of the meeting, as I heard it expressed there, was that teachers need to let students get at the books. Paper after paper assumed that though *everybody* has the right to literacy, modern schools are conspiring to keep it from them. According to this view, schools and teachers are engaged in a systematic, covert attempt to *keep* people illiterate. Not just unable to read and write—the meaning we most commonly associate with "illiteracy"— but unable to use language to assert their own political presence in society. Unable to interpret or challenge the language of social policy. Unable to use language to engage in searching political debate. Unable to articulate their own needs or values. Unable to examine even the dissatisfaction or desire of their own lives. The subject of the conference was more than the ability to read and write. It was the inability, lacking the power of language, to think about one's own experience.

Murphy finds this theme and its variations "unnerving."[69] It moves him to question the means and ends of his own educating, to consider the danger of literacy as an unsettling force, and to wonder about the accuracy and severity of the charge.

Though Murphy recalls feeling at odds with the cynicism of one speaker, he admits "that much of what he had said about the triviality and waste of education seems true to me." But he also demurs: "I don't think the waste is *systematic,* as he claimed. I don't think the triviality is *deliberate.*" Yet even when he detected patent overstatement in the speaker's critique, he felt alienated by the speaker's knowledge and the peremptory complexity of his thought. He wanted to challenge but didn't. His frustration grew into anger. And, as his litotes has it, "I wasn't alone."[70] However many others might be implied, he certainly felt kinship with the woman seated next to him, who shared with him her similar anger and left before the speaker finished.

Murphy's reflections on that event lead him to realize that what alienated him most from that speaker—and others—was his "estranging language," leftist theoretical jargon "both strange and colloquial" that made Murphy feel "powerless and silent." In other words, it put him and his like-alienated colleague(s) in the position of the "unable" he discussed earlier, as he explains: "The conference made us feel again like students. Not just ignorant, but excluded. It made us realize how easily our own students may be dispossessed by us. We lecture about themes with which we are familiar, in language we have come to make our own. We pause: Any questions? Silence. We go on." Thus he clinches his interpretation of the parable and concludes:

> It was precisely to *keep* people powerless and silent that the monks of Eco's monastery built that labyrinthine library. The book they were most eager to keep hidden was the only surviving copy of Aristotle's treatise on comedy [a portion of his *Poetics* that in fact has not survived, if it was ever written]. The root of its danger was that it celebrated laughter and thus exorcised fear and in so doing gave ordinary people the power to speak. To speak. To be freed thereby from their helpless submission to the learned in Church and State. In the guise of a murder mystery, Eco tells the story of the power of language that is at the center of contemporary debates about literacy.
>
> The speakers I heard were charging that the schools and teachers of today are still trying to keep people illiterate. It is a terrible claim. I don't want it to be true. But the most surprising thing I learned about it at the "Right to Literacy" conference is the ironic evidence that it might very well be so: we do it even to ourselves.[71]

When I first read Murphy's essay, my reaction was one of amused irritation: here is yet another squawk—though an eloquent one—from yet another mossbacked colleague intolerant of critique and theory, rancorous toward their "overpaid" practitioners, wanting from the conference not what he sees as outré self-indulgence but a lesson plan for Monday morning, stubbornly unwilling to join in the play of new perspectives. I featured the author not as a neoconservative so much as someone headed for professional burnout—and I sympathized, perhaps too smugly.

On a second reading I realized that, however inaccurate or not the particulars of my profile of the author, the whole essay made a parable of sorts for me to (re)interpret. The story of student alienation tells also of Murphy's, of many educators', and—a fortiori—of the public's, the world's. It is a story of alienation occasioned only superficially by a lack of one kind or another of cultural information (names, dates, places, jargon—tokens) but more profoundly by a feeling of being *uninvited* to join the play of new perspectives, to contribute "newness," to open up to the other, to experience difference, to enter the unknown. Bristling with warning, it is a story not simply of keeping people from books (though that, in several senses, is part of the problem and must be dealt with) but of not helping people learn what to *do* with them when they "get at" them. The story is not about a crisis in cultural literacy force-bloomed or fabricated by Hirschian panels and commissions: it is about a crisis in *apeironic literacy,* a far more significant phenomenon.

Insofar as "schools and teachers" work "to *keep* people illiterate," they do so, of course, much more to keep them apeironically illiterate than to keep them culturally illiterate in anything like Hirsch's sense. And their efforts are neither as innocent of systematicity and deliberateness as Murphy thinks nor as conspiratorial and covert as others allege. They are systematic and deliberate mostly only by virtue of robotic inertia, however intricately it may be rationalized personally or institutionally; they are conspiratorial and covert mostly only to the extent that they are guided generally by unexamined or unconscious fear and ignorance of the transformative power (whose flip side, by etymology, is *danger*—to the status quo) of large-scale apeironic literacy. Though they must be overcome, such inertia, fear, and ignorance are understandable (indeed, they must be understood to be overcome): apeironic literacy privileges not the unicultural but the multicultural, not sameness but difference, not convergence but divergence, not the known but the unknown, not self but other; functions not to close the case of the past but to open the case of the future; embraces not certainty but uncertainty; does not hide but reveals; listens not to one voice but to many; does not exclude but includes; strives, to recall Murphy again, to change powerlessness and silence into laughter and speech.[72] It strives for both the "more collective, pluralistic, inclusive national discourse" that Bizzell suggests may now be possible and a like *inter*national discourse.[73]

If the democratic saturnalia of apeironic literacy is to happen, locally or globally, we must all open our "libraries" to one another and learn through one another new ways to read the "books" we discover. We must cultivate a Bakhtinian readiness to be surprised by one another. Certainly educators and students must do this, but so must educators and their fellow educators at all levels, in all disciplines, and—in positive but ironic response to the calls from Giamatti, Cheney, and others for wider communication—so must educators and the public as well. An enriched personal and cultural self-consciousness is required, a realization, at the least, of the extent to which our cultures are already rhizomatically interpenetrated and to which one cannot be known without knowing others, a furtherance of cultural holism and globalism that both criticizes and respects all cultures, an enlarging affirmation of and attentiveness to what exists beyond any given person or culture.

CHAPTER 8

Evaluation, Assessment, Accountability

Controversy abounds in the realm of educational evaluation, assessment, and accountability, as do the delusions that fuel much of that controversy. It would be easy to cite examples of the fatuousness of most of the rationales and procedures for these three activities in virtually any educational system in the world. Such controversy inevitably characterizes activities that strongly influence parental expectations, the careers and lives of individual students and educators, institutional budgets, and the development of whole cultures. But such controversy would function more fruitfully if informed by the long-overdue recognition that most of those rationales and procedures are not only fatuous but—especially when misused, as they frequently are, in terms of their own avowed purposes—variously counterproductive and injurious. Largely irrelevant to apeironic education, they nonetheless continue, by virtue of their systemic entrenchment, strongly to retard the shift from teaching, whose ends they ill serve in any case, to instructing. More appropriate alternatives have been proposed, and I would like to discuss several, along with the critiques that help to shape and motivate them.

But first let me address briefly a matter of definitions. Though much used interchangeably, *evaluation* and *assessment* should be distinguished. Etymologically, the former has to do with "deciding the value of" something, the latter with "sitting in judgment of" it. This distinction may seem a fine point to some, wholly debatable to others, but it is translated, albeit obliquely, into practice to a certain extent—and should be more consistently so—

when, on the one hand, *evaluation* provides a student with information that reflects or predicts his or her performance as a learner and suggests ways to improve it (thus promoting formative *self-*evaluation) and, on the other, *assessment* of a student's performance provides *someone else* with information about such performance that may be used variously—for apprising parents, awarding scholarships, and so on. Much the same holds, mutatis mutandis, for the evaluation and assessment of individual educators, courses, degree programs, institutions, school districts, and so on—though, in general, evaluation tends to be (and should be, is more effective as) a relatively small-scale and personal activity and assessment a relatively large-scale and impersonal one. By this distinction, evaluation is part of the process of education, assessment not necessarily so, a difference that indexes the problems typically attendant upon a more harmful interchangeability: using the results of evaluation for purposes of assessment or vice versa. Finally, *accountability,* in this context most frequently spoken of as "teacher accountability," carries a version of that distinction: it may involve either "being required to explain (render an account of) what one does" (a situation that promotes worthwhile communication and self-awareness) or "being required to have what one does judged (and controlled) by someone else" (a situation that may or may not be productive, depending on who is judging [and controlling]). So, with these definitions in mind, let me proceed.

The most enduring and significant controversies have to do with the evaluation and assessment of student learning; all the rest follow from them. Some recent foci for such controversies: out-of-date or unrepresentative norms for national achievement tests, the practice of teaching specific items in the tests, the intrusion of imposed competency testing into educational programs whose goals are irrelevant to it, national tests (Graduate Record Examinations, for instance) that reflect little awareness of the current state of the disciplines their questions concern, tests whose standards are culturally biased or otherwise unfair (for instance, Florida's competency test for college students has been severely criticized in this regard), and so on. It is not surprising that many controversies focus on the problems of standardized tests since such tests are familiar to the public and tend powerfully—mostly, in the United States, through the considerable industry of the Educational Testing Service—to determine, directly and indirectly, the rationales and procedures for all manner of educational evaluation and assessment.

Intelligent and potentially influential polemics gradually are sifting out of the welter of controversies. In *The Hurried Child: Growing Up Too Fast Too Soon,* David Elkind finds American schools "increasingly industrialized and product oriented" and thereby reflecting and contributing to "the contemporary bias toward having children grow up fast." A principal consequence of such industrialization and orientation is that "testing has become mechanized (machine scored) and all pervasive." To understand the real cost of this situation, according to Elkind, one must first acknowledge its ironies: "The industrialization of our schools is not surprising, for universal schooling in the United States was introduced, in part, to prepare children for the new ways of living and working brought about by the machine age. What is surprising about our schools today is that they continue to follow a factory model at a time when factory work, as it was once known, is becoming as obsolete as farming without a tractor." Thus American schools "suffer from the same structural problems that make our industries an easy mark for foreign competition": they tend to be "top-heavy administratively and excessively hierarchical and authoritarian"; their drive for uniformity in procedures and standards discourages pedagogical creativity; they are prevented from changing by all manner of petty politics. Reform in such a system tends to parallel in its logic and inefficacy the "restructuring" of American industry and "means more basics, more hours, more homework, more testing—more of everything that is creating the problem." This classic application of the American philosophy of *more* has created "a classic case of the cure being worse than the disease."[1] And, I might add, the privatization of public education, for which some neoconservatives call, surely would do nothing to correct this situation and would make it—and other situations—worse.

I am a little troubled by Elkind's medical metaphor, and I disagree with him that "schools are always (and necessarily) behind the times because they transmit accumulated knowledge and skills" —since I believe that apeironic education can effectively counter that "always (and necessarily)." Also, while I do not disagree with the general purport of his argument that "our children do poorly in school today, in part at least, because they are repeatedly made aware that what they learn outside of school is more up to date than what they learn in school," what he means by "up to date" lacks sufficient elaboration. But I very much agree that the debilitating ironies outlined above justify the conclusion that "our schools . . . are out of sync with the larger society and represent our past rather than our future"[2] (putting aside the issue of *how* they do or do not "represent"). And Elkind is surely right that "more testing" has contributed significantly to that situation.

How so? The factory model of education mandates a uniformity of "product" anomalous in an age of diversity, and standardized testing is the key mechanism for monitoring that uniformity— indeed, for controlling it. The system thus engendered "ignores individual differences in mental abilities and learning rates and learning styles," and it provides for the diagnostic categorization of "defective vessels" who might learn quite well in different circumstances. Elkind offers a telling capsule history of standardized testing from Alfred Binet and Henri Simon's development of the norm-referenced test of "Mental Age," through William Stern's application of the dubious notion of IQ and the first use of "group tests" during World War I, to the subsequent introduction of "machine-scored group tests," which last innovation, in spite of misgivings and caveats from Binet onward, "has become a major force in contemporary education." That force, the culmination of a problematic evolution, remains the weapon of choice for those basic-skills "pragmatists" who, horrified at the lamentations of reports like *A Nation at Risk,* want to find out what's wrong on the assembly line and, by God, hold *someone* responsible for fixing it. "The hurricane of testing that reform has unleashed" has, of course, encouraged measures not so much to increase learning as "to increase test scores," which means that students are pushed harder and sooner to get higher scores on more and more tests administered more and more frequently at lower levels—a disastrously counterproductive cycle, since "children discover very quickly that passing tests, rather than meaningful learning, is what school is all about." As educators and educational administrators dance willy-nilly to the mechanistic tune of accountability, children who are "too dumb" are damned early on and "think of themselves as defective before they have had a chance to show what they can do"; the others "are more concerned with grades than with what they know"; "dishonesty and cheating" thrive; and this whole pressured scurry activated by "the abuse of testing,"[3] while "out of sync with the larger society," is very much *in* sync with the moral entropy, sociopathic despair, knee-jerk monotonies, and cardiac futilities of a futureless culture.

Perhaps I construe Elkind too apocalyptically in that final chain of phrases. I doubt that he would think so. Nor would Albert Shanker. In October 1989, speaking at an ETS conference in his role as president of the American Federation of Teachers, he called for an immediate end to standardized multiple-choice achievement testing as conventionally practiced. In his widely publicized speech, which stressed that he was not opposed in principle to achievement testing nor to accountability (indeed, he has advocated for some time a national test for teacher certification), he argued that conventional testing is administered too frequently, that it is too mechanical to measure more than superficial knowledge, and that it hinders innovative educational reform by discouraging teachers from venturing beyond the kind of learning it addresses. And he urged that schools demand—and publishers produce—tests that could effectively measure higher-level abilities in such areas as reading, writing, and mathematical problem solving. Hardly radical enough, his criticisms and proposals nonetheless signal a growing need for evaluation and assessment appropriate to many educators' increasingly apeironic praxis, and they echo the criticisms (Merrell and Schank come to mind) and proposals of others.

Ken Macrorie, long a vociferous opponent of conventional testing, distinguishes between two kinds of "teachers": "*teachers* in the usual sense—persons who pass on the accepted knowledge of the world and get it back from students on tests"—and "*enablers* who help others to do good works and extend their already considerable powers." The kind of educating habitual to the former is perpetuated by conventional testing and vice versa—and as Macrorie explains, that situation involves a perverse and reductive hierarchization:

> Most traditional education fails to produce works any more significant than rote test answers and knowledge (or more often, recollection) of disconnected bits and pieces of information. That fact is both cause and effect of those powerful instruments called "Minimum Competency" or "Scholastic" and "College Aptitude" tests. They are administered impersonally to thousands of students who are by the nature of the process destined to be seen as

educational units—average, above average, or failing. These tests can't measure a person doing good works. They are designed not to teach, but to judge. Unwittingly, administrators and teachers, as well as the general populace, have elevated them to such a position of unquestioned authority that we now find many courses in schools and universities tailored to prepare students for these standard tests rather than to produce good works that help people become ongoing, creative learners. A sadder notion of education can hardly be imagined. The result is that traditional educational experience appears even more useless to learners than it actually is.

And, of course, this reciprocal but hierarchized relationship is cognate with what Macrorie calls "the Lecture-Test-Grade System," a "structure that runs throughout our educational institutions like a spine. . . . It supports the weak, but central, nervous ganglion of conventional school. It doesn't support enabling."[4]

Enablers think little of conventional tests because, while they may "reveal . . . ignorance" of some kind, "they are seldom instruments for learning." Enablers are interested, however, in "devising unconventional ones that demand initiative from learners" and "tell . . . about students' ability to do something with knowledge or a skill." And enablers design their daily assignments to test students more effectively than any standardized exercise in recalling tokens. In Macrorie's view conventional tests, like lectures and grades, the other two "instruments of the inquisition," create more "fright and boredom" than productive learning. Moreover, they encourage, especially in the form of proficiency tests, merely " 'minimal competency,' a goal which steadily scales down the expectations of teachers and students," whereas testing in "Moebian education," in which enablers help students engage in a subjective/objective interplay of their own ideas and experiences with those of others, involves expectations that "are solid and positive and high, and they include fumbling and making mistakes." To put it another way, conventional tests elicit compliant regurgitation of undigested information, whereas Moebian tests encourage risk taking, awareness of the intelligence at play in errors, creative use of information—maximal habilitation instead of minimal competency, students who are "finders, rather than simple keepers of someone else's knowledge."[5]

Mike Rose's critique parallels Macrorie's but expectably more concerns "marginal" students. "We set out to determine what a child knows in order to tailor instruction," he generously grants, "but we frequently slot rather than shape, categorize rather than foster." Such slotting and categorizing immure "poorer" students especially as surely as physical prisons, and in spite of pieties about—and erratically supported efforts, like the generally laudable federal Head Start program, to promote—"equal access to America's educational resources," predictable imprisoning ironies obtain for those students:

> Judgments about their ability are made at a very young age, and those judgments, accurate or not, affect the curriculum they receive, their place in the school, the way they're defined institutionally. The insidious part of this drama is that, in the observance or the breach, students unwittingly play right into the assessments. Even as they rebel, they confirm the school's decision. They turn off or distance themselves or clam up or daydream, they deny or lash out, acquiesce or subvert, for, finally, they are powerless to stand outside the definition and challenge it head-on.

Even teachers who "see through this behavioral smokescreen" are too bureaucratically trammeled to alter the situation, and so "the children gradually internalize the definition the school delivers to them, incorporate a stratifying regulator as powerful as the overt institutional gatekeepers that, in other societies, determine who goes where in the educational system."[6] The complex differences in student lives that Rose believes should function as fundamental factors in formulating educational strategies are reduced by conventional assessment, norm- or criterion-referenced, to simplistic labels with the force of destiny.

Ubiquitously implicated in this mess is the imperative for mechanical quantification, a concern of Elkind's that needs amplifying. As Rose notes, test scores—and the ever-burgeoning numerical data associated with them—"in an academic bureaucracy . . . are valued terms of debate." They provide grist for "the policy documents and the crisis reports," which thereby wind up "focused too narrowly on test scores and tallies of error and other such measures." The operation of this imperative is for the most part eerily sealed off from the problematics of conventional standardized tests or local instruments of assessment (their validity, reliability, fairness, and so on), for recent decades have seen the proliferation of a "vast and wealthy industry" concerning "the business of underpreparation" in which the drive to quantify became very strong, a reality unto itself, and what you couldn't represent with a ratio or a chart—what was messy and social and complex—was simply harder to talk about and much harder to get acknowledged. Patricia Cline Cohen, the historian of numeracy, notes that in America there is the belief that "to measure is to initiate a cure." But a focus on quantification—on errors we can count, on test scores we can rank-order—can divert us from rather than guide us toward solutions. Numbers seduce us into thinking we know more than we do; they give the false assurance of rigor but reveal little about the complex cognitive and emotional processes behind the tally of errors and wrong answers. What goes on behind the mistakes simply escapes the measurer's rule.

And, of course, quantification favors "so-called objective tests" that furnish numbers (doubtless the main reason why many standardized tests, including the reasoning sections of the SAT, still lack essay components) but unfortunately "stress the recall of material rather than the reasoned elaboration of it." Such tests have virtually nothing to do with "how to use knowledge creatively," so that the continuing administration of them very much promotes educational experience that "year after year is the exchange of one body of facts for another—an inert transmission, the delivery and redelivery of segmented and self-contained dates and formulas"—with the result, against which Dewey warned, that students "develop a restricted sense of how intellectual work is conducted."[7] While Rose does not elaborate his alternative for testing, surely it is readily implicit: it would be more personalized, more sensitive to the meaning of errors, more concerned with the demanding complexities of improving learning and less with the convenient simplicities of merely judging competence, far less reliant on any kind of brute quantification, and designed to reflect not so much what one knows as what one can do with what one knows and how one does it—all in terms of always-provisional standards that are open to discussion, even and particularly by students.

Richard Mitchell illuminates the issue of educational measurability by exposing a contradiction:

The educationistic mind is deeply divided against itself. It wants to follow Wundt and believe that teaching and learning are objectively measurable phenomena and that those who study teaching and learning are therefore scientists and worthy of chairs in colleges and universities. At the same time it wants to contend that the profoundly important results of an education, especially the education of a teacher, are attitudes, values, and "philosophies" that transcend cognition.

Continuing with his characteristic tone, Mitchell codifies the result of this contradiction with summary logic: "Measurable things are not important; unmeasurable things are paramount. Let us therefore measure only the unmeasurable."[8] But, given the exigencies of the quantificational imperative, this confused Wundtian logic is translated into practice as what Neil Postman calls "the Technical Thesis": "the idea that it is only through the use of *technique* and *technicalization* that we may find out what is real, what is true, and what is valuable"[9]—or, to follow Mitchell's terms, the idea that measurement, even if it can't measure the unmeasurable, somehow can reveal it.

What happens, of course, as Jacques Ellul and many others have demonstrated, is something else. The application of technique, which Postman defines most simply as "a standardized method for achieving a purpose," tends almost inevitably to give rise to an "aberrant process by which a method for doing something becomes the reason for doing it. At the cultural level, one of the names is *reification*. To reify a procedure or a technique is to elevate it to the status of a purposeful creature, to invest it with objectives of its own." And reification pushes on from an identification of procedure with purpose toward a privileging whereby "procedure is more real than purpose." Consequently, in the realm of educational evaluation and assessment, reification creates a situation in which "the test score is taken for the reality. The student's behavior in various contexts is to be judged against this standard. If life contradicts a test score, so much the worse for life. Life makes mistakes. Instruments do not."[10] And the more bureaucratized conventional education gets, the more it gets in over its head with reified technique, with measurement that is no longer its means but its end—in more than one sense, I would argue and hope.

Though Postman somewhat nostalgically sentimentalizes the usurpation of "the traditional moral code" by the Technical Thesis, particularly through television programming in which "living is construed as purely a technical problem," he does persuasively evidence his argument as to how, in a world dominated by technique, "we lose confidence and competence in our ability to think and judge, we willingly transfer these functions to machines." He wishes fervently that schools would resist, oppose, and correct the bias of the Technical Thesis, but he recognizes that relentless "outside pressures" urge them "to continue to technicalize their operation." Thus students continue to be treated as "objects or commodities, mere units in some statistical compilation," with the result that the solution to educational problems (he cites particularly those targeted by the now-vestigial back-to-basics movement) "lies in improving our statistics, not our students," who "are to learn what will show up as a number"—if it does not, "it does not exist." And thus this bias, Thomas Gradgrind in apotheosis, its imperial metastasis overseen by the unoverseen ETS, "the supreme seat of technicalization of education in the country," defines education, and "its definitions are wholly controlled by what instruments are available to quantify learning; that is to say, it is reductionist and impoverishing." While I agree with Postman that the hegemony of technicalization, which puts "our schools in the service of the very ideology that requires the severest criticism" and preempts deeper learning, "is a rejection of the past,"[11] I would emphasize that it is also—and more alarmingly—a rejection of the future.

Postman's "alternative arguments" betray a good deal of skepticism about the extent to which such institutionalization can be changed. Still, he takes hope, oddly enough, from the schools themselves, whose conservativeness (in a sense different from, perhaps more fundamental than, that pertinent to reactionary bureaucracy) runs against the grain of "revolutionary" technicalization:

> They have a tradition of humane concern and a conservative bias. There is among many teachers a suspicion of technicalization and a keen awareness of its limitations. There is even among parents a certain resistance to submitting their children to the autonomy of technique. It is far from fanciful that the schools can generate a counterargument to the technical thesis, an argument that denies the intrinsic authority of technical definitions, that speaks in favor of ambiguity and complexity, that refuses to accept efficiency as a definitive purpose or technique as a comprehensive philosophy.

Despite his dark anticipation that "the well-heeled revolutionaries will do anything to prevent such arguments from entering the schools," Postman, with his Bakhtinian distrust of rigid simplisms, proposes for the schools not so much increasingly more clever counterstrategies as a development of "suspicion" and "resistance" together into a more sophisticated critical vigilance. In evaluation and assessment this involves awareness of the ways "evaluation procedures take precedence over ideas"; of the principle "that what is to be evaluated, and how, must be decided *after* we determine what is worth doing"; of the "educational thesis" a given test represents "as much through the form of the test as through its content"; of the ways "formal tests, while sometimes useful, can be a snare and a delusion," given the tendency to allow them "to take over the functions of human judgment" and become "*the method* of student assessment"; of grades as "summary statements, but no diagnosis and no prescription"; of the need to avoid teaching "only those things for which there are easily discernible behavioral outcomes," especially since "the study of learning is very far from being a science." Postman proposes that educators "distinguish human education from animal training" and abide by what any "good teacher" knows: "Evaluation is not something that happens on Friday. Every class is a test. Every interaction is a test. Every response is a test."¹²

Conservative in the best sense, Postman's proposal strikes me as a necessary part of an alternative—but only a part. Education of and for the future requires more than just an informed critical vigilance about the rationales and procedures of evaluation and assessment: it requires as well the positive thrust of different rationales and procedures that derive from a different way of thinking about learning. The report of the elementary strand at the English Coalition Conference suggests something of the character of this thrust in its insistence that "the focus and source of all curricular development and assessment must be on the individual learner" and also that "individual assessment must be based on the principles and assumptions about learning theory that support literacy development" as outlined by the conference. And one gathers more from some of the conference's general resolutions. Lamenting how "the increased call for assessment of student learning has often resulted in a curriculum that is test- and assessment-driven" and how, "at present, most tests undermine good teaching by stressing mere recognition or 'decoding' and by implying that reading is a largely passive process of getting 'right' answers," the conference report nonetheless recognizes that "some form of assessment is unavoidable in the interests of accountability"; but it recommends that it be "carried out with moderation and sophistication" in order to "help students learn and teachers teach," that specification of "the understandings—and more important, the *ways of knowing and doing*—that our students should achieve" be the professional responsibility of their teachers, that a group of teachers and researchers representing all levels "develop statements and goals that can serve as a basis for better assessment," and that goals be stated "in ways that reflect the complex, highly constructive processes of reading."[13] Such insistent recommendations disclose that the new positive thrust is very much a theoretical one; that is, it is informed by an increasingly rigorous self-consciousness about what is being evaluated or assessed, how and why, and it works to inform rationales and procedures with the most sophisticated and productive theory possible. That thrust *is* new, and it figures significantly in the general shift toward apeironic learning.

Joseph D. Novak and D. Bob Gowin provide a useful sense of historical context here. For them "evaluation rests on the judgment of value. To evaluate, we must have a clear notion of value." However, they observe, "the professional practice of evaluation seldom worries about value. The standard devices (achievement tests, for example) tell us almost nothing about what is worth knowing and how we are to judge the worth of knowledge." In their view "the educational value of any 'object' (lecture, text, lab manual, experiment, book, test, educational event)" is not a matter merely of data transmitted; rather, that value "resides in how well it can help us to realize our power to understand the world we inhabit: It should transform the meaning of our experience so that both we and our world have enriched meaning." For them, as for many others who hold similar views, "meanings are social constructions" whose sharing makes possible both education and educational value. Novak and Gowin's efforts to formulate "a theory of educating" based on David P. Ausubel's notion of meaningful learning are motivated in large part by a desire to understand that value, to distinguish "what . . . does and does not count as educating." The cruciality of such efforts may be gauged by an embarrassing situation that many others also have come to acknowledge and address: method-driven like the research on which it is based, "educational evaluation has not so far been guided by theory. Book after book on educational evaluation fail us because they fail to specify what constitutes an instance of teaching or learning."[14] Novak and Gowin's theory, which I discussed briefly in the preceding chapter, can serve as a guide for, among other things, evaluation. It is not the only one now around, as we have seen, and they particularize it largely for science education; but it is comprehensively enough conceived and researched for its principles to apply broadly, and many of its general emphases or basic features have their counterparts in the theoretical work of others in other areas who are developing alternatives to conventional evaluation and assessment. In their theory Novak and Gowin carefully distinguish "standard methods of testing, measuring, and evaluating, which seek to elicit information from students that exactly mirrors a text or lesson," from their own "heuristic," which "asks students to reorganize new information using what they already know." Thus that heuristic—which involves what they call "Vee diagramming," a method of conceptual mapping, evolved from Ausubelian learning theory, that allows students (and their instructors) to analyze and construct knowledge (of, say, cell physiology) graphically—insists that students experience evaluation as "a process that is creative and idiosyncratic and that requires that understanding be expressed through a variety of ways of thinking and doing." In terms of this rationale, "educational value is determined by what the learners *do* with lessons, not by the exact fit between a lesson and its replication on a test." Such value "is a transformation of the quality of experience that empowers students to give meaning to themselves and to their world, and the value of education can only be judged by its power to bring about educational consequences." Novak and Gowin readily admit that their heuristic "is to some extent arbitrary" and could be otherwise configured, but the point is that, as an instrument of evaluation, it attempts to "take cognizance of our understanding of how humans create and appraise knowledge and the psychological processes by which they come to understand knowledge."[15] I would argue that the intelligently elaborated theory informing their heuristic, here absent many details, does a far better job of that than any so-called (mostly unconscious and ill-considered) theory that informs conventional testing, and it mandates, to borrow Novak and Gowin's helpful terminology, a shift from the simplistic quantitative measurement of informational *replication* to the more complex qualitative measurement of epistemological *transformation*.

This latter, apeironic project is fraught with important implications, not the least of which is the diminution and perhaps the eventual archaization of assessment in the sense I discussed earlier. But there are others as well. With the shift to apeironic evaluation, students are tested not so much for what they know as for how they use what they know to deal with the unknown. Certainly they need to "know" things, but they should learn them as much as possible through their applicability to some meaningful practice, not through rote. And why should everyone know the same things? Even in medical and legal education students don't, past a certain point, and in the best programs in those areas most of what an outsider would see as mere dues-paying memorization is very much knowledge engaged through such practice—and enlarged because it is. Also, the relationship between apeironic evaluation and instructing involves reciprocality and mutual productivity, whereas that between conventional evaluation or, especially, assessment and teaching involves a perverse, and in some ways pernicious, even violent, hierarchy, one that promotes the delusion of absolute standards. And, finally, apeironic evaluation is concerned with appraising and furthering the enrichment of intelligence as a phenomenon arising, as Robert de Beaugrande and Wolfgang Dressler believe, "not merely from rapid, accurate storage and recovery of specific knowledge—an unfortunate misconception in both psychology and education—but rather from the *ability to apply or adapt a small set of powerful skills and procedures to any particular task at hand.*"[16] Interestingly enough, young children wonderfully enjoy that ability—before it gets hobbled by conventional formal education and its hyper-Grad(e)grindian paraphernalia of testing and scoring.

Much of the foregoing discussion applies, mutatis mutandis, to the evaluation and assessment of educators as well. Conventional quantitatively based tests do a poor job of evaluating or assessing—or predicting—their performances. Though Lee S. Schulman, the ETS, and others have developed new multimedia tests that attempt to reflect subject knowledge, awareness of pedagogical principles and methods, and subtler aspects of approach and attitude, I am skeptical about their efficacy—until they are redesigned as instruments for the apeironic evaluation of instructing that are predominantly qualitatively based and rely more on careful individualized review by informed and experienced professional peers than on any numbers glowing on a screen.

Most conventional educational assessment, of students or educators, is driven by a notion of accountability that has little to do with the sort of learning I advocate and a great deal to do with delusions about efficiency and productivity. Geraldine Jonçich Clifford and James W. Guthrie offer a telling history of this notion in the United States during recent times:

> The decade of the 1970s, like the period 1900–1920, was characterized by a series of particularly intense efforts to render schools more efficient. As had been the case historically, proponents of productivity again diagnosed schools as poorly operated, and the injection of private-sector management techniques, described in bureaucratic babble, was the prescribed reform medicine. School administrators were admonished, and in some instances mandated by state legislatures, to utilize program performance budgeting systems (PPBS), program evaluation review techniques (PERT), management by objectives (MBO), and other technocratic "remedies" derived from the private or defense sectors. Yet education does not meet most of the production assumptions upon which such technical management procedures are based. Hence the accountability fad washed through the system, leaving virtually no residue. Not even performance-based teacher education (PBTE) systems, whatever they were intended to be, lasted.
>
> Proponents of heightened productivity next advocated expanded testing of students. The rationale was that educators could be pressured to perform more effectively if the system's "output," or student achievement, could be subjected to more intense public scrutiny. Thirty-five states responded during the 1970s to the call for standardized testing programs. Indeed, revisions of the late 1980s in the National Assessment of Educational Progress (NAEP), to permit state-by-state comparisons, represent an unprecedented expansion of the strategy of accountability through testing—compromising the heretofore sacrosanct principle of local control of public education. This is a consequence of public distrust of student achievement which, as measured by the press's barometer, the Scholastic Aptitude Test scores, continued a nearly two-decade-long decline into the 1980s, followed by only small recoveries.[17]

This history of futility continues (some NAEP officials and others, especially at the federal level, prone to be uncritically enamored of Japanese and European approaches to testing, still express the hope that absolute, even unchanging, assessment standards for educators and students, along with more centralized bureaucracy, can be used to prod the educational system into higher efficiency and productivity), and it will continue indefinitely—until education generally has undergone a shift of emphasis from teaching to instructing, from conventional to apeironic evaluation, and has sufficient support, economically as well as philosophically, from a public that understands, with the help of committed educators, the *value* of that shift and holds them accountable in terms of it.[18]

Still, however far we are from that situation, the accountability movement that began in the 1970s has had at least one positive effect. By exposing inadequacies in the training, qualifications, and practice of educators, especially in the public schools, it has stimulated considerable interest in new and more effective approaches to professional development—as witnessed by the rise, at scattered sites across the United States, of professional development schools (PDSs). Such primary or secondary schools, crucial to the Holmes Group agenda for professional reform and strongly endorsed by John I. Goodlad's comprehensive 1990 report *Teachers for Our Nation's Schools,* operate through alliances (precarious though increasing in number) between local school systems and universities, serving, like medical-school hospitals in a way, as laboratories for innovation and renewal.[19] Trammeled as it is with problems of definition and, even more so, of procedure (as the National Board for Professional Teaching Standards, established in 1987 by the Carnegie Forum on Education and the Economy, continues to rediscover), accountability has served to focus more thoughtful attention, from both the academic and public sectors, on the (lifelong) education of educators and on other aspects of their professional circumstances. At times intelligent action accompanies that attention, at least up to a point, and it is motivated by what, in the United States if not elsewhere, amounts to a breakthrough understanding: if educators are to be held accountable for what they do—or, in a harsher version, are told to do—then they must have what they need to do it and work free of the control of any confused bureaucracy; that is, they must be "empowered."

Typically, particularly in public schools, educators are not—in several respects. An exemplary exception is the school district of Rochester, New York, where a remarkable experiment is under way, a model of reform that holds some promise as a model of transformation. It began in 1985 with the efforts of Peter McWalters, the superintendent of schools, to get a new teachers contract and within two years involved the committed interest of Governor Mario Cuomo, the presidents of the University of Rochester and Eastman Kodak (which has its home office there), the head of the local Urban League, the president of the Rochester Teachers' Association, and other movers and shakers—all determined that public education in Rochester, with its considerable cultural diversity, would no longer be more of the same but something different. The plan for change, announced in January 1988 in *A Region Prepared,* echoes, as it responds to and builds upon, the recommendations of the Carnegie Forum's 1986 report *A Nation Prepared: Teachers for the 21st Century.* Its provisions, which include an emphasis on "at-risk" students and, predictably, preparation for the workplace, depend ultimately on accountability, but their enactment entails notable differences from the situations in most of the 15,500-odd school districts (many of them condemned by economic and other inequities to maintain the population of at-risk students) in the United States: decentralized decision making and "school-based management"; high and informed standards for faculty hiring and retention; vigorous recruitment of minority faculty members; salaries far above the national average; intelligent support from and interaction with local businesses (which, in the United States, too rarely invest systematically in education), the public, and a major research university; a PDS atmosphere that encourages research (not in remote, white-coat settings but in the classroom), risk taking, and change; extensive new-faculty mentoring by "lead teachers" and creative, ongoing collegiality; minimal hobbling of educators with trivial and nonprofessional responsibilities; and so on. Clearly, however, the Rochester system in practice is not the sort of totalized educational utopia the above inventory might suggest. Its pervasive stress on job-related education checks its apeironic possibilities; many predict that its optimistic momentum will not hold, finding it still riddled with problems and its means and ends lacking in specificity. Some judge it already foundered. Still, given the chaos with which it began (high dropout rate, miserable faculty morale—the usual urban catastrophe), an extraordinary turnaround has been accomplished, one well worth monitoring.

But the important point here is that the Rochester experiment, however problematic its methodology of accountability proves to be (certainly local evaluation and assessment procedures apart from peer review have been a matter of contention in recent years), provides generously for the sine qua non of accountability: the empowerment of those held accountable. Empowered educators enjoy (self-)respect and high morale, strive to be conscious of their own learning processes and more pedagogically sensitive to their subjects, are not compelled to be merely vessels open to administrative will (or whim), and work free of the too-typical self-contempt of educators who fear that someone will step forward to announce that the emperor of education has no clothes on. Without adequate empowerment, there never can be useful accountability. With it, there always can be, for well-enabled professional educators want to be acknowledged for their accomplishments and productively responsive to appropriate criticism; that is true a fortiori for instructors, whose work constantly ventures beyond tried and predictable patterns. A long history of mixed attitudes toward education—certainly in the United States but elsewhere as well—argues that empowerment of the kind achieved in Rochester is anomalous and will be short-lived. But with the recently increasing interest of postsecondary students in education as a profession, a growing awareness of the implications of a worldwide shortage of educators, innovative programs for teacher education, and increasing excitement about the possibilities of apeironic learning, there is reason to believe otherwise. Empowerment entails a difficult bootstrapping, to be sure, but so do all important cultural (and personal) transitions.

CHAPTER 9

Re(-)mediation

As we have seen, education based on teaching involves severely limited notions of what success in learning might be. Its notions of failure in learning are no less limited, but they inform its practice much more extensively, with the result that conventional evaluation and assessment, from daily grading to the whole armamentarium of standardized tests, tend to be a matter more of detecting weaknesses ("errors," "mistakes," "wrong answers") to be "corrected" than of discovering strengths to be encouraged and built upon. Students generally, at all levels, can testify to this bias and typically are more deeply conditioned and troubled by it than they can articulate. That holds all the more for students who are "marginal," "underprepared," "at risk," those most subject(ed) to what Mina Shaughnessy calls "the remedial model," among whose worst features are that it "isolates the student" from his or her larger educational context, "imposes a 'fix-it station' tempo and mentality upon both teachers and students," and, most lamentably, obstructs the discovery of "the intelligence and linguistic aptitudes" operating "below the surface of . . . failures"—that is, of *strength in* (apparent) *weakness.* [1]

Mike Rose also remarks on "the ease with which we misperceive failed performance" and stresses, perhaps more intensely than Shaughnessy, "the degree to which this misperception both reflects and reinforces the social order." He is particularly concerned with the problems of the remedial model in American literacy education at the college level, but his argument pertains in principle to its problems in virtually all education: "Class and

culture erect boundaries that hinder our vision—blind us to the
logic of error and the everpresent stirring of language—and encourage the designation of otherness, difference, deficiency." To
counter this situation he proposes an overturning shift: "To truly
educate in America, then, to reach the full sweep of our citizenry,
we need to question received perception, shift continually from
the standard lens."[2]
What do we see when we make that questioning shift of perspective? With Rose's help we see a modern history of language
research and pedagogy that parallels and complements that of
remediation, a history, familiar to Neil Postman, dominated, in
spite of motions to the contrary, by simplistic notions of grammatical etiquette, "positivism," industrial principles of efficiency,
"tallies and charts"—all with very little "consideration of the social context of error" and with an exaggerated responsiveness, in
terms of "an economic decision-making model," when issues of
accountability are pressed "in times of crisis: when budgets crunch
. . . or, particularly, when 'nontraditional' students flood our institutions." And we see, of course, a metaphor and its implications exposed:

> The designation *remedial* has powerful implications in education—to be
> remedial is to be substandard, inadequate—and, because of the origins of the
> term, the inadequacy is metaphorically connected to disease and mental de-
> fectiveness. The etymology of the word *remedial* places its origins in law and
> medicine, and by the late nineteenth century the term generally fell into the
> medical domain. It was then applied to education, to children who were thought to
> have neurological problems. But *remedial* quickly generalized beyond the
> description of such students to those with broader, though special, educa-
> tional problems and then to those learners who were from backgrounds that
> did not provide optimal environmental and educational opportunities.
>
> As increasing access to education brought more and more children into the
> schools, the medical vocabulary—with its implied medical model—remained
> dominant. People tried to *diagnose* various *disabilities, defects, deficits,* and
> *handicaps,* then tried to *remedy* them. . . . The remedial paradigm was be-
> ginning to include those who had troubles as varied as bad eyes, second
> language interference, and shyness. The semantic net of *remedial* was ex-
> panding and expanding.

Rose readily details this telling history—noting, for example, that
remedial sections were nicknamed by the logic of quarantine,
"sick sections" in the 1930s, "hospital sections" in the 1940s, and

so on—and concludes that, "though we have, over the last fifty years, developed a richer understanding of reading and writing difficulties, the reductive view of error and the language of medicine is [*sic*] still with us. . . . We seem entrapped by this language, this view of students and learning."[3]

And yet, of course, Rose's own critique helps us escape this entrapment. Through its lens we gain a perspective on how the medical model has blinded "those who dwell on differences" negatively:

> Ironically, it's often the reports themselves of our educational inadequacies . . . that help blind us to cognitive and linguistic possibility. Their rhetorical thrust and their metaphor conjure up disease or decay or economic and military defeat: A malignancy has run wild, an evil power is consuming us from within. . . . The character of the alarms and, too often, the character of the responses spark in us the urge to punish, to extirpate, to return to a precancerous golden age rather than build on the rich capacity that already exists. . . . The reports urge responses that . . . focus on pathology rather than on possibility. Philosophy, said Aristotle, begins in wonder. So does education.

So Rose, echoing Shaughnessy, suggests that we turn over pathology to find possibility, turn over fear to find wonder. And he advocates overturning the medical model of remediation not just because of the destructiveness documented by its problematic rhetorical history but also because, as he argues convincingly, it "is simply not supported by more recent research in language and cognition."[4]

Certainly that model must be continually challenged by reason of the oppressive boundaries and discouraging labels it imposes on students—who after a while, like Rilke's captive panther, come to see only the bars on their cages and nothing beyond—but it must be challenged all the more for being unsupported by cognitively oriented research. Indeed, the relevance and usefulness to education of even that research is increasingly being questioned when it shows insufficient cultural self-awareness. Rose accuses some contemporary cognitive theorists of creating "models of mind" that promote "cognitive reductionism," since, among other "difficulties," their "theories end up levelling rather than elaborating individual differences in cognition"—and this "at a time when cognitive researchers in developmental and educational psychology, artificial intelligence, and philosophy are posing more elaborate and domain-specific models of cognition." He faults such theorists for oversimplifying the conclusions derived from their models—"a tendency to accept as fact condensed deductions from them"—and he argues that their "theories inadvertently reflect cultural stereotypes that should, themselves, be the subject of our investigation." Thus, according to him, through the research of theorists concerned with cognitive development, distinctions between orality and literacy, hemisphericity, and so on, "the complexity of cognition—its astounding glides and its blunderous missteps as well—is narrowed, and the rich variability that exists in any social setting is ignored or reduced." And thus, because of "the hidden influences of culture on allegedly objective investigations of mind," Rose insists that "we must ask ourselves if speculation about cognitive egocentrism and concrete thinking and holistic perception embodies unexamined cultural biases about difference—biases that would be revealed to us if we could adopt other historical and social perspectives." Acknowledging that all theory, however powerful, is tentative, both "evocative and flawed," he poses questions to help us adopt those other perspectives, such as "Do our practices . . . honor the complexity of interpretive efforts even when those efforts fall short of some desired goal? Do they foster investigation of interaction and protean manifestation rather than investigation of absence: abstraction is absent, consciousness of print is absent, logic is absent?"[5] He is far from alone in urging the adoption of such perspectives, new sociological lenses, as a quick review of contemporary work on "learning disabilities" would demonstrate.[6] Greg Sarris speaks for many other educators who carefully scrutinize cognitive theory and research when he observes that "it has become increasingly difficult to dismiss student difficulties as mere cognitive dysfunctions; such attributions, now more thoroughly contextualized, have lost their objective value. A student's difficulty in the classroom is just as likely to be social, and ultimately political, in nature."[7] The relationship between domain-specific and domain-general knowledge involves a complexly balanced interplay that we do not yet understand well, but Rose and Sarris argue compellingly that, if that relationship is to be as productive as possible, educational practice must attend more fully, with keener rhetorical awareness, to the particularities of the positions and situations from which students are encouraged to elaborate and apply general strategies of learning.

From Cultural (Il)literacy to Re(-)mediation

To break out of the prison of the medical model with its dark *d*-words (without, I would hope, abandoning relevant medical knowledge), to more sensitively contextualize cognitive theory and research, to reconceive wholly "the traditional orientations to error and remediation," and thus to transform the practice of democratic education, "we'll need," according to Rose,

> many conceptual blessings: A philosophy of language and literacy that affirms the diverse sources of linguistic competence and deepens our understanding of the ways class and culture blind us to the richness of those sources. A perspective on failure that lays open the logic of error. An orientation toward the interaction of poverty and ability that undercuts simple polarities, that enables us to see simultaneously the constraints poverty places on the play of mind and the actual mind at play within those constraints. We'll need a pedagogy that encourages us to step back and consider the threat of the standard classroom and that shows us, having stepped back, how to step forward to invite a student across the boundaries of that powerful room. Finally, we'll need a revised store of images of educational excellence, ones closer to egalitarian ideals—ones that embody the reward and turmoil of education in a democracy, that celebrate the plural, messy human reality of it.[8]

A wild-side vision of apeironic possibility, if ever there was one! And it is cognate with Shaughnessy's vision of nontraditional education for nontraditional students, with its emphasis on how "error should or can become a subject for instruction." In her vision of education, concerned immediately with the postsecondary level but powerfully relevant to all levels, student learning problems comprise occasions for educators "to become better teachers" and more informed critics of their own profession. Her vision insists that the teacher not "slip . . . into the facile explanations of student failure that have long protected teachers from their own mistakes and inadequacies." It proposes, by inversion, a different kind of teacher, one "who begins to look at his students' difficulties in a more fruitful way: he begins to search in what students write and say for clues to their reasoning and their purposes, and in what *he* does for gaps and misjudgments. He begins teaching anew and must be prepared to be taxed beyond the limits he may have originally set for himself."[9] For such a teacher no student is "traditional."

A version of that strategy, very much an instructorly one, figures in Mariolina Salvatori's portrayal of the classroom as a pedagogical site where "the *remedial* approach is replaced by one of *mediation* as both teachers and students learn to ask and to answer questions that make texts speak, and speak away silences with 'voices' that *mediate* and *remediate* understanding in continuous, enriching dialogues."[10] By this logic, then, Shaughnessy's inversion may be recast more dynamically as a sort of chiasmic shift: the teacher's detached *remediation* becomes the instructor's involved *re-mediation,* just as pedagogical self-certainty becomes self-questioning.

That hyphen, which I insert to stress Salvatori's distinction, marks a crucial distinction between two pedagogical worlds: one in which the teacher tries to "heal" the student "against" error and, to follow through the etymology here, another in which the instructor "again" gets "in the middle" of error. One is a closed world of "objective" diagnosis and judgment (conventional evaluation), the other an open world of continually renewed intersubjective understanding and intervention (apeironic evaluation). To take an extreme but sobering view, in one world students, not educators, fail; in the other, vice versa. But this view, while illustrating a radical shift of emphasis, is indeed too extreme—and too simplistic—for the paramount significance of the second world is that it hosts a situation in which educators, no longer remediating to ensure sameness but re-mediating to enrich the experience of difference, join with students to make the mutual play of error productive.

Entrance into this second, other world thus requires the recognition that, as Postman puts it, *"all learning is remedial,"* a claim he persuasively explains:

> If I may dare to contradict Professor Dewey's best-known aphorism, we do not learn by doing: we learn by *not* doing. By trial and error. By making mistakes, correcting them, making more mistakes, correcting them, and so on. The "and so on" is important here, because the process of making mistakes has no end. There is no one who learns how to write or read or calculate or think once and for all. . . . To be sure, some . . . make fewer mistakes than others. But there is no one who reaches a point where remediation is not necessary.
>
> Every student in a classroom, therefore, has learning difficulties—the A students as well as the F.

Though Postman's vocabulary is quite conventional, his notion of remediation invokes the re-mediational/interventional model much more strongly than the remedial/medical model—as we soon see:

From Cultural (Il)literacy to Re(-)mediation

If teachers grasped this idea, they would inevitably pay more attention to mistakes and errors than they do at present, and would be closer to a professional position in advising students about how to improve themselves. In fact I believe it would be entirely possible to teach any course—not only English or math, but history, economics, biology, and physics—as a study in mistaken beliefs, debilitating prejudices, and inadequate skills. This is perhaps what the old-line progressives had in mind when they instructed us to "start where the student is." That is sound advice, because where the students "are" is where their errors are. What a student does not know, and cannot do, is where education begins.[11]

The recognition that all learning is remedial is one of Martin Mueller's "moments of return" with a difference: it involves both *recognizing* (remembering) what all education is about and *re-cognizing* (rethinking) how to be about it.

PART 4

Apeironic Learning: A New Paideia

I find stirrings in my brightest younger colleagues of desires not so much to attack the canon of critical works as to find a way out of what they regard as an intellectual impasse. It is as if they are looking for something else to know.
　　　　　Hazard Adams, *"Canons: Literary Criteria/Power Criteria"*

In all the fighting over education we are simply saying that we are not yet satisfied—after about a million years of struggling to become human—that we have mastered the fundamental human task, learning. It must also be clear that we will never quite learn how to learn, for since Homo sapiens *is self-changing, and since the* more *culture changes, the* faster *it changes, man's methods and rate of learning will never quite keep pace with his need to learn. This is the heart of the problem of "cultural lag."*
　　　　　Jules Henry, Culture against Man

With "the closing of the American mind": the opening of the global mind.

CHAPTER 10

Countercurriculum(s)

How further re(-)cognize education?

Let me begin, again, indirectly—with a brief but powerful lesson from David Laurence. (And it is perhaps useful here to keep in mind that *lesson* carries the inscribed meaning of the Latin *lectio,* "a reading.") After discussing the realpolitik of "the struggle over the curriculum" as (melo)dramatized by the press during the late 1980s, he comes to his own re(-)cognitive moment. "Many times over the past months," he recalls, "a sentence of Rousseau's has swum into my memory: 'If we knew how to be ignorant of the truth, we would never be the dupes of lies'" (the sentence, ironically enough, is from Allan Bloom's translation of *Émile ou de l'éducation*). Laurence continues, glossing as he goes:

> Conceptual structures speed understanding but no less speedily lure the mind into error. No degree of vigilance seems able to protect us, so vulnerable are we to the charm verbal frameworks exert. We are wise not to rely too much on our own powers to resist when resistance resembles nothing so much as an effort to catch sight of Kierkegaard's elf who wears a hat that makes him invisible. . . . It seems safer to look to persons outside our own points of view to prod us into awareness and the capacity for self-criticism.

He then offers a "simple example . . . to expose the frightening ease with which," in a phrase from Ellen J. Langer, "the rhythm of the familiar lulls us into mindlessness":

> Let this word trap illustrate our proclivity for unwittingly falling prey to the knowledge that is deceived:

Q.   What do we call the tree that grows from acorns?
A.   Oak.
Q.   What do we call a funny story?
A.   Joke.
Q.   What do we call the sound made by a frog?
A.   Croak.
Q.   What do we call the white of an egg?
A.
Really?[1]

Thus, as this koan-like dialogue illustrates, the need to think anti-thetically, to counter the hypnosis of the familiar, habitual, com-monsensical, conventional, received, traditional—lest we be "de-ceived" or, to recall the negative meaning of *trāditio, betrayed* into "error" subtler and more consequential than that to which this trap leads. And what counters, what is "outside our own points of view," should urge and enable not only "the capacity for self-criticism" but also "awareness": a double, oxymoronic (both negative and affirmative, disillusioning and creative) dynamic of consciousness that, to synthesize Laurence's provisions, might be called self-aware involvement or skeptical wonderment. Both supplementing and supplanting the given, this dynamic is above all apeironic, and it will not thrive—nor will we—without coun-tercurricular education. Let me explain.

Many people now live in—and increasingly more aspire to live in or are, willy-nilly, by the forces of economic hypertrophy, being dragged into—a world characterized by what Tony Schwartz, one of Alvin Toffler's epigones, characterizes as "acceleration syn-drome." A global phenomenon that variously affects even the Third World, its symptoms, with a little "outside" perspective, readily come to the foreground: "Life in a state of constant over-drive. There's more information than ever to absorb, more de-mands to meet, more roles to play, the technology to accomplish everything faster, and never enough time to get it all done. And the cycle feeds on itself." Computers, fax machines, cellular phones, frenetic diet and exercise programs, two-income families, on and on—all manifestations of and goads to not just change but change that is accelerating, to the point that change itself is changing (faster). And conventional education, not only in America but worldwide, is not enabling humankind to deal with this monster it has created. Recalling the dupes of Laurence's word trap, Schwartz notes that "clerical workers who use computers, for example, report with increasing frequency that they find themselves adapt-ing their own rhythms to those of the computer—trying, in a sense, to become more like the high-performance machines they oper-ate."[2] Other symptoms and by-products besides such automatism that Schwartz observes generally include short attention span, unengaged busyness, emotional superficiality, lack of introspec-tion, single-vision Type-A compulsions galore. This world direly lacks sufficient critical self-awareness and creative alternativity, let alone the possibility of silent contemplation "upon a peak in Darien," where Keats, by an error cultural-literacy Gradgrin-dians savor pointing out, has his "stout Cortez" be the first to view the Pacific.

And, of course, the Pacific—and all for which Keats has it stand—has changed, is changing, will change, rapidly. As Bill McKibben argues in *The End of Nature,* there is a still larger acceleration syndrome involved, one in which humankind is pro-foundly implicated:

> I believe . . . that we are at the end of nature.
>
> By the end of nature I do not mean the end of the world. The rain will still fall and the sun shine, though differently than before. When I say "nature," I mean a certain set of human ideas about the world and our place in it. But the death of those ideas begins with concrete changes in the reality around us—changes that scientists can measure and enumerate. More and more fre-quently, these changes will clash with our perceptions, until, finally, our sense of nature as eternal and separate is washed away, and we see all too clearly what we have done.

McKibben's overarching concern is with the greenhouse effect and associated phenomena, but that concern is more than scien-tific in the usual sense: "It is too early to tell exactly how much harder the wind will blow, how much hotter the sun will shine. That is for the future. But the *meaning* of the wind, the sun, the rain—of nature—has already changed." Though the traditional idea of nature as "wildness" has proven "durable in our imagina-tions" and "has outlasted the exploration of the entire globe," that idea increasingly confronts a nature that we "have deprived . . . of its independence," which quality "*is* its meaning." The "natu-ral" and the "man-made" are now confused to the point of indis-tinction, "the laws of nature . . . rewritten." Thus summer is being "replaced by something else that will be called 'summer,'" and "those 'record highs' and 'record lows' that the weathermen are always talking about—they're meaningless now. . . . They imply a connection between the past and the present which doesn't exist." The "new 'nature' "—born of the extinction of species, deforestation, acid rain and other pollutions, the shopping-mall life-style—"won't be predictably *anything,* and therefore it will take us a very long time to work out our relationship with it, if we ever do." Bereft of a relevant past, "we are left with a vast collection of 'mights,' " even an apocalyptic vision of the vacuity of all meaning: "The idea that nature—that *anything*—could be defined will soon be outdated. Because anything can be changed."[3] The truth of anything thereby becomes conditioned by commonplace truthlessness.

McKibben holds to no simple fatalism about this situation and hopes that we can "change our habits"—largely through the practices of a "deep ecology" that asks fundamental questions about the human experiment and proposes a radically deindustrialized civilization. And, of course, he seeks to help us understand the cruciality of that "change," sometimes reminding us poignantly of the cost of forgetting the past: "As it ["nature as we have known it"—though one might substitute science, history, literature, music . . .] disappears, its primal importance will become clearer—in the same way that some people think they have put their parents out of their lives and learn differently only when the day comes to bury them."[4] Such an analogy is moving enough, but, however much we may wish to preserve something, to "keep it the same" (and a lot depends on whose/what past/nature/tradition we are talking about), we are never wholly able to; and, to the extent that we can, what we preserve may be of little help, indeed may be very much counterproductive.[5] To play off McKibben's analogy, we keep our parents meaningfully in our lives not just by being their children but also by learning to relate to them in other, quite different ways.

The past, however interpreted, cannot tell us all we need to know of how to sift useful information from the daily avalanche of it, how to formulate a deep ecology for a world that has no traditional frontiers, or how to, say, articulate and enact a global feminism. Nostalgia is certainly no help, and just as certainly not all change is "bad." To understand what (version) of the past is important to us as we "work out our relationship" to what has never happened before—indeed, to work out that relationship not just by a sort of bricolage but by the apeironic bootstrapping of "making it up as we go," without rehearsal—requires education other than and quite different from that of the past, which is still mostly what we have and which is still mostly Gradgrindingly spinning its wheels as automatically and self-destructively as one of Schwartz's clerical workers. The past, increasingly already an archaeology, may serve in various ways as a sense of "origin" (perhaps even as a gauge) for the events of our labile world, but it tells little of our "destination," of how to fly by the seat of our pants in the night of accelerating uncertainty that concerns Schwartz and McKibben. The past—conventionalized, traditionalized, habitualized, *naturalized* as the present with which it is already out of sync—determines curriculums, what the monolithically minded term *the* curriculum; what we need now are countercurriculums that balance (even as they exceed complementarity or supplementarity to modify, incorporate, or supplant) the former. (I have inserted parentheses into my chapter title in order to suggest both the shared apeironic spirit of the countercurricular and the desirability of its diversity. I will admit, however, that I am traditionalist enough not to like the non-Latinate spelling that this both-and trick entails.)

The American public, in spite of evidence seemingly to the contrary, may well be growing more interested in and open to countercurricular education. In 1989 a Media General–Associated Press poll indicated that most of the 1,084 respondents doubted the validity of standardized testing and were worried that students, though "absorbing facts," are not "learning to think." Practically everyone is beginning to figure out that urban schools desperately must have alternatives to their curricular malaise. High school principals, typically among the most conservative of educators, are calling more and more for "education for change." Even the stodgy LSAT (Law School Admission Test) and MCAT (Medical College Admission Test) recently have been revised to take more account of applicants' abilities to interpret and critique creatively, to engage in problem-based learning—with revisions in the latter reflected in recent changes in the curriculum at the Harvard Medical School. And one can get a feel for the character, momentum, and scale of the countercurricular shift and its evolving pedagogy from a 1989 brochure announcing The Ninth Annual and Seventh International Conference on Critical Thinking and

Apeironic Learning: A New Paideia

Educational Reform, which was sponsored by the Center for Critical Thinking and Moral Critique (the name since shortened to just Center for Critical Thinking) at Sonoma State University and featured over a hundred distinguished educators. The following selections, attributed to Richard W. Paul, director of the center, are exemplary:

> Critical thinking ought to be the heart and core of educational reform. When students are adept at thinking critically, they are adept at gathering, analyzing, synthesizing, and assessing information, as well as identifying misinformation, disinformation, prejudice, and one-sidedness. With such skills, students have the tools of lifelong learning.
>
> A critical education respects the autonomy of students. It appeals to reasons and evidence. It encourages students to discover as well as to process information. It provides occasions wherein students use their own thinking to work their way to conclusions; to defend positions on issues; to consider a wide variety of points of view; to analyze concepts, theories, and explanations; to clarify issues and conclusions; to evaluate the credibility of sources; to raise and pursue root questions; to solve non-routine problems; to transfer ideas to new contexts; to make interdisciplinary connections; to evaluate arguments, interpretations, and beliefs; to generate novel ideas; to clarify and critique texts; to question and discuss each other's views; to compare perspectives and theories; to write extended essays; to compare ideals with actual practice; to examine assumptions; to distinguish relevant from irrelevant facts; to explore implications and consequences; and to come to terms with contradictions and inconsistencies. Unfortunately, most professors feel they do not have the time to focus on the critical thinking of their students. They feel that their primary responsibility is to "cover" subject matter in didactic lectures. . . .
>
> This didactic mindset of most professors dovetails perfectly with the passive "tell-me-what-is-important-so-I-can-tell-it-back-to-you-on-tests-and-papers" attitude on the part of most students. Most are totally unprepared for assignments that require them to think critically. They assume that one way or another either the textbook or the professor will tell them what they are to say or do. . . .
>
> Administrators have their own role in this problem. They usually feel too burdened down with day-to-day matters to spend time investigating how classes are taught. Furthermore, given the imperial nature of departmental decision-making, most administrators feel they would be asking for trouble to raise questions in this domain. So, if there aren't complaints from students, they take a "hands-off" attitude. The result is a synergistic relationship between professors, students, and administrators. Each has a vested interest in the status quo.
>
> Nevertheless, fundamental changes in instruction are required if students are to be prepared to function successfully in a world in which the pace of change is continually accelerating. Critical thinking *is* becoming an imper-

ative in every dimension of everyday life. The average person now changes his career three to seven times in a lifetime. Everywhere information is multiplying and at the same time becoming rapidly obsolete. Half the information that students are laboriously memorizing today will be out-of-date in about six years (Will they know which half?). In their political and civic life, student will have to make decisions on increasingly more complex and pressing problems of environmental damage, diminishing resources, over-population, global competition, cultural misunderstanding, ideological conflicts, and the danger of nuclear holocaust. Society will no longer be able to afford masses of people whose obsolescent thinking endures until they themselves pass away. Critical, flexible, adaptable thinking will become a practical necessity.

Paul's text has some of the frenzied tone of what I would call the futuristic sublime, and, as is typical of the brochure each year, it reveals more than a little questionable positivistic and rationalistic bias. But cumulatively it argues cogently for a shift from a curricular model of education (and not just postsecondary education) as, again in Paul's words, "a mere piling up of more and more bits and pieces of information" to a countercurricular one of education as "a process of deciding for ourselves what to believe and do"—along with a correlative shift, by a computer analogy, from a pedagogy of data storage (teaching) to a pedagogy of heuristic procedures (instructing).

Such reconception (oppositional, critical, heterogeneous, divergent) of curriculum(s) necessarily involves a repudiation of objectivist notions of *the* curriculum (or even *The* Curriculum)—there never has been nor ever will be an ideal curriculum, save in authoritarian fantasy. And it necessarily involves relativism as well, but here that term must be understood, in a sense subtler and less confused than Bloom's, as designating not cultural anarchy or axiological entropy but a re(-)cognition (another one) of the diversity of the human experiment. Barbara Herrnstein Smith can help make this point. Observing an epidemic tendency toward "the privileging of the self through the pathologizing of the Other" (and one could productively substitute alternatives for self and Other—canonical and noncanonical, for example, or *our* culture and *their* culture), she asks us to remember "that there are many people in the world who are not—or are not yet, or choose not to be—among the orthodoxly educated population of the West" and to rethink, imperatively, the propensity "routinely" to take the fact that the texts of such education "*do not have value for them* . . . as evidence or confirmation of the cultural deficiency—or, more piously, 'deprivation'—of such people. " Indeed, she stresses the importance of the authority promoting that propensity being "*always* subject to interrogation and *always* at risk" and of us asking ourselves "whether—and at the cost of what else—any of us ever does or *could* 'give sense to our lives' in some *single, particular* way." Criticizing those (here, specifically, Richard Rorty) who ignore "the mobility, multiple forms of contact, and numerous levels and modes of interconnectedness of contemporary life" and who therefore forget "that contemporary communities are not only internally complex and highly differentiated but also continuously and rapidly reconfigured," she offers the affirmative example of Clifford Geertz. His anthropological theory and practice respect and deal with the labile complexity of those communities, and he acknowledges, with her, "that at any given time as well as over the course of anyone's life history, *each of us* is a member of many, shifting communities, each of which establishes, for *each* of its members, multiple social identities, multiple principles of identification with other people, and, accordingly, a collage or grab-bag of allegiances, beliefs, and sets of motives."[6]

For Herrnstein Smith "Re[-]cognition of this situation requires a conception of 'community' and an image of individual social life and mental life that is considerably richer, more subtly differentiated, and more dynamic than that articulated by contemporary communitarians." It requires as well a concomitant conception or image of education, of countercurricular paideia, in which " 'the best' is always both heterogeneous and variable" and which involves " 'relativism' in the sense of a conception of the world as continuously changing, irreducibly various, and multiply configurable."[7] Such relativism, contingently conceiving the contingency of the world, deeply informs countercurricular thinking and strongly suggests both the necessity and opportunities of a general—and courageous—countercurricular praxis.

And that praxis *is* developing. Humanities educators increasingly realize the importance of students treating "every text in its full complexity" and of encouraging "a full range of voices in our classrooms."[8] Science educators increasingly realize the importance of women and minorities engaging in scientific learning and of putting an end to the Nicolas Bourbaki–like male dominance of their enterprise.[9] And many educators increasingly realize that education involves not one culture but, in Mike Rose's words, "one culture embracing another"—not acculturation but transculturation (which requires a pedagogy of cultural interface)—and that "underprepared students" must be acknowledged as already "competently literate" in ways that demand respect and, with informed attention, can be extended into deeper learning.[10] There is growing impatience with various kinds of "tracking" at all educational levels, and educators are more and more interested in mixing students in cooperative or collaborative learning environments. And anyone with eyes to see surely realizes that the typical postsecondary student is—and is increasingly being re(-)cognized as—not a "traditional" one at all but one who is older (in the United States, where a fourth of college students are over thirty, even the "four-year student" now takes five to six years to get an undergraduate degree), less predictably prepared, and less and less likely to be Caucasian (consider the University of California at Berkeley, where less than half the student body is white) and male. The *uni*versity is becoming—and must become more—a *di*versity.

Countercurricular praxis is "heterogeneous and variable," and yet a shared spirit animates all its manifestations, a Bakhtinian imperative to increase the number and variety of voices speaking in the conversation of learning; to listen better to their contributions; to incorporate those contributions into an ever larger, richer, more open awareness of the world. Thus, for Donald Lazere, such praxis involves "acting as a counter force to the biases of special interests in the majority."[11] For Gerald Graff it involves "what we have come to call 'theory'—the self-consciousness generated when consensus breaks down"—which in turn involves a sense of the dialogics of texts, the interplay of "opposing voices" (however subtle or silenced) in them, that urges the study not of "the isolated text (or author)" but of "the virtual space or cultural conversation that the text presupposes."[12] (By this logic, a curriculum is constituted to a great extent by texts, a countercurriculum by *con*texts, including the range of events encompassed by the term *reader response*.) For Paul Feyerabend, who wishes *"to overcome the chauvinism of science that resists alternatives to the status quo,"* it involves the adoption of "the 'counter-rule' that urges us to introduce hypotheses which are *inconsistent* with well-established *theories."*[13] And, of course, that Bakhtinian imperative figures variously in interdisciplinary educational projects.

That imperative certainly would operate in the large-scale countercurricular praxis that Neil Postman proposes—with a twist. Defining any curriculum as "a specially constructed information system whose purpose, *in its totality,* is to influence, teach, train, or cultivate the mind and character of our youth," he discerns two major curricular estates, television and school, both of which "not only have curriculums but are curriculums; that is, they are total learning systems." Because "television is not only a curriculum but *constitutes the major educational enterprise now being undertaken in the United States"*—and the world, I would add—he calls it "the First Curriculum. School is the second." He rehearses lengthy, intelligent, but fairly predictable criticisms of the TV (general electronic) curriculum (that it threatens to produce "a population of 'right-brained' people," that its "teaching . . . must lead inevitably to a disbelief . . . in the need for confronting complexity," that it suppresses the cognitive world of the word and makes us "both mute and powerless," that it encourages us "to prefer media-life to reality itself," and so on). And he laments that "the school curriculum yields [to it] at almost every point and in the worst possible way—by trying to mimic the forms of the electronic curriculum and therefore to indulge its biases." He elaborates:

> School courses are reduced to twenty-minute modules so that children's attention will not wander. Required courses are eliminated and replaced with inconsequential electives. Teachers become entertainers. Programmed machines and other techniques are introduced. Audio-visual aids flood the classroom. . . .
> There even develops a widespread interest in what are called "alternative curriculums." But the school as we normally think of it (or used to think of it) is now, itself, an alternative curriculum, one whose teachings very much need to be preserved in the face of the onslaught of the First Curriculum.

The title of Postman's book *Teaching as a Conserving Activity,* from which I am quoting, expectably adumbrates this line of argument; but, whatever specific "alternative curriculums" he intends to deride here (perhaps appropriately), his conception of what the school curriculum ought to be vis-à-vis that of the electronic media is far from conventionally conservative:

> The schools should always provide an alternative educational bias to the educational bias of the rest of the culture. This is the countercyclical or

thermostatic view of schools and . . . is justified by the principles of social ecology. Without opposition, the biases of a culture turn in on themselves, overrun the culture, and become dangerously oppressive. . . . The schools should focus their attention on the information environment and, in particular, on the *structure* of the information environment. This means that educators would be centrally concerned with the topology of information—its form, its speed, its magnitude, its direction, its accessibility, its continuity—and ultimately, with the bias of mind that any information configuration would tend to promote.

Quoting André Gide's maxim against complacent knowledge ("The only real education . . . comes from what goes counter to you"), Postman even suggests that this countercurriculum be enacted through an essentially apeironic pedagogy: "The task of a teacher . . . is to generate, and help students generate, questions"— including curricular questions—"which can lead to awareness," and that of the school is to "provide a vision of something different and a concept of something better."[14]

Though I have reservations about some aspects of Postman's proposal (the occasional nostalgia it indulges, for instance, or its tendency to privilege linear rationality over the paratactic and paralogical), it is certainly cogent on the whole. And notice that he, significantly, does not advocate that the First Curriculum be somehow simply ended but rather that it be studied, understood, re-envisioned in terms of the second. Recalling Graff, Warnock, Kaufer, and many others, he is proposing that the hidden conflicts of the First Curriculum be the concern of the second, that the readerliness of the first be supplemented or supplanted by the writerliness of the second, that the givens of the first become the issues of the second—that, in other words, the second curriculum have as its purpose a global informational literacy. Since humankind *is* information (genetic, neural, printed, electronic, whatever), Postman's proposal for a counterenvironmental, oppositionally balancing countercurricular praxis seems wholly *practical*. And in its grappling with the complex interrelationships between curriculum and countercurriculum, it creatively engages matters crucial to the continuing evolution of the apeironic paideia.

Let me stress the importance and necessity of the both-and character of countercurricular praxis, touched on above, to the development of such a paideia. (The late poet laureate Howard Nemerov observed once during a heated political discussion that, whether you walk on your right foot or your left, you need both.) Certainly education on a wide scale is now undergoing what may be described, by borrowing a little casually from Thomas Kuhn's *Structure of Scientific Revolutions,* as a paradigm shift, though the specific features and advance of that shift vary considerably by educational level and cultural situation (the literary canon in American high schools has changed only sluggishly, for instance, and education in Asia generally is a long way from being apeironic). That shift, I argue, ought to be informedly applauded and encouraged, for much education in the world is, in many ways, as deluded and futile as France's efforts to preserve its language from change and "contamination" (especially by English). But I do not mean by that judgment that traditional or conventional education (or French, for that matter) should be abolished but that it necessarily must be extended, built upon, made different for an ever-different world—by a process, a radical shift of *emphasis,* that takes the form of a turning-over, hierarchical inversion, *renversement.* Nor do I mean at all that apeironic education should work toward past-lessness or ahistoricality; quite the contrary, it should deal, like a play by Sam Shepard, with the past (including its own past) in terms of the equivocalities through which it (its values, epistemologies, and so on) exists as a (con)text in relation to the present (con)text becoming a future one.

Let me illustrate and expand this difficult but crucial point. First, a lesson (a "reading") in etymology that concerns English but whose implications explode well beyond English-speaking cultures. It begins with a re(-)cognitive aside in an essay on literary history by Gary Shapiro in which he notes that the world *lore* "signifies *both* that which is remembered, handed down and preserved and that which has been lost."[15] Now, *lore* derives from the Old English *lār,* a word closely related to the Old English *leornian,* "to learn," and it still carries several of the more specific meanings of *lār:* "learning," "science," "art of teaching," "preaching," "study," "story," "history," and so on. (And, interestingly enough, the Old English word for *school* is *lārhūs,* "lorehouse.") Thus, inscribed in this both-and etymology is the both-and nature of learning as process and product: it both preserves and loses, is both preserved and lost. "New" learning continually both preserves and loses "old" learning in the cyclical overturning of it by extension and transformation. When that action occurs radically and rapidly in a world in which the old learning is insufficient to deal with the unfamiliar and unknown, then the new learning may be characterized as apeironic. But that action *does* and *must* both preserve and lose, and so must its associated countercurricular praxis.

This both-and-ness might be considered also in terms of Susan Noakes's idea of "timely" reading. Lore loss can be understood to some extent as a result of a past/present gap inherent in the human condition, a situation synopsized, by my interpretation, in the opening lines of Nemerov's poem "Ultima Ratio Reagan": "The reason we do not learn from history is / Because we are not the people who learned last time."[16] Noakes conceives this situation as one defined by a polar tension between reading a text for its meaning for its author and intended readers *then* and reading it for its meaning for us *now*—activities that she calls, respectively, borrowing from theological hermeneutics, "exegesis" and "interpretation." Following this conception, she argues that the reading of a text (especially, for her, a canonical literary text) as "timeless" is a profoundly problematic activity since "reading must be understood as the constantly transformed product of historical change, not a timeless process focused on timeless texts but rather a 'timely' activity—the most complex encounter with time in which many Westerners consciously engage." Furthermore, even though a then/now gap separates exegesis (typified by "Boccaccio's humanistic quest for the perfectly reconstructed text") and interpretation (typified by "Baudelaire's occasionally exuberant celebration of a kind of reading that knows no rules or boundaries"), the pure version of either, she claims, is "not merely stultifying" but "impossible." That impossibility, well known also in its there/here analogue to translators, arises because each kind of reading "mirrors and depends upon the other," a both-and relationship that she explains as follows:

An exegete is concerned with the text's historical character and position but not with his or her own. Thus, an exegete, although perhaps labeled a "historicist," will in fact try to evade history in the most fundamental way. At moments when the exegete realizes that the total historical reconstruction of a text is impossible, she or he becomes an interpreter. While perhaps continuing to give the text's historicity a passing nod, out of scholarly habit, the interpreter's principal goal will be to identify a relationship between the text and what is contemporary to the interpreter. While not denying that the text has its own historical character, the interpreter is likely to be skeptical about her or his ability to know it, implying that it is not the interpreter who evades history but history that evades the interpreter. At both exegetical and interpretive poles, then, the reader's stance with regard to history is unsteady, serving to impel a restless movement, a kind of oscillation between the two.[17]

Thus, by this hermeneutic movement, which may recall Richard Lanham's oscillatory *Through/At* vision of the text or Albert Rothenberg's janusian ability creatively to juggle conflicting images or concepts, the timely reader shuttles unsteadily but imperatively between, to return to Nemerov, what "the people who learned last time" learned ("from history") and what can be learned ("from history") this time. Both "learnings" are required: each "mirrors and depends upon the other."

Noakes (punningly) concretizes and underlines the importance of timely reading by invoking the figure "of the book as clock":

> The numbers on a clockface are understood by all to be relative: twelve may indicate midnight or noon; it may further indicate midnight or noon on the eighteenth of April or the fourth of July; finally, it may indicate these hours on these dates in 1835 or 1972. It is easy to keep in mind that these numbers are elements in an ongoing process of sign production, and everyone who "reads" a clockface does so. Exactly the same is true of words in a book, and anyone who reads them must read them as but elements in the process of sign production. Yet rarely is this fact about books explicitly recognized. If it were, the broadly cultural consequences of such recognition would be considerable.

Certainly they would be so for education, whether one is speaking of a "book" or some other text, verbal or not. And the "timely" education urged by such re(-)cognition would be very much apeironic since it would involve an expansive updating "entailing loss as well as productivity," a both-and process that Noakes describes as follows:

> the subject seeking to be conscious of its own temporality and of that of the texts it encounters must be always making its continuity in the present, and consciously doing so, while deliberately encountering an ever-widening range of information from the past, information that announces its discontinuity with the present. . . . The range of information that must be encountered must indeed remain "ever-widening" in that as one element of information becomes incorporated into the continuity being made in the present, it loses its character as temporally discrepant from the present; and different ones must be encountered to serve anew the old function, entirely essential to

"timely reading," of recalling to the reader his or her temporal discrepancy from the text.

This difference-sensitive process is fundamental to countercurricular praxis, which not only reads the past in terms of both the past and the present but also reads *them* in terms of the present-becoming-the-future, the "ever-widening range" of information never before encountered by anyone. Such praxis—a matter, among other things, of questioning the canonical from the perspective of the noncanonical (an activity crucial to Noakes's work as a feminist theorist) and curriculum from that of countercurriculum—is inevitably ideologically oriented to some extent and requires "explicit education in the principles of hermeneutics."[18] Not at all as large an order as one might think, that education could well begin when students learn—as they should, even in our digital age—how to read a clockface.

Or an old movie, say one made around 1950 and concerned with World War II, which can be "read" both for what it meant then and for what it means now. Or a current movie, video documentary, or television program, which can be experienced both with suspended disbelief (just watched, through surrender to illusionism, in go-with-the-flow fashion) and with critical consciousness (analyzed in terms of prop design, camera angle, lighting, ideological motivation, and so on). Either case involves an oscillatory both-and movement, each pole of reading impelling a return to the other in a cycle of rereading that continually challenges and unsettles knowledge (even, to extend from these cases, the most intelligent "scientific" knowledge, which not so much judges its past or alternatives as "wrong" as it reciprocally rereads them and [re]builds, by supplementation and supplantation, in relation to them). Without such movement, learning is unipolar, merely "curricular." Countercurricular learning requires both "running *with*" and "running *against*."

This both-and dance of countercurricular praxis involves some delicate balances, especially in a time when its countermoves, with their contradictory and paradoxical bipolar forces, are occurring more frequently and growing stronger. Perhaps no one has helped educators and the public understand those balances more than Peter Elbow, whose book *Embracing Contraries: Explorations in Learning and Teaching* is most relevant here.

Elbow begins his exploration with the conviction, born of his experience as an educator, "that we must *adjust* our picture of what is natural in learning and teaching—of what goes on in the mind: our picture needs to be messier, more complicated, more paradoxical." His discussion of the learning process concerns "how we can coax the mind to transform itself or restructure its own contents through various kinds of interaction between contraries." Restricting himself "to a purely cognitive view of curriculum" (though he very much believes that cognitive and affective learning, however usefully distinguished, are "optimally a single complex process" and mutually reinforcing), he argues that this transforming and restructuring can be greatly promoted by adding "nondisciplinary" courses. Such courses—which, he is careful to note, would "supplement disciplinary courses, not replace them"—are ones "in which a single concrete particular [as distinguished from the unfocused generality of many *inter*disciplinary courses] is seen from the point of view of the widest range of conflicting models, metaphors, hypotheses, conceptual schemes, sets, and disciplines." Countering "the exclusive curricular emphasis on disciplinary structure or high-order generalization," they, along with disciplinary courses designed to encourage "transfer in learning" (not a controversial process for Elbow), would work to develop what he defines as the two principal abilities involved in a student's "real learning," both apeironic, the second pronouncedly so: *"the ability to apply already-learned concepts to the widest range of data"* (behind which "is *the capacity to construct new experience from symbols"*) and *"the ability to construct new concepts"* (which inventional activity "probably goes against the grain of his thinking"), abilities Elbow correlates respectively with "Piaget's two basic processes of assimilation and accommodation: as it were, eating the environment and being eaten by the environment."[19]

Just as students who "learn well" must, by another both-and doubleness, both *"give in* or submit to teachers" and *"resist* or even reject" them, so they must develop both those conceptual abilities, which involve their own kinds of resistance and submission. The second, however, is the special concern of countercurricular praxis; it is Elbow's too, as his elaboration of the striking figure above, following on his disagreement with what he considers to be Paulo Freire's overemphasis on student autonomy, shows:

Countercurriculum(s)

Freire's education-as-cognitive-dissonance is assimilation: the organism brings what is outside into itself on its own terms; it eats the world and digests it and makes the eaten portion of the world take on the shape of the organism; the organism keeps its own shape, identity, autonomy. In contrast, education-as-emulation or participation is Piaget's accommodation: the organism grows by letting its guard down, letting its outlines and identity become fuzzy; it participates in other people or things; allows itself to be swallowed by what is different from the self—to merge or expand into what is different.
As Piaget recognizes, these two aspects of growth are dialectically or developmentally linked.

And these conflicting but linked abilities/educations/processes, which can be very subtly interimplicated (as the chiasmas in the first sentence of my present paragraph illustrates), require instructing that is concomitantly conflictual, complexly tensional, dialectical. Thus countercurricular praxis works beyond just helping students "know something" in order to enable them to discover a perspective for "knowing *about* . . . [their] knowing"—it stresses "meta-knowledge or second-stage learning too." It requires the instructor to develop in him- or herself both "the supportive and nurturant side and the tough, demanding side" and to realize and enact the reciprocal empowerment of contraries productively "somehow blending or merging."[20] A difficult praxis, as Elbow repeatedly admits.

But Elbow offers stimulating, even wise, ideas for such praxis. Particularly helpful, for educators and students alike engaged in inquiry, are those concerning dialectic and those concerning the interplay of belief and doubt. Dialectic, in his use of the term, is most pertinent when "we are trying to know something that is especially hard to check or verify": it entails dealing with "as many *different* and *conflicting* knowings as possible" in order to "try to get a sense of the unknown behind them." This procedure, as Elbow's argument for it makes clear, functions apeironically:

My claim is that many important insights or breakthroughs end up as a movement of thought from one frame of reference—originally taken as the whole frame of reference or the most universal way to conceive the matter—to a larger one. There appears to be a contradiction between the original and the new frame of reference—and/or between the original one and some consequence or branch of the new one. But the original one can finally be understood as a subset of the larger one, a special case that does not contradict it if correctly restricted. If breakthroughs often have this shape, then the following strategies are likely to be fruitful: to watch for potential contradictions in a given system; to heighten them by affirming both sides rather than trying to resolve or eliminate them immediately; to develop in general an attraction for contradiction . . . ; and even to try negating or turning things upside down just to see what new comes to light. The goal is to encourage the growth of new and larger frames of reference out of the interaction of contradictions, but one should remember, nevertheless, not to be in too much of a hurry to get rid of the contradiction and find a new frame of reference.[21]

If one translates "the original and the new frame of reference" into *the curriculum and the countercurriculum,* then the cogency of this line of argument (complete with the admonition to exercise both-and patience) for countercurricular praxis is vivid enough.

Elbow construes belief and doubt, perhaps too easily hyperbolized to naïve credulousness and radical Cartesian skepticism, as profoundly interrelated opposites equally necessary to intelligent learning. "Doubt and the need for certainty reinforce each other" in this construal, and he draws attention to "important etymological links which reflect the psychological links" between the two, by way of the word *critical:* " 'Critical' comes from a word meaning to cut or separate into two parts in order to judge; 'doubt' is cognate with 'two' ('double'—also in German: *zweifel* and *zwei*); and 'critical' is cognate with 'certain.' " He evidences this linkage with somewhat deconstructive analyses of arguments presented as calm, serious, or earnest that betray a "trace" of "anger," "flippancy," or "nonconviction" and by the fact that "a paradoxical principle of extreme rigor" pertains in doubting an interpretation of a text: "you may not reject a reading till you have succeeded in believing it." And, recalling his earlier discussion of Piagetian assimilation and accommodation, he argues persuasively that this linkage builds ontogenetically:

Psychologically or developmentally, we learn to doubt after believing gets us into trouble. Yet doubt and belief seem to alternate dialectically as we grow up. We define ourselves by saying Yes—for example to parents and teachers—but then by saying No, and then back and forth. Babies begin by putting everything in their mouths, but they move on to spitting out or rejecting. There is the period called "the terrible twos" when the tiny person says nothing but No—she seems literally to be flexing a doubting or rejecting muscle. This usually subsides, yet often recurs around age four. And then comes the striking period of adolescent refusal. In short, we relate to the world by merging and incorporating, but also by rejecting and quarreling.

Finally, the educational power of doubt and belief comes through making them "methodological" as, respectively, "the rhetoric of propositions" and "the rhetoric of experience," both of which have apeironic functions: "Putting our understandings into propositional form helps us extricate ourselves and see contradictions better; trying to *experience* our understandings helps us see as someone else sees."[22]

Though belief and doubt, like other contraries with which Elbow deals, may have their own "terrible twos" (so that, for instance, depending on one's point of view, either their "apparent opposition" *or* their *"equivalence"* can be ascribed to a "trick of language") that invite quibbling, he insists, convincingly, on the "phenomenological difference" between them. For him both, each in its own way, respond to the need, emphasized by critical theorists like Freire and Jürgen Habermas, "to learn to criticize or 'problematize' one's own normally-taken-for-granted surroundings"; they thereby serve as "methods for distancing oneself from one's context or achieving metacognition." Thus methodological belief and doubt, like Derridean "declaration" (what a text affirms) and "description" (its questioning of what it affirms) or subjectivity/objectivity and Habermasian intersubjectivity, mirror the relation between curriculum and countercurriculum in apeironic countercurricular praxis. In Elbow's terms, that praxis must involve not just denying a point of view but inhabiting another as well, a conditional "act of imagination or game-playing" or temporary "self-delusion" that can change the way students understand and help them "to see the truth in a point of view which at first they find alien, absurd, or repellent." Its purpose is not just "the opening and restructuring of the mind" but also the cultivation of "the ability to allow one's thinking and perceiving to be restructured" continually. Achieving that purpose requires student and educator alike to break out of the habit of either "naive belief" or "knee-jerk skepticism" and immerse "in the dangerous element" of methodological belief, however provisional, that animates Elbow's dialectic. Finally, well aware that he is riskily "threading a common-sense path between hermeneutical relativism or deconstruction on the one side, and monism or positivism or absolutism on the other" (so that his reader embracing contraries embraces two Elbows as well), Elbow reminds his fellow educators that "they

Apeironic Learning: A New Paideia

fall prey to self-deception with surprising frequency—not because they lack skill in critical thinking, but because they lack the benefit of methodological belief to teach them how to bring critical thinking to bear on their own positions"[23]—that is, how to be *op*positional pedagogues, for counter-curricular praxis must involve oppositional pedagogy in some form.

CHAPTER II

Hermetic Pedagogies

Oppositional pedagogies come in a number of colors—to which rainbow I am contributing. In the broadest sense any pedagogy that counters traditional or conventional theory and practice is oppositional, whether called alternative or radical or, more specifically, contextual, response-based, collaborative, conflictual, and so on. As we have seen, Peter Elbow, Paul Feyerabend, and many others have offered theoretical rationales and practical procedures for such pedagogies. Marked by what Thaïs E. Morgan terms "the heterogeneity of our times," they all nonetheless share the impulse to enact pedagogical "reorientations"—through strategies for both forgetting ("in some sense") and preserving the past, "overlapping" collaboration and conflict, redefining the student as a subject, exploring the possibilities of "the postmodern 'noisy classroom,'" letting "the margins become the center," conceiving "mobility and heterogeneity as a positive opportunity more than as a crisis or a decadence," or even interrogating the idea of pedagogy itself.[1]

Still, however, some insist on more specificity. For instance, Robert Con Davis, noting that " 'oppositional' thought . . . draws from contemporary semiotic, deconstructive, and Marxist theory but also, though less obviously, from a tradition of oppositional 'logic' first theorized by Aristotle as a kind of algorithm of interpretive relations," characterizes "oppositional pedagogy" as exemplary of such thought and defines it as "the attempt by Paulo Freire, Pierre Bourdieu, and many others to theorize but also to initiate radical social change through pedagogy, through what students are taught and how they are taught it." Acknowledging with Louis Althusser and others that education plays the—or at least *a*—paramount role in implementing the ideology of the dominant culture and that therefore oppositional pedagogy is caught in the "dilemma of . . . trying to destroy and reconstitute an activity even while performing it," he nonetheless discerns in the activities of such pedagogy the evolution of "an implicit but powerful manifesto . . . , perhaps the only thorough and consistent critique of educational practices to emerge in the last twenty-five years."[2]

Tracing its origins to "third-world attempts to reject foreign domination in education and radical attempts to rethink the nature of social change in France after the May 1968 student/worker uprisings," Davis outlines the tenets for that manifesto. Derived from many sources, most notably Freire, they emphasize, among other things, the development of *conscientização* instead of the imposition of " 'civics' lessons," "the active participation of students as the oppressed struggling in their own liberation" instead of alienated learning, the exchanging of educator and student roles, and the importance of "ideological resistance" as "a crucial indicator of the direction critique can and should take at any one moment." For Davis, following Graff as he interprets him, "oppositionalism" (lest, I would add, it merely reinforce its own marginality) requires the both-and-ness of "dominant and alternative practices responding to each other in a series of ruptures and resistances," and it "shows that pedagogy does not exist neutrally or ideally. It is not a fixed entity but a social practice and a cultural construct, a dynamic and unfinished (hence impossible to 'fix') activity—an enactment-as-practice of ideology in culture." Thus, even though he attempts to "fix" oppositional pedagogy by a specific definition, he stresses its necessary self-criticizing changefulness, its adumbration of "practices for which we as yet have no models," practices that "gradually take shape as a kind of access to the future—an access to that which is already being 'opposed' even before it can be made known or teachable."[3]

As if in response to Davis's caution, Ronald Strickland argues that there are "at least two currents of recent pedagogical theory which suggest new models of teaching precisely by challenging the traditional assumptions of canonical knowledge and pedagogical authority." And he addresses those currents in terms that invite consideration of the broader enterprise of which they are part:

Psychoanalytic critics have rethought the traditional opposition of "knowledge" and "ignorance," by seeing "ignorance" as an active form of [largely ideological] resistance to knowledge, and by identifying the individual student's resistance to knowledge as analogous to the repression of the unconscious. In a more directly political vein, Marxists and feminists have called for an oppositional pedagogy which can understand the way the concept of knowledge is implicated in the reproduction of the dominant ideology, and which can empower students to resist the neoconservative and corporate-sector demand for an educational system that shapes students to fit the needs of a capitalist and patriarchal society.

Hearing here a mandate for "a radically unconventional orientation for the teacher," he outlines "a strategy of confrontational pedagogy,"[4] one that draws specifically on those two currents of theorizing but suggests principles that are or should be more widely operative.

Strickland's overall strategy, Graffian in its emphasis on exposing the suppressed conflicts between educator and student, involves "theorizing the classroom" (something little done before the 1960s or, intensely, before the 1980s) in order "to acknowledge conflict and to open up the classroom for a productive contestation and interrogation of existing paradigms of knowledge (as opposed to the mere reproduction of knowledge, or the transmission of information as knowledge)." Citing Shoshana Felman's argument that "the single most important contribution of psychoanalysis to education is that psychoanalysis reveals 'the radical impossibility of teaching,'" he considers why teaching, as he interprets Felman's use of the word (in a sense that overlaps with my own), cannot work:

The "teaching" Felman refers to is the conventional notion of teaching as the transmission of existing knowledge from an authoritative, "knowing" teacher to an "ignorant" student who desires to know. What psychoanalysis calls for, instead, is a radical rethinking of the concepts of knowledge and ignorance. Traditional theories of pedagogy implicitly assume the existence of a substantial, fixed, and absolute body of knowledge which can be mastered by the student. But, when knowledge is conceived as an absolute category, teaching can only be indoctrination; there is no discursive space in which new knowledge can be produced.

As Strickland points out, following Felman, the notion of knowledge as such a category has been "exploded" by Jacques Lacan (among, I would add, many others)—with the consequence that its corollary notion of ignorance requires reinterpretation. No longer merely a blankness or emptiness or silence, "ignorance may be seen as the dominant order's term for the suppressed other against which it defines itself," an active "unconscious resistance to the dominant order." And this re(-)cognition of ignorance has powerful pedagogical implications, not the least for the conventional model of remediation:

> The point at which the student's "ignorance" manifests itself, the point at which the student desires to ignore the knowledge proffered by the teacher, is precisely the point at which any real learning has to take place. It is the point at which minds are changed. The difficulty comes in flushing this resistance out and confronting it in the classroom. Students are conditioned, by traditional patterns of pedagogy, as well as by the conventional structures of society, to defer, as "unknowing" subjects, to the teacher as a "subject who is supposed to know," in Lacan's phrase. . . . But insofar as this deferral goes unchallenged, students are not really learning anything new.[5]

That point is, in other words, where an alternative or reverse pedagogy should intervene and challenge the deferral, partly by insisting that the student, in effect, become Lacan's "sujet supposé savoir."

While Strickland offers a number of useful particularized strategies whereby an oppositional and confrontational pedagogy can deal productively with the conflicts that inform resistance in English literary studies, I want to abstract from his discussion recommendations that suggest principles important for countercurricular praxis in virtually any disciplinary area and any culture and at virtually any level. First of all, such pedagogy should problematize "the idealist-humanist conception of consciousness as prelinguistic and of the individual subject as an originator of language rather than an effect of language." It should reveal the curriculum (and the countercurriculum!) as consisting of "constructions . . . rather than distinct and substantial bodies of knowledge, which exist independently of our work as scholars and teachers." The educator should "acknowledge his or her implication in the institutional assumptions and conceptual frames which produce our particular constructions of knowledge," question their "intellectual boundaries," and create "the possibility for alternative knowledges produced in other cultural sites." He or she should encourage students in "strong/symptomatic reading," reading that accounts for their positions as readers and "attends to the symptoms of disorder" in the text and thus "strives for an epistemological break between the reader and the text," creating a "space of rupture" in which "knowledge can be produced, and not merely reproduced." Finally, an oppositional and confrontational pedagogy should work, as Elbow also emphasizes, for a model of the educator as "the interrogating intellectual who could recognize his/her subject position as the product of discursive conflict" and whose role is not merely to transmit information to students but to "challenge them to recognize and rethink their assumptions."[6]

This last recommendation suggests a principle of special importance that involves others suggested above and is essential to apeironic education: the effectiveness of countercurricular praxis depends crucially on a shift of emphasis from the pedagogical model of the teacher as Pygmalion to that of the instructor as Hermes. Let me explain these borrowings from Greek mythology. Pygmalion is the legendary king of Cyprus who fell in love with a statue of a beautiful woman that, according to Ovid's *Metamorphoses,* he sculpted by his own idealizations and that, in response to his prayer for a wife resembling it, Aphrodite brought to life. Hermes is a multiform "mercurial" figure (appropriately so, as we shall see), among other things the messenger of the gods and tutelary of the arts and sciences, an interpreter variously interpreted (*hermeneutics* and related words are associated etymologically with his name) who mediates between the known and the unknown; above all else, perhaps, he is inventional. In terms of this distinction, the pygmalionic teacher strives to reproduce him- or herself (his or her knowledge, tradition, values) in the student, whereas the hermetic instructor strives to enable the student to be independently (self-)productive. The first is a *shaper* of students (traditional pedagogy is shot through with the rhetoric of *forming* students by "feeding" them knowledge) in his or her own image, the second a *shape-shifter* who challenges students constantly to re(-)cognize the images by which they construct (and thereby close or open) their selves/worlds. One can see an example of the first in the mechanomorphic Thomas Gradgrind and of the second, up to a point, in Socrates (or, through all his self-effacing ironies and scant positive doctrine, in the great interrogating educator he sought but never found—or perhaps, to return to recent times, in the less egotistical side of the character John Keating [modeled, *freely,* on Samuel Pickering, a professor of English at the University of Connecticut] in Peter Weir's film *Dead Poets Society*).

Let me further illustrate and elaborate this distinction, especially in order to suggest variously the character of the hermetic instructor, a more complex and less familiar figure than the pygmalionic teacher. Elbow, for instance, rejects the pygmalionic role when he advises himself against coaxing students "to be my mouthpiece" in discussions and advocates the hermetic when he argues that some educational goals must be achieved "with a wise indirection" and that educators should reveal their "doubts, ambivalences, and biases" to their students, admitting they "are still learning, still willing to look at things in new ways, still sometimes uncertain or even stuck, still willing to ask naive questions, still engaged in the interminable process."[7] Thus, unlike the teacher, that epistemological puppeteer whose (pretense of) absence from the immediate drama of knowledge is all too familiar, the hermetic instructor opens (*dis*closes) the process of that drama and thereby, to reapply Barthes's wonderfully apt figure for the semiologist "speaking of signs with signs," resembles "Chinese shadowcasters when they show both their hands and the rabbit, the duck, and the wolf whose silhouettes they simulate."[8] Certainly many of the differences between *professing* and *enabling* mark the distinction with which I am concerned. So do those between, to play with terms from Northrop Frye, the teacher as ἀλαζών (*alazon*) or the redoubtably present *magister gloriosus,* the "imposter" who "imposes" opinions (postures) on students, and the instructor as εἴρων (*eiron*) or the self-deprecating "dissembler" who may well, like Hermes or Kierkegaard's elf, wear a hat that makes him or her become unexpectedly invisible (and silent!) in the shifting perspectives of interpretive negotiation and thus disappear into the students' learning. The former deals in object lessons; the latter, like the fallible but endlessly clever trickster-transformer coyote ubiquitous in Native American mythologies, deals in, to appropriate a phrase from Hugh Munby, "lessons as moving objects."[9]

The pedagogical attitude of the hermetic instructor is diversely suggested by Josué V. Harari and David F. Bell in their discussion of the significance of Hermes in the work of the French polymath Michel Serres. They characterize Hermes in his many roles as, among other things, a "weaver of spaces," a "philosopher of *plural* spaces," a "guide" who "keeps moving; he connects, disconnects, and reconnects the endless variety of spaces he traverses." And their description of Serres and his wide-ranging work on "disorder," a term that includes many of the phenomena and epiphenomena (including, indirectly, learning itself) that engage the postmodern science of chaos explored by James Gleick in his well-known *Chaos: Making a New Science,* intriguingly parallels that characterization: he "think[s] of knowledge not in terms of order and mastery, but in terms of chance and invention"; his discourse, "to measure up to the world of which he speaks," is "multiple," a discourse for which "the simple, the distinct, and the monosemic are no longer acceptable values" and so "are replaced by concepts and logics of fuzziness, complexity, and polyvalence"; querying and (re)constructing that world, in the spirit of Feyerabend but more complexly, through his "anti-method," he "assumes his multiple identities as he works through a myriad of inter(re)ferences."[10] A paradigmatic apeironic educator-learner, Hermes/Serres ceaselessly patchworks together a mosaic of changing isomorphisms to map indeterminacies never dreamt by Laplacean tradition.

For the hermetic instructor the traditional (performance or demonstration of the) authority or mastery of the teacher is just as much in question as the determinacy of knowledge. The new pedagogy, like the psychoanalysis from which it gleans insights, "aims precisely to cancel the special privilege of the masterful subject"; it is, in Davis's words, "a pedagogy for teaching that which cannot be known in advance."[11] Conscious of the repertory by which the "teacher produces the effect of authority," the hermetic instructor enacts an undoing of it that "will resemble what Derrida has called 'double writing,' a simultaneous postulation and displacement of positions"; that is, he or she "must take up the position of authority in order to displace it, and thus to teach the student how to doubt Mastery." By this and other means, he or she enacts, in part, as Gregory S. Jay observes, a *renversement* of the psychoanalytic project: "Where the psychoanalyst seeks to stabilize a shattered self, the pedagogue hopes to unsettle the complacency and conceptual identities of the student. Like psychoanalysis, education can only begin with self-doubt, and its disciplinary self-analyses should be interminable." The independence the student develops through such pedagogy involves not any kind of traditional self-sufficiency and self-possession but the critical-minded-ness of an "(in)determinate subject" engaged in the "production rather than consumption" of knowledge. The pedagogy of that development provides "an opportunity to debate meanings and values, and," Jay argues persuasively, "once students overcome their initial fright the response is usually one of relief and excitement"—especially in the case of American students, "since American pedagogy has largely abandoned critical thought out of its obeisance to vocationalism or its tired allegiance to banalities that bore even the instructors who repeat them." Breaking the pygmalionic cycle, such pedagogy, like psychoanalysis, in a way that recalls Chambers's palimpsestic pedagogy, "at once demystifies the hermeneutic process and puts the *student* into the position of the subject who is supposed to know"[12]—rather than into that of the taught, the "teachee," the passive object of a lesson, the one who is not *respons*ible to/for knowledge. In the most minimum practical terms, breaking that cycle involves educators avoiding repetition in themselves of those who educated them, surrendering compulsive control of classroom discourse, trusting students to contribute more (texts, thoughts, feelings, attention), centering class on what *they* do.

Psychoanalysis, particularly as rewritten by Lacan, himself a Hermes figure, provides many of the insights that inform and vivify recent pedagogical (re)thinking, insights that help define the enterprise of the hermetic instructor. Felman is a key interpreter in that regard. Observing that "for Lacan psychoanalysis is an invention that, in its practice, *teaches people how to think beyond their means,*" she argues that those who construe Freudian analysis as somehow undoing what education establishes—and thus see Freud as an "anti-pedagogue"—fail to understand (by a more, to borrow a term from Alfred Jarry, "pataphysical" logic) "that there is no such thing as an anti-pedagogue: an anti-pedagogue is *the* pedagogue par excellence." Realizing that "human knowledge is, by definition, that which is untotalizable, that which rules out any possibility of totalizing what it knows or of eradicating its own ignorance," the anti-pedagogue, in many ways *the* hermetic instructor par excellence, understands that ignorance "is no longer simply opposed to knowledge: it is itself a radical condition, an integral part of the very structure of knowledge," and "can teach us something, become itself instructive." What does it "teach"? That "teaching . . . is not the transmission of ready-made knowledge. It is rather the creation of a new condition of knowledge, the creation of an original learning disposition," what I would call an apeironic *ganas*. That, "contrary to the traditional pedagogical dynamic, in which the teacher's question is addressed to an answer from the other—from the student—which is totally reflexive, and expected," the knowledge that comes from the student addressed as a Lacanian "Other" is "that which comes as a surprise, that which is constitutively the return of a difference," confirming the indispensability of "the position of alterity" for learning and the "essentially, irreducibly dialogic" nature of knowledge. That, to focus on what Felman regards as "the most radical, perhaps the most far-reaching insight psychoanalysis can give us into pedagogy," the hermetic instructor educates (Elbow has said as much in his own way) by exemplifying the interminability of learning, an exemplification with powerful implications concerning the slippery position of the Lacanian "subject," as she explains:

> The analysand is qualified to be an analyst as of the point at which he understands his own analysis to be inherently unfinished, incomplete, as of the point, that is, at which he settles into his own didactic analysis—or his own analytical apprenticeship—as fundamentally interminable. It is, in other words, as of the moment the student recognizes that *learning has no term,* that he can himself become a teacher, assume the position of teacher. But the position of the teacher is itself the position of the one who learns, of the one who teaches nothing other than the way he learns. The subject of teaching is interminably—a student; the subject of teaching is interminably—a learning.[13]

The classicist William Arrowsmith once told me that a teacher teaches, finally, only who he *is* by virtue of what he learns—an almost quintessential definition of the pygmalionic teacher, in contrast to the hermetic instructor, who, as Felman, drawing on Lacan's notion of style, nicely puts it, "teaches nothing other than the way he learns," a way that, to avoid its own pygmalionism, must proceed in interminable dialogue with other(s') ways. Thus the lesson of "ignorance."

And that dialogue operates by a complex both-and-ness. At its best it involves not just exchange but a janusian simultaneity of voice that reminds one of great acting, in which text and subtext (like plot and subplot or masque and antimasque) are played together, both with and against each other. Its aspects are helpfully explored by G. Douglas Atkins in a generally positive discussion of Felman's ideas, which he qualifies and extends:

> An interesting, if much less sophisticated, parallel to Felman's description of teaching as the creation of a "learning-disposition" occurs in the work of the priest/educator/writer Henri J. M. Nouwen, who believes that "we have paid too much attention to the content of teaching without realizing that the *teaching relationship* is the most important factor in . . . teaching." Though I applaud Father Nouwen's emphasis on "our fundamental human condition . . . as the foundation of all learning in which both students and teachers are involved," I do not want to privilege *either* the "teaching relationship" or "the content," since I believe them to be of equal importance.

Though Atkins agrees with Felman "that the 'teaching relationship' is dialogical," he proposes that "teaching, in its various aspects, involves not just a delicate balance between the (apparently competing) interests and needs of teacher and student but also a particular structure," a reciprocally overturning one saliently countercurricular and hermetic in character:

> I would describe that structure as resembling Wordsworth's resolution, in a fine surmise, of "mutual domination" and "interchangeable supremacy" as occurring between the demands of, and the opportunities presented by, the forces of imagination and nature. In teaching, that structure, which involves an oscillation of power and authority, entails the aggrandizement of neither student nor teacher, content nor form (or style), at the expense of the other. No master-slave relationship here, then. To put it differently: Teaching occurs in and as a play of differences that neither becomes absolute nor collapses into identity.

As Atkins is quick to explain parenthetically, his argument thus "involves the claim that teaching consists of principles and strategies notably similar to those that characterize poststructuralist theory," a project within the general enterprise of "theory," which he defines earlier but quite pertinently here as a matter of not only particular "principles and strategies" of but also the "*practice* of both self-consciousness and self-criticism" that "acts . . . as critique of practice, including its own."[14]

Indeed, theory in various versions (psychoanalytic, poststructuralist, postpositivist, feminist, Marxist, and so on)—for Atkins always inclined "to become metatheory" and yet increasingly applied to the work of preventing "particular theories from evading the question of their own framing"[15] (both by the pressure, powerfully in effect since the demise of foundationalist empiricism, of what I have called elsewhere the "theoristic imperative")[16]—operates for Joan De Jean both to expose the pygmalionic "inability to encourage individuality and refusal to view the student/other as anything but a projection of the teacher and his desires" and to explore the hermetic ability to encourage "the *clinamen*" ("swerve") from such projection "that makes a teacher of the student" and openness to "the moment when a hand will shoot up, signaling a question . . . that introduces an entirely new perspective on the material under consideration."[17] Theory operates for Barbara Johnson to make "the pedagogical moment" not just one in which the student summarily fills in the blank (the silence) with what is supposed to be known but one "that marks the place where what is not known is evoked as the blank that makes the story go on forever," a herme(neu)tic blank that "is precisely what must—and cannot—be taught" and yet "can somehow, nevertheless, be captured."[18] Thus, by such operations, theory apeironically *stories* (in several senses) pedagogy, as Angela S. Moger tells us:

Pedagogy and narrative are coincident in their reliance on the mechanism of desire as a modus operandi. Teaching and telling exist, endure, function, by means of perpetually renewed postponement of fulfillment. If desire comes into being and is sustained as a result of inaccessibility or otherness of the object which one would like, in principle, to tame or consume, can't we rightly contend that narrative operations and didactic operations intersect in their implicit intention to refrain from closing the gap which is the goal of their explicit *pre*tentions? Once the object of desire has been appropriated, it loses its status as desirable. Now, meaning is to narrative as fulfillment is to desire; possession means death. Stories work by going through the motions of imparting information which they only promise but never really deliver. A story is a question to be pursued; if there is no enigma, no space to be traversed, there is no story.

Teaching is another such "optical" illusion; it functions by a similar sleight of hand. The pedagogical stance is a pretext that there is something substantive to be deciphered and appropriated. But wisdom, like love and the story, is not found in nature; it has no empirical status. Like the beloved or the narrative, it exists only in the eye of the beholder; I am a teacher only in the mind of one who thinks I might teach him something he does not know. But since I do not possess the knowledge he desires, to teach is only to continue to generate the desire for wisdom. Pedagogy, like narrative, functions by means of withholding rather than by means of transmission. It works by multiplying the enigmas (obstacles) rather than by eliminating them. Teaching, then, is the subject's telling of the desire for the object rather than the subject's telling of the object.

Such storying tells of a shift in emphasis interimplicated with that from pygmalionic teaching to hermetic instructing: from education whose "immediate goal . . . is the satisfaction of the quest for knowledge" to education whose "fundamental goal is the denial of that satisfaction in favor of the renewal of questing itself," from static "possession" to dynamic "teasing and withholding." [19] Other parallel and interimplicated stories abound.

Counterbalancing Pygmalion's shaping of his creation/student as a dependent woman, damned whether she does or does not assert herself, feminist theory now works tirelessly to articulate oppositional pedagogies that can enable independent learning (for all people, not just women). Moreover, they are distinctly hermetic in conception and style—no surprise when one realizes that Hermes, especially through the alchemists (for whom he was Mercury), is, in yet another aspect of his multiple nature, strongly associated with the "feminine principle." [20] Feminist pedagogies are not new, but the extent of their present increasing influence and sophistication is—a burgeoning that can be traced to, among other places, Adrienne Rich's repeated call in the 1970s for a feminization of education. Recognizing that women, so long culturally marginalized, need a new curriculum, "a reorganization of knowledge, of perspectives and analytical tools that can help us know our foremothers, evaluate our present historical, political, and personal situation, and take ourselves seriously as agents in the creation of a more balanced culture," she recognized also that "a radical reinvention of subject, lines of inquiry, and method will be required." The pedagogical style of "feminist teaching," she argued, would have to be "antihierarchical," and such teaching would work to help women do something quite other than "think like men," long prisoned by their tunnel vision of abstraction and deluded objectivity: it would help women "think like a woman in a man's world," which

means thinking critically, refusing to accept the givens, making connections between facts and ideas which men have left unconnected. It means remembering that every mind resides in a body; remaining accountable to the female bodies in which we live; constantly retesting given hypotheses against lived experience. It means a constant critique of language, for as Wittgenstein (no feminist) observed, "The limits of my language are the limits of my world." And it means that most difficult thing of all: listening and watching in art and literature, in the social sciences, in all the descriptions we are given of the world, for the silences, the absences, the nameless, the unspoken, the en-coded—for there we will find the true knowledge of women. And in breaking those silences, naming our selves, uncovering the hidden, making ourselves present, we begin to define a reality which resonates to *us,* which affirms *our* being, which allows the woman teacher and the woman student alike to take ourselves, and each other, seriously: meaning, to begin taking charge of our lives.[21]

The pedagogies that have developed in the wake of Rich's call are not only theorized as feminist but (as the reader recalling one of this book's epigraphs will note) "Nietzsche-ized," and they are concerned, more and more, to help *all* students "think like a woman in a man's world"—that is, learn seriously in a gender-conscious, critical, oppositional, apeironic way "as agents in the creation of a more balanced culture."

If the development of feminist pedagogies has gone through a phase of repudiating (masculine, phallocentric) tradition (includ-ing more orthodox, patriarchal Freudianism, already discredited somewhat by scientific scrutiny), it certainly has come around to a more both-and, gender-balanced attitude. As Margo Culley and Catherine Portuges observe, "The phrase 'feminist pedagogy' couples the contemporary and the traditional, joining current po-litical movements with a concern for the transmission of knowl-edge more ancient than the Greek word for teaching." Though using "transmission" questionably here, they elsewhere certainly conceive the purpose of feminist pedagogy as not just to transmit but "to reorganize all knowledge." And they see that purpose as very much aligned "with shifts in student concerns and student populations" during the 1960s and 1970s, along with which "came the need to rethink the organization and delivery of 'knowledge,' as traditionally vested in the composition of the academic canon across the disciplines"—all of which "highlighted the need for new ways of teaching." Praising Freire and others for their con-tributions to active "learner-centered education," they nonethe-less argue for more efforts "to bring theories of teaching and learning together with a heightened consciousness of gender," especially in the sciences and in "settings outside formal school-ing" and at the elementary and secondary levels.[22] Advocating the transformative preservation of tradition, they also accord with Frances Maher's argument that "appropriate teaching styles to recover the female experience can also be applied to the education of all people."[23]

The hermetic thrust of such styles and the theory that informs them manifests readily in Maher's pedagogy, which is "collaborative, cooperative, and interactive" and "draws on a rich tradition going back to Paulo Freire, John Dewey, even Socrates, of involving students in constructing and evaluating their own education." It draws most strongly on Freire's pedagogical theory, especially in her critique and eschewal of American education as relying too much on what he calls a "banking" concept of education, whose enactment oppressively enforces passive and silent learning (particularly, for her, in the case of women), and in her advocacy of what he calls a "problem-posing" concept of education, whose enactment liberates students into active and dialogical learning. Thus, instead of a pygmalionic pedagogy by which "the teacher (representing the oppressor) is the sole authority and the 'Subject' [for whom students are the objects] . . . of the learning process," who "chooses the content which the oppressed students passively accept" (that is, who "makes deposits of predetermined information into the empty vaults of the students' minds"), she advocates a hermetic one that, like her research methodology, "aims for the construction of knowledge from multiple perspectives through cooperative problem-solving." And she stresses the importance of such pedagogy and methodology in the social sciences and particularly in the natural sciences, where single (male) interpretive perspectives tend to dominate. For her, "research, teaching and learning all become part of the same educative process," an apeironic one that asks "students not only to answer questions, but to pose them; to become creators and constructors, as well as learners, of knowledge."[24]

Maher's advocacy is echoed in the pedagogies of many other feminists. In *Women's Ways of Knowing*, Mary Field Belenky and her coauthors survey a broad range of research on pedagogical styles and recommend, among other things, more attention to students' "intuitive" ways of knowing that diverge from "so-called objective modes of knowing," encouraging students to move Philomela-like from "silence" to "voice," helping them (as William Perry and others have urged) learn how "the meaning of an event depends on the context in which that event occurs and on the framework that the knower uses to understand that event," less emphasis on an anesthetizing bureaucratic "banking" method of education and more on a "midwife"-like " 'problem-posing' method," and a shift from "traditional separate education" (in which "the student tries to look at the material through the teacher's eyes") to "connected education" (in which he or she "is treated from the start not as subordinate or as object but as 'independent, a subject' ").[25] Radically "experimental feminist discourse," particularly that of Luce Irigaray, suggests extraordinary possibilities for hermetic pedagogy, since, complexly self-subverting as it can be, it "intends," as Robert de Beaugrande argues, "not to block or disable the process of understanding, but to *obvert* it: to swing into view sides and facets that are normally turned away and unseen." Indeed, he views feminism, in its sophisticated grappling with problems of "repression and violence," as paralleling numerous other "models" (not only Marxism in various flavors and deconstruction, which, however co-opted, are, like feminism, "on the 'other' side of our dominant ideology") that can contribute to its "momentum" and, implicitly, to its burgeoning pedagogies:

A physical model might be the quantum theory dealing with concurrent realities ("wave functions") and virtual particles. An astronomical model might be the open, ever-expanding cosmos, most of whose mass is apparently undetectable. A psychological model might be the flipping between figure and ground during the perception of ambiguous images. A geometric model might be the range of non-Euclidian geometries in which strange mutations of space proliferate. An aesthetic model might be the portrayable yet impossible worlds of Escher and Borges.

Such models hold great promise for apeironic education—if we refrain from trying to contain them as merely "unplanned ruptures in our ultimately well-grounded sense of the world"—for "they converge upon creative spaces into which we can be restituted from our common sense's inertia and passion for sameness."[26] They tell us, as does Irigaray, to "turn everything upside down, inside out, back to front."[27] They suggest pedagogies like those of Hélène Cixous and other French feminists that, as Clara Juncker puts it, "reach our students from unexpected angles."[28] Thus they urge us not just to invert, evert, reverse but also, as Sandra Alcosser argues, "to shift the balance this way, that way; to swerve, disrupt, multiply; to renounce the privilege of the single unified voice/self and so to affirm and yes even unequivocally to celebrate not only what we know already of difference but all that it is not yet possible to know."[29]

With the development and diversification of feminist and other new pedagogies has come—and will continue to come—inevitable re(-)cognitions and revisions of the hermetic role. Thus, for instance, Noakes proposes that the currently evolving feminist hermeneutics, "the result of efforts to challenge the androcentric foundations of traditional hermeneutics, might well be called 'iristics' "—after Iris, the messenger of the gods (particularly Hera) in Homer's *Iliad* (who was soon to be eclipsed, in the *Odyssey,* by Hermes) and prior to that, it is thought, a personification of the rainbow. Associated with that "infinite variety of colors," Iris suggests, for Noakes, an exegetic and interpretive "variety as an analytical starting point rather than an afterthought"[30] and, for me, the cognate possibility of a radically multiperspectival pedagogy enacted by an *iristic* instructor.

And Iris as a rewritten feminist Hermes has an African-American counterpart: Esu-Elegbara, "the divine trickster figure of Yoruba mythology," who appears in numerous avatars in various black cultures in Africa, the Caribbean, and South America and whose "most direct Western kinsman," according to Henry Louis Gates, Jr., "is Hermes." Defined as "the text's interpreter *(Onitumo),* 'the one who translates, who explains, or "who loosens knowledge," ' " this fascinating figure "recurs throughout black oral narrative traditions" in, among other situations, "a primal scene of instruction for the act of interpretation." Mythologically the original instructor-interpreter, Esu, playing many roles analogous to those of Hermes, mediates opposites in both-and janusian fashion and instantiates qualities of or associations with the hermetic instructor, with a (black) difference: as the originator of African "close reading," he "is the Yoruba figure of indeterminacy itself, *ayese ayewi,* or *ailemo,* literally 'that which we cannot know' "; he "rules the process of disclosure, a process that is never-ending, that is dominated by multiplicity"; above all, for Gates, Esu, in his "depictions in sculpture as possessing two mouths," epitomizes "Signifyin(g)," the black rhetorical gesture of Bakhtinian double-voicing, repeating with a difference. Signifyin(g), with its *g* in parentheses to indicate that the word is dialectally pronounced without it, differs from conventional (white) signification, which "depends for order and coherence on the exclusion of unconscious associations which any given word yields at any given time," in that Signifyin(g) "luxuriates in the inclusion of the free play of these associative rhetorical and semantic relations." Palimpsestic, Lacan's "Other of discourse," it constitutes "the black trope of tropes" and works by pastiche, parody, "riffing upon tropes," "rewriting the received textual tradition" to revise the given or same into the new or different. Serving "to create a space for the revising text,"[31] Signifyin(g) might be considered (though Gates is no more than I any kind of essentialist— that is, one who believes, for instance, that only black people can understand or do black things) *the* characteristic move of the (black) hermetic instructor, in contrast to the (white) pygmalionic teacher, who only signifies. (Still, each kind of move, like a jazz composition and the old standard on which it is based, depends on the other—for, by this analogy, material for improvisation and the possibility of continuation through transformation, respectively.) And, of course, Signifyin(g) can Signify itself and thus contribute to the further revision of the hermetic role.

Thus contemporary pedagogical revision is, in many respects, a mode of Signifyin(g), whatever theorized pedagogies one has in mind—feminist, black, postmodernist, poststructuralist, postpositivist, Marxist, and so on. And thus the antipedagogue is a (floating) Signifier, a role that Serres surely instantiates, though without an explicit pedagogy. Much the same might be said of the late Michel Foucault, in whose philosophical work—especially *The Order of Things; The Archaeology of Knowledge; The Discourse on Language; Language, Counter-Memory, Practice;* and *Power/ Knowledge*—one can find abundant thought pertinent to hermetic pedagogy.[32] While a full survey of that work is not possible here, highlighting some of its features, with the help of Karlis Racevskis and Uta Liebmann Schaub, should demonstrate that pertinence and suggest both the usefulness and the limitations of Foucauldian strategies, many already widely practiced, in regard to apeironic education.

Approaching him in part by way of Lacan, Racevskis argues that Foucault "grounds his writing not in the claim of an Imaginary, authorial creation, but in the awareness of the Symbolic— the silent void against which we are able to constitute our meanings"—that is, to define the Imaginary and the Symbolic somewhat simply, not in "an awareness of the Same" but in "that of the

Other," not in "the realm of conscious certitude" but in "that of intersubjective relations." Thus the tentativeness of Foucault's difficult writing mirrors and illustrates his attempt to break out of consciousness "dominated by the Imaginary mode," which is constituted "at an early stage of infancy, during a period that Lacan calls the mirror-phase, when the child acquires an identity by seeing himself reflected in the perception of others," and which "tends to be rigid, finite, and fixed in precise patterns that form stereotypes of thought," and to engage "the Symbolic dimension [that] both reveals and bridges the gap that separates our consciousness from the world." In that more fluid, contingent dimension, with its relativities and reversibilities, he, like the hermetic instructor, "sees himself dispersed by a field of signifiers," at play in a multitude of relations and exchanges in which "our very humanity is not so much an ontological given as an epistemological construct." His purpose—very much a pedagogical one, it seems to me—"is to direct our thinking away from the internal 'meaning' of a discourse to its external conditions of possibility." So his study of economics, art, psychiatry, whatever in his polymathic range, is "archaeological" (in this special sense) rather than historical, interpretively seeking not (referential) content but what, prior to it, configures it.[33]

The strategies of Foucauldian archaeology may be codified in various ways that suggest their resemblance to and/or usefulness as strategies of Signifyin(g), hermetic pedagogy, apeironic education. They involve "a movement away from the Imaginary and toward the Symbolic." They "undermine all those approaches and methods that have been valued by a cultural tradition and are set in secure and seemingly natural patterns of thought." They provide "a perspective that inverts accepted hierarchies and sequences." They expose the "self-delusion" of much Western thought. They work through "paradox" rather than *"doxa"* (received opinion, conventional thinking), even that of Marxism, which Foucault inverts by examining social processes not " 'from the top' as it were, by positing sovereign principles such as 'history' or 'class,' " but "from below, by examining the micro-mechanisms of power." Though they "retain certain elements of the traditional approaches," they apply them limitedly, caricature them, fragment and localize them. They make a game of knowledge that can break out of its own rules. Contrary to accusations of nihilism, they constitute "an affirmative and committed approach to human affairs." And through all the substitutions by which these strategies operate to, as Racevskis argues, replace "the Imaginary with the Symbolic" ("meaning with event, reason with unreason"), they do not accomplish any simple supersession, since, as I stressed earlier in regard to most of the aspects of the shift I have charted, the substitution of the second term for the first does not function to get rid of it but, without forgetting it, to make possible through this homospatial process "a new conceptualization." For Racevskis, again relying on Lacanian terminology, that means "a perspective on a third component—the Real, that is, the reality of the subject as it is constituted at the conjunction of the Imaginary and the Symbolic."[34]

The effectiveness of these strategies depends crucially on a special awareness, according to Racevskis: "an awareness of the Symbolic, of all that conditions and predisposes our ways of knowing and speaking," "an awareness of the need to think genealogically, that is, relentlessly to reexamine our historical antecedents, to review the story of all that has brought us to our present modes of conceptualization." Furthermore, the "genealogical vocation" enabled by such awareness requires "a pedagogical process," and Foucault's is characteristically paradoxical and hermetic: "it makes the intellect into an attribute of the common man, it supports what he has called the 'struggles against the privileges of knowledge,' but by its own example, it shows this critique to be effective only when involved in the rigorous and demanding life of the disciplines of knowledge, only when it realizes itself as a 'relentless erudition.'"[35]

In a passage in his book *This Is Not a Pipe,* Foucault, much given to laughter at the surprise of the otherwise, narrates a classroom scene, as it were, that dramatizes or performs (all language being, finally, performative) the onset of such a process, the transformation of a conventional pedagogical situation into one involving "relentless erudition" (from Latin *eruditio,* both "learning" and "instruction," whose more literal meaning of a state of being "freed from roughness" is less apt here), its opening into the apeironic. It dramatizes as well the difficult excitement of the transition from pygmalionic teacher to hermetic instructor. The scene concerns a well-known surrealist painting, "Magritte's second version of *This Is Not a Pipe*" (the 1966 version, known also as *Les Deux mystères*), though I would argue that, in its general purport, it could concern virtually any pedagogical "object" (a scientific theory, historical account, literary interpretation, legal opinion):

> In placing the drawing of the pipe and the statement serving as its legend [in French, "Ceci n'est pas une pipe"] on the very clearly defined surface of a picture (insofar as it is a painting, the letters are but the images of letters; insofar as it is a blackboard, the figure is only the didactic continuation of a discourse), in placing the picture on a thick, solid wood tripod, Magritte does everything necessary to reconstruct (either by the permanence of a work of art or else by the truth of an object lesson) the space common to language and the image.
>
> Everything is solidly anchored within a pedagogic space. A painting "shows" a drawing that "shows" the form of a pipe; a text written by a zealous instructor "shows" that a pipe is really what is meant. We do not see the teacher's pointer, but it rules throughout—precisely like his voice, in the act of articulating very clearly, "This is a pipe." From painting to image, from image to text, from text to voice, a sort of imaginary pointer indicates, shows, fixes, locates, imposes a system of references, tries to stabilize a unique space. But why have we introduced the teacher's voice? Because scarcely has he stated, "This is a pipe," before he must correct himself and stutter, "This is not a pipe, but a drawing of a pipe," "This is not a pipe but a sentence saying that this is not a pipe," "The sentence 'this is not a pipe' is not a pipe," "In the sentence 'this is not a pipe,' *this* is not a pipe: the painting, written sentence, drawing of a pipe—all this is not a pipe."
>
> Negations multiply themselves, the voice is confused and choked. The baffled master lowers his extended pointer, turns his back to the board, regards the uproarious students, and does not realize that they laugh so loudly because above the blackboard and his stammered denials, a vapor has just risen, little by little taking shape and now creating, precisely and without doubt, a pipe. "A pipe, a pipe," cry the students, stamping away while the teacher, his voice sinking ever lower, murmurs always with the same obstinacy though no one is listening, "And yet it is not a pipe." He is not mistaken; because the pipe floating so obviously overhead (like the object the blackboard drawing refers to, and in whose name the text can justifiably say that the drawing is truly not a pipe) is itself merely a drawing. It is *not* a pipe. No more on the board than above it, the drawing of the pipe and the text presumed to name it find nowhere to meet and be superimposed, as the calligrapher so presumptiously had attempted to bring about.
>
> So, on its beveled and clearly rickety mounts, the easel has but to tilt, the frame to loosen, the painting to tumble down, the words to be scattered. The "pipe" can "break": The common place [*sic*]—the banal work of art or everyday lesson—has disappeared.

Numerous transitions occur in the Foucauldian unfolding of this scene: aesthetically, from a painting instantiating a "resemblance [that] serves representation" to a "similitude [that] serves repetition" and that plays against the former, obedient to "no hierarchy" of "primary reference" and propagating "from small differences among small differences"[36] (or, more hyperbolically, from a theme to "variations set free from a theme"); hermeneutically, from Foucault's "death of interpretation" (which involves the belief "that there are signs, signs that exist primally, originally, really, as coherent, pertinent, and systematic marks") to the "life of interpretation" (which involves the belief "that there are only interpretations");[37] in Lacanian terms, from the Imaginary to the Symbolic; pedagogically, not just from the pygmalionic to the hermetic but from the curricular to the countercurricular.[38] Indeed, rereading several times this story of the ob(li)vious exploding into bafflement and a text into subtexts (through which the self-subverting pedagogue both learns and instructs more than he knows), of presence and absence interplaying, of the certain becoming as fractalized as the play of caustics in moving water, of the Bakhtinian carnivalesque irrupting into a staid "pedagogic space" (a postmodern version of Sissy Jupe's world invading Gradgrind's), the reader may find in it almost a synopsis of my appendicized chart—remembering, however, that Foucault narrates, as I said earlier, only on "onset": still to come is what the instructor *and* the students can do to discover or invent what "all this [that] is not a pipe" otherwise *is,* a "ghost chapter," as Umberto Eco calls it, that the reader may write.[39]

The instructor, in any case, *must* enable the students to go on. Hermetic pedagogy certainly (negatively) critiques the positive *re*productive thrust (of the Imaginary) enacted by pygmalionic pedagogy, but it also enacts a positive *productive* thrust of its own. In the case of Foucault, frequently misconceived as a nihilist, that thrust is quite subtle at times, though Racevskis argues well for its efficacy. It takes getting used to, but it can be enacted, in some appropriate form, at any educational level, in any learning situation, even if only as a subtext of critique to be desedimented and discussed (as Elbow says, all doubt depends on belief of some kind). Uta Liebmann Schaub identifies that subtext in the work of Foucault, "the man and the teacher," as an "Oriental" one, "a counterdiscourse that appropriates Oriental lore in opposition to Western strategies of control" and thus invokes "an image of the other of Occidental thinking." Rejecting much of traditional Western rationalist thought and its "delusive discourses," it nonetheless (or because of that) works, like Buddhism, to "think of coexisting opposites": its *transgression* of traditional limits involves an *affirmation* of limitlessness (the apeironic). The positive thrust of Foucault's subtext is toward "a new way of thinking," a new "language of the future" that "will operate in paradoxes." Such language, Schaub argues, "has the same goal as does the practice of Zen, where meditation on a seemingly meaningless koan is supposed eventually to precipitate the disciple's shock of enlightenment. 'Perversity' becomes purposeful pedagogy," with the further intent of "leading from shock to transformation."[40]

Elaborating this subtext through various versions during his career, Foucault "has walked a narrow line between play and purpose, between pure sophistry and the praxis of Oriental schools such as Zen." His subtext, as Schaub construes it, is not the only way for the instructor to help students go beyond negative critique to positive transformation through apeironic "shock," but it does exemplify, in progressing somewhat by Lanham's dialectic of playfulness/earnestness, the "unsettling style" of the pedagogical trickster, in whose work "the question of seriousness . . . must concern not the seriousness of meaning but the seriousness of praxis." For Foucault that praxis is finally a critique of all Western civilization, one whose exposures indicate that "this civilization needs to recognize and produce its positive counterimage." Given what he has accomplished in that regard, Schaub is reluctant to fault him for his tendency "to stop at criticism and to refrain from describing that counterimage [beyond his subtext] and the means of realizing it." But I am not quite so generous, for I believe that the hermetic instructor has the responsibility of recognizing and producing that counterimage, of describing it and the means of realizing it—not alone but dialogically along with students sufficiently enabled and engaged by his or her discourse to contribute meaningfully to that work. Whatever merit may obtain in a "concealed pedagogy"—and hermetic instructing can be discomfitingly trick(sterl)y—Foucault's should be taken as a limit case. As Schaub concludes, "his enterprise can be called emancipatory" in that "he has not left behind prescriptions of how to proceed, or methods to apply, or a theory to stand on,"[41] but that result, in spite of what may be gleaned by struggling with his subtext, is, if left naked, perhaps too negatively apeironic to be generally useful in education. Nonetheless, I would value its open challenge to the creativity of almost any student far more than the result advocated by Hirsch and his ilk.

A less "concealed" hermetic pedagogy has been explored by Gregory L. Ulmer, whose proposals for revisionary praxis in his *Applied Grammatology* not only illustrate the positive thrust of well-conceived instructing but suggest its possibilities for the further (ultra-Ulmer) development of apeironic education. He is interested in tentatively elaborating an eclectic educational rationale that, punning in French, he terms " 'post(e)-pedagogical,' in order to indicate that it is both a move beyond conventional pedagogy and a pedagogy for an era of electronic media (with *poste* meaning in this context television station or set)." More specifically, he is interested in the possibility of "a grammatological pedagogy," but he ranges well beyond the work of Derrida (who, through his formative participation in GREPH [the Groupe de recherches sur l'enseignement philosophique, which, starting in 1974, advocated radical philosophical education at all grade levels in France] and otherwise, is surely the most pedagogically oriented of all contemporary philosophers) in opening "the question of the nature of the educational presentation (the manner of transmission of ideas) adequate to a poststructuralist epistemology."[42] Ulmer's treatment of that question is intricate and lengthy, but extracting some of his emphases, even at the cost of neglecting important and polemical details, will prove quite worthwhile, particularly in underscoring and transcribing previous emphases of my own.

Ulmer makes clear in his preface the positive thrust of his pedagogy, for he is intent on "replacing 'deconstruction' with 'grammatology' as the principal name for Derrida's program." By that replacement he wishes "not to impose a binary opposition on Derrida's thinking, but to reread his *oeuvre* from a perspective that turns away from an exclusive concern with deconstruction," a word with which Derrida himself has long been uncomfortable. Ulmer puts forward grammatology, which Derrida regards as the more " 'affirmative' . . . dimension" of his work, as "a more inclusive notion, embracing both deconstruction and 'writing' (understood not only in the special sense of textualist *écriture,* but also in the sense of a compositional practice)"—that is, writing as both Derrida's protowriting, the fundamental dynamic of *différance* (both "difference" and "deferral") that constitutes human consciousness, and as the kind of playful creative activity exemplified by Derrida when he deals with "literary or artistic texts (which he mimes) . . . as generative forms for the production of another text." By this *renversement,* as it were, of Derrida, Ulmer seeks to go beyond the analysis of the problems (inconsistencies, ironies, and so on) occasioned by what a text suppresses and "to construct a fully operational mode of thought on the basis of the excluded elements (in the way that the non-Euclideans built consistent geometries that defied and contradicted the accepted axioms)." He sees this project, his "applied phase of grammatology," as analogous to Derrida's writing as "scripting," a research process more "dramatic" than the "conceptual" one of "the printed book": it is "the pedagogical equivalent of this scripting beyond the book, adequate to an era of interdisciplines, intermedia, electronic apparatus." Choosing that rather than deconstruction (and its pedagogy) involves for him a distinctly apeironic shift of paradigms, "a move that, as Thomas Kuhn pointed out, does not solve the old problems but exchanges for them an entirely new set of problems"—a challenging situation "making this a particularly happy time to be a pedagogue."[43]

Still, sobering realizations must accompany thinking about this shift. As in the case of deconstructive pedagogy too, the "introduction of heterogeneous forces into the 'teaching body' in order to deform and transform it," however undertaken, entails "the risk that such forces might be reappropriated or be unreceivable"—largely because of "the generally conservative nature of the educational institution." And well-entrenched attitudes maintain a split between the scientific-dialectical and literary-rhetorical modes of knowing and presenting knowledge that grammatological pedagogy violates by its radical interdisciplinarity. Also, it is one thing to admit, as surely even the most idealistic pygmalionic teacher would, that "every pedagogical exposition, just like every reading, adds something to what it transmits" but quite another, given institutionalized conservatism, to make what is added ("the supplement") the privileged educational concern—that is, to enact "a pedagogy committed to change rather than to reproduction." Such realizations variously story a "lag between inquiry and presentation . . . which a new pedagogy must confront," a problem that concerns Serres, in Ulmer's phrasing, "as the disparity between a recent epistemology (which is thoroughly interdisciplinary, based on the free exchange of concepts across all fields of knowledge) and an older pedagogy (which is highly specialized)."[44] In other words, the challenge of the shift is to cross a formidable gap.

But the happiness that Ulmer finds in that challenge inheres in the opportunity it affords "to help pedagogy negotiate the same paradigm shift that altered the arts and sciences at the beginning of our century, leaving pedagogy behind in the age of Hegel," which age he so names because of Hegel's interest in what Ulmer terms "the problem of pedagogy in general," the essentially pygmalionic problem "of a communication between a teacher (the one who is supposed to know) and a student (the one who thinks he is supposed to learn what the teacher knows)." In response to that challenge and opportunity, Ulmer proposes "transmission that is itself invention." Observing that "teaching in the age of Hegel . . . has a retrospective, rather than a prospective, function" (that of faithfully transmitting tradition), he advocates *the classroom as a place of invention rather than of reproduction.*" With that advocacy comes the necessity of breaking away from the Hegelian role of the teacher as an authoritative model, "a concrete embodiment of the ideal self with which the students must identify (from Socrates to Freud and beyond, transference is an important element in the pedagogic effect)," and of defining the role of the instructor, by my conception, as more like that of a semitransparent, multifaceted mirror that reflects for the student (thus, to borrow M. H. Abrams's categories, more lamp than mirror) the myriad aspects of his or her interminable process of self-development while adding to it (a role, I would argue, especially critical in elementary education). But the new role involves more than that. Since, as Ulmer notes, echoing Derrida, "the ideal of an educated person held by a given era . . . is always predicated on the basis of a theory of truth," that role must be defined further in relation to a question both vexing and exciting: "What might be the ideal of an educated person proposed by a poststructuralism that puts in question the very notion of truth . . .?"[45]

Applied Grammatology in all its detail might well be read as nothing else than an exploration of that question (and questions that follow from it), an exploration to which I cannot hope to do justice here, but Ulmer's somewhat indirect response can be inventoried (with apologies) fairly succinctly. He is surely insistent that Hegelian pedagogy (with its associated notions of curriculum and educator role) can*not* define or promote that "ideal." Grammatological pedagogy, on the other hand, at least tries to— by shifting "away from the exclusive domination of mind . . . to a mode that includes the body (desire and the will to knowledge)"; by encouraging the teacher "indoctrinated to believe he can only repeat a message" to "produce one himself"; by moving from a (Hegelian) concern with "the universal" to a concern with "the singular and the anomalous"; by discouraging a "discipleship" model of education (with its oedipal logic of authoritarian epistemological reproduction) in favor of a model for a more "thoughtful relationship to knowledge," even a "paradoxical pedagogy" of the kind put forward by Bernard Pautrat, another member of GREPH, that "attempts to teach the 'unteachable *relation* to truth' "; by acknowledging that "the most significant aspect of pedagogic communication is finally not the message but the 'medium,' understood in the largest sense as the scene of teaching"; by ensuring that, if "the classroom is inevitably a theater" (as Pierre Bourdieu and Jean-Claude Passeron contend), it be "an avant-garde theater" that functions "to erase the stage and transform the neutrality and distance separating actor and audience, master and pupil"; by not excluding "truth" but by putting it "in its place, inscribed in a more general system whose principle is the quotation mark," and effecting *"a displacement of educational transmissions from the domain of truth to that of invention "*; by returning to "the old tradition" of the pedagogy of *memoria* but by transferring "some of its principles into a new dimension" (that of *inventio,* which Ulmer conceives not as a making-out-of-nothing activity but, following Serres, as an *ars interveniendi,* an activity of intervention, interference, translation), so that mimesis is realized, through one of Ulmer's endless puns, "not as copy but as *copia*—the love of abundance (*apeiron*) which characterized the Renaissance"; by recognizing "knowledge . . . not as a representation of something else but as itself a mode of action in the cultural world" and its "organization and classification . . . [as] *interested* activities"; by "reversing the usual order and direction of knowledge gathering," so that, following Derrida, the vector of relation is not from the unknown to the known but from the known to the unknown.[46]

Thus the grammatological pedagogue—and Ulmer in his own

praxis—uses all manner of (what I am tempted to call "encyclo-pedagogical") strategies, models, multimedia materials, unpre-dictable assignments—a boundless array of hermetic *bricolage*—in engaging students in their development as poststructuralist "educated persons." How, then, would I summarize his ideal of such a person? Toward that end, let me quote a passage from Gerald Holton's *Thematic Origins of Scientific Thought,* which Ulmer also quotes, that concerns two distinct aspects of "science":

> One is the private aspect, science-in-the-making, the speculative, perhaps largely nonverbal activity, carried on without self-consciously examined methods, with its own motivations, its own vocabulary, and its own modes of progress. The other is the public aspect, science-as-an-institution, the inher-ited world of clarified, codified, refined concepts that have passed through a process of scrutiny and have become part of a discipline that can be taught, no longer showing more than some traces of the individual struggle by which it had been originally achieved.[47]

Ulmer finds in this distinction a summatory analogue: "Gram-matology is committed to a pedagogy that will shift its focus from the latter to the former aspect of science—that will collapse disci-pline into invention." Insofar as he demonstrates that his applica-tion of grammatology, his post(e)-pedagogy, "is not simply a utopian ideal"[48]—and he does, persuasively, at least for the postsecond-ary level—he strives through his pedagogy to exemplify and to realize in his students a cogent ideal of the educated person as one who knows how to do "science-in-the-making." Though I might quibble at least with Holton's dismissal of "self-consciously ex-amined methods," he suggests—if I may generalize his distinction and tinker with the ideal I attribute to Ulmer—an ideal of the apeironically educated person that virtually any version of her-metic pedagogy could endorse and continue to rethink: he or she is a person who both critically knows "knowledge-as-an-institu-tion" and, more important, creatively, playfully engages "knowl-edge-in-the-making."

That "playfully" is crucial. As Ulmer observes elsewhere, draw-ing on Jaeger, the Greek word for play (παιδιά, *paidia*) relates closely to *paideia,* both once referring to activities of the child (παῖς, *pais*). (And, I should note, there are additional similar etymological connections whose kind not only Ulmer but Jules Henry and many others would like to see revitalized: the word *school* derives from the Greek word for "leisure," σχολή, *skhole;* the Latin word *ludus* means both "play" and "school"; and so on.) Plato and Aristotle found the connection appropriate enough, but each strove to sublate *paidia* into *paideia* for the purposes of higher learning (dialectic, which is monologically resolvable in Socratic but not in apeironic learning). It is almost as if one can hear, in the middle of all the dialogical fun of learning, the historical *Yeah, but seriously, folks,* . . . just before the teacher's dry dominance begins, so that by the time of the height of the Roman Empire even elementary school, the *ludus litterarius,* had undergone sublation and was hardly fun. That sublation, which has counterparts in cultures throughout the world, has resulted, through historical repetition and intensification, in the profound repression of the play element in learning, the *paidia* in *paideia,* in favor of an oppressive, frequently insincere earnestness that, at its worst, leads to exactly the kind of consciousness-razing educational havoc documented by Elkind in *The Hurried Child.* Ulmer, following Derrida, desediments that sublation to "expose" it and develops pedagogical strategies to undo it and let *paidia* supplement *paideia,* thereby opening the possibility of an "amateurization" of civilization, a world of pleasureful learning (one, I would add, following Hans-Georg Gadamer, not of *the* play, which is already rigidly structured, but of play as ongoing creativity). Thus Ulmer would "deconstruct the work/play, serious/frivolous opposition" and, somewhat like Lanham, bring it into a more productive balance—particularly, for him, in the humanities—through a pedagogy, thoroughly hermetic in spirit, that carnivalizes education (that is, I would add, makes it subversively festive and, following Bakhtin's sense of the word, dehierarchizes and creatively interanimates its voices, turns "dialectics" into "dialogic," "earnest" learning into Nietzsche's *gaya scienza*). Such pedagogy "is a response to the electronic paradigm, whose chief characteristic, with respect to education, is information overload, or knowledge explosion," with which it enables students to deal by encouraging them to see that "the inner 'mystery' of any discipline is not its order or coherence but is its disorder, incoherence, and arbitrariness" and by letting them "confront . . . the provisional, permeable character of all knowledge, the creative 'ground' (*apeiron*) of the formation of a discipline"—and thereby develop an affirmative ease with contradiction, paradox, irony. I agree with Ulmer that such pedagogy is not a utopian dream—indeed, it is a necessity in the postmodern age—but I continue to ponder and ask the reader to continue to ponder his most (self-)critical reflection on his project: "The problem with this pedagogy, however, may be identified by one of Nietzsche's queries: Who will teach the teachers?"[49]

The question haunts. Ulmer suggests, with disarming humility, that he does not address it adequately. Doubtless I too do not. And yet, insofar as educators should be students and students (self-)educators (and thus pedagogy already metapedagogy, pedagogy about pedagogy), perhaps both of us—and many others—do. Especially if the reader is a "teacher of teachers" who is *ready* to read (and write!) the text(s) of a new education. Ready to understand—and educate by such understanding—that, as Barthes puts it, "today our world is a global village. It's a profuse world. . . . The world is too surprising, its unexpectedness is so excessive that it goes beyond the codes of popular wisdom."[50] Ready to resist "the human obsession"—which Gustave Flaubert satirizes in *Bouvard and Pécuchet,* his narrative study of "received ideas" and the hebetude that supports them—"with 'wanting to conclude' . . . in areas where truth is subject to constant revision and restatement, or is simply unverifiable."[51] Ready, again as Barthes puts it, to "teach not skepticism but doubt bolstered by *jouissance*" and, "shaking up truth" like Nietzsche, thus "to make difference shimmer, that plural in the Nietzschean sense, without ever letting it decline into simple liberalism."[52] Ready to practice the contingencies of (Barthes again) "a *floating* (the very form of the signifier),"[53] so that, in Vincent B. Leitch's phrasing, the "whole pedagogical project goes in the direction of deracination and desedimentation, on one hand, and pleasure and play, on the other."[54] And yet, to recall Moger, ready to say to his or her students what Pygmalion cannot say, what Socrates says to Alcibiades as "the only way to assure that he might eventually proceed toward self-knowledge,"[55] what Barthes says "silently to who is no longer or is not yet the other: *I keep myself from loving you.*"[56] Ready to risk the wild side of education.

CONCLUSION

Changing All Those Changes

Risking the wild side of education requires preeminently an attitudinal shift in emphasis—alas, Deweyan but with a difference—
with which I have been concerned all along: from "education as a
function of society" to "society as a function of education."[1] A
dangerous business in any case, appalling to some, surely difficult
to enact, susceptible to co-optation and ironies (of blame and otherwise). But mild-side education has proven inadequate, one way
or another, for practically everyone, neoconservatives and Marxists alike. As Coombs argues persuasively, the world crisis in education, which is "a *continuing* crisis," is occasioned and maintained by many disparities, all of which may be seen as features of
a general disparity between educational systems and their environments. And he proposes several shifts of emphasis to overcome that disparity: from "schooling" to *"learning,"* from "insti-
tution-bound, age-bound" education to "education as a *lifelong*
process," from formal education to various kinds of informal and
"nonformal" (organized but outside-the-usual-system) education,
from "one-shot" innovations to innovation "as a continuing process," from the formal educational system to "a nationwide 'learning network'" that would be "broad and flexible" enough "to
accommodate . . . the highly diverse and constantly growing and
changing learning needs and interests of all members of the population, from their earliest infancy to their old age." Coombs repu-
diates any assertion that education, however changed, "is a cure-
all for the world's ills,"[2] but I would claim that education globally
must, through shifts of the kind he proposes and others as well,

252

not only match its environment better but play *the* principal role in helping people shape it—indeed, *save* it. What else should? What else will?

Such privileging of education over society, as it were, requires their mutual restructuring—in such ways and to such extents that the prospect of the whole undertaking could easily daunt us to despair. But sooner or later—and I hope sooner—we must realize that *we have no alternative* if we want the human experiment to survive and flourish. And the education thus privileged cannot be the same old stuff: it will be an education that is critical (for we are dealing with an ongoing *crisis*), self-conscious, revisional, creatively open to the different and unknown. Which is not to say that the traditional/past/known of any culture should be forgotten or abandoned—an undesirable and, really, impossible goal—but that it should be reread, reframed (even, when it comes to that, in derisive quotation marks), and reinvented in relation to the non-traditional/present/unknown. The critic Geoffrey H. Hartman, a hermetic instructor if ever there was one and for some a practitioner of what Christopher Norris calls "deconstruction 'on the wild side,' "[3] offers a version of the distinction involved here when he speaks of "the difference in talmudic writings between *haggada* (story, troping, free elaboration) and *hallaka* (law, the truth of the letter, the unmodifiable character of ritual)." The two may be opposed, but, as Hartman knows, each depends on the other: there is no vital, practicable tradition, whose power is not to dominate by mortmain but to animate forward, without (further) interpretive development of what has come before. One must "incorporate *and* revise" (my emphasis).[4] Though I have little sympathy for neoconservative nostalgia, I fear the destitution of any society stripped of its cultural ancestors and believe that education should preserve them *transformatively* into the future. But there is no simply going back to them. Newton's laws still apply in the post-Einsteinian world, but only in terms of a continuously changing understanding of their limits and conditions, their supplementation (and eventually, perhaps, supplantation) by other "laws." Likewise, mutatis mutandis, Euclid's geometry, Muhammad's ethics, Montezuma's architecture, Shakespeare's wisdom, Kōrin's aesthetics.

Significant learning is less and less a matter of accepting (peremptory) "truth," more and more a matter of contesting it, of

discovering what else or otherwise is "true." And that shift—
which educators increasingly should help their students, who
show many signs of starting a new, more lasting era of political
activism, gauge, engage, and shape—is gaining in momentum,
however much opposed by some. Consider in what a short time
the policies of *glasnost* and *perestroika* and their aftermath changed
what for so long had been taught as the "laws" of communism, or
how research in low-temperature physics has changed what were
taught, with equal dogmatism, as the "laws" of superconductiv-
ity. Conventional education, like the conventional knowledge it
transmits through its conventional structures of authority, no longer
suffices. Broadening and enriching debate about this situation (to
include as much as possible even those who would suppress debate), we should strive, in light of constant overturns of the kind
occasioned by research in low-temperature physics, to restructure education in the natural sciences along the lines suggested by
Paul Feyerabend and Lewis Thomas; in light of those of the kind
prompted by *glasnost* and *perestroika,* however problematic their
aftermath, we should strive, especially in the United States, as
Walter LaFeber argues, "to rethink not just the foreign policies
we have pursued since the advent of the Cold War, but also our
scholarship and the curriculum we teach," with a particular concern for "decreasing vocational and pre-professional education
during the high-school and undergraduate years and offering additional semesters of broader, cross-cultural education."[5] And
more, of course.

For some years Edward B. Fiske, education editor of the *New
York Times,* has stressed in various fora the outdatedness of the
American educational system, its need for radical restructuring
(especially at the primary and secondary levels), and its neglect of
opportunities for exemplary participation in the new model for
international education (involving cross-cultural satellite campuses and other developments) now being explored. While I do
not agree with some of Fiske's more conservative ideas, I applaud
the general thrust of much of what he has said about the importance of the American educational system, already the most diverse anywhere, serving, restructured, as a model system for an
astonishingly diverse world. And I hope that I have surveyed in-
formatively and instigatingly many ways in which that restructuring already proceeds and suggested useful ideas for guiding its

continuation on a scale that will lead to a system that can serve as a global model.[6] By that I do not mean that all cultures should copy a new American educational system—core curricula worldwide have already converged too far into monotonous similarity—but that they might be helped by it (be partly enabled by it as hermetic instructor) to envision and implement new systems of their own. Likewise the United States would be foolish to copy wholesale the system of any other culture, particularly that, however Western in origin, of Japan, which depends for its not-unproblematic success on an (increasingly unstable) ideological homogeneity impossible in American culture, but it would do well to learn from that system and adapt some of its features—use it, like others, in Merry White's words, "as a mirror, not as a blueprint."[7] Granting that one must respect the inevitable disjunctions that arise between different political paradigms, I nonetheless agree with W. J. T. Mitchell that the (self-)deluded educational pretensions of American neoconservatism are growing wearisome and increasingly irrelevant to "the global decolonizing" now well under way. And I hope, with him, that the United States will accept a "graceful imperial decline" and that its educational system—both "higher," his special province, and otherwise—"can aspire . . . in the next century" to become, among other things, "a world school for intelligent, peaceful, and productive decolonization."[8]

Finally (I would conclude, insofar as any text can close), we must remember that the turnings-over and overturnings I have been discussing involve systemically corrective, complexly reverberant adjustments. They will not just happen and stop: they will persist through ever-changing and interimplicated terms of opposition; they will generate further turnings-over and overturnings. Thus the dynamic of apeironic learning. Its advantage, much like that of deconstruction, in Sharon Crowley's characterization, "is that it permits us to oppose tradition to its suppressed alternatives, and from this opposition to generate yet other alternatives"[9]—alternatives that in turn form another tradition, and so on ad infinitum, the unknown becoming known but never yet quite familiar. Jacques Derrida, explaining his *"general strategy of deconstruction"* for dealing with "a violent hierarchy," offers apt advice about this process:

One of the two terms governs the other (axiologically, logically, etc.), or has the upper hand. To deconstruct the opposition, first of all, is to overturn the

Conclusion

hierarchy at a given moment. To overlook this phase of overturning is to forget the conflictual and subordinating structure of opposition. . . . When I say that this phase is necessary, the word *phase* is perhaps not the most rigorous one. It is not a question of a chronological phase, a given moment, or a page that one day simply will be turned, in order to go on to other things. The necessity of this phase is structural; it is the necessity of an interminable analysis: the hierarchy of dual oppositions always reestablishes itself. Unlike those authors whose death does not await their demise, the time for overturning is never a dead letter.[10]

Not a comfortable situation, but one potentially vibrant with responsiveness, imagination, and intelligent change. If the enterprise of all this seems too daunting, too difficult to begin or to take up again, we might remember also the advice of the poet William Stafford, an educator as wise in his (apparent) simplicity as Derrida in his complexity, at the opening of his poem "Knowing":

> To know the other world you turn
> your hand the way a bird finds angles
> of the wind. . . .[11]

APPENDIX

Aspects and Versions of the Shift in Emphasis from Teaching to Instructing

Teaching involves (concerns, stresses, etc.)	Instructing involves (concerns, stresses, etc.)	Citation
presenting the ob(li)vious	obverting the ob(li)vious	
"errors"	"expectations"	Mina Shaughnessy
the familiar	the unfamiliar or the familiar "defamiliarized"	Viktor Shklovsky
running on automatic pilot	the "deautomatization" of teaching	
hierarchy	hierarchical inversion or heterarchy	
imparting or imposing tokens	turning over tokens	
reality as given	reality as constituted	
knowledge as souvenirs	knowledge as revisionary activity	
"imparting knowledge" (the monological classroom)	students interactively "asking the questions" (the dialogical classroom)	John I. Goodlad
practice	praxis	
conventional learning	apeironic learning	
"totality"	"infinity"	Emmanuel Levinas
the known	the unknown	
the mild side (Apollonian)	the wild side (Dionysian)	Friedrich Wilhelm Nietzsche
what is settled	unsettling what is settled	

257

Appendix

Teaching involves (concerns, stresses, etc.)	Instructing involves (concerns, stresses, etc.)	Citation
reinforcing un(self-)conscious myths	(self-)consciously demythologizing or re-mythologizing	
inculcating "orthodoxy"	encouraging the student "to challenge orthodoxy"	Robert Scholes
definite or well-scripted situations	indefinite or ill-scripted situations and devising metascripts	
"facts"	"facts" as situated and motivated fictions	
hidden conventions	exposed conventions	
adapting old knowledge to new circumstances	creating new knowledge for new circumstances	
the dominant ideology	counterdominant possibilities	
building a structure for the student	enabling the student to rebuild or build beyond a given structure	
"Learning I"	"Learning II" and "Learning III"	Gregory Bateson
"fixed procedures"	"creativity in general"	Floyd Merrell
"associative thought" ("within the confines of a given matrix")	"bisociative thought" ("of independent matrices")	Arthur Koestler
"convergent production"	"divergent production"	J. P. Guilford
"autocentric perception"	"allocentric perception"	Ernest G. Schachtel
thinking in discrete categories	"janusian [or 'homospatial'] thinking"	Albert Rothenberg
"the secondary process"	"the primary process" (toward synthesizing "the tertiary process")	Silvano Arieti
"*neutral* naming"	"perspective by incongruity"	Kenneth Burke
"vertical thinking"	"lateral thinking"	Edward DeBono
going with "the mainstream"	going "against the mainstream"	Roger Schank
"answering the questions of others"	"posing one's own questions"	Roger Schank
"handing down knowledge . . . seemingly cast in stone"	"encouraging children to formulate their own knowledge"	Roger Schank
formulas as what students "are tested on and measured by"	formulas as "pieces in a game"	Roger Schank
learning to follow the rules	learning "to play with the rules as well as follow them"	
accepting old knowledge as given	"tweaking" old knowledge "into relevance or applicability"	Roger Schank

Appendix

avoiding "anomalies" or reductively incorporating them into "one's present model"	actively searching for and hypothesizing about "anomalies"	Roger Schank
finding out "what the answers are"	finding out "what the questions are"	Roger Schank
a silent lack of understanding	a dialogical exploration of "what is not understood"	Roger Schank
"passive" education	"active" education	Roger Schank
"teacher-initiated" learning	"student-initiated" learning	Roger Schank
"fear of failure"	freedom from "fear of failure"	Roger Schank
a subject ("object," "topic," etc.)	the subject ("person," "mind," etc.)	
"a subject"	the ways students "might know themselves as subjects"	Gary Waller
"liberal" education	"liberatory" education	Paulo Freire
"information"	"the substructures of ideas on which information stands"	Theodore Roszak
educational reform	educational transformation	
"acquiescence"	"originality"	Jules Henry
transmitting the past	rereading the past	
consensus	debate	Gerald Graff
a static, unicultural paideia	a dynamic, multicultural paideia	
"a vast disorganized external apparatus for living"	*sprezzatura*	Werner Jaeger/ Richard A. Lanham
"prejudices" or "just reading"	"hermeneutic consciousness"	Allan Bloom/ Joel C. Weinsheimer (Hans-Georg Gadamer)
institutionalized humanism	the "struggle for openness" and "political self-determination"	Paul A. Bové
the canon as "a stable, finished work of art" or as "revealed cultural truth"	the canon as "a work of postmodern art" or as "a participatory drama"	Richard A. Lanham
"knowledge"	"the way knowledge is held"	Richard A. Lanham
reproduction	invention	
"facts"	"procedures for acquiring or demonstrating facts"	Robert-Alain de Beaugrande and Wolfgang Ulrich Dressler

259

Appendix

Teaching involves (concerns, stresses, etc.)	Instructing involves (concerns, stresses, etc.)	Citation
undergraduate-level teacher education through general "methods" courses	graduate-level teacher education in subject fields and their specific pedagogies	The Holmes Group
the separateness of the sciences and humanities	the complex complementarity of the sciences and humanities	Northrop Frye
"ideologically petrified science"	"anarchistic" (or dadaistic) science	Paul Feyerabend
"hard facts"	"provisional and tentative" conclusions	Lewis Thomas
"the so-called basics"	"the things that are *not* known"	Lewis Thomas
history as "content"	history as cultural formations	
convergent modes of discourse	divergent modes of discourse	Mikhail Bakhtin
vanishing-point perspective	"rondure" perspective	Erwin Panofsky
textual content	textual *dis*content	
learning "about" something	building a strategy of learning	
History	historicism(s)	
the assumed known	the troublingly unknown	
closed advocacies	open explorations	
reading "to reconstruct the author's intention"	reading "against the grain of [the author's] intention"	Brook Thomas (Jacques Derrida)
separate disciplines	"blurred genres"	Clifford Geertz
"the texts of official history"	what "the texts of official history . . . exclude, . . . censor, exorcize"	Philippe Sollers
history as "true and immutable"	history as "heterogeneous, and constantly changing"	Joan W. Scott
linear, deterministic models of behavior	nonlinear, probabilistic models of behavior	
society "as an elaborate machine or a quasi-organism"	society "as a serious game, a sidewalk drama, or a behavioral text"	Clifford Geertz
social life as a formal system	social life as "just a bowl of strategies"	Clifford Geertz
the (world-)text as an artifact	the (world-)text as a cybernetic semiotic system	
dogmatic philosophizing and psychologizing	"realistic modelling of the diverse but systematic strategies people actually apply"	Robert-Alain de Beaugrande and Wolfgang Ulrich Dressler

Appendix

"*deterministic* [models]"	"*probabilistic* models"	Robert-Alain de Beaugrande and Wolfgang Ulrich Dressler
"static descriptions of . . . structures"	"dynamic accounts of *structure-building operations*"	Robert-Alain de Beaugrande and Wolfgang Ulrich Dressler
"*rules* and *laws*"	"*regularities, strategies, motivations, preferences,* and *defaults*"	Robert-Alain de Beaugrande and Wolfgang Ulrich Dressler
"*strict categories*"	"*dominances*"	Robert-Alain de Beaugrande and Wolfgang Ulrich Dressler
ignoring or arguing away "*fuzziness*"	systematizing "*fuzziness*"	Robert-Alain de Beaugrande and Wolfgang Ulrich Dressler
the universe as objective, physical, and material	the universe as relational, informational, and perceptual or conceptual	
a Cartesian worldview	a Batesonian worldview	
the logical conditions of knowledge as "truth"	the sociocognitive conditions of knowledge as interpretation	
"*mimesis*" (the text's extensional "*meaning*")	"*semiosis*" (the text's intensional "*significance*"	Michael Riffaterre
"checking language against reality"	"what language does *to* reality"	Michael Riffaterre
"teacher-telling"	"learner-interpreting"	Malcolm Coulthard
"surface grammatical structures"	"underlying semantic roles" and "pragmatics and interaction"	Malcolm Coulthard
the humanities in the place of "the silenced woman"	the humanities' insistence on a both-and "discourse"	Susan Sage Heinzelman
"clear images" of chaos	"broken images" of a new order	Robert Graves
curricular compartmentalization or modularity	curricular interconnection	Gerald Graff
literature as "self-interpreting"	literature in relation to "the larger cultural conversation"	Gerald Graff
" 'direct' experience" of the text	contextualized experience of the text	Gerald Graff
"an unthinking consolidation of tradition"	"the revision of disciplinary boundaries"	Karen Lawrence

Appendix

Teaching involves (concerns, stresses, etc.)	Instructing involves (concerns, stresses, etc.)	Citation
"mere reproduction of the text"	repetition of the text "in a manner appropriate to the times"	Martin Mueller
preservation of the past	transformation of the past	
what texts are read	*how* texts are read	
what texts mean	how meaning is assigned to texts	
imitation (the *what* of knowing)	explanation (the *how* of knowing)	Roger Schank
suppressing "the principle of difference"	dramatizing "the principle of difference"	Gerald Graff
"agonistic" relations between teachers and students	an interplay of issues pursued "in the widest possible variety of perspectives"	Walter Ong / Thomas O. Sloane
"cultural unanimity"	the intersection of "cultures and classes"	Mike Rose
canonical coherence based on authoritarian (Mosaic) consensus	canonical coherence based on democratic (mosaic) interconnectedness	
cultural assimilationism	"eclectic ideology"	James A. Banks
differences that "distinguish"	differences that "relate"	Myra Jehlen
un(self-)conscious theory	(self-)conscious theory	
passive reception	active, creative questioning	
"grand narratives"	"little narratives"	Jean-François Lyotard
an established, traditional curriculum	a provisional, "chaotic" curriculum	David Laurence (James Gleick)
the "abstractly" determinate	the "concretely" indeterminate	
no questioning of "ideological assumptions"	alertness to "ideological assumptions"	George Levine et al.
"the desperate need to return to old unities"	willingness "to live with uncertainty"	George Levine et al.
"irritable reaching after fact and reason"	"negative capability"	John Keats
resolving "what is read into glossy ideas"	"reading as a form of life"	Geoffrey H. Hartman
"a kerygma"	"an enigma"	Geoffrey H. Hartman
"disentanglement from"	"progressive *knotting into*"	Thomas Pynchon
reading by "the straight line . . . approach"	reading by the "detour" that leads into "hermeneutic 'infinitizing'"	Geoffrey H. Hartman

Appendix

deductive "philosophical style"	interruptive "philosophical style"	Geoffrey H. Hartman (Walter Benjamin)
the referentiality of the text	the self-referentiality of the text	
centered structures	decentered structural free play	Jacques Derrida
the explicit and literal text	implicit and figurative intertexts	
communication as the sending and receiving of information	communication as the interactive negotiation of meaning	
ingenuousness	irony	
consistency	contradiction	
decidability	undecidability	Kurt Gödel
"the old mode"	"the advance"	William Carlos Williams
affirming the canon	questioning the canon	
canonical pedagogy	"palimpsestic pedagogy"	Ross Chambers
reading as a "sequential process"	reading as a "non-linear process"	John M. Slatin
the arts as static knowledges	the arts as open(ing) experiences	
"one"	"more than one"	Ursula K. Le Guin
nationalistic propaganda	global acculturation	
knowing (declaratively) *about*	knowing (procedurally) *how*	Gilbert Ryle
"the readerly"	"the writerly"	John Warnock (C. A. Bowers and Roland Barthes)
the reader as "a consumer . . . of the text"	the reader as "a producer of the text"	John Warnock
the "extensive curriculum"	the "intensive curriculum"	E. D. Hirsch, Jr.
reading as "matching what was written with one's own knowledge"	reading as "rewriting the text"	R. J. Tierney et al.
"teaching as surgery, suppression, replacement, deficit filling"	learning as "the recreating of meaning"	Jerome Bruner
the student "as a recipient of knowledge transmission"	the student as "an agent of knowledge making"	Jerome Bruner
students as "*consumers* of . . . culture"	students as "*creators* of new cultural forms"	Jerome Bruner (Roland Barthes)
"prescriptive" pedagogy	"collaborative" pedagogy	Patricia Bizzell
"cultural literacy"	"*critical* literacy"	E. D. Hirsch, Jr./ Donald Lazere
"collection codes"	"integration codes"	Basil Bernstein

263

Appendix

Teaching involves (concerns, stresses, etc.)	Instructing involves (concerns, stresses, etc.)	Citation
"passive receivers"	"active learners"	Wayne Booth
rote learning of language	"practicing" and "self-consciously reflecting on" language and adapting it "to a variety of stituations"	Richard Lloyd-Jones and Andrea A. Lunsford
new knowledge	*ganas* ("appetite") for learning	*Stand and Deliver*
"common humanity"	social diversity	Richard Lloyd-Jones and Andrea A. Lunsford
learning as the "passive ingestion of 'facts'"	learning as "the process of actively constructing meaning from experiences"	Richard Lloyd-Jones and Andrea A. Lunsford
the traditional canon	an expanded canon	
traditional texts	traditional texts "in relation to theoretical concerns"	Richard Lloyd-Jones and Andrea A. Lunsford
the classroom as "a place in which knowledge is disseminated"	the classroom as "a place in which . . . knowledge is created"	Richard Lloyd-Jones and Andrea A. Lunsford
traditional "cultural information"	apeironic cultural *knowledge*	E. D. Hirsch, Jr.
"cultural literacy"	"pluralistic literacy"	E. D. Hirsch, Jr./ Paul B. Armstrong
"memorizing vocabulary"	"learning how to control and generate synthesizing patterns"	Paul B. Armstrong
langue (grammar, vocabulary)	*parole* (communicational situations)	Ferdinand de Saussure
"one discourse"	"more than one ['discourse']"	Robert Scholes
canonical texts	noncanonical texts	
"old materials"	"a stock of existing categories to alter and extend"	Paul B. Armstrong
"mastery of content"	using "what one knows to meet unexpected challenges"	Paul B. Armstrong
"common ground"	"negotiating different perspectives"	Paul B. Armstrong
"science and knowledge today as a search . . . for consensus"	"science and knowledge today as a search . . . for 'instabilities,' as a practice of *paralogism*"	Fredric Jameson (Jean-François Lyotard)
conventional perspectives	"decentered perspectives"	Helene Moglen
reading	(re)reading "differently"	Jacques Derrida

264

Appendix

the denotative	the connotative and the "stereoscopic"	David Bleich
logocentric univocality	deconstructive equivocality	Jacques Derrida
receptive reading	conflictive and integrative reading	
positive logic	either/or, both-and, and "fuzzy" logic	
giving students "readings"	giving students "tools for producing their own [readings]"	Robert Scholes
"text within text"	"text upon text" and "text against text"	Robert Scholes
learning "about literature"	learning by "working with literature"	Robert Scholes, Nancy R. Comley, and Gregory L. Ulmer
"Through vision"	"At vision"	Richard A. Lanham
"Through vision" or "At vision"	"Through/At vision"	Richard A. Lanham
"Edenic" humanism	"Post-Darwinian" humanism	Richard A. Lanham
"culture as suppression"	culture as "expression"	Richard A. Lanham
a curriculum based on "philosophy" (a philosophical paideia)	a curriculum based on "rhetoric" (a rhetorical paideia)	Richard A. Lanham
Platonic rhetoric	Gorgian rhetoric	
conventional pedagogy	"a poetic pedagogy"	Richard A. Lanham
cultural literacy as "sharing ['a cultural background']"	cultural literacy as "contributing ['to common issues']"	David S. Kaufer
"cultural facts and associations"	"cultural conversations"	David S. Kaufer
"received knowledge"	"'surprising' knowledge"	David S. Kaufer
cultural homogeneity	cultural heterogeneity	
positivist behaviorism	constructivist cognitivism	David P. Ausubel
rote learning	meaningful learning	David P. Ausubel
conventional "concepts and practices"	"acquiring the capacity to generate and use new ['concepts and practices']"	Joseph D. Novak
low-informativity (high-probability, low-surprise) texts and concepts	high-informativity (low-probability, high-surprise) texts and concepts	Robert-Alain de Beaugrande and Wolfgang Ulrich Dressler
the learner as "pupil"	the learner as "student"	Jacques Barzun
"the giving out of predigested hokum"	"genuine, hand-to-hand teaching" of "principles"	Jacques Barzun

Appendix

Teaching involves (concerns, stresses, etc.)	Instructing involves (concerns, stresses, etc.)	Citation
top-down bureaucratic pedagogy and curricula	"a cooperative, dialogic pedagogy" and "curricula not afraid of the forbidden"	Andrew Sledd
cultural literacy	apeironic literacy	
the unicultural	the multicultural	
"teacher-delivered knowledge"	"self-propelled" learning	Theodore R. Sizer
a pedagogy of "telling"	a pedagogy of "coaching"	Theodore R. Sizer
schools that "represent our past"	schools that "represent . . . our future"	David Elkind
"teachers" ("the Lecture-Test-Grade System")	*"enablers"*	Ken Macrorie
low expectations	high expectations	Ken Macrorie
conventional testing	"Moebian" testing	Ken Macrorie
minimal competency	maximal habilitation	
students as "keepers" of knowledge	students as "finders" of knowledge	Ken Macrorie
evaluation and assessment based on the student's "recall of material"	evaluation and assessment based on how the student can "use knowledge creatively"	Mike Rose
the "technicalization" of education	"suspicion" of and "resistance" to the "technicalization" of education	Neil Postman
assessing for the " 'right' answers"	assessing for "understanding" and "the *ways of knowing and doing*"	Richard Lloyd-Jones and Andrea A. Lunsford
method-driven educational research and evaluation	theory-driven educational research and evaluation	Joseph D. Novak and D. Bob Gowin
testing "to elicit information from students"	testing that "asks students to reorganize new information using what they already know"	Joseph D. Novak and D. Bob Gowin
"educational value . . . determined . . . by the exact fit between a lesson and its replication on a test"	"educational value . . . determined by what the learners *do* with lessons"	Joseph D. Novak and D. Bob Gowin
"reception learning"	*"discovery learning"*	Joseph D. Novak and D. Bob Gowin
the quantitative measurement of informational *replication*	the qualitative measurement of epistemological *transformation*	

Appendix

conventional evaluation (of what the student knows)	apeironic evaluation (of how the student deals with the unknown)	
intelligence as arising from the "rapid, accurate storage and recovery of specific knowledge"	intelligence as arising from "the *ability to apply or adapt a small set of powerful skills and procedures to any particular task at hand*"	Robert-Alain D. Beaugrande and Wolfgang Ulrich Dressler
school-university alliances based on "simple scenarios"	school-university alliances based on "tolerance for ambiguity," "the logics of muddling-through," etc.	Burton R. Clark
educational research in remote, white-coat settings	educational research in the classroom	
accountability without empowerment	accountability with empowerment	
"failures"	"the intelligence and linguistic aptitudes" operating "below the surface of . . . failures"	Mina Shaughnessy
"tables and charts" concerning error	"the social context of error"	Mike Rose
"the *remedial* approach"	*"mediation"*	Mariolina Salvatori
remediation	re-mediation	
education beginning with what a student knows and can do	education beginning with "what a student does not know, and cannot do"	Neil Postman
nature "as eternal and separate"	nature as "changed" in *"meaning"*	Bill McKibben
how to "live with the rules"	how "the rules may not make sense"	James Gunn
rules	the discovery or invention of new rules (and metarules)	
"more and more bits and pieces of information"	"critical thinking"	Richard W. Paul
data storage	heuristic procedures	
the curriculum	countercurriculum(s)	
one culture	"one culture embracing another"	Mike Rose
acculturation	transculturation	
tracking	cooperative or collaborative learning	
"traditional" students	"nontraditional" students	
"the isolated text (or author)"	"the virtual space or cultural conversation that the text presupposes"	Gerald Graff

Appendix

Teaching involves (concerns, stresses, etc.)	Instructing involves (concerns, stresses, etc.)	Citation
the curriculum as constituted by texts	the countercurriculum as constituted by *con*texts	
"well-established *theories*"	"hypotheses which are *inconsistent* with well-established *theories*"	Paul Feyerabend
acquiescence to "the First [TV] Curriculum"	enhancement of "the second [school] curriculum" to "focus . . . on the *structure* of the information environment"	Neil Postman
"exegesis"	"interpretation"	Susan Noakes
"timeless reading" (exclusively either "exegetical" or "interpretive")	"timely reading" (oscillatorially both "exegetical" and "interpretive")	Susan Noakes
"disciplinary courses"	"nondisciplinary" courses	Peter Elbow
"knowledge" (knowing "something")	"meta-knowledge" ("knowing *about* . . . knowing")	Peter Elbow
"the original . . . frame of reference"	"the new frame of reference"	Peter Elbow
"declaration"	"description"	Jacques Derrida
subjectivity/objectivity	intersubjectivity	Jürgen Habermas
"naive belief" or "knee-jerk skepticism"	"methodological belief"	Peter Elbow
conventional pedagogy	oppositional pedagogy	
" 'civics' lessons"	*conscientização*	Robert Con David/ Paulo Freire
"eliminating any and all paradoxes"	"the path leading to paradox"	Floyd Merrell
suppression of educator-student conflicts	"theorizing the classroom"	Ronald Strickland
"the mere reproduction of knowledge, or the transmission of information as knowledge"	the "interrogation of existing paradigms of knowledge"	Ronald Strickland
ignorance as a blankness or emptiness	ignorance as "the suppressed other" or "unconscious resistance to the dominant order"	Ronald Strickland
the teacher as "the subject who is supposed to know"	the student as "the subject who is supposed to know"	Gregory S. Jay (Jacques Lacan)
"the individual subject as an originator of language"	"the individual subject as . . . an effect of language"	Ronald Strickland

Appendix

the curriculum as "distinct and substantial bodies of knowledge"	the (counter)curriculum as "constructions"	Ronald Strickland
knowledge that exists "independently"	"constructions of knowledge" in which the educator should "acknowledge his or her implication"	Ronald Strickland
affirming "intellectual boundaries"	creating "the possibility for alternative knowledges produced in other cultural sites"	Ronald Strickland
the teacher as Pygmalion	the instructor as Hermes	
the teacher making students his or her "mouthpiece"	the instructor admitting he or she is "still learning"	Peter Elbow
predetermining student growth	accepting and encouraging divergent student growth	
teachers as epistemological puppeteers	instructors as "Chinese shadow-casters"	Roland Barthes
the teacher as ἀλαζών (*alazon*) or *magister gloriosus*	the instructor as εἴρων (*eiron*) or "dissembler"	Northrop Frye
object lessons	"lessons as moving objects"	Hugh Munby
determinate science (Laplacean tradition)	"disorder" and the science of chaos	Michel Serres / James Gleick
"knowledge, . . . in terms of order and mastery"	"knowledge . . . in terms of chance and invention"	Josué V. Harari and David F. Bell (Michel Serres)
"the simple, the distinct, and the monosemic"	"concepts and logics of fuzziness, complexity, and polyvalence"	Josué V. Harari and David F. Bell (Michel Serres)
method	"anti-method"	Josué V. Harari and David F. Bell (Michel Serres)
the role of pedagogue	the role of "anti-pedagogue"	Shoshana Felman
ignorance as something "opposed to knowledge"	ignorance as "part of the very structure of knowledge"	Shoshana Felman
"the transmission of ready-made knowledge"	"the creation of a new condition of knowledge, . . . of an original learning disposition"	Shoshana Felman
the text (plot, masque)	the subtext (subplot, antimasque)	
"the content of teaching"	"the *teaching relationship*"	Henri J. M. Nouwen
foundationalist empiricism	the theoristic imperative	
"the student/other as . . . a projection of the teacher"	making "a teacher of the student"	Joan De Jean

Appendix

Teaching involves (concerns, stresses, etc.)	Instructing involves (concerns, stresses, etc.)	Citation
"the pedagogical moment" as when the student fills in the blank	"the pedagogical moment" as marking "the place where what is not known is evoked as the blank that makes the story go on forever"	Barbara Johnson
"the subject's telling of the object"	"the subject's telling of the desire for the object"	Angela S. Moger
a hierarchical pedagogical style	an "antihierarchical" pedagogical style	Adrienne Rich
women who "think like men"	women who are "thinking critically, refusing to accept the givens"	Adrienne Rich
(masculine, phallocentric) tradition	a gender-balanced attitude	
a pedagogy "for the transmission of knowledge"	a pedagogy "to reorganize all knowledge"	Margo Culley and Catherine Portuges
a "banking" concept of and approach to education	a "problem-posing" concept of and approach to education	Paulo Freire
competitive and repressive pedagogy	"collaborative, cooperative, and interactive" pedagogy	Frances Maher
students as "learners"	students as "creators and constructors"	Frances Maher
"silence"	"voice"	Mary Field Belenky et al.
"separate education"	"connected education"	Mary Field Belenky et al.
new "models" as "unplanned ruptures"	new "models" as possibilities for "creative spaces"	Robert de Beaugrande
"the single unified voice/self"	a celebration "of difference"	Sandra Alcosser
hermeneutics	"iristics"	Susan Noakes (Gary Shapiro)
"signification"	"Signifyin(g)"	Henry Louis Gates, Jr.
the given or same	the new or different	
"the Imaginary"	"the Symbolic"	Michel Foucault (Jacques Lacan)
humanity as "an ontological given"	humanity as "an epistemological construct"	Karlis Racevskis (Michel Foucault)
"the internal 'meaning' of a discourse"	the "external conditions of possibility ['of a discourse']"	Karlis Racevskis (Michel Foucault)

Appendix

pygmalionic pedagogy	hermetic pedagogy	
"doxa"	"paradox"	Michel Foucault
examining social processes "from the top"	examining social processes "from below"	Karlis Racevskis (Michel Foucault)
"resemblance"	"similitude"	René Magritte (Michel Foucault)
theme	"variations set free from a theme"	James Harkness (Michel Foucault)
the "death of interpretation"	the "life of interpretation"	Michel Foucault
the "everyday lesson"	the Bakhtinian carnivalesque	Michel Foucault/ Mikhail Bakhtin
"discipline"	"astonishment"	Michel de Certeau (Michel Foucault)
"the seriousness of meaning"	"the seriousness of praxis"	Uta Liebmann Schaub (Michel Foucault)
"conventional pedagogy"	a "post(e)-pedagogical" educational rationale	Gregory L. Ulmer
a "conceptual" research process	a "dramatic" research process	Gregory L. Ulmer
"the old problems"	"an entirely new set of problems"	Gregory L. Ulmer (Thomas Kuhn)
"a pedagogy committed to . . . reproduction"	"a pedagogy committed to change"	Gregory L. Ulmer (Pierre Bourdieu and Jean-Claude Passeron)
"pedagogy . . . in the age of Hegel"	"grammatological pedagogy"	Gregory L. Ulmer (Jacques Derrida)
"retrospective" learning	"prospective" learning	Gregory L. Ulmer
"the classroom as a place of . . . reproduction"	*"the classroom as a place of invention"*	Gregory L. Ulmer (Pierre Bourdieu and Jean-Claude Passeron)
the teacher as "a concrete embodiment of the ideal self"	the instructor as a semitransparent, multifaceted mirror	Gregory L. Ulmer
the student as mirror	the student as lamp	M. H. Abrams
"the exclusive domination of mind"	the mind *and* "the body (desire and the will to knowledge)"	Gregory L. Ulmer
the teacher's ability to "repeat a message"	the instructor's ability to "produce one ['a message'] himself"	Gregory L. Ulmer
"the universal"	"the singular and the anomalous"	Gregory L. Ulmer
a "discipleship" model of education	a model of education for a more "thoughtful relationship to knowledge"	Gregory L. Ulmer (Bernard Pautrat)

Appendix

Teaching involves (concerns, stresses, etc.)	Instructing involves (concerns, stresses, etc.)	Citation
the pedagogic "message"	the pedagogic "medium" ("the scene of teaching")	Gregory L. Ulmer
the classroom as "inevitably a theater"	the classroom as "an avant-garde theater"	Gregory L. Ulmer (Pierre Bourdieu and Jean-Claude Passeron)
"the domain of truth"	*"the domain of . . . invention"*	Gregory L. Ulmer
"the old tradition" of the pedagogy of *memoria*	"a new dimension" of the pedagogy of *inventio*	Gregory L. Ulmer
mimesis "as copy"	mimesis as "*copia*—the love of abundance (*apeiron*)"	Gregory L. Ulmer
"knowledge . . . as a representation of something else"	"knowledge . . . as itself a mode of action in the cultural world"	Gregory L. Ulmer
moving from the unknown to the known	moving from the known to the unknown	Jacques Derrida
"science-as-an-institution"	"science-in-the-making"	Gerald Holton
mathematics as "the rigorous science of Euclid"	"mathematics in the making"	G. Polya
"discipline"	"invention"	Gregory L. Ulmer
the classroom as "workshop"	"the classroom as "textshop"	Gregory L. Ulmer (Roland Barthes)
"objects"	"events"	Gregory L. Ulmer (Alfred Korzybski)
paideia	*paidia*	Gregory L. Ulmer (Jacques Derrida)
specialization	"amateurization"	Roland Barthes
the play	play as ongoing creativity	Hans-Georg Gadamer
"dialectics"	"dialogic"	Dominick LaCapra (Mikhail Bakhtin)
"earnest" learning	*gaya scienza*	Friedrich Wilhelm Nietzsche
"order or coherence"	"the provisional, permeable character of all knowledge"	Gregory L. Ulmer
a world comprehensible through "the codes of popular wisdom"	a world whose "unexpectedness is so excessive"	Roland Barthes
"received ideas"	"truth . . . subject to constant revision and restatement, or . . . simply unverifiable"	A. J. Krailsheimer (Gustave Flaubert)

Appendix

"education as a function of society"	"society as a function of education"	Kenneth Burke (John Dewey)
"schooling"	*"learning"*	Philip H. Coombs
"institution-bound, age-bound" education	"education as a *lifelong* process"	Philip H. Coombs
formal education	informal and "nonformal" education	Philip H. Coombs
"one-shot" innovations	innovation "as a continuing process"	Philip H. Coombs
the formal educational system	"a nationwide 'learning network'"	Philip H. Coombs
the traditional/past/known	rereading, reframing, reinventing the traditional/past/known	
hallaka	*haggada*	Geoffrey H. Hartman
incorporation	revision	Geoffrey H. Hartman
preserving cultural ancestors	*transformatively* preserving cultural ancestors	
(peremptory) "truth"	what else or otherwise is "true"	
"vocational and pre-professional education"	"broader, cross-cultural education"	Walter LaFeber
imperialism	"global decolonizing"	W. J. T. Mitchell
"the hierarchy at a given moment"	overturning "the hierarchy at a given moment" through "an interminable analysis"	Jacques Derrida
"the world"	"the other world"	William Stafford

273

Notes

Preface
A Progressive Knotting Into

1. Gayatri Chakravorty Spivak, Translator's Preface, *Of Grammatology,* by Jacques Derrida, trans. Gayatri Chakravorty Spivak (Baltimore: Johns Hopkins University Press, 1976), pp. ix–x. Her indented quotation is from Jean Hyppolite, "The Structure of Philosophic Language According to the 'Preface' to Hegel's *Phenomenology of the Mind,*" in *The Structuralist Controversy: The Languages of Criticism and the Sciences of Man,* ed. Richard Macksey and Eugenio Donato (Baltimore: Johns Hopkins University Press, 1970), p. 159.

2. See Michael L. Johnson, "The Theoristic Imperative and the Paralogical Play of 'That Dangerous Supplement,' " *North Dakota Quarterly* 56, no. 3 (Summer 1988): 34–35. Apart from whatever differences they may seem to have in one version or another, cognitivism and social constructionism increasingly dovetail in their premises that knowledge and self are very much local and nonfoundational constructions. Brain physiologists such as José M. R. Delgado for some time have embraced such premises, which do not necessarily discount the role of innate and/or universal structures in the development of knowledge and self but regard them as strongly shaped by other factors—and certainly do not regard them as constituting some sort of central human "core." Those premises are wryly capsuled in Tom Wolfe's characterization of the beliefs of the Bororo Indians of Brazil "that there is no such thing as a private self," that the mind is "an open cavity . . . in which the entire village swells and the jungle grows," and that, therefore, "without the entire village, the whole jungle, occupying the cavity, they had no minds left" (*The Bonfire of the Vanities* [New York: Farrar Straus Giroux, 1987], p. 491).

3. Stefano Agosti, "Coup upon Coup: An Introduction to *Spurs,*" in Jacques Derrida, *Spurs: Nietzsche's Styles,* trans. Barbara Harlow (Chicago: University of Chicago Press, 1979), p. 23.

4. Roland Barthes, "Literature/Teaching," in *The Grain of the Voice: Inter-*

views, 1962–1980, trans. Linda Coverdale (New York: Hill & Wang, 1985), p. 239.

Chapter 1
Obverting the Ob(li)vious

1. Hunter S. Thompson, Introduction, *Generation of Swine: Tales of Shame and Degradation in the '80s* (New York: Summit Books, 1988), pp. 10, 11.

2. J. Mitchell Morse, "A Little Night Teaching," *American Scholar* 55 (1986): 403, 405.

3. See Martin Joos, *The Five Clocks* (New York: Harcourt Brace Jovanovich, 1967).

4. See Mina P. Shaughnessy, *Errors and Expectations: A Guide for the Teacher of Basic Writing* (New York: Oxford University Press, 1977), esp. pp. 1–13, 290–93.

5. Neil Postman, *Teaching as a Conserving Activity* (1979; reprint, New York: Dell, 1987), p. 16.

6. See Jerome Kagan, *The Nature of the Child* (New York: Basic Books, 1984).

7. Werner Jaeger, *Paideia: The Ideals of Greek Culture,* trans. Gilbert Highet, vol. 1 (Oxford: Blackwell, 1939), pp. xiv, xvii.

8. Postman, *Teaching as a Conserving Activity,* p. 16.

9. H. G. Wells, *The Outline of History* (New York: Garden City, 1931), p. 1169.

10. Philip H. Coombs, *The World Crisis in Education: The View from the Eighties* (New York: Oxford University Press, 1985), p. 9.

11. Gene Lyons, "Why Teachers Can't Teach," in *The Higher Illiteracy: Essays on Bureaucracy, Propaganda, and Self-Delusion* (Fayetteville: University of Arkansas Press, 1988), p. 211. This essay was originally published in *Texas Monthly,* September 1979, pp. 122–28, 208–20.

12. Ibid.

13. Coombs, *World Crisis,* p. 9.

14. Henry Adams, *The Education of Henry Adams,* ed. Ernest Samuels (Boston: Houghton Mifflin, 1974), p. 300.

15. See Joseph Epstein, Introduction, *Masters: Portraits of Great Teachers,* ed. Joseph Epstein (New York: Basic Books, 1981), p. xii. The same point is made, passim and less directly, in Gilbert Highet's *Art of Teaching* (New York: Knopf, 1950), a "commonsensical" and simplistic (though not all wrongheaded) book that stops short of really exploring its subject.

16. Jérôme Carcopino, *Daily Life in Ancient Rome: The People and the City at the Height of the Empire,* ed. Henry T. Rowell, trans. E. O. Lorimer (New Haven, Conn.: Yale University Press, 1940), p. 104. Pistoclerus's question (in the original, "Tibi ego an tu mihi servus es?") may be found in Plautus, *Bacchides* 162, after which may be found Lydus's "tricky" answer.

17. The most affecting enactment of this inversion in modern literature is

Harold Pinter's play *The Servant*, which might well be interpreted educationally. See his *Five Screenplays* (New York: Methuen, 1971), pp. 1-60.

18. Translator's note in Phillippe Sollers, *Writing and the Experience of Limits*, ed. David Hayman, trans. Philip Barnard with David Hayman (New York: Columbia University Press, 1983), p. 9.

19. A sense of how out of balance present practice is, how strongly biased toward "teaching," may be gained from the extensive research of John I. Goodlad, who reports in *A Place Called School: Prospects for the Future* (New York: McGraw-Hill, 1984) that "the data from our observations in more than 1,000 classrooms support the popular image of a teacher standing or sitting in front of a class imparting knowledge to a group of students" whose activities are dominantly "marked by passivity." Though this situation varies somewhat by level, "on the whole, teachers at all levels apparently did not know how to vary their instructional procedures, did not want to, or had some kind of difficulty doing so"—a characterization that contrasts dramatically with that of rare "successful classrooms," where goals are shared, the individual and the group interact supportively to achieve them, teachers ask engaging questions and mediate open discussions, and students are able "to turn things around by asking the questions" (pp. 105, 106, 108, 109). The prevalence of the kind of classroom that Goodlad finds far more typical doubtless accounts in large part for the (seemingly) effortless satirical portrayal of it in the 1986 movie *Ferris Bueller's Day Off*: high school teachers endlessly ask and answer their own dull questions while the students sit in mouth-breathing boredom.

20. See Martin Heidegger, *Early Greek Thinking*, trans. David Farrell Krell and Frank A. Capuzzi (New York: Harper & Row, 1975), p. 54; G. S. Kirk, J. E. Raven, and M. Schofield, *The Presocratic Philosophers: A Critical History with a Selection of Texts*, 2d ed. (New York: Cambridge University Press, 1983), pp. 109-17; and Jacques Derrida, *Dissemination*, trans. Barbara Johnson (Chicago: University of Chicago Press, 1981), p. 365. Kirk, Raven, and Schofield, like Derrida in his own way, stress "the lack of positive identification" (p. 11) of the *apeiron*—a notion I would extend: apeironic learning should be thought of as not so much an apprehension of positive knowledge as an engagement with difference. John Wild gets at this distinction in his discussion of Emmanuel Levinas's distinguishing between the quest for "totality," which involves "a mode of thought which tries to gather all things around the mind, or self, of the thinker," and the quest for "infinity," which involves "an externally oriented mode which attempts to penetrate into what is radically other than the mind that is thinking it" (Introduction, *Totality and Infinity: An Essay on Exteriority*, by Emmanuel Levinas, trans. Alphonso Lingis [The Hague: Martinus Nijhoff; Pittsburgh: Duquesne University Press, 1969], p. 16).

21. Robert Scholes, *Textual Power: Literary Theory and the Teaching of English* (New Haven, Conn.: Yale University Press, 1985), p. 1.

22. Morris Berman, *The Reenchantment of the World* (1981; New York: Bantam Books, 1984), pp. 212, 213, 214, 275-76. It is worth noting that Berman stresses the necessity, even for the "triggering of Learning III," of not abandoning "traditional archaic practices" (p. 290). Gregory Bateson's three categories of learning are detailed in his *Steps to an Ecology of Mind: Collected Essays in*

Anthropology, Psychiatry, Evolution, and Epistemology (1972; Northvale, N.J.: Jason Aronson, 1987), esp. pp. 287-308.

23. Floyd Merrell, *Semiotic Foundations: Steps toward an Epistemology of Written Texts* (Bloomington: Indiana University Press, 1982), pp. 82-83, 84, 86, 87.

24. Ibid., pp. 87, 102. See Ludwig Wittgenstein, *Zettel*, ed. G. E. M. Anscombe and G. H. von Wright, trans. G. E. M. Anscombe (1967; Berkeley and Los Angeles: University of California Press, 1970), p. 82.

25. Merrell, *Semiotic Foundations,* pp. 102-3. The quotation from Karl R. Popper is from his "fundamental theorem" of learning as set out in his *Objective Knowledge: An Evolutionary Approach* (Oxford: Clarendon Press, 1972), p. 71.

26. The best single source for a survey of these matters is *The Creativity Question,* ed. Albert Rothenberg and Carl R. Hausman (Durham, N.C.: Duke University Press, 1976), which brings together representative work from Koestler, Guilford, Schachtel, Rothenberg, Arieti, and many others. See also Kenneth Burke, *Perspectives by Incongruity,* ed. Stanley Edgar Hyman (Bloomington: Indiana University Press, 1964), esp. pp. 94-99.

27. Roger Schank, with Peter Childers, *The Creative Attitude: Learning to Ask and Answer the Right Questions* (New York: Macmillan, 1988), pp. xi, 5, 6, 7, 17, 347. Educators frequently speak of how few students are "gifted," "exceptional," "intellectual," and so on—the usual terminology of creativity— without realizing the extent to which virtually *all* students, even those diagnosed as having "learning disabilities," are (or still are, in spite of being hobbled by cultural institutions) capable of creative engagement. Indeed, so-called special education is beginning to change its thinking, radically and not without resistance, about the issues of "exceptionality"—see, for instance, Thomas M. Skrtic, "The Crisis in Special Education Knowledge: A Perspective on Perspective," *Focus on Exceptional Children* 18, no. 7 (March 1986): 1-16, an article that touches on some of those issues and calls for expansion of its postmodernist critique "to the entire system of public education in this country" (p. 15).

28. Schank, *Creative Attitude,* pp. 15, 26, 28, 27, 36, 346.

29. I agree with David Elkind that typically "the balance" of pedagogical attention "shifts progressively from student to subject as the students become more advanced," but I suggest that the balance should be adjusted and stress more strongly than he that "teachers at all levels of education should be aware of individual students as well as being knowledgeable about subject matter" (*The Hurried Child: Growing Up Too Fast Too Soon,* rev. ed. [Reading, Mass.: Addison-Wesley, 1988], p. 67). Thus, like many who advocate reform in schools of education, I believe that elementary-level educators should be more "knowledgeable about subject matter," but I also endorse wholeheartedly efforts at the postsecondary level to be more "aware of individual students." The undergraduate program in English at Carnegie Mellon University, with its multifaceted core courses concerned with textuality, exemplifies such efforts: acknowledging that "this world is not the one most of us here grew up in," the faculty, according to Gary Waller, is committed to "teaching our students . . . not only a subject but ways by which they might know themselves as subjects" ("Knowing the Subject: Critiquing the Self, Critiquing the Culture," *ADE Bulletin,* no. 95 [Spring 1990], pp. 15, 16). The two knowledges of "subjects" are profoundly interdependent, for educators as for students.

30. The scandal of computer literacy has been well documented. Some years ago many educators were concerned that only economically advantaged students in public schools were learning to program, while "poor" students just played games on the machines. On the whole, I think, the situation was—and is—worse than that, as Theodore Roszak shows in *The Cult of Information: The Folklore of Computers and the True Art of Thinking* (New York: Pantheon Books, 1986), pp. 47–71, a discussion that contributes to his argument that students, especially younger ones, are learning about "information" but not how to deal with "the substructures of ideas on which information stands," with expectable consequences for the development of "critical reflection" (p. 106).

31. This situation could be exemplified almost interminably, but an especially memorable "practical" example may be found in the financial universe of discourse. Many people in finance know the so-called Rule of Seventy-two, whereby one can divide the simple interest rate on invested money into the number seventy-two and have as a quotient the approximate number of years required for that money to double in amount. But typically those people have been taught that rule *as a rule* and lack the instructing that would enable them to know how it derives from a power series and how its range of accuracy is constrained and to explore how it might be made more accurate and hence more useful. Increasingly, I suspect, the rule is simply falling into disuse, since calculators may displace human computation as an anachronism—with the result that humankind generally now faces the possibility of learning neither new math nor "old math."

32. Karlis Racevskis, *Michel Foucault and the Subversion of Intellect* (Ithaca, N.Y.: Cornell University Press, 1983), p. 165.

33. Postman, *Teaching as a Conserving Activity*, pp. 11, 13, 14, 15.

34. Ibid., p. 11. As I hope to show, there are many reasons for believing that "the next time around," which already is arriving, will be different. One of the reasons is that even many state boards of education are starting to get the drift of the shift. For instance, I was surprised and heartened to find in the middle of a 1989 report from the Kansas State Board of Education a chart of "Value Shifts and Their Directions for Education," most of whose paired entries, presented below, could be transplanted aptly into the chart that constitutes my Appendix:

From	To
Schooling	Learning and human resource development
Accreditation or "seat time"	Performance and competency achievement
Schooling as preparation for adult roles	Schooling as preparation for lifelong learning
Limited achievement	No limits to learning
Sorting	Open opportunity systems
Measures of factual recall	Assessment of thinking and information processing skills
Teacher as content deliverer	Teacher as manager of learning
Teacher-centered learning	Learner-centered learning

(continued)

From	To
Teacher responsible for structuring knowledge	Teacher responsible for teaching students to structure knowledge (information processing)

A fair amount of predictable progressive gobbledygook about restructuring and teacher empowerment and political hype about economic leadership contextualize the chart (as well as a noticeable paucity of attention to attendant implications for teacher education), but it does suggest the dimensions of the report's seemingly sincere and somewhat imaginative engagement with "the difficult process of envisioning what education must be to meet changed community and societal conditions." (*Kansas Schools for the 21st Century* [Topeka: Kansas State Board of Education, 1989], p. 7.)

Chapter 2
Homo Deludens: The Trivial Pursuit of Paideia

1. Werner Jaeger, *Paideia: The Ideals of Greek Culture,* trans. Gilbert Highet, vol. 1 (Oxford: Blackwell, 1939), pp. xiii, xiv, xviii, xxvii.

2. Werner Jaeger, *Paideia: The Ideals of Greek Culture,* trans. Gilbert Highet, vol. 2 (New York: Oxford University Press, 1943), pp. 70, 294.

3. Donald Lazere, "Conservative Critics Have a Distorted View of What Constitutes Ideological Bias in Academe," *Chronicle of Higher Education,* 8 November 1988, p. A52.

4. Jules Henry, *Culture against Man* (New York: Random House, 1963), pp. 283, 284, 285, 286, 287.

5. For a discussion of the "exaptation" of languages as cognitive modeling systems for the purposes of communication, a controversial notion, see Thomas A. Sebeok, "In What Sense Is Language a 'Primary Modeling System'?" in *Proceedings of the 25th Symposium of the Tartu-Moscow School of Semiotics, Imatra, Finland, 27th–29th July, 1987,* ed. Henri Broms and Rebecca Kaufmann (Helsinki: Arator, 1988), pp. 67–80. He borrows the term, which refers to the appropriation of an evolutionary adaptation for a subsequent and different function (an adaptation of an adaptation), from Stephen J. Gould and Elisabeth S. Vrba, "Exaptation: A Missing Term in the Science of Form," *Paleobiology* 8 (1982): 4–15.

6. Robert M. Nielsen and Irvin H. Polishook, "Academic Autopsies," *Chronicle of Higher Education,* 29 June 1988, p. A24.

7. Gene Lyons, "The Higher Illiteracy: On the Prejudice against Teaching College Students to Write," in *The Higher Illiteracy: Essays on Bureaucracy, Propaganda, and Self-Delusion* (Fayetteville: University of Arkansas Press, 1988), pp. 46, 47, 48, 52, 53, 55, 57. This essay was originally published in *Harper's,* September 1976, pp. 33–40.

8. Gene Lyons, "Why Teachers Can't Teach," in *Higher Illiteracy,* pp. 187, 188, 190, 191, 196, 202, 207, 210. This essay was originally published in *Texas*

Monthly, September 1979, pp. 122–28, 208–20. Lyons's judgment of schools of education, much like that found in Rita Kramer's more recent *Ed School Follies: The Miseducation of America's Teachers* (New York: Free Press, 1991), neglects mercilessly many aspects of their long-evolving dilemmas. For a more balanced view see Geraldine Jonçich Clifford and James W. Guthrie, *Ed School: A Brief for Professional Education* (Chicago: University of Chicago Press, 1988), which deals particularly with the predicament of such schools trying to respond to the demands of both their research university environments and their public school constituencies, at the expense, in the authors' opinion, of the latter. But see also, in this connection, *The Professors of Teaching: An Inquiry,* ed. Richard Wisniewski and Edward R. Ducharme (Albany: State University of New York Press, 1989), a collection whose contributors grapple passim with the same predicament and whose editors conclude that, since "scholarship is the *sine qua non* of the professorial life," it has to be combined with fieldwork and that schools of education should "shift from a grudging acceptance of this dual responsibility to a spirited embrace of it" and thereby (along with such measures as the elimination or considerable improvement of low-quality institutions, especially those unaccredited—for whatever the sanction is worth—by the National Council for the Accreditation of Teacher Education) "transform the world of teaching and learning" (Wisniewski and Ducharme, "Where We Stand," pp. 150, 152)—surely a recommendation, however hyperbolic in its hope, germanely responsive to Lyons's indictment.

9. Richard Mitchell, *The Graves of Academe* (Boston: Little, Brown, 1981), pp. 27, 26, 39, 47–48.

10. Ibid., pp. 67, 66, 66–67.

11. Ibid., pp. 69, 71.

12. Ibid., pp. 78, 83, 82.

13. Ibid., pp. 85, 87, 88, 91, 198, 199, 202.

14. Carolyn J. Mooney, "Conservative Scholars Call for a Movement to 'Reclaim' Academy," *Chronicle of Higher Education,* 23 November 1988, p. A1. Catharine R. Stimpson points out numerous ironies in the conservative (mis)use of the term *politically correct,* arguing that it "was first used as a term of self-criticism among Marxists and progressives" to refer to "a hack, one who mindlessly hewed to the party line," but is now used by conservatives to "accuse the left of being incapable of self-criticism," in her "Now 'Politically Correct' Metaphors Insult History and Our Campuses," *Chronicle of Higher Education,* 29 May 1991, p. A40. Though the term at some time may have been used without derogation, it was a joke when I first encountered it; and it will, I predict, quickly fall into disuse. But be that as it may, the term, when now used seriously by anyone, bespeaks a desire for a simple attitudinal solution to complex cultural problems. Hence, to the extent that such a solution is institutionalized and enforced, it surely harbors genuine dangers: suppression of free speech, discouragement of individuality, imposition of a monolithic "liberal" ideology on the curriculum and society at large. Still, the present threat of such dangers has been much exaggerated by the phantom-manufacturing right. And few on the left or right seem to notice how little attention is paid to political correctness by many of those about whom one is supposed to be politically correct—or to find a measure of humor in some of the epiphenomena of political correctness (in the ideological slippage that sanctions "blonde jokes," for example, or in what I call

the hyperethnicity bandwagon effect, whereby, among other manifestations, an increasing number of apparent Caucasians are suddenly, for the first time, identifying themselves in terms of a real, imagined, or scantily documented minority ancestry, Native American being of late the most "in," as the last decennial census dramatically shows).

15. A. Bartlett Giamatti, *A Free and Ordered Space: The Real World of the University* (New York: Norton, 1988), pp. 299, 280, 34, 25, 26.

16. Ibid., pp. 25, 28.

17. Ibid., pp. 38, 45–46.

18. Allan Bloom, *The Closing of the American Mind: How Higher Education Has Failed Democracy and Impoverished the Souls of Today's Students* (New York: Simon & Schuster, 1987), pp. 19, 20, 21.

19. Ibid., pp. 22, 25, 27, 30, 34.

20. Ibid., pp. 40, 43, 42. Oddly enough, Gary Kates, who has observed Bloom in the classroom, contends that there he "took an open approach to the classics" quite unlike that proposed in his book, where "he mummifies the history of ideas" ("The Classics of Western Civilization Do Not Belong to Conservatives Alone," *Chronicle of Higher Education*, 5 July 1989, p. B2). In any case, Bloom's notion that educators ought somehow to clear away "critical concepts" in order to expose nature pure and simple is appallingly silly. An effective antidote is Joel C. Weinsheimer's *Gadamer's Hermeneutics: A Reading of "Truth and Method"* (New Haven, Conn.: Yale University Press, 1985), a book that explores at length not only the interpretive methods of the natural sciences, aesthetics, historicism, and other epistemological enterprises but also the extent to which, once they reflect on their own methods, they become hermeneutical in a much more complex way. Presumably Bloom would have educators avoid both those methods and reflection on them in favor of his "prejudices"—and thereby protect their students from the conversations of "hermeneutic consciousness," an apeironic "openness to new experience, to the unexpected, to possibility, and to the future" (pp. 205, 204).

21. Bloom, *Closing of the American Mind*, pp. 141, 143, 147, 153, 155.

22. Ibid., pp. 337, 336, 337, 338.

23. Ibid., pp. 339, 343, 344, 343, 344, 346.

24. Ibid., pp. 346, 379, 380.

25. Ibid., pp. 370, 380, 381, 382. Further examples of the self-undermining gestures that punctuate Bloom's book may be found in Karen Swann, "The Sublime and the Vulgar," *College English* 52 (1990): 7–20. She explores the history, from Edmund Burke to the present, of the sublime-slime dialectic that Bloom resuscitates, exposing the ironies of interdependence of his dreamy elitist idealism about education and everything pop that he abhors. Prominent among those ironies is "Bloom's commercial success," which indicates "that the boundaries between the high and the low are more permeable and the man of culture's relation to both fields more complex than he himself lets on" (p. 9). Such gestures punctuate also Bloom's more recent *Giants and Dwarfs: Essays, 1960–1990* (New York: Simon & Schuster, 1990), a book that offers nothing new.

26. Robert Scholes, "Three Views of Education: Nostalgia, History, and Voodoo," review of *The Closing of the American Mind* by Allan Bloom, *Professing Literature: An Institutional History* by Gerald Graff, and *Cultural Literacy:*

What Every American Needs to Know by E. D. Hirsch, Jr., *College English* 50 (1988): 323, 326, 332.

27. See Martin Gardner, "The Curious Mind of Allan Bloom," review of *The Closing of the American Mind* by Allan Bloom, in *Gardner's Whys & Wherefores* (Chicago: University of Chicago Press, 1989), pp. 256–61.

28. Kenneth Alan Hovey, "The Great Books versus America: Reassessing *The Closing of the American Mind,*" in *Profession 88,* ed. Phyllis Franklin (New York: Modern Language Association, 1988), pp. 41, 40–41.

29. William K. Buckley, "The Good, the Bad, and the Ugly in Amerika's *Akadēmia,*" in *Profession 88,* ed. Franklin, pp. 46, 47, 51.

30. Helene Moglen, "Allan Bloom and E. D. Hirsch: Educational Reform as Tragedy and Farce" in *Profession 88,* ed. Franklin, pp. 60, 61, 62–63.

31. Sidney Hook, *"The Closing of the American Mind:* An Intellectual Best-Seller Revisited," *American Scholar* 58 (1989): 127, 128, 130, 134.

32. Paul A. Bové, *Intellectuals in Power: A Genealogy of Critical Humanism* (New York: Columbia University Press, 1986), pp. ix, xi, xii, xiii, xv.

33. Ibid., pp. 1, xvii, 1–2.

34. Ibid., pp. 2, 8, 36, 37, 173, 172, 173.

35. Russell Jacoby, *The Last Intellectuals: American Culture in the Age of Academe* (New York: Basic Books, 1987), pp. 221, x, xii, xiii.

36. Ibid., pp. 5, 6, 7.

37. Ibid., pp. 237, 19.

38. Ibid., pp. 196, 198, 199, 200, 201, 203, 205, 208, 207.

39. Richard Ohmann, "Graduate Students, Professionals, Intellectuals," *College English* 52 (1990): 256. According to Ohmann, Jacoby very much underestimates the public impact of "critical intellectuals" since the early 1960s.

40. Jonathan Swift, *A Tale of a Tub,* in *Jonathan Swift,* ed. Angus Ross and David Woolley (New York: Oxford University Press, 1984), p. 143.

Chapter 3
The Natural Sciences

1. See Ina V. S. Mullis and Lynn B. Jenkins, *The Science Report Card: Elements of Risk and Recovery: Trends and Achievement Based on the 1986 National Assessment* (Princeton, N.J.: Educational Testing Service, 1988).

2. See Archie E. Lapointe, Nancy A. Mead, and Gary W. Phillips, *A World of Differences: An International Assessment of Mathematics and Science* (Princeton, N.J.: Educational Testing Service, 1989).

3. See John A. Dossey, Ina V. S. Mullis, Mary M. Lindquist, and Donald L. Chamber, *The Mathematics Report Card: Are We Measuring Up?: Trends and Achievement Based on the 1986 National Assessment* (Princeton, N. J.: Educational Testing Service, 1988).

4. See *Everybody Counts: A Report to the Nation on the Future of Mathematics Education* (Washington, D.C.: National Academy Press, 1989).

5. There is considerable debate about the exportability, to the United States or elsewhere, of the Japanese model of education (either generally or in specific

disciplinary areas). Whatever its merits—the greatest of which is a pervasive awareness of the importance of education (*kyōiku*, which means "culture" as well), especially by Japanese mothers, who, for good or ill, make a profession of their children's educational development and accomplishments—it has serious problems. Most notably, like the American model, it fosters, in spades, "excessive academic pressure" that has little to do with engaged, productive learning, with the consequence that students who graduate from high school (a *high* percentage) and go on to a university (a relatively *low* percentage) experience there a sort of postpressure "four-year vacation" that little encourages subsequent educational growth—a paradigmatic illustration of the cost of "premature education structuring" (David Elkind, *The Hurried Child: Growing Up Too Fast Too Soon*, rev. ed. [Reading, Mass.: Addison-Wesley, 1988], pp. 57, 59, 60).

6. Encouraging in this regard is Robert-Alain de Beaugrande and Wolfgang Ulrich Dressler's claim that "the shift away from 'facts' toward the procedures for acquiring or demonstrating facts has finally begun in the sciences at large. . . . This trend, so long overdue, has proven enormously productive in opening the foundations of sciences to critical discussion at a time when a point of diminishing returns has become noticeable in many fields. . . . On a more detailed plane, the same trend is emerging in education" (*Introduction to Text Linguistics*, updated and trans. Robert-Alain de Beaugrande [London: Longman, 1981], p. 222n).

7. Mathematicians have a poor record of effectively sharing their work and its implications with nonspecialist students and the lay public, a situation addressed with sensitivity and humor by John Allen Paulos in his best-selling *Innumeracy: Mathematical Illiteracy and Its Consequences* (New York: Hill & Wang, 1988).

8. See *Science for All Americans* (Washington, D.C.: American Association for the Advancement of Science, 1989). I should note here that, while the Holmes Group was well conceived—especially in its demands, outlined originally in *Tomorrow's Teachers: A Report of the Holmes Group* (East Lansing, Mich.: The Holmes Group, 1986), for the enhancement of graduate-level teacher education, an end to the conventional baccalaureate in education, more undergraduate learning in subject fields, more attention to the pedagogical principles specific to those fields (instead of general "methods" courses), higher standards for professional tiering, more productive linkage between educational research and practice, and so on—it has not, for the most part, proven to be an effective organization. The reasons for that, which include internal political squabbles and a lack of sufficient membership commitment (budgetary and otherwise) to the agenda for reform, are various, partly adumbrated by Geraldine Jonçich Clifford and James W. Guthrie in their *Ed School: A Brief for Professional Education* (Chicago: University of Chicago Press, 1988), p. 346. When I attended the 1988 national meeting, a colleague observed, perhaps with more sense of irony than I registered at the time, "There's no place like Holmes." Alas, there still is not (a "place," a utopia ["no-place"]), like it wanted to become.

9. Edward A. Feigenbaum and Pamela McCorduck, *The Fifth Generation: Artificial Intelligence and Japan's Computer Challenge to the World*, rev. and updated ed. (New York: New American Library, Signet, 1984), pp. 247, 249, 251.

10. Northrop Frye, "Speculation and Concern," in *The Stubborn Structure:*

Essays on Criticism and Society (Ithaca, N.Y.: Cornell University Press, 1970), pp. 55, 50, 55.

11. Paul Feyerabend, *Against Method: Outline of an Anarchistic Theory of Knowledge* (Atlantic Highlands, N.J.: Humanities Press, 1975), pp. 19, 307, 308, 20, 21.

12. Lewis Thomas, "Humanities and Science," in *Late Night Thoughts on Listening to Mahler's Ninth Symphony* (New York: Viking Press, 1983), pp. 143, 146, 147–48.

13. Ibid., pp. 148–49, 150.

14. Ibid., pp. 151, 152, 153, 154–55. In the United States the imperative for a citizenry more radically and critically educated in the natural sciences is made all the more crucial by the unwillingness of the federal government, so busy mandating reports about science education, to maintain adequate agencies for advising its own branches about scientific (and attendant technological) issues. It also does a poor job of heeding such advice as *is* available from agencies like the shrunken Office of Science and Technology Policy and the newer President's Council of Advisers on Science and Technology. In this connection see *Science and Technology Advice to the President, Congress, and Judiciary,* ed. William T. Golden (New York: Pergamon, 1988).

15. James Boyd White, *When Words Lose Their Meaning: Constitutions and Reconstitutions of Language, Character, and Community* (Chicago: University of Chicago Press, 1984), p. 278.

Chapter 4
The Social Sciences

1. Diane Ravitch, "Tot Sociology: Or What Happened to History in the Grade Schools," *American Scholar* 56 (1987): 343, 344, 345, 346, 347, 349.

2. Ibid., pp. 350, 351, 353, 354, 351, 353.

3. Larry McMurtry, *Anything for Billy* (New York: Simon & Schuster, 1988), p. 366.

4. Guy Davenport, review of *Gibbon's Solitude: The Inward World of the Historian* by W. B. Carnochan, *American Scholar* 58 (1989): 470. It is interesting to note in this connection that Gibbon achieves his insight through a perspective that, as Davenport explains Carnochan's adaptation of an observation from Erwin Panofsky concerning the retinally determined concavity of vision, involves "ultimately a rondure, not the pinching in of a vanishing point" (470). It might be useful to think of apeironic instructing in history as favoring the openness of biologically based rondure perspective rather than the closedness of vanishing-point perspective, which latter seems to be (unconsciously) favored by traditional teaching, probably as a consequence of the general acceptance as "natural" of an artistic convention inherited from the Renaissance. This construal suggests an analogy with Mikhail Bakhtin's distinction between histories as convergent modes of discourse and novels as divergent ones: the texts of traditional history and teaching instantiate more the first mode, while those of apeironic historicism and instructing instantiate more the second (which is not to imply that they are any less "true"—quite the contrary).

5. Lest the reader think I am inadvertently reinventing the wheel, I should say that the idea of reading history in terms of such rhetorical actions, though it has been little enacted educationally, especially at primary and secondary levels, is not wholly new. Indeed, as Susan Noakes notes in her discussion of the centrality of historical problems to Derridean deconstruction, "reflections on the impulse . . . to 'read' certain things as symptoms of what is lost, have been an important part of the territory of the historiographer since long before they were associated with the term 'deconstruction' " (*Timely Reading: Between Exegesis and Interpretation* [Ithaca, N.Y.: Cornell University Press, 1988], p. 219).

6. Brook Thomas, "The Historical Necessity for—and Difficulties with— New Historical Analysis in Introductory Literature Courses," *College English* 49 (1987): 509, 510–11, 513, 514, 519, 520, 521. This perspective necessarily entails the recognition, neatly codified by Dominick LaCapra in *Rethinking Intellectual History: Texts, Contexts, Language* (Ithaca, N.Y.: Cornell University Press, 1983), that "there are no purely documentary texts. . . . The artifacts through which we approach historical reality are themselves historical realities," therefore do not represent in any simple way "some privileged reality such as 'society' or 'ordinary life,' " and should themselves, especially if canonical, be studied through "contestatory readings" and "reopened" to reveal their assumptions (metaphysical and otherwise) and discontinuities (pp. 340, 344, 345).

7. See, for example, Martin Mueller, "Yellow Stripes and Dead Armadillos: Some Thoughts on the Current State of English Studies," *ADE Bulletin,* no. 92 (Spring 1989), pp. 8–9. Surely the most severe position on the "blurred genres," to use Clifford Geertz's phrase, now involved in the melding of the projects of the humanities and social sciences into a larger textualist superdiscipline is that of Stanley Fish, who argues that "being interdisciplinary is more than hard to do; it is impossible to do"—by reason of perspectival paradoxes (for instance, a given practice "cannot 'say' the Other but can only say itself")—and that "proponents of radical pedagogy" should be aware of that ("Being Interdisciplinary Is So Very Hard to Do," in *Profession 89,* ed. Phyllis Franklin [New York: Modern Language Association, 1989], p. 19). The argument has more Zenonian interest than purport for practical usefulness; still, however, it should serve to qualify profoundly any naïveté about the ambitions and limitations of interdisciplinarity.

8. Phillippe Sollers, *Writing and the Experience of Limits,* ed. David Hayman, trans. Philip Barnard with David Hayman (New York: Columbia University Press, 1983), p. 124.

9. Quoted in Karen J. Winkler, "Dispute over Validity of Historical Approaches Pits Traditionalists against Advocates of New Methods," *Chronicle of Higher Education,* 11 January 1989, pp. A5, A7.

10. Quoted in ibid., p. A7.

11. For example, having high school students write revisions of passages in their history textbooks from several interpretive positions helps them see "how history is constructed out of conflicting sets of data" and understand "that historical knowledge (and by implication, all knowledge) is a construction" about which they should "think critically" (John Reiff, "Remembering Things Past: A Critique of Narrow Revision," *Research in the Teaching of English* 24 [1990]: 101, 106).

12. Ellen K. Coughlin, "Anthropologists Explore the Possibilities, and Question the Limits, of Experimentation in Ethnographic Writing and Research," *Chronicle of Higher Education,* 30 November 1988, p. A5.

13. Gordon Hewes, "The Rashōmon Problem," review of *Works and Lives: The Anthropologist as Author* by Clifford Geertz, *American Book Review* 10, no. 5 (November-December 1988): 11, 19.

14. Clifford Geertz, "Blurred Genres: The Refiguration of Social Thought," in *Local Knowledge: Further Essays in Interpretive Anthropology* (New York: Basic Books, 1983), pp. 20, 22–23, 25, 9, 21. What "is happening to the way we think about the way we think" *is,* in many ways, textualization, an interdisciplinary, thickly cross-referenced extrapolation of what Robert Scholes calls "the semiotic assumption that all the world's a text" (*Protocols of Reading* [New Haven, Conn.: Yale University Press, 1989], p. 1). To the profound extent that all the world indeed is a text (or is read as a text, experienced as a cybernetic semiotic system and not just as an artifact)—from the realm of subatomic physics to that of the human genome to that of Michel de Certeau's "semiocracy" controlled by sociopolitical institutions and on out to the stars—all learning, even at the elementary level, should involve some self-conscious knowledge of and exploratory thinking in semiotics, the ecumenical study of sign systems (monetary, immunological, mathematical, architectural, whatever) as structures or processes for making meaning. This argument is engagingly elaborated in a monograph by T. A. Sebeok, S. M. Lamb, and J. O. Regan entitled *Semiotics in Education: A Dialogue* (Claremont, Calif.: The Claremont Graduate School, 1988), which is concerned, as Regan observes in his opening remarks, both with how "the variety of modes or ways of human thinking, creating, communication can be appreciated by implementing a semiotic perspective in education" and with how semiotics can help in "understanding educational problems" (p. 2).

15. Robert-Alain de Beaugrande and Wolfgang Ulrich Dressler, *Introduction to Text Linguistics,* updated and trans. Robert-Alain de Beaugrande (London: Longman, 1981), pp. 110, xiv–xv. Thus the interpretive conventions to which Geertz alludes engage the universe (social and otherwise) more as relational, informational, and perceptual or conceptual than as objective, physical, and material. Their worldview is more Batesonian than Cartesian, more concerned with the sociocognitive conditions (constraints, thresholds, and so on) of knowledge as interpretation than with the logical conditions of knowledge as "truth." Also, in Michael Riffaterre's terms, they tend to emphasize *"semiosis"* over *"mimesis,"* being more attentive to "what language does *to* reality" than to "checking language against reality," a privileging of the text's intensional *"significance"* over its extensional *"meaning"* (*Semiotics of Poetry* [Bloomington: Indiana University Press, 1978], pp. 4, 2, 7, 2).

Chapter 5
The Humanities

1. Northrop Frye, "Speculation and Concern," in *The Stubborn Structure: Essays on Criticism and Society* (Ithaca, N.Y.: Cornell University Press, 1970), pp. 42, 53.

2. Robert E. Proctor, *Education's Great Amnesia: Reconsidering the Humanities from Petrarch to Freud, with a Curriculum for Today's Students* (Bloomington: Indiana University Press, 1988), p. xiii.

3. Ibid., pp. xiv, xv. The "vogue for 'quantitative reasoning' in the social sciences" surely has been around too long to be labeled such. For a more informed and still pertinent view of it—and of the history of movement counter to it—see Floyd W. Matson, *The Broken Image: Man, Science and Society* (New York: Braziller, 1964).

4. Proctor, *Education's Great Amnesia*, pp. xv, xvi–xvii. Petrarch thus may be portrayed as the founder (one of them, anyway) of what some Christian fundamentalists have of late called secular humanism, though his works (especially those that engage Proctor, *Secret* [*Secretum*] and *On His Own Ignorance and That of Many Others* [*De sui ipsius et multorum ignorantia*]) show him to have been much more acutely and intelligently aware than his smug latter-day condemners of both the conflicts involved in his divergence from classical tradition (and the Christian, preoccupied with the wobble in its own inner/outer distinction) and the implications for education.

5. Proctor, *Education's Great Amnesia*, pp. xvii, xviii.

6. Ibid., p. xviii.

7. Ibid., pp. 171, 173, 172, 173, 175, 174, 179.

8. Ibid., pp. 183, 185, 188, 198.

9. In this connection see William Damon, *The Moral Child: Nurturing Children's Natural Moral Growth* (New York: Free Press, 1988), a work, some of whose insights are applicable beyond childhood, that counters in scholarly fashion the conservative and traditionalist accusation that liberal and leftist moral education is corrupting—or leaving open to corruption—America's youth. The research that Damon surveys has not received much attention from educators, however, partly because of a behaviorist, non-Piagetian bias in American educational psychology (see Karen J. Winkler, "Experts on Moral Development Find Common Ground under Fire from Critics of America's Schools," *Chronicle of Higher Education,* 26 October 1988, pp. A4, A8). An opposite situation is beginning to obtain (once again, many would argue) in language education, where for several decades research has argued that the pedagogies of both native and non-native languages "should shift from teacher-telling to learner-interpreting within a syllabus whose prime goal is the development of strategies for discourse processing, rather than an assembly of items," with the result that increasingly the focus of effective language education is less on the *teaching* of grammar (probably the way Proctor would favor for Greek and Latin) and more on the immersion-oriented *learning* of "communicative competence." The research urging that shift, with its emphasis not on "surface grammatical structures" (a narrowly conceived *grammatica*) but on "underlying semantic roles" and "pragmatics and interaction" (a broadly conceived *rhetorica*), now more closely parallels, I would suggest, social-constructionist than Piagetian research in moral development—though educators are not attending sufficiently to either. (Malcolm Coulthard, *An Introduction to Discourse Analysis* [London: Longman, 1977], pp. xii, 138, 154.)

10. See Proctor, *Education's Great Amnesia,* pp. 190-97.

11. However much at odds with Bennett on many issues, I must give him his due: some of his criticism of spending in education, especially that on non-

academic endeavors (not to mention research-funding scams, more of which come to light almost daily), hits the mark. Though it betrays a Bennett-like bias in its judgments about the professoriat and curricular matters, an article that provides embarrassing corroboration is Jay Amberg, "Higher (-Priced) Education," *American Scholar* 58 (1989): 521–32.

12. Susan Sage Heinzelman, "Two Turns of the Screw: Feminism and the Humanities," *ADE Bulletin*, no. 91 (Winter 1988), p. 18.

13. Gerald Graff, *Professing Literature: An Institutional History* (Chicago: University of Chicago Press, 1987), pp. 4, 5.

14. Ibid., p. 6.

15. Ibid., pp. 7, 8, 9.

16. Ibid., pp. 9–10, 11. The phrase quoted from Robert Scholes may be found in his *Textual Power: Literary Theory and the Teaching of English* (New Haven, Conn.: Yale University Press, 1985), p. 33. Though Graff's discussion throughout *Professing Literature* focuses to a great extent, as one would expect, on the internal historical logic of a discipline and tends to be oriented toward faculty issues, I think his interest in the political dimensions of the issues he foregrounds and in student participation in debating them is well evidenced in this and the preceding paragraphs. Hence I disagree strongly with Bruce Henricksen's opinion that "Graff's 'dialogue' is a one-way hookup between faculty and student; it is only professors who speak, and their words remain uncontaminated either by the voice of the student or by social discourses originating outside the academy" ("Teaching against the Grain," in *Reorientations: Critical Theories and Pedagogies*, ed. Bruce Henricksen and Thaïs E. Morgan [Urbana: University of Illinois Press, 1990], p. 31). Graff, like Henricksen, advocates a more Bakhtinian classroom, hardly a monological one designed to smother the possibilities of wider conversation and social action.

17. Graff, *Professing Literature*, pp. 11, 13, 15.

18. Karen Lawrence, "Curriculosclerosis; or, Hardening of the Categories," *ADE Bulletin*, no. 90 (Fall 1988), pp. 13, 16.

19. Martin Mueller, "Yellow Stripes and Dead Armadillos: Some Thoughts on the Current State of English Studies," *ADE Bulletin*, no. 92 (Spring 1989), p. 6–7. For further discussion of the opposing scientific ("natural science") and humanistic ("human science") views of the past, see Joel C. Weinsheimer, *Gadamer's Hermeneutics: A Reading of "Truth and Method"* (New Haven, Conn.: Yale University Press, 1985), esp. pp. 26–27. The more I ponder Mueller's invocation of this opposition, in the light of Weinsheimer's discussion, the more I discern a delusion in the conservative accusation (that education neglects the past) being aimed more at any specific antitraditional leftist agenda, real or imagined, than at the general dominance of the scientific view, however problematic, that history is linear, cumulative, and progressive and the past therefore always superseded, abandoned, or both. Bloom seems to aim at both targets; but he is not typical in that regard, since an unreflective proscientific attitude tends to characterize the self-warring amalgam of the conservative spirit.

20. Mueller, "Yellow Stripes," p. 7.

21. Ibid., pp. 7, 11.

22. Peter Carafiol, "The Constraints of History: Revision and Revolution in American Literary Studies," *College English* 50 (1988): 614.

23. Nelson and Waller are quoted, directly and indirectly, in Scott Heller, "Scholars Defend Their Efforts to Promote Literature by Women and Blacks, Decry Attack by Bennett," *Chronicle of Higher Education,* 17 February 1988, pp. A1, A16. The what/how distinction here has an important parallel in Roger Schank's argument, set forth in his *Explanation Patterns: Understanding Mechanically and Creatively* (Hillsdale, N.J.: Erlbaum, 1986), that understanding, by either artificial or human intelligence, is gauged better by a test of explanation (the *how* of knowing, the concern of his "Explanation Test") than by a test of imitation (the *what* of knowing, the concern not only of traditional teachers but also of artificial-intelligence theorists who long have been obsessed—misguidedly, according to Schank—with the so-called Turing test or "Imitation Game" as the criterion of whether or not a computer manifests humanlike comprehension).

24. Gerald Graff, "Conflicts over the Curriculum Are Here to Stay; They Should Be Made Educationally Productive," *Chronicle of Higher Education,* 17 February 1988, p. A48. His notion of conflict and debate as a conversation of differences that defers any collapsing into indifferent consensus should be distinguished carefully from what Walter J. Ong, in "Agonistic Structures in Academia: Past to Present" (*Daedalus* 103, no. 4 [Fall 1974]: 229–38), calls "the old kind of ceremonial enmity between teacher and (male) student," inherited from the medieval university, that by the end of the 1960s "was largely outmoded or even outlawed"—along with its "extreme noetic conservatism" and the combative male "insecurity" that perpetuated it (pp. 229, 230, 235). What has emerged on the other side of the 1960s is a less Spartan, more open, connective, collaborative, playful, feminized kind of dialogue (indeed, one that has been evolving since women began entering academia). It thrives not on ceremonial attacks and counterattacks but on the more Ciceronian interplay of issues pursued "in the widest possible variety of perspectives" (Thomas O. Sloane, "Reinventing *inventio,*" *College English* 51 [1989]: 469).

25. Mike Rose, *Lives on the Boundary: The Struggles and Achievements of America's Underprepared* (New York: Free Press, 1989), pp. 233, 234. On the criteria involved in selecting texts for different kinds of canons, see Wendell V. Harris, "Canonicity," *Publications of the Modern Language Association* 106 (1991): 110–21.

26. Rose, *Lives on the Boundary,* p. 235.

27. Ibid., pp. 236, 237–38.

28. The example of the Los Angeles school system, with its insatiable need for bilingual educators, should startle and sober anyone who believes that the problems of cultural diversity in American education are either readily manageable or passing—or that its opportunities are not worth pursuing. The typical American attitude, most severely instanced by the fact that one-third of the states recently have passed legislative propositions concerning English as the country's "official language," is assimilationist—in marked contrast to the attitudes prevalent in most of the countries of the of the world, where multilingualism is general. The melting-pot philosophy involved here is all the more problematic when one realizes that immigrant students are not just from "other countries": frequently they come from countries that are racked by war, starvation, death squads, God knows what horrors—which may well have been occasioned, in part at least, by the ineptitudes of American foreign policy. Many native-born

minority students have experienced situations almost as bad. In any case, the time of assimilationism—if it ever had a time—has passed.

Still, widespread calls for cultural pluralism in American education—especially those from conservatives like Ravitch and Charles E. Finn, Jr., now president of the Madison Center, with their concern that ethnic particularism or chauvinism makes a hypocritical hodgepodge of the curriculum (see, for example, Diane Ravitch, "Multiculturalism: E Pluribus Plures," *American Scholar* 59 [1990]: 337–54)—tend to feel assimilationist in ultimate intent. Ideological resistance to pluralism and its implications is nearly as strong, on the whole, as it was at the beginning the 1980s, when James A. Banks argued that "most of the educators who control the schools are assimilationist oriented and see forms of pluralistic education as inconsistent with their basic values, commitments, and beliefs" (*Multiethnic Education: Theory and Practice* [Boston: Allyn & Bacon, 1981], p. 84). Given such resistance, he may well be right that change in policies and curricula, at least in the immediate future, can be effected most fruitfully if "guided by an eclectic ideology that reflects both the cultural pluralist position and the assimilationist position, but that avoids their extremes" (p. 73). If such a multiethnic ideology were (internally) transactional à la Graff and Rose, it surely could avoid both the beige cultural unification advocated by Ravitch, Finn, and others and the treaty-driven cultural amorphousness promoted by the sort of thoughtless and depersonalized accommodation that has become pathological in American high schools and made their faculties multiethnic babysitters rather than creative mediators. (See Arthur G. Powell, Eleanor Farrar, and David K. Cohen, *The Shopping Mall High School: Winners and Losers in the Educational Marketplace* [Boston: Houghton Mifflin, 1985], a book that shrewdly exposes the travesties born of noncommittal cultural bargaining and stresses the need for more meaningful interaction not only between educators and their students but among educators themselves.) The sine qua non for the educational success of any such ideology, particularly if it pushes toward the pluralist end of Banks's spectrum, is that it be, as systems analysts say, a *system* (with a purposeful, however changeful, dynamic) and not just a *heap*—a necessity of which Graff, Rose, and others are very much aware.

29. Myra Jehlen, "How the Curriculum Is the Least of Our Problems," *ADE Bulletin*, no. 93 (Fall 1989), p. 7.

30. See Scott Heller, "Experts Convened by Endowment Head Are Divided in Assessing the Health of the Humanities," *Chronicle of Higher Education,* 9 March 1988, pp. A4, A11. In regard to Cheney's imposing her diagnosis on these proceedings, see, for example, Gerald Graff, "How to Deal with the Humanities Crisis: Organize It," *ADE Bulletin*, no. 95 (Spring 1990), p. 9, where he notes that "several panel members (myself included) persistently and strongly objected to . . . Cheney's tendentious conclusions. These conclusions dominated the published report, which gave no hint that objections had been made." And he adds that "this is but one instance of Cheney's flagrant abuse of the NEH to impose an ideological agenda on the humanities in the name of supposedly universal values and 'our' common culture."

31. Barbara Herrnstein Smith, "President's Column: Curing the Humanities, Correcting the Humanists," *MLA Newsletter,* Summer 1988, pp. 3, 4.

32. Lynne V. Cheney, *Humanities in America: A Report to the President, the*

Congress, and the American People (Washington, D.C.: National Endowment for the Humanities, 1988), pp. 2, 4, 5.

33. Ibid., pp. 7, 8, 9, 10. A special irony inheres in Cheney's choice of an example of the sort of text that "colleagues in the same discipline" have trouble understanding. It is a sentence from an article I wrote, "Hell Is the Place We Don't Know We're In: The Control-Dictions of Cultural Literacy, Strong Reading, and Poetry," *College English* 50 (1988): 309–17. According to Cheney, the sentence—found on pp. 314–15 and accurately cited by her—is from "a long, theoretical article" (somewhat theoretical, I admit, but eight and a half pages is hardly long) pointed out to her by "Jaime O'Neill, an English professor at Butte College in Oroville, California," who found the article "incomprehensible . . . , even though its subject—how to teach English—is one in which he is immersed professionally" (*Humanities in America,* pp. 9, 10). I know nothing about the extent of O'Neill's professional immersion in my subject, which involves a good deal more than just "how to teach English," but I do know that my sentence, though long (unlike the article) and complex, is surely comprehensible if the reader is attentive to its context (from which Cheney has removed it). It is just as comprehensible as the article itself when I first presented it as the keynote address, in almost exactly the same form, at the annual Composition and Literature Conference at the University of Kansas in October 1987. The three-hundred-odd people in attendance—educators from regional high schools, junior colleges, community colleges, colleges, and universities—apparently had little trouble understanding it. Indeed, it was very well received, so much so that, after appearing in *College English,* the article was immediately reprinted in *Kansas English* (73, no. 2 [March 1988]: 61–70). In consummation of the irony, I have received numerous letters from colleagues in the region and beyond—all of whom are employed, at various levels, in public institutions—thanking me for its helpfulness in their classroom practice. None mention whether or not it has influenced their "narrowly focused research." Finally, it seems absurd to use my article as a springboard for lamentation about the academy/society dichotomy: I was writing for my professional peers; if the text had been intended for a more general audience or readership, I would have written it otherwise—much as a physicist would in explaining the intricacies and possible applications of, say, magnetohydrodynamic theory, a preoccupation of his or her peers, to a more general audience or readership.

34. Cheney, *Humanities in America,* pp. 11, 12, 14.

35. Ibid., pp. 17, 18, 22.

36. Ibid., pp. 27, 28, 29. The reader may wish to consult also Cheney's *American Memory: A Report on the Humanities in the Nation's Public Schools* (Washington, D.C.: National Endowment for the Humanities, 1987).

37. David Laurence, "From the Editor," *ADE Bulletin,* no. 91 (Winter 1988), pp. 1, 2, 3. See also his "From the Editor," *ADE Bulletin,* no. 95 (Spring 1990), p. 3, where, in this same vein, he suggests, borrowing an outline from an un-named colleague, the possibility of a postsecondary English curriculum that, among other characteristics, "will not rest on a metanarrative" but "will tell many noncumulative stories" (an echo of Jean-François Lyotard's idea that "grand narratives," comprehensive "stories" of scientific knowledge, are now giving way to more provisional "little narratives"—see his *Postmodern Condi-*

tion: A Report on Knowledge, trans. Geoff Bennington and Brian Massumi [Minneapolis: University of Minnesota Press, 1984], p. 60); will "orchestrate contrasts" and "set the local against the local" (in the fashion of Clifford Geertz in his *Local Knowledge: Further Essays in Interpretive Anthropology* [New York: Basic Books, 1983]); and "will be chaotic in the technical sense, in that it will pay close, analytical attention to relations among disparate levels of scale . . . and to the appearance, disappearance, and reappearance of pattern across disparate scales" (see James Gleick, *Chaos: Making a New Science* [New York: Viking Press, 1987]). Laurence's suggestion concerning the shift from an established, traditional curriculum to a provisional, "chaotic" one thus reflects a more general shift in scholarly and scientific attention from the "abstractly" determinate to the "concretely" indeterminate, a shift instantiated in linguistics, for instance, in a movement from "virtual" to "actual(ized)" systems of language.

38. Phyllis Franklin, "From the Editor," *MLA Newsletter,* Winter 1988, p. 5.

39. George Levine et al., *Speaking for the Humanities* (New York: American Council of Learned Societies, 1989), pp. 1, 3, 4.

40. Ibid., pp. 5, 6, 8.

41. Ibid., pp. 9, 10, 11, 12.

42. Ibid., pp. 14, 13, 13–14. No one has developed or exemplified this pattern of argument more eloquently—or, perhaps, controversially—than Geoffrey H. Hartman, for whom it has considerable pedagogical import. In his *Criticism in the Wilderness: The Study of Literature Today* (New Haven, Conn.: Yale University Press, 1980), a book whose approach he characterizes as "personal and macaronic," he argues that "all knowledge" is "knowledge of a text, or rather of a textuality so complex and interwoven that it seems abysmal"; that indeterminacy in the interpretation of a text involves "delay" that may he conceived as "thoughtfulness itself, Keats's 'negative capability,'" a project of reading "to understand what is involved in reading as a form of life, rather than to resolve what is read into glossy ideas"; and that such "suspensive discourse," which he equates with criticism, assists us in hermeneutically "finding an enigma where we expected a kerygma" and enables "the inspiring teacher in the humanities" to "always be pointing to something neglected by the dominant point of view, or something blunted by familiarity, or despised by fashion and social pressure"—an activity of both "uncovering and preserving" (pp. 5, 202, 270, 272, 274, 283, 300).

43. Levine et al., *Speaking for the Humanities,* pp. 15, 16, 18, 20.

44. Ibid., pp. 22, 24.

45. See ibid., pp. 25–29.

46. Ibid., pp. 29, 30, 31.

47. Thomas Pynchon, *Gravity's Rainbow* (New York: Viking Press, 1973), p. 3. One may find abundant correlatives to Pynchon's contrajunctive turn here, which might well serve as the most general statement of the "progressive" tendency of the apeironic: reading not by "the straight line . . . approach" but by the "detour" that leads into "hermeneutic 'infinitizing'" of the text's labyrinth or "philosophical style" in the mode of Walter Benjamin that is not deductive but interruptive (Hartman, *Criticism in the Wilderness,* pp. 244, 281), not the seemingly straightforward referentiality of the text but its increasingly more deeply tangled and recursive self-referentiality, not centered structures but de-

centered and disseminated Derridean structural free play, not the explicit and literal text but its implicit and figurative intertexts, communication not as the sending and receiving of information but as the interactive negotiation of meaning, not ingenuousness but irony, not consistency but contradiction, not decidability but (more or less Gödelian) undecidability, and so on.

48. William Carlos Williams, "The Black Winds," in *The Collected Poems of William Carlos Williams,* ed. A. Walton Litz and Christopher MacGowan, vol. 1, *1909–1939* (New York: New Directions, 1986), p. 191.

49. Levine et al., *Speaking for the Humanities,* pp. 32, 33, 34, 33.

50. See, for example, Lynne V. Cheney, "Current Fashions in Scholarship Diminish the Value of the Humanities," *Chronicle of Higher Education,* 8 February 1989, p. A40. Pretty much the same drumbeating characterizes her *50 Hours: A Core Curriculum for College Students* (Washington, D.C.: National Endowment for the Humanities, 1989) though the report is perhaps a little more moderate in tone. Cheney amply exemplifies efforts she regards as praiseworthy, and the report is hard to fault in some particulars—for instance, in its scolding of some institutions for allowing courses in "physical education" and the like to fulfill general-education requirements, typically a grab bag, and in its recognition of the need for more rigorous and comprehensive education in mathematics and laboratory-based science courses. But the humanities canon offered has the usual pseudo-Periclean flavor, albeit with the inclusion of token texts from Mayan civilization, blacks, women, and so on. The fear of "politics" turns up again, along with Cheney's apparently incorrigible belief that her principal texts about the human condition really do not require much interpretation. In any case, the report is largely old hat, for postsecondary institutions had been undertaking reforms much like those she proposes since at least 1985.

51. Some idea of the fruitfulness of this comparative method in the teaching of American and Native American literature may be found in *Approaches to Teaching Momaday's "The Way to Rainy Mountain,"* ed. Kenneth M. Roemer (New York: Modern Language Association, 1988). Evidence for the substantial but inadequately theorized and debated influence of the computer on the humanities is readily available; cogent examples may be found in recent issues of the journal *Computers and the Humanities* and, especially regarding its usefulness to the pedagogy of intra- and intertextuality (a distinction that is becoming increasingly blurred), in George P. Landow, "Changing Texts, Changing Readers: Hypertext in Literary Education, Criticism, and Scholarship," in *Reorientations,* ed. Henricksen and Morgan, pp. 133–61, a treatment that suggestively interrelates the concerns of cognitive learning theory, critical theory, and poststructuralism.

52. Ross Chambers, "Irony and the Canon," in *Profession 90,* ed. Phyllis Franklin (New York: Modern Language Association, 1990), pp. 23, 21, 24.

53. John M. Slatin, "Reading Hypertext: Order and Coherence in a New Medium," *College English* 52 (1990): 872, 874.

54. See Ellen K. Coughlin, "Scholars in the Humanities Are Disheartened by the Course of Debate over Their Disciplines," *Chronicle of Higher Education,* 13 September 1989, pp. A1ff. Donald Lazere makes and ably documents much harsher judgments of how the right has manipulated the debate, especially during "the canon wars of 1988," when the National Association of Scholars was

cranking up, big-city newspapers were beginning to get on the canonical band-wagon, and "neoconservative ideologues" of all kinds—however "self-deluded"—were engaged in "ham-fisted assaults" toward the end of "delegitimizing views outside the ideological consensus," assaults that—however much "ostensibly defending high-minded disinterestedness"—show "all the rhetorical marks of a partisan smear campaign: making lurid accusations calculated to maximize public-ity; evaluating expressions of the opposing side with malice aforethought . . . ; misquoting or misrepresenting the opposition . . . [and on and on]" ("Literary Revisionism, Partisan Politics, and the Press," in *Profession 89,* ed. Phyllis Franklin [New York: Modern Language Association, 1989], pp. 49, 51, 53, 54, 53, 49).

55. Well-meant and sobering, though naïve and somewhat curmudgeonly, caveats on this matter may be found in Dwight Eddins, "Yellow Wood, Diverging Pedagogies; or, The Joy of Text," *College English* 51 (1989): 571–76. His emphasis on an oxymoronic "pre-theoretical human experience" in reading is quaint, but one can scarcely fault his insistence that the student, prior to any elaborate, self-conscious treatment of a text, be encouraged to experience, if possible, "its concrete vividness, its immediacy, its urgency, its painful relevance" (p. 574).

Chapter 6
The Arts

1. Northrop Frye, "Speculation and Concern," in *The Stubborn Structure: Essays on Criticism and Society* (Ithaca, N.Y.: Cornell University Press, 1970), pp. 44, 49, 53.

2. *Toward Civilization: A Report on Arts Education* (Washington, D.C.: National Endowment for the Arts, 1988), p. 19.

3. Ibid., p. 13.

4. Ibid., pp. 14, 15, 17, 18.

5. Ibid., pp. 18–19.

6. Ibid., pp. 25, 26, 29.

7. See ibid., pp. 35–45.

Chapter 7
Cultural (Il)literacy

1. E. D. Hirsch, Jr., "Reading, Writing, and Cultural Literacy," in *Composition and Literature: Bridging the Gap,* ed. Winifred Bryan Horner (Chicago: University of Chicago Press, 1983), pp. 141, 142, 143.

2. Ibid., pp. 144, 145, 146, 147.

3. John Warnock, "Cultural Literacy: A Worm in the Bud?" *ADE Bulletin,* no. 82 (Winter 1985), p. 2.

4. Ibid., pp. 3, 4.

5. Ibid., p. 4.

6. Roland Barthes, *S/Z*, trans. Richard Miller (New York: Hill & Wang, 1974), p. 4. Warnock's quotation stops short of a sentence whose potential for polemicization is perhaps not directly relevant to Warnock's purpose but is never absent from mine: "We call any readerly text a classic text." Nor does he invoke a further characterization of the writerly that surely would serve his purpose: "the writerly text is *ourselves* writing, before the infinite play of the world (the world as function) is traversed, intersected, stopped, plasticized by some singular system (Ideology, Genius, Criticism) which reduces the plurality of entrances, the opening of networks, the infinity of languages" (p. 5).

7. Warnock, "Cultural Literacy," pp. 4, 5. Lest his exhortations concerning writerliness seem to some only emanations of "theory," I should point out that impressive empirical research on reading, besides Britton's, supports him. See, for example, R. J. Tierney, T. Raphael, Jill LaZansky, and P. Cohen, "Authors' Intentions and Readers' Interpretations," in *Understanding Readers' Understanding: Theory and Practice,* ed. Robert J. Tierney, Patricia L. Anders, and Judy Nichols Mitchell (Hillsdale, N.J.: Erlbaum, 1987), pp. 205-26. Their protocol-based investigations demonstrate persuasively "that successful reading is more akin to composing than regurgitation of what was stated or merely matching what was written with one's own knowledge"; that is, such reading involves responses that have "a reflexive quality as if readers were rewriting the text that they were reading" (pp. 223, 222). Their references include many reports and other publications that thoroughly document and intelligently explore effective comprehension as a compositional (writerly) process.

8. Warnock, "Cultural Literacy," pp. 5, 6. His invocation of Bruner is reverberantly pertinent. Like many others, Bruner acknowledges a profound crisis in the disparity between "a changing society whose future we cannot foresee" and the means by which students are being prepared, inadequately, to deal with that society and its future. Attempting "to find a key to this crisis in the language of education," he views a given culture as "an ambiguous text that is constantly in need of interpretation by those who participate in it" and argues, therefore, "that induction into the culture through education" should proceed in "the spirit of a forum, of negotiation, of the recreating of meaning." He judges the dominant "traditions of pedagogy," with their emphasis on the "*transmission* of knowledge" and their "view of teaching as surgery, suppression, replacement, deficit filling, or some mix of them all"—along with their behaviorist theories and methods of "reward and punishment"—to be outmoded and largely inimical to that spirit. "What we still lack," except for embryonic hints in the work of Lev Vygotsky and a few others, "is a reasoned theory of how the negotiation of meaning as socially arrived at is to be interpreted as a pedagogical axiom"—a lack very much germane to the writerly approach to cultural-literacy education and addressed by Bruner in his proposing that educators give more attention to the student as "an agent of knowledge making as well as a recipient of knowledge transmission." Indeed, he proposes a whole new "language of education," a terminology, an inventory of concepts quite apt for apeironic instructing, that includes "learning by inventing," "being able to reflect on one's own knowledge," the "process of objectifying in language or image what one has thought and then turning around on it and reconsidering it," and realizing "that self is a construction." His focus as a

constructionist on the importance of metacognitive learning concerns precisely the thrust of writerliness: if students at all levels are not to become mere *"consumers of . . . culture"* (as Barthes, Michael Cole, and others have written of them as becoming), they must be helped to become *"creators* of new cultural forms" (Jerome Bruner, *Actual Minds, Possible Worlds* [Cambridge, Mass.: Harvard University Press, 1986], pp. 121, 122, 123, 124, 127, 129, 130).

9. Warnock, "Cultural Literacy," p. 6.

10. E. D. Hirsch, Jr., *Cultural Literacy: What Every American Needs to Know* (Boston: Houghton Mifflin, 1987), pp. xiv, 142.

11. Quoted in Scott Heller, "Author Sets Up Foundation to Create 'Cultural Literacy' Tests," *Chronicle of Higher Education,* 5 August 1987, p. 2. The foundation's functions have multiplied, of course, so that now, among other activities, it publishes cultural-literacy readers on various list-related topics.

12. James Wolcott, "The Young and the Wasted," *Vanity Fair,* September, 1987, p. 24.

13. Hirsch, *Cultural Literacy,* pp. 175, 173.

14. In this connection see Elizabeth Greene, "Proponent of 'Cultural Literacy' Finds Disciples in the Nation's Schools," *Chronicle of Higher Education,* 16 November 1988, pp. A13ff. According to her, Hirsch accuses his opponents of being "more interested in intellectual game-playing than in studying the problems in the nation's schools and devising practical solutions," and she quotes him, tellingly, in regard to the sort of practicality entailed: " 'If you say, "Let the Hispanics and the blacks have their own culture; their culture is just as good as ours," that's fine except they won't make any money,' he says" (p. A17). Equally telling is her anecdotal insert near the end of the piece, which observes that in *The Dictionary of Cultural Literacy* the capital of Florida is identified incorrectly as Jacksonville, reports that Hirsch blamed the mistake on Joseph F. Kett ("who he said was responsible for proofreading the social-sciences copy"), and quotes Hirsch as explaining that "your mind may go numb, I suppose, reading the damn things" ("Capital of Florida? Wait, Don't Tell Me," p. A17).

15. Wayne C. Booth, Foreword, *The English Coalition Conference: Democracy through Language,* ed. Richard Lloyd-Jones and Andrea A. Lunsford (Urbana, Ill.: National Council of Teachers of English; New York: Modern Language Association, 1989), pp. viii–ix.

16. Scott Heller, "English Teachers Favor Emphasis on How to Read, Write, Think, Rather than on Becoming Familiar with Specific Literary Works," *Chronicle of Higher Education,* 5 August 1987, p. 10.

17. Some of the material in this paragraph and those immediately preceding it was adapted from pp. 311–13 of my article "Hell Is the Place We Don't Know We're In: The Control-Dictions of Cultural Literacy, Strong Reading, and Poetry," *College English* 50 (1988): 309–17.

18. Hirsch, *Cultural Literacy,* pp. 109, 130, 126–27, 128.

19. John Warnock, review of *Cultural Literacy* by E. D. Hirsch, Jr., *College Composition and Communication* 38 (1987): 486, 487, 488, 489, 490.

20. [Robert D. Denham], "From the Editor: Notes on Cultural Literacy," *ADE Bulletin,* no. 88 (Winter 1987), pp. 3, 4, 6, 7.

21. Robert J. Yinger, "The Conversation of Learning: A Reaction to Hirsch's *Cultural Literacy,*" *Holmes Group Forum* 2, no. 2 (Winter 1988): 20, 21.

22. Patricia Bizzell, "Arguing about Literacy," *College English* 50 (1988): 145, 147, 150, 151.

23. Robert Scholes, "Three Views of Education: Nostalgia, History, and Voodoo," review of *The Closing of the American Mind: How Higher Education Has Failed Democracy and Impoverished the Souls of Today's Students* by Allan Bloom, *Professing Literature: An Institutional History* by Gerald Graff, and *Cultural Literacy* by E. D. Hirsch, Jr., *College English* 50 (1988): 327, 328, 330, 331.

24. Patrick Scott, "A Few Words More about E. D. Hirsch and *Cultural Literacy,*" review of *Cultural Literacy* by E. D. Hirsch, Jr., *College English* 50 (1988): 336, 338.

25. Ibid., p. 338.

26. Donald Lazere, letter in "Comment and Response," *College English* 51 (1989): 215, 216. See also, in the same issue, David Leiwei Li's far less forgiving letter about standardization and Hirsch's chauvinism (pp. 210–14).

27. Jeff Smith, "Cultural Literacy and the Academic 'Left,' " in *Profession 88,* ed. Phyllis Franklin (New York: Modern Language Association, 1988), pp. 25, 26, 27.

28. Barbara Herrnstein Smith, "Presidential Address 1988: Limelight: Reflections on a Public Year," *Publications of the Modern Language Association* 104 (1989): 286.

29. Patricia Bizzell, review of *The Social Construction of Written Communication* ed. Bennett A. Rafoth and Donald L. Rubin, *College Composition and Communication* 40 (1989): 485.

30. Paul B. Armstrong, "Pluralistic Literacy," in *Profession 88,* ed. Franklin, p. 29.

31. Andrew Sledd and James Sledd, "Hirsch's Use of His Sources in *Cultural Literacy:* A Critique," in *Profession 88,* ed. Franklin, pp. 33, 38.

32. William K. Buckley, "The Good, the Bad, and the Ugly in Amerika's Akadēmia," in *Profession 88,* ed. Franklin, p. 49.

33. Helene Moglen, "Allan Bloom and E. D. Hirsch: Educational Reform as Tragedy and Farce," in *Profession 88,* ed. Franklin, pp. 59, 60. The quotations are from Hirsch, *Cultural Literacy,* p. 142.

34. James A. Schultz, "Stick to the Facts: Educational Politics, Academic Freedom, and the MLA," in *Profession 88,* ed. Franklin, p. 69. The foregoing critiques elicited an extended comment from Hirsch, which in turn elicited replies from several of the contributors who discussed his work (see "Profession Forum," in *Profession 88,* ed Franklin, pp. 77–82), but none of that, in my opinion, significantly refutes, in the first instance, or qualifies or amplifies, in the second, those critiques. Related subsequent correspondence from Hirsch and Scholes may be found in, respectively, *MLA Newsletter,* Spring 1989, pp. 26–28, and *MLA Newsletter,* Summer 1989, pp. 21–22. The latter letter especially interests because in it Scholes criticizes Hirsch's use in *Cultural Literacy* (p. 69) of Basil Bernstein's work in the sociology of language to support his notion of culture. Scholes argues persuasively, as he has elsewhere (see "Three Views of Education," pp. 331–32), that Bernstein, who "has a good deal to say about the ways in which schools should change to improve education," advocates a mode of cultural education quite different from the one Hirsch imputes to him. Besides

emphasizing the importance of the educator's knowing the cultures that form the students' minds in order to help them learn another culture (an emphasis Rose certainly would endorse, as would educational psychologists in the innovative school of David P. Ausubel), Bernstein "does not suggest that requiring the ingestion of a body of information would be a useful mode. In fact, he calls this mode of teaching the 'collection code' of education (as opposed to the one he favors—the 'integration code')" (p. 21). Bernstein's characterization of the former code, which Scholes quotes at length, shows it to involve knowledge as "private property, with its own power structure and market situation . . . , such that the ultimate mystery of the subject is revealed very late in the educational life." What is thus delayed—and thus reserved for "only the few"—is apeironic learning, the experience of that mystery as "not coherence but incoherence: not order, but disorder, not the known but the unknown." The many educated solely "under collection codes" never "*experience* in their bones the notion that knowledge is permeable, that its orderings are provisional"; for them "socialization into knowledge is socialization into order, the existing order, into the experience that the world's educational knowledge is impermeable"—a situation that he suggests is "another version of alienation" (Basil Bernstein, *Class, Codes and Control: Theoretical Studies towards a Sociology of Language* [New York: Schocken, 1975], pp. 213, 214).

35. Booth, Foreword, *English Coalition,* ed. Lloyd-Jones and Lunsford, p. x.

36. Richard Lloyd-Jones and Andrea A. Lunsford, Introduction, *English Coalition,* ed. Lloyd-Jones and Lunsford, pp. xviii, xix, xx, xxi.

37. Ibid., pp. xxii, xxiii. It is interesting to note that the imperative for students to "read widely" is typically American. In Europe, for example, the imperative is more for intense reading of a limited number of texts. The difference may be accounted for in part by a somewhat mythic difference in cultural "confidence"; that is, Americans feel a need for broad textual acculturation, while Europeans, already broadly textually acculturated, want another, deeper reading of this passage or that. The English Coalition Conference report appears to advocate, laudably, curricular and pedagogical interplay of these two attitudes.

38. *English Coalition,* ed. Lloyd-Jones and Lunsford, pp. 2, 3, 4, 5.

39. Ibid., pp. 17, 20, 22, 19, 22.

40. Ibid., pp. 25, 26, 27, 28, 29, 30, 36.

41. Armstrong, "Pluralistic Literacy," pp. 29, 30, 31. The quotation from Robert Scholes is from his *Textual Power: Literary Theory and the Teaching of English* (New Haven, Conn.: Yale University Press, 1985), p. 144. The sort of juxtaposition that Armstrong advocates can readily be accomplished by, for instance, thematically pairing canonical and noncanonical texts in virtually any course—an approach used productively by William Andrews in courses in black and white American literature at the University of Kansas and by J. Douglas Canfield in eclectic humanities courses at the University of Arizona. Also, "the limits of translatability" that Armstrong is careful to mention have been potential at least since the so-called Whorfian Hypothesis was formulated a half century ago—see George Steiner, *After Babel: Aspects of Language and Translation* (New York: Oxford University Press, 1974), esp. pp. 88–94—though Gordon H. Bower and Randolph K. Cirilo conclude confidently (and happily for

Armstrong's concept of cultural literacy) that research on cross-cultural text comprehension shows "as yet no convincing evidence that textual schemata differ fundamentally [that is, cognitively or neurocognitively] across cultures" ("Cognitive Psychology and Text Processing," in *Handbook of Discourse Analysis,* ed. Teun A. van Dijk, vol. 1, *Disciplines of Discourse* [New York: Academic Press, 1985], p. 99).

42. Armstrong, "Pluralistic Literacy," pp. 31–32. Peter Elbow's discussion of "metaphorical thinking" may be found in his *Embracing Contraries: Explorations in Learning and Teaching* (New York: Oxford University Press, 1986), pp. 22–32, esp. pp. 29–30.

43. Fredric Jameson, Foreword, *The Postmodern Condition: A Report on Knowledge,* by Jean-François Lyotard, trans. Geoff Bennington and Brian Massumi (Minneapolis: University of Minnesota Press, 1984), p. xix.

44. Sledd and Sledd, "Hirsch's Use of His Sources," pp. 38, 39.

45. Moglen, "Allan Bloom and E. D. Hirsch," p. 63.

46. See Johnson, "Hell Is the Place," esp. pp. 314–16. Interestingly enough, very much the strategy I propose in that article is applied in an ingenious analysis of it by Vera Neverow-Turk (see her letter in "Comment and Response," *College English* 52 [1990]: 206–8), who finds in it a "completely inadvertent" but ideologically revealing "gender-bias" and even proposes "a fourth level of reading that harrows hell [the place the naïve reader/writer doesn't know he or she is in] and brings the captives out of bondage to a patriarchal language that inscribes oppression even in the discourse of liberation" (pp. 206, 208). See also Michael L. Johnson, "The Art of Rereading: Prolegomenon to a Contemporary Pedagogy of Poetry," *Journal of Aesthetic Education* 19, no. 4 (Winter 1985): 37–49, where through numerous examples I explore the application to poetry— but with only an inchoate consideration of my concept of third-level reading. The notion of reading "differently" *(autrement)* is borrowed from Jacques Derrida (see his *Of Grammatology,* trans. Gayatri Chakravorty Spivak [Baltimore: Johns Hopkins University Press, 1976], p. 87). The denotative-connotative-"stereoscopic" progression is adapted from David Bleich's idea of language as a Cassirerian "symbolic form" that can create knowledge that is "always a re-cognition because it is a seeing through one perspective superimposed on another in such a way that the one perspective does not appear to be prior to the other" (a process described by Jean Piaget as "the internal reciprocal assimilation of schemata"), the kind of knowledge occasioned "when we 'get' a joke"; such "stereoscopic knowledge" involves language evoking the "perspectival possibilities" of always interdependent denotation and connotation (David Bleich, "Cognitive Stereoscopy and the Study of Language and Literature," in *Convergences: Transactions in Reading and Writing,* ed. Bruce T. Petersen [Urbana, Ill.: National Council of Teachers of English, 1986], pp. 101, 99, 101). Detailed discussion of Albert Rothenberg's notion of the janusian mentality may be found in his *Emerging Goddess: The Creative Process in Art, Science, and Other Fields* (Chicago: University of Chicago Press, 1979), where he characterizes it as undertaking "a quest for control" over *"two or more opposite or antithetical ideas, images, or concepts simultaneously"* (pp. 49, 55).

47. See Hirsch, *Cultural Literacy,* p. 200.

48. Robert Frost, "The Road Not Taken," in *Complete Poems of Robert Frost*

1949 (New York: Henry Holt, 1949), p. 131. Interestingly enough, Lawrance Thompson and R. H. Winnick, in their *Robert Frost: A Biography* (New York: Holt, Rinehart & Winston, 1982), argue, fairly convincingly, that Frost intended this poem, which he first titled "Two Roads," to be taken as an amusingly ironic portrayal of the "posture of his romantic friend" and fellow poet Edward Thomas—though Thomas took the poem, before Frost explained the "gentle joke" to him, not as a teasing parody but, anticipating most of its subsequent readers, as a straight, even "staggering," statement of Frost's own viewpoint (pp. 234, 235).

49. Scholes, *Textual Power,* p. 24. See also his innovative *Text Book: An Introduction to Literary Language,* coauthored with Nancy R. Comley and Gregory L. Ulmer (New York: St. Martin's Press, 1988), which expands the logic of his progression into what the authors, in their opening "Letter to the Instructor," stress is "not a book *about* literature" but "a text for working *with* literature" (p. v).

50. Richard A. Lanham, *Literacy and the Survival of Humanism* (New Haven, Conn.: Yale University Press, 1983), p. 62.

51. Ibid., pp. 4, 9, 15, 13, 43, 47.

52. Ibid., pp. 12–13, 145, 103, 57.

53. David S. Kaufer, "Cultural Literacy: A Critique of Hirsch and an Alternative Theory," *ADE Bulletin,* no. 94 (Winter 1989), p. 23.

54. Ibid., p. 24, 25.

55. Ibid., pp. 25, 26.

56. Ibid., p. 26. Kaufer's discussion is indebted to Robert Pattison, "On the Finn Syndrome and the Shakespeare Paradox," review of *Cultural Literacy* by Hirsch and *Closing of the American Mind* by Bloom, *Nation,* 30 May 1987, pp. 710–20.

57. Kaufer, "Cultural Literacy," p. 27.

58. Ibid., p. 28.

59. Howard Gardner has explored an alternative to Hirsch's project based on his research into Chinese education. Realizing that a country as pluralistic as the United States cannot (and should not) hope to achieve a national consensus about what *content* students should learn, he proposes that American education should emphasize a national *understanding* of the processes through which knowledge is constructed in exemplary disciplines. Like Kaufer, he believes that students should work toward widening, deepening, and more complexly integrating such understanding by participating in and contributing to these processes, practicing and advancing them, as well as possible. See his *To Open Minds: Chinese Clues to the Dilemma of Contemporary Education* (New York: Basic Books, 1989).

60. Eugene R. Kintgen, Barry M. Kroll, and Mike Rose, Introduction, *Perspectives on Literacy,* ed. Eugene R. Kintgen, Barry M. Kroll, and Mike Rose (Carbondale: Southern Illinois University Press, 1988), p. xviii.

61. An admirable freshman-level textbook whose use surely counters this attitude and practice is *Rereading America: Cultural Contexts for Critical Thinking and Writing,* ed. Gary Colombo, Robert Cullen, and Bonnie Lisle (New York: St. Martin's Press, Bedford Books, 1989).

62. Roger C. Schank, *Reading and Understanding: Teaching from the Perspective of Artificial Intelligence* (Hillsdale, N.J.: Erlbaum, 1982), pp. 12, 122, 170, 176.

63. Joseph D. Novak, *A Theory of Education* (Ithaca, N.Y.: Cornell University Press, 1977), pp. 24, 17, 25, 24. The quotation from David P. Ausubel is from his *Educational Psychology: A Cognitive View* (New York: Holt, Rinehart & Winston, 1968), p. vi.

64. Robert-Alain de Beaugrande and Wolfgang Ulrich Dressler, *Introduction to Text Linguistics,* updated and trans. Robert-Alain de Beaugrande (London: Longman, 1981), p. 213. In fairness to Hirsch, I should say that the definition of *readability* they attribute to him does not fully present his notion of "*relative* readability" (my emphasis): "*Assuming that two texts convey the same meaning, the more readable text will take less time and effort to understand*" (E. D. Hirsch, Jr., *The Philosophy of Composition* [Chicago: University of Chicago Press, 1977], p. 85). But, as I say, that attributed definition is "essentially" the one he endorses, and de Beaugrande and Dressler do spare him an exposure of the wholly dubious assumption, for any reader seeking more than the rough gist of a text, that prefaces and enables his notion above.

65. Jacques Barzun, *Teacher in America* (Boston: Little, Brown; Atlantic Monthly Press, 1945), pp. 20, 21, 22, 23, 24, 23, 25.

66. Robert Pattison, "The Stupidity Crisis," *ADE Bulletin,* no. 89 (Spring 1988), pp. 3, 4, 6, 9.

67. Andrew Sledd, "'Readin' not Riotin'': The Politics of Literacy," *College English* 50 (1988): 495, 497, 495, 497, 499, 496, 498, 499, 503, 506.

68. Ibid., pp. 505, 506.

69. Richard J. Murphy, Jr., "The Right to Literacy," *MLA Newsletter,* Fall 1989, p. 12. In this connection see Mark Holmes's essay, of which Murphy appears unaware, "The Fortress Monastery: The Future of the Common Core," which concludes a collection entitled *Cultural Literacy and the Idea of General Education,* ed. Ian Westbury and Alan C. Purves (Chicago: National Society for the Study of Education, 1988). While occasionally offering fresh perspective on the reasons for general education not having a common curriculum (the lack of "a reasonably coherent, consensual vision of society's ideal image" in most of the West, the"common school" no longer serving "as a microcosm of the larger society," the absence of a "current, sustaining *myth* to uphold the ideology of a common core of schooling," and so on), Holmes winds up embracing what he calls "the character myth" as an organizing principle for the development of a common core, a somewhat Bloomian one "founded on the virtue that leads to truth and wisdom" and maintainable—oddly enough, in this context—only by "a few fortress monasteries," schools "both public and independent, . . . which will integrate the important aspects of our cultural heritage" (pp. 239, 245, 247, 248, 255). Too appalled at the problems of differentiated education to discern any opportunities in them, he proposes a "re-monasticization" of knowledge that would ensure the cultural illiteracy of the general populace.

70. Murphy, "Right to Literacy," p. 12.

71. Ibid., pp. 12, 13. Some of Murphy's distress about the negativity of the conference seems to have been addressed in the second, more ambitious national conference on literacy undertaken by the MLA and state affiliates of the NEH. Held in 1990 at the University of Pittsburgh and entitled Responsibilities for Literacy: Communities, Schools, and Workplaces, it engaged a wider range of

issues concerning access to literacy, even setting the stage for practical cooperation between the MLA and the AFL-CIO.

72. Commenting on recent "Hollywood high school movies," Pattison notes that "the first lesson of the kind of education described in these movies is that a sense of humor is the highest educational value. It's not a bad lesson. Certainly it's a lesson the humanist can live with" ("Stupidity Crisis," pp. 7, 8).

73. Patricia Bizzell, "Beyond Anti-Foundationalism to Rhetorical Authority: Problems Defining 'Cultural Literacy,'" *College English* 52 (1990): 663.

Chapter 8
Evaluation, Assessment, Accountability

1. David Elkind, *The Hurried Child: Growing Up Too Fast Too Soon*, rev. ed. (Reading Mass.: Addison-Wesley, 1988), pp. 47, 48. Perhaps the most blatant instantiation of the "factory model" at all levels is the lockstep fashion in which the typical "school day" runs. With the exception of some small institutions (Colorado College, for instance, which since 1970 has operated by a "Block Plan" that allows considerable scheduling flexibility within three-and-a-half week segments), even higher education, however otherwise free from the lockstep mentality of lower levels, functions mostly by the regular ringing of bells that prompt students to move in intermingling herds from one classroom to another. Criticizing American high schools for the bureaucratic structures that maintain their "mediocre sameness," the "conveyer-belt" pace that has students passively "taking" subjects rather than actively studying them (and thus getting "teacher-delivered knowledge" rather than becoming "self-propelled" or "generative" learners), a temporally pinched pedagogy of "telling" rather than a more fluid one of "coaching," and related problems born of an obsession with unitizing and quantifying, Theodore R. Sizer sums up the whole system in one short clause: "the clock is king" (*Horace's Compromise: The Dilemma of the American High School* [Boston: Houghton Mifflin, 1984], pp. 6, 83, 216, 113, 109, 97). He does an admirable job of dramatizing the ironies (inefficiencies multiplied by an archaic Gradgrindian cult of efficiency) of this situation, which is too easily blamed on the scale of institutions (though that contributes) rather than on a failure of pedagogical imagination, public distrust, anachronistic administrative strategies, misplaced budgetary priorities. I join Sizer in calling for institutions at all levels to try alternative plans, plans he is now helping dozens of middle and secondary schools implement, for organizing educational time and effort—and *place* as well, for that matter.

2. Elkind, *Hurried Child*, p. 48.

3. Ibid., pp. 48, 50, 51, 52, 53, 54, 55–56. The extent to which the system, in its administrative structures, is rife with "the abuse of testing" is witnessed also by the prevalence in state testing programs of results that show "above-average performance" for most students, a situation, doubtless partly due to meaningless and outdated norms, that instantiates "the 'Lake Wobegon effect'—named of course after Garrison Keillor's description of the imaginary town of Lake Wobegon where 'all the children are above average'" (p. 53).

4. Ken Macrorie, *Twenty Teachers* (New York: Oxford University Press, 1984), pp. xi, xii, 238.

5. Ibid., pp. 238, 239, 238, 246.

6. Mike Rose, *Lives on the Boundary: The Struggles and Achievements of America's Underprepared* [New York: Free Press, 1989), p. 128.

7. Ibid., pp. 186, 187, 200, 191, 190. The quotation from Patricia Cline Cohen is from her book *A Calculating People: The Spread of Numeracy in Early America* (Chicago: University of Chicago Press, 1982), p. 225.

8. Richard Mitchell, *The Graves of Academe* (Boston: Little, Brown, 1981), pp. 55, 56.

9. Neil Postman, *Teaching as a Conserving Activity* (1979; reprint, New York: Dell, 1987), p. 84.

10. Ibid., pp. 85, 86-87, 90.

11. Ibid., pp. 93, 94, 96, 97, 98.

12. Ibid., pp. 85, 97, 98-99, 193, 194, 196, 201, 202, 205, 202, 205, 201.

13. *The English Coalition Conference: Democracy through Language,* ed. Richard Lloyd-Jones and Andrea A. Lunsford (Urbana, Ill,: National Council of Teachers of English; New York: Modern Language Association, 1989), pp. 6, 7, 41, 42, 41, 42.

14. Joseph D. Novak and D. Bob Gowin, *Learning How to Learn* (New York: Cambridge University Press, 1984), pp. 109-10. Their generalization holds, in my opinion, even for such now-classical schemes as Benjamin Bloom's "taxonomy" of learning objectives.

15. Novak and Gowin, *Learning How to Learn,* pp. 111, 2, 111, 112. Thus they favor *"discovery learning"* over *"reception learning"* (p. 7), a distinction that parallels Macrorie's between "finders" and "keepers."

16. Robert-Alain de Beaugrande and Wolfgang Ulrich Dressler, *Introduction to Text Linguistics,* updated and trans. Robert-Alain de Beaugrande (London: Longman, 1981), p. 210.

17. Geraldine Jonçich Clifford and James W. Guthrie, *Ed School: A Brief for Professional Education* (Chicago: University of Chicago Press, 1988), p. 10.

18. In this connection see Jacques Derrida, "The Principle of Reason: The University in the Eyes of Its Pupils," trans. Catherine Porter and Edward P. Morris, *Diacritics* 13, no. 3 (Fall 1983): 3-20. This subtle discussion of academic responsibility, beyond that of representing or reproducing society, pertains in some respects to all educational institutions, not just the university. It ought to be required reading for the National Council on Education Standards and Testing.

19. Such alliances are precarious because they run counter to a long-institutionalized close coupling between American primary and secondary levels and a much more labile and complex coupling between either of those levels, especially the secondary, and the postsecondary, a situation rife with polemical disjunctions, especially concerning student preparation for postsecondary education. This situation—largely attributable to most primary and secondary schools being locally controlled and trying (perhaps democratically but amorphously, in a blandly accommodating and increasingly problematic fashion) to be comprehensive, all things to all people—differs markedly from that in many other countries (Sweden, France, and Japan, for instance), where the secondary-

postsecondary coupling, for understandable though not always laudable reasons (systems on a more manageable national scale, specialized high schools, traditions of invidious streaming or tracking, whatever), is much stronger. For an admirable collection of comparative studies of the issues involved, see *The School and the University: An International Perspective,* ed. Burton R. Clark (Berkeley and Los Angeles: University of California Press, 1985). Clark details nicely the vicious cycle of what he rightly sees as "a distinctive American problem" in this regard, one that he suggests be addressed by, among other things, "new combinations of comprehensive and specialized secondary schools," but he discerns a worldwide trend in secondary-postsecondary coupling "toward increasing complexity," toward more kinds of coupling with subtler ambiguities. Rather than despair at this state of affairs, however, he proposes that the trend be understood "as a process of maturation," reminding us that "we continually underestimate what a mature educational system does." Acknowledging that the trend "will continue to unsettle the school and the university and the relations between them," he advises against nostalgia ("since traditional images rely on simple scenarios that will not again obtain") and advocates an apeironic attitude characterized by "tolerance for ambiguity"; an interest in "the ideal of dispersed power," "the logics of muddling-through," "the metaphors of loose coupling and organized anarchy"; and "ideological support for unclear variety, even the legitimation of disorder in formal systems"—a sense of the "virtues" of uncertainty ("Conclusions," pp. 291, 319, 320, 321, 322, 323).

Chapter 9
Re(-)mediation

1. Mina P. Shaughnessy, *Errors and Expectations: A Guide for the Teacher of Basic Writing* (New York: Oxford University Press, 1977), pp. 293, 292.

2. Mike Rose, *Lives on the Boundary: The Struggles and Achievements of America's Underprepared* (New York: Free Press, 1989), p. 205.

3. Ibid., pp. 208, 209, 208, 209, 208, 209, 210.

4. Ibid., pp. 222–23, 210.

5. Mike Rose, "Narrowing the Mind and Page: Remedial Writers and Cognitive Reductionism," *College Composition and Communication* 39 (1988): 294, 267, 294, 295, 294, 295, 296, 297.

6. See especially Gerald Coles, *The Learning Mystique: A Critical Look at "Learning Disabilities"* (New York: Pantheon Books, 1987).

7. Greg Sarris, "Storytelling in the Classroom: Crossing Vexed Chasms," *College English* 52 (1990): 173.

8. Rose, *Lives on the Boundary,* pp. 211, 238.

9. Shaughnessy, *Errors and Expectations,* pp. 13, 292.

10. Mariolina Salvatori, "The Dialogical Nature of Basic Reading and Writing," in *Facts, Artifacts and Counterfacts: Theory and Method for a Reading and Writing Course,* ed. David Bartholomae and Anthony R. Petrosky (Portsmouth, N.H.: Heinemann and Boynton/Cook, 1986), p. 139.

11. Neil Postman, *Teaching as a Conserving Activity* (1979; reprint, New

York: Dell, 1987), p. 203. His argument that error is essential to learning has an important sort of obverse: lack of error is not necessarily indicative of learning. I am thinking generally of students who "know" the "right" answers and yet never seem to learn deeply, certainly not apeironically, but this obverse may pertain with a vengeance in remediation. In that connection recent research on "style shifting" among students who are speakers of Black American English—and therefore are apt to be subject(ed) to remediation to help them acquire Standard American English—raises an issue with far-reaching implications: "If school success is in part a function of children more frequently using grammatical forms that are commonly associated with Standard American English," then one must ask "whether such usage is itself linked to learning styles or aptitudes or readiness, or whether, instead, success in school is more likely among children who adopt a mode of behavior that satisfies in their teachers a sense of what is appropriate in the classroom, regardless of the fact that that behavior may be irrelevant to learning" (Daniel Hibbs Morrow, "Black American English Style Shifting and Writing Error," *Research in the Teaching of English* 22 [1988]: 338).

Chapter 10
Countercurriculum(s)

1. [David Laurence], "From the Editor," *ADE Bulletin,* no. 92 (Spring 1989), pp. 1, 3. His citations are as follows: Jean-Jacques Rousseau, *Emile: or, On Education,* trans. Allan Bloom (New York: Basic Books, 1979), p. 54; Søren Kierkegaard, *The Concept of Irony,* trans. Lee M. Capel (Bloomington: Indiana University Press, 1968), p. 50; and Ellen J. Langer, *Mindfulness* (Reading, Mass.: Addison-Wesley, 1989), p. 21.

2. Tony Schwartz, "Acceleration Syndrome," *Vanity Fair,* October 1988, p. 147.

3. Bill McKibben, *The End of Nature* (New York: Random House, 1989), pp. 8, 48, 58, 59, 60, 96, 133, 168–69.

4. Ibid., pp. 170, 181, 70.

5. Thus—and McKibben argues as much, indirectly—the need to figure science fiction in countercurricula. James Gunn, in *Science Fiction: Its Past, Present, and Future* (Kansas City, Mo.: Midwest Research Institute, 1988), calls science fiction "the literature of discontinuity" because, unlike traditional fiction, which "is concerned with the attempt by the characters to discover what the rules are" and "describes how they learn about them and how they live with the rules," science fiction "begins with the assumption that the rules may not make sense, are incomplete, or are inappropriate" and so "is about new situations" (p. 2). In such situations the discovery or invention of new rules (and metarules) is imperative.

6. Barbara Herrnstein Smith, *Contingencies of Value: Alternative Perspectives for Critical Theory* (Cambridge, Mass.: Harvard University Press, 1988), pp. 38, 53, 161, 167, 168.

7. Ibid., pp. 168, 179, 183.

8. Jay Parini, "Academic Conservatives Who Decry 'Politicization' Show Staggering Naïveté about Their Own Biases," *Chronicle of Higher Education,* 7 December 1988, p. B2.

9. See, for example, Shirley M. Malcom, "Who Will Do Science in the Next Century?" *Scientific American,* February 1990, p. 112.

10. Mike Rose, *Lives on the Boundary: The Struggles and Achievements of America's Underprepared* (New York: Free Press, 1989), pp. 225, 188.

11. Donald Lazere, "Conservative Critics Have a Distorted View of What Constitutes Ideological Bias in Academe," *Chronicle of Higher Education,* 8 November 1988, p. A52.

12. Gerald Graff, *Professing Literature: An Institutional History* (Chicago: University of Chicago Press, 1987), pp. 253, 257. "To emphasize conflict over consensus" is not, in his view, "to turn conflict into a value, nor certainly is it to reject consensus where we can get it—as would the silly recent argument that identifies consensus with repressive politics. It is simply to take our point of departure from a state of affairs that already exists" (p. 258)—and he would argue that, though the "departure" is under way, there is a long way to go.

13. Paul Feyerabend, *Against Method: Outline of an Anarchistic Theory of Knowledge* (Atlantic Highlands, N.J.: Humanities Press, 1975), pp. 47, 35.

14. Neil Postman, *Teaching as a Conserving Activity,* (1979; reprint, New York: Dell, 1987), pp. 51–52, 70, 74, 77, 80, 81, 105, 159, 162, 165.

15. Gary Shapiro, "What Was Literary History? A Critical Synthesis," *Social Epistemology* 2 (1988): 14.

16. Howard Nemerov, "Ultima Ratio Reagan," in *War Stories: Poems about Long Ago and Now* (Chicago: University of Chicago Press, 1987), p. 6.

17. Susan Noakes, *Timely Reading: Between Exegesis and Interpretation* (Ithaca, N.Y.: Cornell University Press, 1988), pp. 11, xi, xii, xiii, 13, 12. Her notion of "oscillation" is similar to the broader notion of "double perspective" developed by David Bleich in his *Double Perspective: Language, Literacy, and Social Relations* (New York: Oxford University Press, 1988).

18. Noakes, *Timely Reading,* pp. 216, 233–34, 243.

19. Peter Elbow, *Embracing Contraries: Explorations in Learning and Teaching* (New York: Oxford University Press, 1986), pp. xiii, 3–4, 9, 12, 14, 18, 14, 23, 33.

20. Ibid., pp. 65, 96–97, 121, 159, 234.

21. Ibid., pp. 243, 251–52.

22. Ibid., pp. 256, 259, 261, 263–64.

23. Ibid., pp. 266, 267, 269, 271, 274, 279, 278–79, 282, 281, 284, 291, 300.

Chapter 11
Hermetic Pedagogies

1. Thaïs E. Morgan, "Reorientations," in *Reorientations: Critical Theories and Pedagogies,* ed. Bruce Henricksen and Thaïs E. Morgan (Urbana: University of Illinois Press, 1990), pp. 3, 6–7, 9, 20.

2. Robert Con Davis, "A Manifesto for Oppositional Pedagogy: Freire,

Bourdieu, Merod, and Graff," in *Reorientations*, ed. Henricksen and Morgan, pp. 248–49. Davis later returns to the Elbow-like "dilemma" of oppositional pedagogy, analyzing it in terms of "how the oppositional critic—speaking within the dominant discourse but committed to speaking 'beyond' it—is inevitably caught in Epimenides's liar's paradox and says, 'what I am telling you is a lie' " (p. 252—and see Pierre Bourdieu and Jean-Claude Passeron, *Reproduction in Education, Society and Culture*, trans. Richard Nice [London: Sage, 1977], p. 12, on which source Davis draws here). Stanley Fish discusses another version of this dilemma in his "Anti-Foundationalism, Theory Hope, and the Teaching of Composition," in *The Current in Criticism: Essays on the Present and Future of Literary Theory*, ed. Clayton Koelb and Virgil Lokke (West Lafayette, Ind.: Purdue University Press, 1987). He finds the contradiction involved—that, as he codifies it, "anti-foundationalism cannot itself be made the basis of a method without losing its anti-foundationalist character"—at once "curious" and deeply troubling, and he concludes that "here the advice is, if all knowledge is situational [rather than foundational], then let's teach situations" (p. 74).

Well, why not? Fish explores at some length what appears to him as the pedagogically self-enclosed dead end implied by this conclusion, but I take it, as I think Davis would, to imply, like the paradox or contradiction that gives rise to it, a "metasituation" we can and must deal with—that is, "teach." The dilemma is neither a new one nor a cause for despair (though it does, as Barthes would say, make things complicated—or perhaps I should turn about and say also that complexity makes things dilemmatic). Indeed, in our era of what Floyd Merrell calls the "Emergent Perspective" (close to a synonym for the apeironic)—in which undecidability, inconsistency, and so on "are the order of the day"—theoretical scientists and mathematicians, still much more than humanists like Fish (though he is more playfully at home with such qualities than most of his colleagues), understand "how . . . natural is the path leading to paradox, and how devious, *ad hoc*, elusive, and unnatural it is to attempt eliminating any and all paradoxes" (Floyd Merrell, "An Uncertain Semiotic," in *Current in Criticism*, ed. Koelb and Lokke, pp. 252, 253). In any case, worse than the problems of the dilemma in the classroom would be the avoidance of them there—that is, following the example of Galileo, who, as Merrell recalls, "taught Ptolemaism in the classroom while independently believing in his own interpretation" (p. 249).

3. Davis, "Manifesto," pp. 250, 251, 254, 262, 264, 265.

4. Ronald Strickland, "Confrontational Pedagogy and Traditional Literary Studies," *College English* 52 (1990): 291.

5. Ibid., p. 292. The quotation from Shoshana Felman is from her "Psychoanlaysis and Education: Teaching Terminable and Interminable," in *The Pedagogical Imperative: Teaching as a Literary Genre*, ed. Barbara Johnson, a special issue of *Yale French Studies*, no. 63 (1982), p. 21. Lacan's relevant discussion may be found in, among other sources, his *Four Fundamental Concepts of Psycho-Analysis*, ed. Jacques-Alain Miller, trans. Alan Sheridan (New York: Norton, 1978), pp. 230–43.

6. Strickland, "Confrontational Pedogogy," pp. 293, 294, 296–97, 298, 297.

7. Peter Elbow, *Embracing Contraries: Explorations in Learning and Teaching* (New York: Oxford University Press, 1986), pp. 78, 135, 149–50. The almost inevitable outcome of teachers making students into their mouthpieces is

dramatized in George Bernard Shaw's *Pygmalion,* a play very much about a student, the cockney flower girl Eliza Doolittle, learning to speak as (but also *what*) her teacher, Professor Henry Higgins, wishes: though she comes to speak her teacher's prestige dialect (and dress like a "lady"), he is unable to see her as other than a flower girl who mouths his language—hence, she marries Freddy Eynsford-Hill, who accepts her as far more than the speaking statue that was all Higgins expected her to be. Thus, ironically, the problem with pygmalionic teaching is not so much that it turns statues into living beings as that it turns living beings into statues. Hermetic instructing, on the other hand, expects students to develop dynamically and independently. And that expectation, openly expressed by an instructor who accepts and encourages their divergent growth— though necessarily in relation to his or her own more or less consciously intended images of them—is crucial to their doing so. Indeed, in many ways expectation, however communicated, is *the* most crucial (and prophetic) factor in education—see Robert Rosenthal and Lenore Jacobson, *Pygmalion in the Classroom: Teacher Expectation and Pupils' Intellectual Development* (New York: Holt, Rinehart & Winston, 1968), esp. p. 180.

8. Roland Barthes, "Lecture in Inauguration of the Chair of Literary Semiology, Collège de France, January 7, 1977," trans. Richard Howard, *October* 8 (1979): 13.

9. Hugh Munby, "Metaphor and Teachers' Knowledge," *Research in the Teaching of English* 21 (1987): 397. Northrop Frye's discussion of the *alazon* and *eiron* may be found in his *Anatomy of Criticism: Four Essays* (Princeton: Princeton University Press, 1957), pp. 172–75, 226–28.

10. Josué V. Harari and David F. Bell, "Introduction: Journal à plusieurs voies," in Michel Serres, *Hermes: Literature, Science, Philosophy,* ed. Josué V. Harari and David F. Bell (Baltimore: Johns Hopkins University Press, 1982), pp. xxxiii, xxix, xxx, xxxvi, xxx.

11. Robert Con Davis, "Pedagogy, Lacan, and the Freudian Subject," *College English* 49 (1987): 755.

12. Gregory S. Jay, "The Subject of Pedagogy: Lessons in Psychoanalysis and Politics," *College English* 49 (1987): 786, 789, 790, 791, 798, 799.

13. Shoshana Felman, *Jacques Lacan and the Adventure of Insight: Psychoanalysis in Contemporary Culture* (Cambridge, Mass.: Harvard University Press, 1987), pp. 15, 72, 78, 79, 80–81, 82, 83, 88. The position of Felman's teacher-learner in relation to "the subject of teaching" thus might be compared to Rabbi Tarphon's characterization of the interpreter in relation to the text: "You are not required to complete the work, but neither are you free to desist from it" (cited in Harold Bloom, *A Map of Misreading* [New York: Oxford University Press, 1975], p. 46).

14. G. Douglas Atkins, "Introduction: Literary Theory, Critical Practice, and the Classroom," in *Contemporary Literary Theory,* ed. G. Douglas Atkins and Laura Morrow (Amherst: University of Massachusetts Press, 1989), pp. 17– 18, 11, 9. The quotations from Henri J. M. Nouwen are from his *Creative Ministry* (1971; reprint, New York: Doubleday, 1978), pp. 5 (emphasis added), 19. The interpretation of Wordsworth, as Atkins acknowledges, is indebted to Geoffrey Hartman's *Wordsworth's Poetry, 1787–1814* (New Haven, Conn.: Yale University Press, 1964).

15. Atkins, "Introduction," pp. 8, 11.

16. See Michael L. Johnson, "The Theoristic Imperative and the Paralogical Play of 'That Dangerous Supplement,'" *North Dakota Quarterly* 56, no. 3 (Summer 1988): 22–36. Paula A. Treichler suggests the force of this imperative, virtually foreseeing the possibility of education in which there are no "theorists" because all educators are such, when she observes that "the classroom is an ideal site for investigating how theory works, what languages it speaks, what claims it makes, what stategies it adopts. When the classroom itself is made the site for self-conscious theorizing, it becomes difficult to sustain a belief that nontheoretical practice is possible" ("Teaching Feminist Theory," in *Theory in the Classroom,* ed. Cary Nelson [Urbana: University of Illinois Press, 1986], p. 99).

17. Joan De Jean, "*La Nouvelle Héloïse,* or the Case for Pedagogical Deviation," in *Pedagogical Imperative,* ed. Johnson, pp. 109, 116.

18. Barbara Johnson, "Editor's Preface: Teaching as a Literary Genre," in *Pedagogical Imperative,* ed. Johnson, p. vii.

19. Angela S. Moger, "That Obscure Object of Narrative," in *Pedagogical Imperative,* ed. Johnson, pp. 135–36, 137.

20. J. E. Cirlot, *A Dictionary of Symbols,* trans. Jack Sage (New York: Philosophical Library, 1962), p. 198.

21. Adrienne Rich, *On Lies, Secrets, and Silence: Selected Prose, 1966–1978* (New York: Norton, 1979), pp. 141, 145, 244, 245.

22. Margo Culley and Catherine Portuges, Introduction, *Gendered Subjects: The Dynamics of Feminist Teaching,* ed. Margo Culley and Catherine Portuges (Boston: Routledge & Kegan Paul, 1985), pp. 1, 2, 3, 6.

23. Frances Maher, "Classroom Pedagogy and the New Scholarship on Women," in *Gendered Subjects,* ed. Cully and Portuges, p. 29.

24. Ibid., pp. 30, 31, 33, 35, 42. See Paulo Freire, *Pedagogy of the Oppressed,* trans. Myra Bergman Ramos (New York: Herder & Herder, 1970), esp. p. 59—an ironic source, really, since, as Maher notes (p. 47), Freire says nothing explicitly about women and tends, except when using "people," to speak of "men." Apparently he has since become more self-conscious about issues involved in the education of women (and certainly he has fervent advocates among women—Ann E. Berthoff comes to mind), but even in *A Pedagogy for Liberation: Dialogues on Transforming Education* (South Hadley, Mass.: Bergin & Garvey, 1987), a book he authored with Ira Shor, where he explicitly addresses such issues (see pp. 163–68), I find his position a little difficult to evaluate—partly, no doubt, because it is defined significantly by his being a man from Brazil, which he characterizes as "a strong *machista* society" and "authoritarian" in no small way because of that (p. 165). In any case, Maher's stress on the need for feminist pedagogy in the natural sciences is crucial, for there most female students still experience an alienation aptly described by Sylvia Plath in her autobiographical novel *The Bell Jar* (1963; reprint, New York: Bantam, 1971) in a passage that begins with her narrator Esther Greenwood recalling that "the day I went into physics class it was death" (p. 28).

25. Mary Field Belenky, Blythe McVicker Clinchy, Nancy Rule Goldberger, and Jill Mattuck Tarule, *Women's Ways of Knowing: The Development of Self, Voice, and Mind* (New York: Basic Books, 1986), pp. 6, 10, 219, 224. I should note that Belenky et al. strongly stress that "connected teachers are believers"—

though their treatment of belief is more informal and less developed than Elbow's—and that women find belief more educationally productive than doubt (or "cognitive conflict"), and they are not convinced that "the doubting model . . . is appropriate for men, either" (pp. 227, 228). My own position, like Elbow's, is that, for either gender, a sensitive balancing (and rebalancing) of the two is required.

26. Robert de Beaugrande, "In Search of Feminist Discourse: The 'Difficult' Case of Luce Irigaray," *College English* 50 (1988): 258, 271.

27. Luce Irigaray, *Speculum of the Other Woman*, trans. Gillian C. Gill (Ithaca, N.Y.: Cornell University Press, 1985), p. 142.

28. Clara Juncker, "Writing (with) Cixous," *College English* 50 (1988): 434.

29. Sandra Alcosser, "Causing Each Tentative Voice to Speak," *AWP Chronicle* 22, no. 2 (October-November 1989): 3.

30. Susan Noakes, *Timely Reading: Between Exegesis and Interpretation* (Ithaca, N.Y.: Cornell University Press, 1988), p. 240. As she notes, the term was suggested to her by Gary Shapiro.

31. Henry Louis Gates, Jr., *The Signifying Monkey: A Theory of Afro-American Literary Criticism* (New York: Oxford University Press, 1988), pp. 5, 8, 9, 5, 11, 21, xxv, 49, 50, 51, 124.

32. Fuller citations of these books by Michel Foucault are as follows: *The Order of Things: An Archaeology of the Human Sciences* (New York: Random House, Pantheon Books, 1971); *The Archaeology of Knowledge*, trans. A. M. Sheridan Smith (New York: Harper & Row, Harper Colophon Books, 1976), which includes *The Discourse on Language*, trans. Rupert Swyer, as an appendix; *Language, Counter-Memory, Practice: Selected Essays and Interviews*, ed. Donald F. Bouchard, trans. Donald F. Bouchard and Sherry Simon (Ithaca, N.Y.: Cornell University Press, 1977); and *Power/Knowledge: Selected Interviews and Other Writings, 1972–1977*, ed. Colin Gordon, trans. Colin Gordon, Leo Marshall, John Mepham, and Kate Soper (New York: Pantheon Books, 1980).

33. Karlis Racevskis, *Michel Foucault and the Subversion of Intellect* (Ithaca, N.Y.: Cornell University Press, 1983), pp. 40, 30, 35, 36, 33, 36, 35, 57, 67.

34. Ibid., pp. 78, 79, 123, 125, 141, 165, 166. On "paradox" and *"doxa,"* see Foucault, *Language, Counter-Memory, Practice*, p. 182.

35. Racevskis, *Michel Foucault*, p. 167.

36. Michel Foucault, *This Is Not a Pipe*, ed. and trans. James Harkness (Berkeley and Los Angeles: University of California Press, 1983), pp. 29–31, 44.

37. Foucault, quoted in James Harkness, Translator's Introduction, ibid., pp. 10, 12. Harkness does not cite specifically the source of the material that he attributes to Foucault.

38. Consider this also as a gloss concerning the transition in Foucault's scene: "The force of pedagogy lies close to farce, and so the pedagogue has always been a comic figure. But if teaching frequently evokes laughter, it is sometimes the critical laughter of a resistance that knows its relation to the 'slippage' in pedagogy between cognition and performance" (Patrick McGee, "Truth and Resistance: Teaching as a Form of Analysis," *College English* 49 [1987]: 677).

39. See Umberto Eco, *The Role of the Reader: Explorations in the Semiotics*

of Texts (Bloomington: Indiana University Press, 1979), pp. 214–15. See also Michel de Certeau, *Heterologies: Discourse on the Other,* trans. Brian Massumi (Minneapolis: University of Minnesota Press, 1986), pp. 193–98, for a discussion of Foucault's habit of displacing "discipline" by "astonishment," of opposing "panoptic leveling with discontinuities revealed in thought by chance," a mild-side-to-wild-side gesture that he "marks with a laugh" (pp. 197, 196, 194). The move that the instructor and students must make, in a Foucauldian or other manner, is from, as it were, "thaumatizing" (wondering) to theorizing (looking self-consciously, rigorously)—but without abandoning the sense of astonishment (or the laughter) triggered by paradox (again and again).

40. Uta Liebmann Schaub, "Foucault's Oriental Subtext," *Publications of the Modern Language Association* 104 (1989): 307, 308, 309, 310, 313, 314.

41. Ibid., pp. 314–15.

42. Gregory L. Ulmer, *Applied Grammatology: Post(e)-Pedagogy from Jacques Derrida to Joseph Beuys* (Baltimore: Johns Hopkins University Press, 1985), pp. 157, 179, 157.

43. Ibid., pp. x, xi, xii, xiii, xiv.

44. Ibid., pp. 160, 162.

45. Ibid., pp. 163, 161, 163–64, 166, 167, 168.

46. Ibid., pp. 168, 171, 173–74, 172, 174, 175, 177, 179, 180–81, 183, 184, 185. See, especially, Bourdieu and Passeron, *Reproduction in Education,* a work that has much influenced Ulmer's thinking about the notion of education as reproduction (and its contradictions), the classroom as theater, and related matters. Ulmer's indebtedness to Derrida (and others) in the formulation of a number of items in my inventory is considerable, as he acknowledges; but it is too diffuse for me to acknowledge in useful form here—the reader is referred to Ulmer's own citations. Still, I should note that Ulmer's interest in the *apeiron*—which he defines, generally following Anaximander, as "the unlimited, the indefinite, the undecidable" (*Applied Grammatology,* p. 150)—apparently comes through Derrida, particularly his *Dissemination,* trans. Barbara Johnson (Chicago: University of Chicago Press, 1981), p. 365, but also his *Edmund Husserl's "Origin of Geometry": An Introduction,* trans. John P. Leavey, Jr. (Stony Brook, N.Y.: Nicolas Hays, 1978), esp. pp. 151–52, and other works. Ulmer's treatment of it (see *Applied Grammatology,* pp. 149–53) is brief and somewhat different from mine, but he does relate it implicitly to the idea of an epistemology "in which knowing and knowledge are oriented not by the *results* as aftereffect, known in advance and to which presentation must conform, but to creativity, innovation, invention, change" (p. 152)—an idea very much aligned with my conceptions of apeironic education and hermetic pedagogy, one that codifies in yet another way the shift from teaching to instructing.

47. Gerald Holton, *Thematic Origins of Scientific Thought: Kepler to Einstein* (Cambridge, Mass.: Harvard University Press, 1973), p. 15. G. Polya makes a similar distinction in his *How to Solve It: A New Aspect of Mathematical Method* (1945; reprint, Princeton, N.J.: Princeton University Press, 1971), a now-classic work whose crisp, broadly applicable heuristic strategies ought to be part of every mathematics educator's pedagogical repertoire, when he speaks of his pioneering efforts to help students, educators, and the public go beyond mathematics as "the rigorous science of Euclid" (in which aspect it "appears as

a systematic, deductive science") and learn "mathematics in the making" or "mathematics 'in statu nascendi,' in the process of being invented" (in which aspect it "appears as an experimental, inductive science")—an approach that, he observes, with telling accuracy still, "is not in fashion nowadays but has a long past and, perhaps, some future" (p. vii). See also Gregory L. Ulmer, "Textshop for Psychoanalysis: On De-Programming Freshmen Platonists," *College English* 49 (1987): 756–69, which draws on Silvano Arieti's notion of the role of the "endocept" (the private, unexpressed "glimmer") in invention and Feyerabend's critique of the overemphasis in academic science on verification (at the expense of invention) and argues for the need to involve "mystory," the "'text' of the student's personal story," in creativity (pp. 765, 767). See Silvano Arieti, *Creativity: The Magic Synthesis* (New York: Basic Books, 1976), pp. 53–65.

48. Ulmer, *Applied Grammatology,* p. 188. See also his "Textshop for Post(e)-pedagogy," in *Writing and Reading Differently: Deconstruction and the Teaching of Composition and Literature,* ed. G. Douglas Atkins and Michael L. Johnson (Lawrence: University Press of Kansas, 1985), pp. 38–64, where he discusses a number of activities (what he calls "as-sign-ments") that suggest how the classroom, as "textshop rather than workshop," can function as a scene for enacting "a *dramatic,* rather than an epistemological, orientation to knowledge." Such activities take account of Holton's insistence on students participating in knowledge and not just consuming it, and they are underwritten by insights from figures like Gaston Bachelard and Alfred Korzybski concerning, respectively, the need "for a new pedagogy that would introduce into the humanities epistemological models derived from science" and the need "to reeducate people to think in a desubstantialized world consisting not of objects but of events." Ulmer realizes that, practically speaking, "it may not be possible, or even desirable, to shift completely to a postmodernized pedagogy"; indeed, he stresses the importance of a both-and approach, with the textshop serving "as a supplement to current practice," a solution required, since the structure of the textshop is "that of parody," for its effectiveness (pp. 39, 49, 51, 52–53).

49. Ulmer, "Textshop for Post(e)pedagogy," pp. 55, 56, 61, 60, 61–62. See Werner Jaeger, *Paideia: The Ideals of Greek Culture,* trans. Gilbert Highet, vol. 2 (New York: Oxford University Press, 1943), p. 317; Derrida, *Dissemination,* p. 156; on "amateurization," Roland Barthes, "Twenty Key Words for Roland Barthes," in *The Grain of the Voice: Interviews, 1962–1980,* trans. Linda Coverdale (New York: Hill & Wang, 1985), pp. 216–18; and, on carnivalization in Bakhtin's sense, Dominick LaCapra, *Rethinking Intellectual History: Texts, Contexts, Language* (Ithaca, N.Y.: Cornell University Press, 1983), pp. 291–324, esp. p. 305, where he discusses how, through laughter, "Dialectics becomes dialogic and carnivalisque."

50. Roland Barthes, "Literature/Teaching," in *Grain of the Voice,* p. 237.

51. A. J. Krailsheimer, Introduction, *Bouvard and Pécuchet,* by Gustave Flaubert, trans. A. J. Krailsheimer (Middlesex: Penguin Books, 1976), p. 16.

52. Barthes, "Literature/Teaching," p. 242.

53. Roland Barthes, "Writers, Intellectuals, Teachers," in *Image/Music/Text,* trans. Stephen Heath (New York: Hill & Wang, 1977), p. 215.

54. Vincent B. Leitch, "Deconstruction and Pedagogy," in *Writing and Reading Differently,* ed. Atkins and Johnson, p. 21.

55. Steven Ungar, "The Professor of Desire," in *Pedagogical Imperative,* ed. Johnson, p. 97.

56. Roland Barthes, *A Lover's Discourse: Fragments,* trans. Richard Howard (New York: Hill & Wang, 1978), p. 234. I am indebted to Ungar for the insight that Barthes's "act of refusal" resembles Socrates' in that both respond positively to the same erotic/epistemological principle of pedagogy: "Only by acknowledging desire in the very moment of denying it can the professor of Desire teach the knowledge of love and love of knowledge, thus fulfilling the nurturing function essential to the learning process as a continuous affirmation of joyful wisdom" ("Professor of Desire," p. 97). This principle of carefully balanced intimacy and formality should not be confused, however, with Paul de Man's stricter and more questionable dictum that "the only teaching worthy of the name is scholarly, not personal"—that is, it "is not primarily an intersubjective relationship between people but a cognitive process in which self and other are only tangentially and contiguously involved" ("The Resistance to Theory," in *Pedagogical Imperative,* ed. Johnson, p. 3). Nor should it be confused with the check on affection necessitated by the constant grade-by-grade, semester-by-semester moving-on of educators and students, a process that Jules Henry sees as promoting a decidedly *destructive* "uninvolvement" (*Culture against Man* [New York: Random House, 1963], p. 318).

Conclusion
Changing All Those Changes

1. Kenneth Burke, *Attitudes toward History* (Boston: Beacon Press, 1961), p. 331. He attributes the distinction to "followers of John Dewey's educational theories" and offers this elaboration:

> we should say that a society is normal when education is a function of society. That is, the principles and directives of the society are operating smoothly, and education prepares the minds of the young by equipping them to maintain these same principles and directives. We are "alienated," "dispossessed" insofar as this order must be reversed, as the followers of Dewey would reverse them. To say that "society" should be a function of "education" is to say, in effect, that the principles and directives of the prevailing society are radically askew (that the society has been despoiled of its reasonableness) and that education must serve to remake it accordingly. (pp. 331-32)

My use of the distinction doubtless complicates it (in no small part because I believe that now no "normal" society exists or, if it did, would exemplify largely the opposite of what Burke predicates of it), but I hope not unduly so. See also Frank Lentricchia's discussion of this distinction and its ironies in his *Criticism and Social Change* (Chicago: University of Chicago Press, 1983), pp. 1-2.

2. Philip H. Coombs, *The World Crisis in Education: The View from the Eighties* (New York: Oxford University Press, 1985), pp. 14, 20, 23, 21, 27, 31. Perhaps the crispest argument for Coombs's emphases on educational illocality,

continuousness, and flexibility resides in this anecdote: "The provocative composer John Cage once observed, with deceptive whimsicality (his characteristic Zen whimsicality, actually) that the trouble with education was that the students weren't always taking the courses at the same times that the professors were offering them" (Stephen Donadio, "The Achievement of Inwardness: The Liberal Arts and American Education" [1987 keynote address], in *Beginning Dialogue: A Report on the CETE Conference on Undergraduate Teacher Education in the Liberal Arts: Creating Models of Excellence,* ed. Mary Ruth Yoe [Middlebury, Vt.: Middlebury College, 1988], p. 22).

3. Christopher Norris, *Deconstruction: Theory and Practice* (New York: Methuen, 1982), p. 98.

4. Geoffrey H. Hartman, *Criticism in the Wilderness: The Study of Literature Today* (New Haven, Conn.: Yale University Press, 1980), pp. 80, 255.

5. Walter LaFeber, "We Need Fresh Scholarship to Understand Changed World Realities," *Chronicle of Higher Education,* 24 May 1989, p. A40.

6. Very much pertinent to the enterprise of apeironic learning is educational administration, which I have discussed little while implying the need for its enlightened interest in and action in terms of the goals of such learning. That topic is too large to treat in detail here, but surely I have at least *suggested* a great deal about how educational administration should function in furthering the changes with which I have been concerned.

7. Merry White, *The Japanese Educational Challenge: A Commitment to Children* (New York: Free Press, 1987), p. 8. White quite rightly warns against trying to import into the United States a system that is defined by a group psychology and axiology alien to American individualism and that sees education as "a force for reducing cultural variety," and she notes that "when Japanese look to the West, they look for models that will provide a more expansive, liberal, individualized form of instruction and give children more room to be creative"; but, acknowledging American need for "a more open view of our own educational system and the cultural conceptions that underlie it," she suggests that much can be learned from the Japanese example: to stress the acquisition of "participatory social techniques," to formulate a more generous notion of potential for learning, to be less Calvinistically obsessed with "classroom orderliness and discipline" (not a priority in Japan and hence "mostly absent" there) and more interested in the general promotion of "high energy engagement," to encourage students to "talk *to each other*" more, to attend more to "cultural values and practices" and less to "the market economy and attendent social mobility," to give "academic subjects priority" and get rid of "silly electives," "to make school a more legitimate place for teachers to work," and to make their profession more "rewarding" financially (pp. 15, 178, 4, 8, 180, 182, 190, 188).

8. W. J. T. Mitchell, "Scholars Need to Explore Further the Links and Dissonance between Post-Colonial Culture and Post-Imperial Criticism," *Chronicle of Higher Education,* 19 April 1989, p. B3.

9. Sharon Crowley, "Jacques Derrida on Teaching and Rhetoric," *ATAC Newsletter* 2, no. 1 (Spring 1990): 2. The complex relation of this dynamic to tradition generally is thereby like that of the works of some deconstructionists to "the ancient rhetorical tradition," as Derrida characterizes it: "it disrupts and it

inherits at the same time" (Gary A. Olson, "Jacques Derrida on Rhetoric and Composition: A Conversation," *Journal of Advanced Composition,* 10, no. 1 [1990]: 18).

10. Jacques Derrida, *Positions,* trans. Alan Bass (Chicago: University of Chicago Press, 1981), pp. 41–42.

11. William Stafford, "Knowing," in *A Glass Face in the Rain* (New York: Harper & Row, 1982), p. 18. The wary reader who has come to this note might heed the end of Stafford's short poem, with its reminder of the trying irony of the apeironic:

> Your hand can make the sign—but begs for
> more than can be told: even the world
> can't dive fast enough to know that other world.

Bibliographic Essay

I know of no work quite comparable to the present study in theme, approach, and comprehensiveness, though there are a few books, such as John S. Mayher's laudable *Uncommon Sense: Theoretical Practice in Language Education* (Portsmouth, N.H.: Heinemann and Boynton/Cook, 1990), that offer somewhat similar treatments of a more restricted range of issues. If pressed, I would cite Gregory L. Ulmer's *Applied Grammatology: Post(e)-Pedagogy from Jacques Derrida to Joseph Beuys* (Baltimore: Johns Hopkins University Press, 1985) as closest in intellectual spirit, but its overall conception and particulars differ a good deal from mine—so much so that such comparison probably would surprise Ulmer. As my copious notes, which the reader is encouraged to consult, indicate, many works, including Ulmer's, have contributed, in one way or another to the development of my arguments. Some of those works, along with a generous selection of others I have not previously cited, are singled out below for their special relevance in that regard. They should prove valuable to the reader who wishes to pursue further certain of the topics and figures I have treated, and a number of them afford specific ideas for apeironic classroom practice that usefully complement and extend my somewhat theoretical text and its accompanying chart and notes.

For the reader who feels too uncomfortably plunged into the vertiginous postmodern world evoked by and embodied in my Preface, I would recommend several works. Sharon Crowley's short and approachable book *A Teacher's Introduction to Deconstruction* (Urbana, Ill.: National Council of Teachers of English, 1989) simplifies its subject about as much as one would dare, explores its implications for the classroom, and is especially good on the application of deconstructive pedagogy to reading and writing—to helping students understand and articulate knowledge as a tentative, communal construct. A readable synoptic history of the poststructuralist situation in which contemporary education finds itself is Jane Tompkins's "Short Course in Post-Structuralism," *College English* 50 (1988): 733–47. Though many works concerned with postmodernity are available, few rival in concision and focus Gregory Jay's "Coloring the Postmodern," *Cream City Review* 13, no. 2 (Fall 1989): 184–88, which dis-

Bibliographic Essay

cusses it, largely in terms of Alice Walker's novel *The Color Purple* and its film adaptation, as "the acceleration of simulation without origin" (p. 184). Two general articles for anyone concerned with the conflicts and rapprochements of cognitivism and social constructionism are Kenneth A. Bruffee's thoughtful survey, which someone ought to update, "Social Construction, Language, and the Authority of Knowledge: A Bibliographical Essay," *College English* 48 (1986): 773–90, and D. N. Perkins and Gavriel Salomon's admirable attempt at productively interrelating domain-general and domain-specific views of learning, "Are Cognitive Skills Context-Bound?" *Educational Researcher* 18, no. 1 (January–February 1989): 16–25. Finally, since I invoke the social-constructionist thought of Mikhail Bakhtin, either directly or indirectly, in a number of contexts, I should suggest two studies of his work that I have found particularly worthwhile: Katerina Clark and Michael Holquist's *Mikhail Bakhtin* (Cambridge, Mass.: Harvard University Press, 1984), an intellectual biography that makes a forceful case for his emergence "as one of the major thinkers of the twentieth century" (p. vii), and Tzvetan Todorov's *Mikhail Bakhtin: The Dialogical Principle,* trans. Wlad Godzich (Minneapolis: University of Minnesota Press, 1984), an exploration of dialogism through a montagelike interplay of selections from Bakhtin's key texts and Todorov's commentaries—so that one has an anthology and a study in the same trim volume.

The notes to chapter 1 cite numerous sources helpful to anyone trying to gain an overview of the present situation of education and to discern a hopeful pattern of changes and possibilities for changes. The works of Neil Postman, Philip H. Coombs, and others were directly helpful to me in that regard, but several works that are not cited doubtless contributed by less direct influence and should be mentioned here. Two extremes in the analysis of the "great teacher" may be found in Joseph Lowman's *Mastering the Techniques of Teaching* (San Francisco: Jossey-Bass, 1985), which surveys well (pp. 1–22) the research on outstanding teaching but is perhaps too tidy and formulaic in its conclusions about what makes for (the much-to-be-questioned notion of) "mastery," and in Robert B. Heilman's essay "The Great Teacher Myth" (largely a debunking review of the film *Dead Poets Society*), *American Scholar* 60 (1991): 417–23. Both of these works, each in its own way, soberingly condition one's thinking about the matter and spur rethinking. John I. Goodlad's *Teachers for Our Nation's Schools* (San Francisco: Jossey-Bass, 1990) might be, in some respects, of more immediate, positive purport.

Additional worthwhile works concerning creativity are Carl R. Hausman's *Discourse on Novelty and Creation* (Albany: State University of New York Press, 1984), which, wisely, investigates creativity as a multiply paradoxical phenomenon rather than one to be either rationalistically explained or categorized as mysteriously beyond understanding; Michael Carter's "Problem Solving Reconsidered: A Pluralistic Theory of Problems," *College English* 50 (1988): 551–65, which eclectically reconceives how "we should see problems as opportunities that should be sought out" and how "people invent them" (pp. 559, 563); and D. N. Perkins's book *The Mind's Best Work* (Cambridge, Mass.: Harvard University Press, 1981), which is irritating in its cuteness but polemically stimulating. The difficulty of "measuring" creativity contributes greatly to its being neglected in formal education and is knotty in the extreme, as Robert T.

Bibliographic Essay

Brown demonstrates in his "Creativity: What Are We to Measure?" in the *Handbook of Creativity,* ed. John A. Glover, Royce R. Ronning, and Cecil R. Reynolds (New York: Plenum, 1989), pp. 3–32, a detailed and comprehensive survey that winds up entertaining the "general implication . . . that we should, however reluctantly, question the presumed existence of any such *thing* as creativity"—though prior to that it calls, more sanguinely, for more intelligently designed or at least less sloppy research on defining, nurturing, and measuring creativity, especially in regard to the underestimated importance of "personal-situational interactions" and "cultural factors" (p. 29).

The reader who wishes to review the Deweyan background to the present study might turn to *Dewey on Education: Selections with an Introduction and Notes,* ed. Martin S. Dworkin (New York: Bureau of Publications, Teachers College, Columbia University, 1959), a small book that has been around awhile but that provides an approachable range of representative texts and, in Dworkin's "John Dewey: A Centennial Review" (pp. 1–18), a useful summary of Dewey's ideas and of reaction to them that argues forcefully for "the need to distinguish Dewey from his followers in progressive education" (p. 17). In spite of its, for me, somewhat off-putting title, J. J. Chambliss's *Educational Theory as Theory of Conduct: From Aristotle to Dewey* (Albany: State University of New York Press, 1987) offers a reading of Dewey and his precursors that encourages continuing thought about the uncertainties involved in learning as self-making. Of related interest are two books, dated in some particulars but remarkably timely in others, by educators whom in some respects I count—without, I hope, undue immodesty—among my own precursors: Alfred North Whitehead's venerable and much-reprinted book *"The Aims of Education" and Other Essays* (New York: Macmillan, 1929), which, besides other things, anticipates Gerald Graff's critique of disconnectedness among academic disciplines and subdisciplines, and I. A. Richards's *Interpretation in Teaching* (London: Routledge & Kegan Paul, 1938), which stresses the need for students to learn more complex interpretive strategies, to be self-conscious about the questions they ask and the meanings of their answers, and "to start from as well as work towards the unintelligible" (p. 7).

Anyone interested in the development of Western notions of paideia should read Werner Jaeger's *Paideia: The Ideals of Greek Culture,* trans. Gilbert Highet, 2 vols. (Oxford: Blackwell, 1939; New York: Oxford University Press, 1943), a work that, however quaint in some respects, can serve as a corrective to the odder classical nostalgias of Allan Bloom and company. An effective countermeasure for conservatives' deluded notions of relativism is a careful reading of Barbara Herrnstein Smith's *Contingencies of Value: Alternative Perspectives for Critical Theory* (Cambridge, Mass.: Harvard University Press, 1988), esp. pp. 150–84, a crucial work for anyone concerned with promoting an apeironic paideia. Another, about which I am not quite so sanguine, is Richard Rorty's *Contingency, Irony, and Solidarity* (Cambridge: Cambridge University Press, 1989). A number of conservatives in addition to Bloom have launched more or less uninformed attacks against deconstruction and its poststructuralist offspring; two of the more clever recent ones may be found in David Lehman's *Signs of the Times: Deconstruction and the Fall of Paul de Man* (New York: Simon & Schuster, Poseidon Press, 1991) and Peter Shaw's *War against the*

Bibliographic Essay

Intellect: Episodes in the Decline of Discourse (Iowa City: University of Iowa Press, 1989). A more balanced representation of the deconstructive enterprise to a general readership may be found in Mark Edmundson's essay "A Will to Cultural Power: Deconstructing the de Man Scandal," *Harper's,* July 1988, pp. 67–71, which also does a good job of exploring what is at stake in the conflicts between literary theorists and the relatively more conservative popular press. There is no shortage of publications concerned with deconstruction, almost all, given the nature of the creature, explicitly or implicitly pedagogical in purport, and I am loathe to "defend" it against detractors; but three works have been especially helpful to me in thinking about issues of tradition and paideia: Gary A. Olson's "Jacques Derrida on Rhetoric and Composition: A Conversation," *Journal of Advanced Composition* 10, no. 1 (1990): 1–21, which makes clear that Derrida hardly opposes tradition but rather sees it as absolutely essential to understanding deconstruction and the inventive activity it enables; *Shakespeare and Deconstruction,* ed. G. Douglas Atkins and David M. Bergeron (New York: Peter Lang, 1988), which offers a wealth of ideas for helping students productively (re)read *the* canonical figure in English literature; and Floyd Merrell's *Deconstruction Reframed* (West Lafayette, Ind.: Purdue University Press, 1985), a brilliant synthetic work that describes all manner of interconnections between deconstruction and concepts in areas as seemingly diverse as quantum physics and Freudian psychology, among many others, along the way offering dozens of thought experiments that dramatize the emergence of new conceptual categories from traditional or conventional ones.

For the reader who wishes to pursue further the polemics of political correctness that emerge in chapter 2 and weave, implicitly or explicitly, through other chapters, I would recommend two books. *Debating P.C.: The Controversy over Political Correctness on College Campuses,* ed. Paul Berman (New York: Laurel, 1992), though perhaps somewhat hastily produced (it lacks an index, for instance), presents 21 pieces, culled from large-circulation journals and newspapers and representing a variety of positions, by Dinesh D'Souza, George F. Will, Edward W. Said, and many others. Berman's "Introduction: The Debate and Its Origins" makes for an informative and good-humored tour of key topics: the charge that postmodern radicals threaten individualism by the imposition of McCarthy-like codes of conduct and speech, the curricular quagmire of "hyperethnicity," historical flip-flops of the phrase itself (used approvingly by Leninists, ironically "among wised-up leftists to denote someone whose line-toeing fervor was too much to bear," then otherwise by those who "relished" the "twist of irony" involved, and so on), the late-1960s background of contemporary "identity politics," the troubling specter of "the young de Man's Euro-style racial thinking," the vicissitudes of affirmative action (which program does need some revamping), the apparent intolerance and hazing that NAS-oriented academics experience from their more postmodern colleagues—all of which Berman, neglecting some influences (most obviously that of British cultural studies), sees as aspects of the political-correctness "syndrome," which is "the fog that arises from American liberalism's encounter with the iceberg of French cynicism" (pp. 3, 5, 11, 17, 24). Sophisticated (and welcome) humor characterizes also much of *Loose Canons: Notes on the Culture Wars* (New York: Oxford University Press, 1992), an engaging and perceptive exploration of the

Bibliographic Essay

issues of multiculturalism at the heart of the political-correctness debate, by Henry Louis Gates, Jr.

To my knowledge there is no comprehensive work on the pedagogy and curriculum of the natural sciences as they are now constituted, though my notes to chapter 3 cite several sources that hint at what such a work might be. Rather than list books on string theory and so on that could serve to jar anyone into realizing the need for a new kind of natural-sciences education, I would merely suggest that the reader venture into James Gleick's *Chaos: Making a New Science* (New York: Viking, 1987). Rich in biographical anecdotes, vigorous (if a little journalistic) in its portrayal of how nonlinear thinking has opened apparent impasses in numerous disciplines and compelled a radical interdisciplinarity, that exciting book abounds with implications for apeironic learning and can readily be mined for topics for discussion and projects for computer simulation or laboratory experimentation. And the reader might have a look at a book that intriguingly relates Gleick's concerns to those of the humanities, N. Katherine Hayles's *Chaos Bound: Orderly Disorder in Contemporary Literature and Science* (Ithaca, N.Y.: Cornell University Press, 1990). Otherwise, J. Bronowski's *Ascent of Man* (Boston: Little, Brown, 1973) remains one of the most engaging (if occasionally irritatingly idiosyncratic) and well-illustrated popular histories of scientific ideas around. Inarguably sexist, it nonetheless does a good job of delineating, with abundant specifics, the evolution of the natural sciences as a multicultural, global enterprise. A more recent one-of-a-kind book that does something similar for mathematics—though without Bronowski's historical sweep—is Marcia Ascher's *Ethnomathematics: A Multicultural View of Mathematical Ideas* (Pacific Grove, Calif.: Brooks/Cole, 1991), which deals more self-consciously with issues of universality and diversity.

For a broader and more detailed development of Diane Ravitch's line of argument about the history curriculum, see the book that she wrote with Chester E. Finn, Jr., *What Do Our 17-Year-Olds Know? A Report on the First National Assessment of History and Literature* (New York: Harper & Row, 1987). For background to that book, see Arthur N. Applebee, Judith A. Langer, and Ina V. S. Mullis's *Literature and U.S. History: The Instructional Experience and Factual Knowledge of High School Juniors* (Princeton, N.J.: Educational Testing Service, 1987), another NAEP report, more perfunctory than usual (concluding little more about pedagogy, for instance, than that "students' descriptions of their coursework in history reflect a very traditional approach to instruction" [p. 34]—that is, mostly, teachers parroting textbooks while students listen) though blandly optimistic. Also relevant here is Ravitch's best-known book, *The Schools We Deserve: Reflections on the Educational Crises of Our Times* (New York: Basic Books, 1985), which winds up lamenting (not without some sympathy from me) the "'technicization' of the curriculum" and asking significant questions about Americans' commitment to education—but simplistically advocating a national consensus on curriculum based on the idea of "heritage" (pp. 313, 315).

A pedagogically useful introduction to New Historicism is Stephen J. Greenblatt's *Learning to Curse: Essays in Early Modern Culture* (New York: Routledge, 1990), which gives a sense of its development over the last two decades. A considerably earlier but still-much-cited work relevant to that development is

Bibliographic Essay

Hayden White's *Tropics of Discourse: Essays in Cultural Criticism* (Baltimore: Johns Hopkins University Press, 1978), which investigates, among other matters, how the writing of history excludes, a process involving epistemological constraints taken up also by Albert Cook in his *History/Writing* (Cambridge: Cambridge University Press, 1988). A crisp discussion of the interdisciplinarity of New Historicism, the need for historicisms, and kindred subjects may be found in Dominick LaCapra's "On the Line: Between History and Criticism," in *Profession 89,* ed. Phyllis Franklin (New York: Modern Language Association, 1989), pp. 4–9. Four books, among many I might mention, that more or less exemplify New Historicist approaches and would be useful in the history classroom are David M. Bergeron's *Royal Family, Royal Lovers: King James of England and Scotland* (Columbia: University of Missouri Press, 1991), an eloquent and methodologically self-conscious biographically oriented study of a watershed period in British history; Donald Worster's *Rivers of Empire: Water, Aridity, and the Growth of the American West* (New York: Pantheon Books, 1986) and *Under Western Skies: Nature and History in the American West* (New York: Oxford University Press, 1992), both of which examine the deeply problematic political, economic, and technological forces driving westward expansion; and the radically revisionary collection *Trails: Toward a New Western History,* ed. Patricia Nelson Limerick, Clyde Milner, Jr., and Charles Rankin (Lawrence: University Press of Kansas, 1991). In the literature classroom one might use Gabriel García Márquez's novel *The General in His Labyrinth,* trans. Edith Grossman (New York: Knopf, 1990), a magical realist's rereading of the life of Simón Bolívar that raises interesting questions about the relation between history and fiction.

Textualist or quasi-textualist studies in the social sciences are not difficult to encounter these days, so I mention here only three, all of which may have some relevance to classroom practice and speak to issues I raised at the end of chapter 4: James W. Fernandez's cultural-anthropological study *Persuasions and Performances: The Play of Tropes in Culture* (Bloomington: Indiana University Press, 1986) and Donald N. McCloskey's *Rhetoric of Economics* (Madison: University of Wisconsin Press, 1985) and *If You're So Smart: The Narrative of Economic Expertise* (Chicago: University of Chicago Press, 1990).

The variety of viewpoints involved in recent debates on humanities education is fairly well represented in two collections: *Criticism in the University,* ed. Gerald Graff and Reginald Gibbons, *TriQuarterly* Series on Criticism and Culture, no. 1 (Evanston, Ill.: Northwestern University Press, 1985), by now almost a "historical" traditionalist/theorist anthology but one still widely used in the graduate classroom, and *The Changing Culture of the University,* ed. Edith Kurzweil, a special issue of *Partisan Review* 58, no. 2 (1991), certainly a more "political" forum, one concerning issues of curriculum and canon, multiculturalism, the role of the media, and so on, which consists of transcribed conversations from the sessions at a conference, partly sponsored by the NEH, with the same title. Also, in this connection, the reader might have a look at *Liberal Education* 77, no. 33 (1991), a special issue that consists of articles, representing various positions, concerning multiculturalism in the humanities, especially in curricula being developed by sixty-three postsecondary institutions through a project coordinated by the Association of American Colleges, funded by the

Bibliographic Essay

NEH, and entitled Engaging Cultural Legacies: Shaping Core Curricula in the Humanities. A detailed account of the building of the poststructuralist English curriculum at Carnegie Mellon University may be found in Gary F. Waller's "Working within the Paradigm Shift: Poststructuralism and the College Curriculum," *ADE Bulletin,* no. 81 (Fall 1985), which unfortunately neglects consideration of the administrative problems involved in such activity. A worthwhile if uneven collection of essays concerned with issues of theory and their implications for both scholarly and pedagogical practice, several with immediate relevance to the humanities classroom, is *Theory in the Classroom,* ed. Cary Nelson (Urbana: University of Illinois Press, 1986). A very readable textbook of essays on theory is *Critical Terms for Literary Study,* ed. Frank Lentricchia and Thomas McLaughlin (Chicago: University of Chicago Press, 1990). In their "Secret Sharing: Reading Conrad Psychoanalytically," *College English* 49 (1987): 628–40, Barbara Johnson and Marjorie Garber offer an excellent example of how the kind of theoretical approach much maligned by some can be used to refresh and enlarge students' reading of a traditional anthology piece, Joseph Conrad's short story "The Secret Sharer." The most controversial recent multicultural literary anthology is *The Heath Anthology of American Literature,* ed. Paul Lauter et al., 2 vols. (Lexington, Mass.: Heath, 1990), a college-level collection, already used widely, that should stimulate much classroom discussion both through its generous representation of noncanonical authors and through its editorial rationale; it will prove, indubitably, to be the forerunner of other, similar anthologies. Besides the works concerning canonicity that I cite in chapter 5, I would recommend also William W. Hallo's "Assyriology and the Canon," *American Scholar* 59 (1990): 105–8, which puts the whole matter in a multimillennial perspective; Richard Lanham's "Rhetorical Paideia: The Curriculum as a Work of Art," *College English* 48 (1986): 132–41, which proposes a move "from curriculum as canon to curriculum as participatory theatre" (p. 140); and John Guillory's "Canon," in *Critical Terms,* ed. Lentricchia and McLaughlin, pp. 233–49, which discusses issues of literacy and reception as well as the school's role in canon formation.

Since I have cited throughout my notes numerous sources concerned with creativity and criticism, I mention here only two works that I think might be valuable to arts educators, both concerned with interdisciplinarity. In *Learning Communities* (San Francisco: Jossey-Bass, 1990) Faith Gabelnick, Jean MacGregor, Roberta S. Matthews, and Barbara Leigh Smith describe in practical terms numerous college-level courses, at various institutions, that thematically integrate the perspectives and issues of several disciplines, some of which suggest ways of thereby enriching arts education; but while encouraging the development of students' critical consciousness through disciplinary interconnection, the book stops short of dealing with questions of canonicity and multiculturality. A work that does do an excellent job of analyzing one of the arts, film, in terms of postmodern cultural questions of immediate interest to college students is Anne Friedberg's article "*Les Flâneurs du Mal(l):* Cinema and the Postmodern Condition," *Publications of the Modern Language Association* 106 (1991): 419–31.

Perhaps the most comprehensive one-volume collection of materials concerned with literacy issues is *Perspectives on Literacy,* ed. Eugene R. Kintgen,

Bibliographic Essay

Barry M. Kroll, and Mike Rose (Carbondale: Southern Illinois University Press, 1988), which includes a lengthy bibliography. On reading as writing, the reader should turn to, among other pertinent work in the collection, David Kaufer and Gary Waller's "To Write Is to Read Is to Write, Right?" in *Writing and Reading Differently: Deconstruction and the Teaching of Composition and Literature*, ed. G. Douglas Atkins and Michael L. Johnson (Lawrence: University Press of Kansas, 1985), pp. 66–92, a somewhat theoretical piece but one that derives from extensive classroom experience. In his "Pleasure and Self-Loss in Reading," *ADE Bulletin*, no. 99 (Fall 1991), pp. 8–12, Barry Weller offers a useful complement to that piece, arguing thoughtfully for the importance of both writerly and readerly reading, for a balance between "the active exercise of a writerly will" and "a kind of readerly receptiveness and self-surrender" that "can sometimes be a part of or even a necessary prologue to self-empowerment" (p. 12). Additional analyses, generally positive, of the English Coalition Conference may be found in "The English Coalition Conference Report: Seven Responses," *ADE Bulletin*, no. 96 (Fall 1990), pp. 25–49, which qualifies some of the conclusions of the official report; a distinctly personal and problematizing analysis is Peter Elbow's *What Is English?* (Urbana, Ill.: National Council of Teachers of English; New York: Modern Language Association, 1990). In his *Preface to Literacy: An Inquiry into Pedagogy, Practice, and Progress* (Tuscaloosa: University of Alabama Press, 1987), Myron C. Tuman offers a balanced critique of different positions on cultural- and critical-literacy issues. An exemplary cross-cultural anthology for college-level students is *Ourselves among Others: Cross-Cultural Readings for Writers*, ed. Carol J. Verburg, 2d ed. (Boston: St. Martin's Press, Bedford Books, 1991), and an unusual periodical resource for the multicultural classroom is *Radical Teacher*, published three times a year and available from Box 102, Kendall Square Post Office, Cambridge, MA 02142. A children's book, unfortunately not a "textbook," that remarkably instances, in a way that would please Jacques Barzun, instructing in principles rather than the teaching of facts and thus represents an alternative to Hirschian cultural-literacy education is David Macaulay's beautifully illustrated survey of physical principles and their applications entitled *The Way Things Work* (Boston: Houghton Mifflin, 1988). Finally, the reader interested in gaining a fuller sense of the MLA's Right to Literacy conference should consult a collection of the papers presented there, *The Right to Literacy*, ed. Andrea L. Lunsford, Helene Moglen, and James Slevin (New York: Modern Language Association, 1990).

As is clear from my discussion in chapter 8 of assessment and evaluation, I find quite valuable David Elkind's critique of them in *The Hurried Child: Growing Up Too Fast Too Soon*, rev. ed. (Reading, Mass.: Addison-Wesley, 1988). Also, concerning strategies of school-university alliance, very much a related matter, especially in the United States, I would again recommend *The School and the University: An International Perspective*, ed. Burton R. Clark (Berkeley and Los Angeles: University of California Press, 1985). While there are a few books around that deal intelligently with discipline-specific methods of conventional assessment and evaluation of student learning—I cut my teeth on P. B. Diederich's *Measuring Growth in English* (Champaign, Ill.: National Council of Teachers of English, 1974)—there is none, to my knowledge, that

Bibliographic Essay

deals with the particular range of issues and kinds of emphases highlighted in chapter 8 and derived, in part, from the various sources cited in its notes.

Besides the works cited in chapter 9 on learning disabilities and remediation, I would suggest two others that any reader interested in the broader issues should know: Kenneth A. Kavale and Steven R. Forness's book *The Science of Learning Disabilities* (San Diego: College-Hill Press, 1985) and James G. Carrier's *Learning Disability: Social Class and the Construction of Inequality in American Education* (New York: Greenwood Press, 1986).

Among a number of works that dramatize the postmodern context of education and the necessity for countercurricular praxis is Kenneth J. Gergen's somewhat maverick social-psychological study *The Saturated Self: Dilemmas of Identity in Contemporary Life* (New York: Basic Books, 1991), which deals not only with specific curricular issues but also with larger issues (of relativism, individualism, contingency of meaning, what he calls the "multiphrenia" of change overload, and so on) that interlock with them. The mazy paradoxes haunting (op)positionality undergo the kind of scrutiny that prompts acute self-awareness in Christopher Butler's *Interpretation, Deconstruction, and Ideology: An Introduction to Some Current Issues in Literary Theory* (Oxford: Clarendon Press, 1984), which exults in exposing the positionality of those who exult in exposing the positionality of others, and James L. Battersby's "Professionalism, Relativism, and Rationality," *Publications of the Modern Language Association* 107 (1992): 51–64, which turns "antiprofessionalism" on its head the better to examine its somewhat Gödelian Achilles' heels. The importance of dynamic both-and vision in curricular (and pedagogical) innovation is well demonstrated by David Bleich in his *Double Perspective: Language, Literacy, and Social Relations* (New York: Oxford University Press, 1988). Some understanding of Jürgen Habermas's thought on intersubjectivity is de rigueur for anyone interested in countercurricular praxis, the pedagogy of critical thinking and literacy, and collaborative learning as a process of eliciting and illuminating differences between and within positions. A work that sets his thought in historical perspective is David Held's *Introduction to Critical Theory: Horkheimer to Habermas* (Berkeley and Los Angeles: University of California Press, 1980). A more specific study is Thomas McCarthy's *Critical Theory of Jürgen Habermas* (Cambridge, Mass.: MIT Press, 1978), which includes a useful bibliography. For a sense of the relevance of Habermasian ideas to the classroom, the reader should see Hugh H. Grady and Susan Wells's "Toward a Rhetoric of Intersubjectivity: Introducing Jürgen Habermas," *Journal of Advanced Composition* 6 (1985–86): 33–47, which treats the Frankfurt School theorist's twin projects of "the critique of positivism and scientism, and the reappropriation of the hermeneutic tradition" in terms of "his theory of communicative competence" (pp. 34, 35), and John Trimbur's "Consensus and Difference in Collaborative Learning," *College English* 51 (1989): 602–16, which concerns using (deferred) "consensus as a critical instrument to open gaps in the conversation through which differences may emerge," an instrument offered to students in the form of "the Habermasian representation of consensus as a counterfactual anticipation of fully realized communication" (p. 614).

The reader wanting a fuller understanding of the Hermes figure behind the hermetic pedagogue might turn to Norman O. Brown's *Hermes the Thief: The*

Bibliographic Essay

Evolution of a Myth (Madison: University of Wisconsin Press, 1947), still the best study of its kind. Jane Tompkins's "Pedagogy of the Distressed," *College English* 52 (1990): 653–60, offers an engaging account of how to shift the "intellectual center of gravity" of a class from the instructor to the students and thereby enlarge their responsibility for its transactions (p. 657). Further discussion of "Signifyin(g)" as elaborated by Henry Louis Gates, Jr., along with some ideas for its application in the literature classroom, may be found in William J. Spurlin's "Theorizing Signifyin(g) and the Role of the Reader: Possible Directions for African-American Literary Criticism," *College English* 52 (1990): 732–42. The reader interested in the counterbalance of an unsympathetic critique of Michel Foucault—whose pedagogical strategies do have, as I admit in my text, limitations—might see John Weightman's essay "On Not Understanding Michel Foucault," *American Scholar* 58 (1989): 383–406. And further discussion of Gregory L. Ulmer's concept of the "textshop," as well as ideas for what he calls "as-sign-ments," may be found in his "Textshop for an Experimental Humanities," in *Reorientations: Critical Theories and Pedagogies,* ed. Bruce Henricksen and Thaïs E. Morgan (Urbana: University of Illinois Press, 1990), pp. 113–32.

Since I invoke Geoffrey H. Hartman in the Conclusion (as an exemplary hermetic instructor) and elsewhere, I should direct the reader to the first and, to my knowledge, only book on his work as a critic and, much more than incidentally, as a pedagogue: G. Douglas Atkins's notable study *Geoffrey Hartman: Criticism as Answerable Style* (New York: Routledge, 1990). Also, though I have neglected direct treatment of the large topic of the administrative role in implementing apeironic learning, as I acknowledge in the notes to the Conclusion, I would urge the reader to think about the matter. If one wishes to pursue the elaboration of what might constitute effective administration in this regard, a good starting point, odd as it may seem, is Michael D. Cohen and James G. March's *Leadership and Ambiguity: The American College President* (Boston: Harvard Business School Press, 1986), especially an appendix by March entitled "How We Talk and How We Act: Administrative Theory and Administrative Life" (pp. 273–90), a contribution that outlines some of the fundamental issues and strategies of what strikes me as a productive postmodern approach to educational administration. Last, I would recommend a book concerned with some of the "bottom-line" questions with which apeironic learning must deal: Elaine Scarry's extraordinary investigation *The Body in Pain: The Making and Unmaking of the World* (New York: Oxford University Press, 1985). A book about the nature of pain, it is also about destruction and creation and, among other things, the "absolute split between one's sense of one's own reality and the reality of other persons" (p. 4), one of the splits that education on the wild side must nonetheless address and attempt to bridge, however tentatively, if not to mend.

Index

Abrams, M. H., 247
Acceleration syndrome, 204–205
Accommodation, Piaget and, 218–19
Accountability, educational, 176, 177, 179–80, 189–93
Accreditation, teacher-college, 32, 281n.8
Acculturation, transculturation and, 211
Acid rain, 5, 206
ACLS (American Council of Learned Societies), 114
Adams, Hazard, 151
Adams, Henry, 9
Adler, Mortimer, 105
Administrators, school, 208, 315n.6
Advertisements, learning from, 159
Aesthetics, 282n.20
AFL-CIO, MLA and, 303n.71
Africa, 238
African Americans, 108; Hirsch on, 297n.14; language of, 306n.11; literature of, 103, 294n.50, 299n.41
Against Method: Outline of an Anarchistic Theory of Knowledge (Feyerabend), 68
Age, of U.S. college students, 211
AIDS, 5, 20, 148; *Cultural Literacy* and, 142
Alazon, teacher as, 228
Alcibiades, 251
Alcosser, Sandra, 237

Algebra, 61. *See also* Equations, algebraic
Althusser, Louis, 224
Amberg, Jay, 289n.11
American Association for the Advancement of Science (AAAS), 65, 66
American Council of Learned Societies (ACLS), 114
American Historical Association, 76
American Scholar, The, 6, 54
Anaximander, 14, 312n.46
Anderson, Richard C., 136
Andrews, William, 299n.41
Anthropic principle, 72–73
Anthropology: cultural, 119; as evolving science, 85; teaching of, 148. *See also* Ethnography
Anti-foundationalism, 308n.2
Anti-intellectualism, 65, 66
Anything for Billy (McMurtry), 78–79
Apeiron, 14, 250, 277n.20, 312n.46. *See also* Education, apeironic; Learning, apeironic; Paideia, apeironic
Aphrodite, 227
Applied Grammatology (Ulmer), 245, 247–48
Arabic, teaching of, 104
Archaeology: Foucauldian, 240; past as, 207
Architecture, 70
Arieti, Silvano, 17, 278n.26, 313n.47
Aristotle, 173, 196, 223, 250
Arizona, University of, 299n.41

Armstrong, Paul B., 149, 154–56, 299–300n.41
Arrowsmith, William, 231
Art(s), 57; entertainment vs., 126; European sponsorship of, 109; "facts" underlying, 70; fine, 125; high-school requirements in, 126–27; humanities and, 119, 124–25, 129; political monitoring of, 126; reasons for teaching, 126, 128; research and, 128; role of, 124–25; and science contrasted, 124–25; teaching of, 124–29; verbal, 125; visual, 127. *See also* Dance; Literature; Music; Paintings
Artifacts, in humanities ambit, 119
Artificial intelligence, 66, 196, 290n.23
Art of Teaching, The (Highet), 276n.15
Asia, education in, 214
Assessment: educational, 176–78, 180, 182, 184–86, 188–90, 192; and evaluation contrasted, 176–77; teaching and, 189–90, 194. *See also* Evaluation; Tests
Assimilation, accommodation and, 218–19
Atkins, G. Douglas, 232
Atom, electronic structure of, 73
Atomic fission, 73
Audiovisual aids, 212
Ausubel, David P., 166–67, 187, 299n.34
Authority, 13

327

Index

Index

Index

Index

Index

of, 88–123, 153–54, 210; "truths" of, 111, 113. *See also* History; Literature; Philosophy

Humanities centers, 119

Humanities in America (Cheney), 108, 113, 118

Humor: as critical pedagogical ingredient, 303n.72; science vs., 68. *See also* Comedy; Jokes

Hypertext, 122

Ideology, humanism and, 116

Ignorance, nature of, 226

Iliad (Homer), 238

Illiberal Education: The Politics of Race and Sex on Campus (D'Souza), 41

Illich, Ivan, 23

Illiteracy: adult, 131–32; political uses of, 172–74, 302n.69

Imagination: as central to art, 124; nature and, 232

Imperialism: cultural, 139; *The Tempest* and, 98

Indians, American. *See* Native Americans

Infants, recalcitrance of, 220

Information: ideas vs., 279n.30; superfluity of, 204

Innumeracy: Mathematical Illiteracy and Its Consequences (Paulos), 284n.7

Instructing (word), 12, 13

Instructing, aim of, 168. *See also* Teaching, and instructing contrasted

Integrity in the College Curriculum: A Report to the Academic Community, 29

Intellectualism, conservative criticism of, 54. *See also* Anti-intellectualism

Intellectuals in Power: A Genealogy of Critical Humanism (Bové), 50–52

Intelligence, and learning contrasted, 16

Interpretation, Foucault on, 243

Involvement in Learning: Realizing the Potential of American Higher Education, 28

IQ (intelligence quotient), 179

Irigaray, Luce, 237

Iris, 238

Islam, 98

Issues, teaching of, 162

Jacobs, Jane, 52

Jacoby, Russell, 50, 52–55, 71, 283n.39

Jaeger, Werner, 8, 25–26, 40, 249

Jameson, Fredric, 53, 156

Japan: computer development in, 66; education in, 62, 63, 107, 255, 283–84n.5, 304n.19, 315n.7; student testing in, 190; U.S. education and, 59, 62. *See also* Kumon Mathamatex

Jarry, Alfred, 230

Jay, Gregory S., 229–30

Jehlen, Myra, 107

Johnson, Barbara, 233

Johnson, Michael L., 66, 292n.33; classroom strategies of, 158–59, 300n.46

Jokes: "blonde," 281n.14; critical analysis of, 159

Joyce, James, 95, 122

Julius Caesar (Shakespeare), 163

Juncker, Clara, 237

Kagan, Jerome, 8

Kansas, state of: educational reform in, 279–80n.34

Kansas, University of, 299n.41

Kates, Gary, 282n.20

Kaufer, David S., 161–65, 213, 301n.59

Keats, John, 159, 205

Keillor, Garrison, 303n.3

Kepler, Johannes, 73

Kett, Joseph F., 141, 297n.14

Kierkegaard, Søren, 203, 228

Kimball, Roger, 108

Kingsley, C. D., 34

Kintgen, Eugene R., 165

Kirk, G. S., 277n.20

Klein bottles, 64

"Knowing" (Stafford), 256, 316n.11

Knowledge(s): alternative, 226; application of proper, 154; creative approach to accepted, 18; determinacy of, 229; domain-specific vs. domain-general, 197; Hartman on, 293n.42; and ideology, 225; and ignorance, 225, 230; information as, 225; as interpretation, 287n.15; love of, 314n.56; mathematicization of, 70; monasticization of, 302n.69; nature of, 13, 230, 248; "new," 162–63; pri-

oritization of, 132–33; as "private property," 299n.34; privileges of, 241; as provisional, 85; psychological aspects of, 188; public contempt for, 126; situationality of, 308n.2; stereoscopic, 300n.46; student participation in, 313n.48; student resistance to, 225; traditional, 14; transmission of, 296n.8. *See also* Information; Learning; Metaknowledge

Knowledge engineering, 66

Koestler, Arthur, 17, 278n.26

Korin, Ogata, 253

Korzybski, Alfred, 313n.48

Kramer, Rita, 281n.8

Kroll, Barry M., 165

Kuhn, Thomas, 214, 246

Kumon Mathamatex, 62

Kurosawa, Akira, 86

Kyōiku, 284n.5

Lacan, Jacques, 225–26, 230, 231, 239, 240

LaCapra, Dominick, 286n.6, 313n.49

LaFeber, Walter, 254

Lake Wobegon effect, 303n.3

Langer, Ellen J., 203

Language(s): barriers of, 152; Bleich on, 300n.46; humanities "celebration" of, 119; limiting nature of, 234; as performative, 241; as political weapon, 172; teaching of, 104, 288n.9. *See also* Vocabulary; Words

Lanham, Richard, 40, 142, 159–61, 216, 244, 250

Last Intellectuals, The: American Culture in the Age of Academe (Jacoby), 50, 52–55

Late Night Thoughts on Listening to Mahler's Ninth Symphony (Thomas), 69

Latin, as high school subject, 93

Latin America, history of, 80

Latin Americans, literature by, 103. *See also* Hispanics, U.S.

Laurence, David, 112–13, 203–204, 292–93n.37

Lawrence, Karen, 99–100

Law School Admission Test (LSAT), 207

Lazere, Donald, 26, 28, 91,

Index

Index

Modern Language Association.
See MLA
Moger, Angela S., 233, 251
Moglen, Helene, 49, 149, 156–57
Montezuma, 253
*Moral Child, The: Nurturing
Children's Natural Moral
Growth* (Damon), 288n.9
Morgan, Thaïs E., 223
Morse, J. Mitchell, 5–8, 19
*Moving Beyond Myths: Re-
vitalizing Undergraduate
Mathematics,* 62
Mozart, Wolfgang Amadeus,
129
Mueller, Martin, 100–102,
200, 289n.19
Muhammad, 253
Multilingualism, 290n.28
Mumford, Lewis, 52, 53
Munby, Hugh, 228
Murphy, Richard J., Jr., 171–
75, 302n.71
Museums, popularity of U.S.,
109
Music: Bloom on popular, 42;
"facts" underlying, 70; stu-
dent appreciation of, 127;
teaching of, 129

NAEP (National Assessment of
Educational Progress), 60,
61, 190; and arts education,
127
Name of the Rose, The (Eco),
171–73
Narrative, pedagogy and, 233
NAS (National Association of
Scholars), 36, 39, 121, 156;
in "canon wars," 294–95n.54
National Assessment of Educa-
tional Progress. *See* NAEP
National Association of Schol-
ars. *See* NAS
National Board for Profes-
sional Teaching Standards,
191
National Council for History
Education, 76
National Council for the Ac-
creditation of Teacher Edu-
cation, 281n.8
National Council of Teachers of
Mathematics, 62
National Council on Education
Standards and Testing,
304n.18
National Council on Social
Studies, 76

National Council on the Arts,
125
National Council on the Hu-
manities, 121
National Endowment for the
Arts (NEA), 125–29
National Endowment for the
Humanities. *See* NEH
Nationality, politics of, 157
National Research Council
(NRC), 61, 62
National Science Foundation
(NSF), 60, 65
National Science Teachers As-
sociation (NSTA), 60, 65
*Nation at Risk, A: The Imper-
ative for Educational Reform,*
28, 125, 179
*Nation Prepared, A: Teachers
for the 21st Century,* 192
Native Americans, 80; Caucasian "identification" with,
282n.14; literature of, 103,
159
Natural sciences, 57, 282n.20;
evolution of, 85; federal government and, 285n.14; vs.
humanities, 46; instruction
in, 59–74, 284n.6; male
dominance of, 236, 310n.24;
Project 2061 and, 65. *See
also* Biology; Mathematics;
Physics; Science(s)
Nature: end of, 205–206; science and, 70, 71
NEA (National Endowment for
the Arts), 125–29
NEH (National Endowment for
the Humanities), 28, 107–
108, 291n.30; censorship
efforts of, 126; Hirsch sup-
port from, 137; literacy con-
ference of, 302–303n.71; vs.
MLA, 121. *See also* Bennett,
William J.; Cheney, Lynne V.
Nelson, Cary, 102, 290n.23
Nemerov, Howard, 213, 215,
216
Neverow-Turk, Vera, 300n.46
New Criterion, The, 54
New Historicism, 81–82
New math, 20, 279n.31
Newspapers, in higher-educa-
tion fray, 121, 295n.54
Newton, Isaac, 100, 253
New York Times, 121
Nietzsche, Friedrich, 44, 46,
48, 250, 251
Nihilism, 44, 240, 243
Nisbet, Robert, 54

Noakes, Susan, 215–17, 238,
286n.5, 307n.17
Norris, Christopher, 253
Northern Illinois University,
Public Opinion Laboratory
of. *See* POL
Nouwen, Henri J. M., 232
Novak, Joseph D., 166–67,
187–88
Novels: history vs., 285n.4;
humanities focus on, 119
NRC (National Research
Council), 61, 62
NSF (National Science Foun-
dation), 60, 65
NSTA (National Science Teach-
ers Association), 60, 65
Nuclear weapons, threat of,
209
Numbers: fun with, 64; nature
of, 63

Obscenity, artistic, 126
"Ode on a Grecian Urn"
(Keats), 159
Odyssey (Homer), 238
Office of Science and Tech-
nology Policy, U.S., 285n.14
Ohmann, Richard, 283n.39
O'Neill, Jaime, 292n.33
Ong, Walter J., 290n.24
Op-ed pieces, critical analysis
of, 159
Operation Desert Storm, 80–81
Organization of American His-
torians, 84
Overpopulation, 209
Ovid, 227

Paedagogi, 11
Paideia, 42, 57, 91, 137;
apeironic, 35, 47, 129 (*see
also* Learning, apeironic);
Bloom and, 47–49; countercurricular, 210; diversity-
driven, 104; education as,
25–27, 29, 31, 35, 55; *paidia*
and, 249–50; relativistic, 43;
at UCLA, 161; white-male,
36
Paideia Group, 105
Paintings: as "art," 125; humanities' focus on, 119
Panofsky, Erwin, 285n.4
Paracelsus, 73
Paradigms, 15
Paradise Lost (Milton), 116
Paradox, as mathematical play,
64

334

Index

Index

Index

Index

338